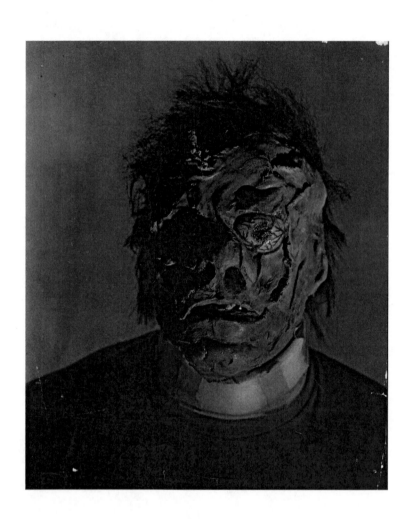

# AMERICAN INTERNATIONAL PICTURES: THE GOLDEN YEARS

## GARY A. SMITH

BearManor
Media

Albany, Georgia

Published in the USA by:
BearManor Media
P.O. Box 1129
Duncan, OK 73534-1129
www.BearManorMedia.com

Cover: Sandra Harrison in *Blood of Dracula*. Photo courtesy of Mark McGee

Frontispiece: Gary Conway in *I Was a Teenage Frankenstein*. Photo courtesy of Mark McGee

ISBN: 1-59393-750-4

Printed in the United States of America

# DEDICATION

*Once again... to Michael*

# ACKNOWLEDGMENTS

A very big thank you to my dear friends Mark McGee, Lucy Chase Williams, and Howard Mandlebaum.

# INTRODUCTION

MORE THAN ANY OTHER COMPANY IN MOTION PICTURE HISTORY, American International Pictures was founded on publicity and hyperbole. James H. Nicholson, the president and co-founder of AIP, was a master of rousing rhetoric. His impassioned speeches to exhibitors, distributors, theater owners, and the like were largely responsible for putting AIP on the map. It didn't seem to matter that his lofty claims and grandiose pronouncements often never came to pass; the man had a definite flair for promotion. And promotion was what AIP was all about.

This is the story of American International Pictures during what I consider to be its "Golden Years," from its 1954 inception through James Nicholson's death in 1972. It is told mainly using material from the files of their New York publicist. This is not an attempt to discuss the merits of AIP's movies or their filmmaking techniques, but instead to trace the history of the company through their continual use of publicity. Not every film is covered here, but I do try to include something on the majority of their major releases. Also, for many of the early films, there are excerpts from personal interviews which have been supplied by Mark McGee and are reproduced here with his kind permission. My personal interjections are in bold face throughout.

# PART ONE

**THE FIFTIES- Mutated Monsters and Troubled Teens**

"We DARE You to See the Most Amazing Pictures of Our Time!"

**Jim and Sam form ARC, which quickly evolves to AIP. Catering to the teen market and drive-in crowd, AIP firmly establishes itself within the Hollywood movie industry.**

# CHAPTER ONE
# 1953-1954

**1953-**

LAWYER SAMUEL Z. ARKOFF REPRESENTED HIS CLIENT, FILM producer Alex Gordon, in a legal dispute with Jack Broder at Realart Pictures. Gordon had submitted a script to Broder entitled *The Atomic Monster* (later filmed as *Bride of the Atom* and eventually released as *Bride of the Monster*). Gordon claimed that Broder had rejected the script, but appropriated the title for a reissue of the Lon Chaney, Jr., movie *Man-Made Monster*. Realart's Sales Manager James H. Nicholson was responsible for re-titling many of the Universal Pictures they had picked up for reissue. Although Nicholson claimed he had never seen the script in question, Arkoff was able to get $500 restitution from Realart for his client. Arkoff had also met a man who shared his ambition to make movies.

Alex Gordon: "Jim [Nicholson] took us into [Jack] Broder's office. Broder told us that Jim was the one who had come up with the title. He asked Jim if he remembered seeing the script and he said that he didn't."

Sam Arkoff: "I said to Broder, 'It may have been just one of those things, Jack; a coincidence. But the fact of the matter is, you did have access to my client's script. We could go to court and you might win, but it's going to cost you money no matter how you look at it.' I was bluffing, but I didn't think he'd want to go to court any more than I did. He got angry and we went around and around, but he finally wrote a check for $500. Jim Nicholson phoned me a few weeks later and we met for lunch. We kept in touch for the next six months and ultimately we decided to go into business together."

**Samuel Z. Arkoff. Photo courtesy of Photofest**

**1954-**

Sam Arkoff and Jim Nicholson decided to form a new film company called American Releasing Corporation (ARC). Their offices were located in the Lawyers' Building, not far from Hollywood and Vine. The company had a total investment of $3000 with $1000 coming from each investor: Jim Nicholson (President), Sam Arkoff (Vice President), and Joseph Moritz (Treasurer). For their first release, ARC struck a deal with fledgling producer Roger Corman to distribute his third movie, *The Fast and the Furious*. Made at a cost of $50,000, Corman hoped to use this picture as the springboard for a multi-picture deal. Although several established companies had offered to purchase the film outright, Corman decided to go with ARC because they offered him a three-picture deal. Corman accompanied Nicholson and Arkoff to New Orleans, Chicago, and New York to obtain financial backing from distributors and theater franchise holders. *The Fast and the Furious* was screened for these potential backers and the trio was able to get enough advance money to finance two more pictures from Corman.

Roger Corman (Producer): "I had offers from Republic and Columbia to distribute *The Fast and the Furious*, but I saw that I was in a trap. If I had to wait for each picture to pay off, I would be making one movie a year. So I gave the picture to Jim [Nicholson] with the stipulation that I would not have to wait for the picture to be released to get my money and I wanted a commitment for two more pictures."

November 1954-

*The Fast and the Furious*
"Widescreen Thrills! Filmed at the Pebble Beach International Sports Car Races."

Produced by Roger Corman   Directed by Edwards Sampson and John Ireland
Starring John Ireland, Dorothy Malone

**Although the film opened to generally mixed reviews, it managed to gross a quarter of a million dollars.**

Film Reviews- *The Fast and the Furious*

*The Hollywood Reporter* (October 28, 1954) by Jack Moffitt
This action-jammed film about sports car racing gives the exhibitor something that will appeal to young audiences on the second half of a double bill. It could have been much better than that.

Producer Roger Corman had a good idea when he conceived the notion of having a fugitive from a murder rap capture a rich girl in a Jaguar and attempt to get across the Mexican border as a contestant in the international motor races.

During the first couple of reels, it looks as though this is going to pay off in a top-flight low-budget production. The opening, played at a mountain hamburger stand, is written with humor, dramatic punch, and clarity. But, unfortunately, the script by Jerome Odlum and Jean Howell fails to deliver a concentrated love story. This is practically a two-character movie in which the development depends on the girl's gradually falling in love with the supposed killer. No incidents are provided to make this seem credible. Those that are attempted are so badly arranged that they move the story by fits and starts without much romantic progression.

This is too bad, because in John Ireland and Dorothy Malone the production has a couple of players who could have done wonders with the right story. Miss Malone, an able little trouper who has been coming through with impressive characterizations lately, seems to realize intuitively what is wrong. She does all an actress can do, without the right lines, to fix it.

There is an old car race in the middle of the film that could still be edited out to advantage. With so much speed in the opening and closing, monotony could be avoided by punctuating the proceedings with a quieter passage.

*Motion Picture Herald*- Sports car enthusiasts may get more satisfaction than other people out of the principal novelty in the picture... and exploitation pointed toward that segment of the public might yield good results.

# CHAPTER TWO
# 1955

ALEX GORDON: "JIM NICHOLSON'S WIFE SYLVIA WAS OUR secretary. I wrote the copy for the press-books and I acted as a casting director and executive producer. Sam Arkoff's brother-in-law, Lou Rusoff, wrote the scripts. Bart Carre was our production supervisor. It was his job to make certain the films didn't go a dime over budget, which he did very well. Joe Moritz was the treasurer. Leon Blender was our sales manager. And once in a while, Jack Broder's secretary, Aggie McCulloch, would do a little moonlighting and balance the books. We all worked for practically nothing."

Leon Blender: "When the money did start coming in, I got $115 a week. I'd go to the exhibitor conventions with Jim and Sam and we'd all stay in the same hotel room. They got the twin beds and I slept on a cot."

March 20, 1955-

**James Nicholson addressed the members of North Central Allied film distributors at their annual convention in Pittsburgh, PA.**

**James H. Nicholson**

"Mr. Chairman, Ladies and Gentlemen, Members of North Central Allied... I feel very honored that I have been asked to be here... as a former Independent Exhibitor myself, I feel more like one of you than a distributor.

"Having spent some time in both the Exhibition and the Distribution field, I've discovered the underlying difference between the two is... the Distributor is an optimist and the

10

Exhibitor is the pessimist. Unfortunately, this is because from the very beginning, the majority of the distributors (present company excepted) have had the upper hand.

"All the commerce is governed by the laws of supply and demand... the sellers' market and the buyers' market. In the motion picture industry, the Exhibitor has been finally shoved so far into the buyers' market, scarcely half the Theaters in the country show a profit of 6% on their investment, yet the Major Companies are making more money than ever in their history... and speaking as a former Independent Exhibitor, WE helped create this Frankenstein Monster.

"Before I explain this any further, I'd like to tell you how AMERICAN RELEASING CORPORATION was conceived and WHY.

"We are a young company with only two pictures in release at this date. We are a company composed and operated by comparatively young people drawn from the fields of Exhibition,

Production, and Distribution. About seven months ago, a group of us who were Independent Exhibitors in Southern California were discussing the same problems of product shortage you are concerned with here today.

"After hearing the various plans to relieve this shortage and the glowing promises of a dozen or more optimists, we found that the situation was getting worse and only lip service was being paid to the problem of enough playable pictures to keep us in business. Every time Allied Artists or Universal would increase its release schedule, the other majors would cut down. Being in Southern California, we naturally had many contacts with the production end of the business.

We determined to make a personal survey.

"It didn't take long to discover that the production end of the business was quickly becoming aware that the public had become very discriminating in its picture-going. As a result, every Major Studio discovered it could function to better advantage as a distribution company and make deals with so-called Independent Production units. Just last week, even Metro Goldwyn

Mayer has changed its policy and has four Independent projects coming up for release. Part of this is justified in that the

11

production of a successful picture is more of an artistic venture than a business venture in today's market.

"However... it has done one thing... it has changed the former Major Studios into a Distributing Company, renting stage space to top Independent Producers.

"If you think this encourages more Independent Production... you will find this is exactly opposite to the truth. In order to break into this inner circle of Independent Producers releasing through a Major, you've got to have a record of top standing and either a sure-fire script and cast or your own financing. In Hollywood, this is called a 'Package Deal' and although this system has been largely responsible for the improved quality of motion pictures, there is no thought of the needs of the Exhibitor insofar as the total output is concerned.

"Now, in order to replace the flow of product formerly made and released by many Major companies, it naturally follows that there must be an even greater amount of Independent Production.

"The average new producer coming into the production field under the present system has a mortality rate of 9 out of 10. If you think you have problems, you should know the problems of the average producer trying to get a start. First, he must have a good script, then he must promote $100,00 to $500,00 in cash. After making his picture, he then goes, hat in hand, to the Distributors. If he's lucky, he has arranged a deal which might guarantee him part of the investment back unless he has had years of experience in negotiating with Distributors. Usually, he finds out that the bookkeeping system used by the Distributor is so designed that no matter what the picture grosses... he will lose money.

"If he has the money, he will try again until he ends up bankrupting both himself and those who have invested with him. If he's too smart for this, he goes into television. A very few break into the big league and obtain multiple picture deals with the Majors.

"TELEVISION, Gentlemen, is where the new production talent is going which is so badly needed to keep your theaters open.

"In respect to the product shortage, we found that the actual shortage is in playable, commercial pictures... not the total number placed into release each year.

"Very revealing figures are available through National Screen Service. Several years ago, there were about 400 features released each year. 300 of these played over 3500 theaters in the country.

"Today, there are still 400 features in release, but because of the increase in foreign and art films together with re-issues, only 200 enjoy more than 3500 playdates. This is not a condemnation of foreign or art films, but it does reflect the fact that the picture which can be played in the majority of theaters is on the decrease... and therefore... the playable pictures are in such demand that they are only available at premium terms... thus your sellers' market... and the 'product shortage.'

"After going into this very complex situation and listening to the often repeated phrase 'the public will only go to see the big hits!' we went into some quite interesting facts and figures. We found that there were scores of pictures made on a modest budget which did quite well at the box office... we played them... we found they produced a profit in our theaters. At the same time, we found that most of the producers in this case did not make a dime. There were two reasons. FIRST: The Distributor had arranged his bookkeeping so that it was impossible for a modest hit to return a profit to the small producer and encourage him to make more pictures. SECOND: Even without that... AND I HOPE THIS SHOCKS YOU... the Independent Exhibitors were the first to turn down Independently made and distributed pictures. In fact, if the same picture was to have been released by a major, Mr. Independent Exhibitor would not only double the playdates, but would go along on the big terms asked by the Majors.

"THIS IS YOUR FRANKENSTEIN MONSTER...

And I am not standing here with clean hands myself... I was an Independent Exhibitor and when the Independent Distributor in my area came to me with a picture, I either turned him down flat or, if he had a picture which I knew was good... I managed to steal it for $25.00, even though I would have paid a Major three times this for the same picture.

"After much soul searching and practical research, several

of my Associates and I in the Exhibition field joined with a few people in production and distribution. We organized AMERICAN RELEASING CORPORATION... not with the idea that it would overnight relieve the product problem... but with the feeling that perhaps we could contribute to its relief and, if all went well, make a profit. To do this, we had to first obtain supply of product which we felt was commercial and playable and would mean something at the box office. We contracted for the production of a few pictures and went into business of December last year. In fact, our first release had its first run two days before we announced our company to the trade press. In case you haven't booked it... we call it *The Fast and the Furious*, starring John Ireland and Dorothy Malone. In terms of number of bookings... it has been a success. By summer, it will have become one of the 200 features released annually which will play over 3500 theaters.

"Our distribution agreement with the producer is such that he will enjoy a profit long before he would have through any Major Distributor. Our second picture is just going into release now. It is an Action Western in Wide Screen Color... *Five Guns West*... with Dorothy Malone and John Lund. And is being booked faster than the laboratory can supply prints. We feel proud that in the space of four months, we've been able to come up with two pictures which fall in the commercial... playable class.

"Next week, we start shooting our Third release, *The Beast With 1,000,000 Eyes*... and in MAY, our Fourth, which is to be in Color and Anamorphic Wide Screen, *Apache Woman*. Later in the year, we will release *One Mile Below... Jungle Queen... Johnny Big Gun...* and *The Day the World Ended...* all pictures which the Exhibitor faction of AMERICAN RELEASING will book with the feeling that they will make a profit at the box office.

"I know this sounds like a commercial for AMERICAN RELEASING... which has barely gotten off the ground as a Distributing Company... but I hope it proves one thing... there IS a way to help the product problem... and we have done something about it, which can be delivered to your theaters in a can... and not a lot of fancy words in the trade press.

"Very simply... our policy is as follows:

ENCOURAGE THE UPCOMING INDEPENDENT PRODUCER!

GIVE HIM A FAIR DEAL WHERE HE MAKES HIS DESERVED PROFIT!

KEEP DISTRIBUTION COSTS AT A MINIMUM!

KEEP THE PRODUCER AWARE OF THE COMMERCIAL AND EXPLOITABLE TYPE OF PRODUCT NEEDED!

AND MOST IMPORTANT... <u>DELIVER THE PICTURES!</u>

"There is no magic formula... no miracle which can be performed to increase the supply of playable product... You, as Exhibitors, must encourage the Independent Exchange in your area... the Independent Producers... the Companies who are coming up... the Allied Artists... the DCA's... the Filmackers... the Lippert's... and the American Releasing Corporation. It seems the Independent Exhibitor who is fighting for an existence should at least have the guts to favor his counterpart in the Distribution business. Surely he will benefit in the long run. Because if he does not encourage the Independent Producer and Distributor, he will further the monopoly and lack of competition, which will lead to harsher terms- production starvation and his own downfall.

"I know the very mention of  TOLL-TV sends shivers down your spines... but I wonder how many of you realize that TOLL-TV is part and parcel and a natural consequence of the same monopolistic situation I have been discussing. If the Independent Producer and in turn the Independent Distributor is not encouraged, this industry can easily be converted to a 'SEE YOUR MOVIES AT HOME' business with fifty or a hundred super-spectacles per year... leaving thousands of dark theaters and Drive-Ins overgrown with weeds.

"When the Major Distributor has control entirely, he is free to move into other fields... when there is competition, he won't dare. Such competition is the backbone not only of our industry, but of all American Industry... if it is allowed to degenerate it becomes a monopoly... and no matter what the arguments... TOLL-TV... the use of the free air... is a monopoly... and could only result from a prior monopoly.

"Now don't leave with the impression that I am asking you to put pictures on your screen which will lose money. All I ask is that on pictures of equal merit, you treat the Independent the same as you would if the picture were released by a Major Distributor... Don't look at trade marks... look at the picture... and all things being equal... give us a break... WE'RE ONE OF YOU... THANK YOU."

**The members of the National Central Allied convention must have felt their heads were spinning after this rousing speech. Nicholson confuses some of his dates. Although he states that ARC went into business in December 1954, *The Fast and the Furious* had already been reviewed in *The Hollywood Reporter* as an ARC film in October. The picture then went into general release in November. He also makes a big point of mentioning that creative bookkeeping prevents producers from realizing any profit. Later, AIP would be accused of this very practice by several of their producers.**

April 1955-

### Five Guns West
"Five condemned men who traded a sentence to die for a thousand to one chance to live."

Produced and Directed by Roger Corman
Starring John Lund, Dorothy Malone, Touch Conners, Bob Campbell, Jonathan Haze, Paul Birch

***Five Guns West* was the second picture in Roger Corman's deal with ARC. With a budget of $60,000 and a nine-day shooting schedule, Corman decided to make the picture in color and direct it himself, although he had no previous experience directing.**

Jonathan Haze (Actor): "*Five Guns West* was the first picture that Roger directed. It was written by a friend of mine, Bobby Campbell, who wrote a good part for me and himself. I staged all the fights in it."

Robert Campbell (Writer-Actor): "I got only $200 for the script. I said to Roger, 'Jesus, Roger, that's not a hell of a lot of money to live on.' I told him that I had noticed that all the actors, because they were in the Guild, made more money than I did, even the bit players. He said, 'You want to play a part?' and I said, 'Why the hell not?' Roger sat with his eyes glued to the script the whole time. I finally told him to forget about the script and watch what the actors were doing."

Film Reviews- *Five Guns West*

*The Hollywood Reporter*- At the outset, we are told that five outlaws must move through a land swarming with Comanches and Union calvary. This raises audience expectations for excitement the picture fails to deliver. There are but two long shots of distant redskins and the fighting consists of a hand-to-hand struggle with one lone Indian. It's a good deal as though you tried to produce *Ben-Hur* by talking about the chariot race.

*Boxoffice*- No matter at which point on the compass this quintet of shootin' irons is aimed, it is not going to blow any gaping holes in the cash drawer records.

*Variety*- [Roger] Corman doesn't supply as much drive to the action as this type of subject requires, so the elements of suspense and tension present in the story aren't fully realized.

*Motion Picture Herald*- The broader, plainer audience that has been the mainstay of the western melodrama ever since Bronco Billy Anderson rode the range is quite likely to give this attraction substantial support.

May 1955-

**Outlaw Treasure**
"Action-Packed Saga of the Lawless West!"

Produced by John Carpenter  Directed by Oliver Drake
Starring Adele Jergens, Glenn Langan, Michael Whalen, John Forbes

**Outlaw Treasure was a Wheeler Company Production that ARC picked up for distribution.**

**Shortly after completing *Five Guns West*, Corman began filming *Apache Woman*, another color western. This time, he had a $80,000 budget and a two-week shooting schedule. Corman had gone over budget on *Five Guns West*, so there was only $29,000 left to make the third picture in his deal with ARC. There is some discrepancy here, as Sam Arkoff's autobiography says that he originally signed Corman on for a four picture deal, while Corman's autobiography says it was a three picture deal.**

Because he was already involved in shooting *Apache Woman*, Corman gave David Kramarsky the task of directing *The Beast With 1,000,000 Eyes*. Kramarsky had previously served as Corman's Production Assistant on *Five Guns West*.

June 1955–

*The Beast With 1,000,000 Eyes*
"Screaming Terror! In Wide-Screen TerrorScope!"

Produced and Directed by David Kramarsky
Starring Paul Birch, Lorna Thayer, Dona Cole

From the pressbook-
SEAT SELLING SLANTS-

SCARE RECORDING- Every town has a radio store where record-making equipment can be rented or used. Make your own record with the following copy... play it at intermission and at every "break." This constant plugging is guaranteed to promote extra business.

"Ladies and Gentlemen... just a moment please... this is your theatre manager... I have a special warning... Your attention please... The Beast With a Million Eyes is coming... If you have a weak heart... please stay at home... thank you."

This stunt has been tried with great success and never fails to get a lot of comment.

Roger Corman: "*The Beast With 1,000,000 Eyes* was a picture for which I put up the money. Dave Kramarsky produced it as my assistant. Dave felt he could make the picture for a very small amount- which he did. I read the script and had some approval as to what was going on."

David Kramarsky (Producer-Director): "Roger took over the

picture. He fired our photographer and brought in Floyd Crosby. They shot 48 pages of interiors in two days at this little studio Lou [Place] had rented on La Cienega. The special effects looked so terrible that I asked the lab to print the scenes darker, but they didn't."

Sam Arkoff: "So Roger laid this picture in our laps, $29,000 worth. And it really wasn't bad. The only trouble was that it didn't have The Beast."

Paul Blaisdell (Special Effects): "Forrest J. Ackerman, who considered himself quite a film critic as well as being America's 'number one fan,' whatever the hell that means, was doing an article for *Spaceway* magazine and I was doing the illustrations for it. Roger Corman contacted Forry, who at the time also thought he was quite a literary agent in terms of science fiction stories and stuff like that, but here was his chance to be a theatrical agent. Forry just looked all around in a wild flap to find somebody that could do a monster for this picture. So I told him okay. I'd give it a whack."

**The Beast With 1,000,000 Eyes was the first movie to employ Paul Blaisdell (1927-1983) to do the special effects. For a mere $200 plus cost of materials, Blaisdell created the miniature space ship and alien seen in the film. Although the million eyes of the title Beast were metaphoric in the movie, the ad art had shown the many-eyed monster. This was cause for some consternation among distributors, who had been sold on the film by the ad art.**

Albert Kallis (Poster Artist): "Jim Nicholson and I would make up most of the titles and decide what the approach for the advertising should be. Then I would design the campaign and we'd show the layouts to the theatre owners."

Sam Arkoff: "Most of the stuff that we did was originals. Why? Because they had to be in order to fit the concept which had already been set. You had the title, the concept, or the artwork.

Now you did the script and it had to follow the title, the concept, or the artwork... and it had to be made for a price."

October 1955–

***Apache Woman***
"Half Breed Emotion Stripped to Raw Fury!"

Produced and Directed by Roger Corman

Starring Lloyd Bridges, Joan Taylor, Lance Fuller, Morgan Jones, Paul Birch, Lou Place

**The script for *Apache Woman* was the first written by Sam Arkoff's brother-in-law, Lou Rusoff (1911-1963). He would be involved with AIP until his untimely death at age 51.**

Dick Miller (Actor): "Jonathan Haze, who had been a buddy of mine in New York, came out to California a little before I did. We met out here and we were bumming around and he said he was working for this young producer-director, Roger Corman. He said, 'Come on up to the office.' So I met Roger. It was laughs. We were sitting around and I thought he was a nice guy. It was a very social thing. He said, 'What do you do?' And I said I was a writer. He said ' I don't need any scripts. I got scripts.' 'That's too bad,' I said. 'What do you need? I can run the camera and I can act.' So my first picture was *Apache Woman*."

Jonathan Haze (Actor): "At that point, I had quite a lot of influence with Roger about actors and writers and all that because he didn't know anything. I was responsible for getting a lot of the people started- Bob Campbell, Chuck Griffin, Dick Miller, Mel Welles, Bruno VeSota- who became part of his stock company."

Alex Gordon (Executive Producer): "We had Lloyd Bridges and Joyce Taylor for our leads. Lance Fuller, who I'd seen in *Cattle Queen of Montana*, was the villain. Jim and Sam were trying to decide whether to sign him or Mike Connors to a contract. They were sure one of them was going to be a big star. I remember there was one day when Lance Fuller had this line-'Take them to the hills.' For some reason, he couldn't remember the line. It took them eighteen takes before he got it right."

Ronald Stein (Composer): "I left some of my music at Roger's office on Thursday and that Sunday I got a call from him around four in the afternoon. He said, 'We're going to give you a chance. We don't have a lot of money. We can pay you $400 at one and a half percent of the producer's profit and a credit as big as Dimitri

Tiomkin's, a card all to yourself.' I would have done it for free. I had ten days to compose thirty minutes of music."

Film Reviews- *Apache Woman*

*Showman's Trade Review*- There are enough exciting western ingredients to satisfy the customers in the action market with action sufficiently fast to hold attention despite some dialogue-heavy spots.

*Boxoffice*- It should be recorded that when the tempo does develop- which is toward the end of the film- it is fast, furious, and exciting.

*Variety*- A familiar plot gets fresh mantling in this rugged western yarn spiked by excellent performances and generally driving treatment.

*The Hollywood Reporter*- Action and direction makes this an okay programmer, though Ronald Sinclair gets a left-handed laugh when Lance Fuller is shown throwing a copy of Milton's *Paradise Lost* through a window (an act bound to win the sympathy of anyone who has tried to read it) and the very next shot shows a bank window smashing four miles away.

October 17, 1955
*Daily Variety 22nd Anniversary Issue*
Trade ad-
Congratulations from the Industry's INFANT! AMERICAN RELEASING CORPORATION
Now in Release
Palo Alto Productions- *The Fast and the Furious, Five Guns West* (Color), *Beast with 1,000,000 Eyes* (In Terrorscope)
Golden State Productions- *Day The World Ended* (Superscope), *Apache Woman* (Color)
Milner Bros. Productions- *Phantom from 10,000 Leagues*

December 1955-

Trade ad-
From the Infant of the Industry! Mr. Exhibitor, You asked for it!
Ready in January- the box office combination of the year! The
TOP Shock Show of ALL TIME! *DAY THE WORLD ENDED*
plus *THE PHANTOM FROM 10,000 LEAGUES.* See your local
AMERICAN exchange!

# CHAPTER THREE
# 1956

Having gotten minimal rentals from exhibitors for their single feature releases, Arkoff and Nicholson decided to try "combinations"- two inexpensive films with similar themes on one double bill. For this, they would ask exhibitors to pay the same higher rental fee as they would pay the major studios for a single picture. *The Day the World Ended* was originally planned as a color widescreen movie, but budgetary restraints relegated the picture to black and white status, although it was still filmed in Superscope. Roger Corman again directed from a script by Lou Rusoff. The budget for the film was $96,000. The higher-than-normal budget (by ARC standards) left little money for a companion feature, so Arkoff and Nicholson approached brothers Jack and Dan Milner with the idea of producing and directing their first film. The Milner Brothers were able to obtain financing to the tune of $75,000 from a group of

**Japanese-American investors, which they used to film the Lou Rusoff script for *The Phantom from 10,000 Leagues*.**

Alex Gordon (Executive Producer): "Nicholson and Arkoff wanted to shoot *The Day the World Ended* in Superscope. It was a widescreen process that was a fraction of the cost of CinemaScope and they felt it would make it seem like a more expensive picture."

January 1956-

***The Day the World Ended/The Phantom from 10,000 Leagues***
"The TOP Shock Show of ALL TIME! See: The world ended by atomic fury! The horrible mutant who seeks a mate! The terrifying beast on the ocean floor! The battle for life at the bottom of the sea! Fantastic world of death and horror!"

*The Day the World Ended*
Produced and Directed by Roger Corman
Starring Richard Denning, Lori Nelson, Adele Jergens, Touch Connors, Paul Birch, Paul Dubov

*The Phantom from 10,000 Leagues*
Produced by Dan Milner and Jack Milner    Directed by Dan Milner
Starring Kent Taylor, Cathy Downs, Michael Whalen, Rodney Bell, Phillip Pine, Helene Stanton

From the pressbook-
NEW HORROR SHOW GUARANTEED SHOCKER!
Hollywood has a history of famous monsters. Since the days of *The Hunchback of Notre Dame* and *Phantom of the Opera*, both starring Lon Chaney, most famous silent day portrayer of horror roles, such pictures have paid off at the box office.
With the advent of talkies, Universal led the field with their sensational *Dracula* and *Frankenstein* pictures, later introducing such characters as "Wolf Man," "Hunchback," "Ape Woman," "The Mummy," and the "Gill man."

26

For many years, mad screen scientists transformed men and women into apes, gorillas, lunatics, and ghouls and horror pictures pretty much followed a formula until the science fiction vogue took over.

Hollywood now had to come up with some new wrinkles to update the old-time horror pictures, which seemed no longer scary to a new generation, which laughed rather than chilled to the old classics.

Finally, the strange man-like mutant of *Day the World Ended* was born with logical story motivations to explain his existence and actions. The situations confronting Richard Denning, Lori Nelson, Adele Jergens, and other cast members COULD happen and are therefore more terrifying to a modern audience than the monsters of old. The strange underwater creature in *Phantom from 10,000 Leagues* could also be a descendant of the prehistoric monsters so brilliantly shown in *The Lost World* and *King Kong*. Starring in the Milner Bros. Production *Phantom from 10,000 Leagues* are Kent Taylor, Cathy Downs, and Michael Whalen.

Preview audiences have hailed *Day the World Ended*, which was photographed in Superscope, and *Phantom from 10,000 Leagues* as a top adult science fiction combination and experts and devotees of such literature consider these two pictures outstanding examples of modern horror on the screen.

MR. EXHIBITOR: *DAY THE WORLD ENDED* and *THE PHANTOM FROM 10,000 LEAGUES* IS A SHOWMANSHIP SHOW FOR SHOWMEN!

**The first week in January, this double feature package opened at six theaters and eight drive-ins in Los Angeles and grossed $140,000 during the first half week. ARC had to order an additional 100 prints of the films to accommodate all of the bookings they had contracted.**

**Lori Nelson is carried off by a monster mutant in *The Day the World Ended*.**

Film Reviews- *The Day the World Ended*

*The Hollywood Reporter*- This low-budgeter should reap its makers a large bundle of dough. With all of its story faults and production inadequacies, its design hits the science fiction trade near perfectly.

*Boxoffice*- Performances by a reasonably competent cast and direction by Roger Corman are acceptable.

Film Review- *The Phantom from 10,000 Leagues*

*Boxoffice*- In describing a situation as this hodgepodge draws to a merciful close, a character intones: "What a mess." If it weren't for the fact that a prescribed amount of space has to be filled, that line of dialogue could aptly serve as the beginning and the end of a critique of this offering.

March 1956-

**Arkoff and Nicholson formally changed the name of their company to American International Pictures, although a few films would still be released under the ARC moniker. Sam and Jim also moved out of the Lawyer's Building to more spacious offices on Sunset Boulevard.**

Sam Arkoff: "We had originally wanted to call our company American International, but there was another company called American Pictures. Ultimately, American Pictures went out of business and that's when we changed the name from American Releasing Corporation to American International."

April 23, 1956
*The Hollywood Reporter*
HORROR PICTURES BECOME THE EXHIBITOR'S DELIGHT- AIP President Tells of Interest

The demand for horror pictures is as standard as that for westerns and there is apparently no end to the exhibitors' need and desire for them, according to James H. Nicholson, president of American International Pictures, which is concentrating on a steady stream of the features.

Nicholson said that a check of exhibitors and branches shows that the straight shockers have the edge over science fiction pictures and the success of this type of feature is responsible for his company's highest gross on a picture since it was founded more than two years ago.

Nicholson reported that exhibitors said they had better business on the horror films as a reliable index than on any other single type. He cited the fact that months after AIP's release of *The Day the World Ended*, the company increased its regular print order by 100 to supply bookings.

This top grosser for the company did $80,000 on April 8 in New York in a saturation booking, despite the fact that this was the weekend of the heavy and unseasonal snowstorm there.

Nicholson said the appetite for the horror pictures is just as keen in foreign markets as it is domestic.

June 1956-

*Female Jungle/The Oklahoma Woman*
"2 All-New SHOCKERS!"

Roger Corman had a $60,000 black and white western in the can entitled *The Oklahoma Woman*. AIP wanted to release another double feature package, but didn't have a second feature ready. They were able to inexpensively pick up the Burt Kaiser production *Female Jungle*, which featured Jayne Mansfield in an early support role. Bruno VeSota had been hired by Kaiser to write and direct the picture, which was shot in six days for $49,000.

*The Oklahoma Woman*
Produced and Directed by Roger Corman
Starring Richard Denning, Peggie Castle, Cathy Downs, Touch Connors, Tudor Owen

*The Female Jungle*
Produced by Burt Kaiser  Directed by Bruno VeSota
Starring Kathleen Crowley, Lawrence Tierney, John Carradine, Jayne Mansfield, James Kodl

David Kramarsky (Production Manager): "Originally, Jayne Mansfield was supposed to play a smaller role. Kathleen Crowley was the lead. We were supposed to film some exteriors in downtown Los Angeles and Kathleen Crowley showed up three hours late. She said she'd been raped by three black men. She became hysterical, so we called her agent and he came and took her away. We still had about half the picture to finish, so we rewrote the script and built up the role that Jayne had. When we were done, there were only two quick shots that we needed of Kathleen Crowley to bridge some scenes, so we hired a double and shot her from behind."

*Gunslinger*
"Hired to Kill the Woman He Loved!"

Produced and Directed by Roger Corman
Starring John Ireland, Beverly Garland, Allison Hayes

**Filmed in six days in February 1956, *Gunslinger* was the last of Roger Corman's westerns and it was also the final film released under the American Releasing Corporation banner.**

Charles Griffith (Writer): "Roger took me to a Randolph Scott western and told me to write the same picture, only change the sheriff's part to a woman. He was going to shoot for three days at Ingram's Ranch in Topanga Canyon. It had a town street with a few acres of scrub around it. And the other three days were going to be shot at Iverson's Ranch out past Chatsworth. So I went out to Ingram's and copied the names off the signs to use for the character's names. That way they wouldn't have to redo the signs. By then, I knew where Roger was at. And I had a look around the land and I figured out that if you looked this way and that you could write the exteriors of the whole picture there and save thirty minutes a day each way, which was a whole shooting day on a six-day picture. Roger was delighted. We shot the whole thing at Ingram's."

Beverly Garland (Actress): "We were between takes and I happened to glance over at Allison [Hayes] and I saw her casually slide off her horse. And she ended up breaking her arm. Later, when there was nobody else around and she was standing there with her arm in a sling, I asked her why she'd done that. She said, 'I was tired of working.' With Roger, you always worked. I mean, you could have one eye hanging and he'd just shoot you from another angle. You really had to be a trooper. But he was a brilliant man."

Allison Hayes (Actress): "[*Gunslinger*] was in the beginning days of Roger Corman when his promise to himself was that he would be a millionaire by the time he was 36 or 37. I broke my arm and had to go to the hospital. He never even called to ask how I was."

Dick Miller (Actor): "I played a Pony Express rider. I couldn't ride for shit, but I was supposed to ride into town at full gallop and execute a change of mount, which the actual riders did every dozen miles or so, I think. I don't know how many times I did it, but Jonathan Haze told me later that everybody had bets on whether or not I'd fall off the horse and Roger was one of the guys who bet I would. That's why he kept making me do it. Roger's a tight man with a buck, but I'll add that once you've made a deal with him, you don't have to worry about anything afterwards. He'll do his best to get the most for the least while the deal is being made, but once it's done, you can work on a handshake."

Film Reviews- *Gunslinger*

*Variety*- Since the material isn't very believable, neither are the performances, although individual personalities help some.

*The Hollywood Reporter*- The script has some interesting characterizations and situations. [John] Ireland is effective as the hired gunman, although his motivations and actions are sometimes a little slow. Miss [Beverly] Garland and Miss [Allison] Hayes are good.

July 1956-

### Girls in Prison/Hot-Rod Girl
"Double Sock... Rock and Thrill Show!"

*Girls in Prison*
Produced by Alex Gordon  Directed by Edward L. Cahn
Starring Richard Denning, Joan Taylor, Adele Jergens, Lance Fuller

*Hot-Rod Girl*
Produced by Norman Herman  Directed by Leslie Martinson
Starring Lori Nelson, John Smith, Chuck Connors, Roxanne
Arlen, Mark Andrews

Film Reviews- *Girls in Prison*

*Variety* (September 12, 1956)- *Girls in Prison* is as routine as
its title, an over length jail yarn with telegraphic situations which
reduce movement to a walk. Characters occasionally get over well
enough for casual interest, however, and film is okay for lowercase
bookings in program runs. Producer Alex Gordon has lined up
a competent cast for the Lou Rusoff screenplay, headed by Joan
Taylor. Miss Taylor shows to advantage and turns in a performance
better than her material. Edward L. Cahn's adequate direction is
backed by acceptable technical assistance headed by Frederick E.
West's camera work.

*Boxoffice-* [*Girls in Prison*] boasts virtually nothing that has
not been previously used in countless offerings dealing with the
lives and inclinations of those in durance vile- both men and
women. But nonetheless, it offers a chance for reasonably good
performances by the experienced troupers, of which there are more
than one might expect in a film of its budgetary classification.

*Los Angeles Examiner-* There is a pretty good story in *Girls
in Prison*, which apparently stemmed from the big earthquake
that rocked the Tehachapi women's prison a few years back. The
dramatic crux of this little situation involves one of the gals in stir,
who is suspected of having some holdup loot cached away. The
people in this drama, some who haven't been heard from for quite
a spell, are Adele Jergens, Helen Gilbert, Jane Darwell, Raymond
Hatton, Richard Denning, Mae Marsh, Lance Fuller, and Joan
Taylor.

Film Reviews- *Hot-Rod Girl*

*Los Angeles Examiner- HOT-ROD GIRL* HAS FILM THRILLS by Lynn Bowers

*Hot-Rod Girl* is about a lot of hot-rod boys who race around on the city streets instead of off someplace where they can just kill each other. As a thriller, it holds up fine and there are some additional kicks in store for the girl audience. Notable among these are John Smith and a new, startlingly good-looking young man named Mark Andrews, who, in spite of playing a heavy, is liable to stir up such a storm that Elvis Presley may have to stop acting and go back to swivel-singing.

*Boxoffice-* As a job of picture making, [*Hot-Rod Girl*] is woefully weak and that concerns scripting, direction, production values, and acting.

July 16, 1956
*The Film Daily*
Trade ad-
Pictures with a purpose... BOX OFFICE RESULTS! Coming this year...
*Flesh and the Spur* (wide vision color)
*Shake Rattle and Rock!* and *Runaway Daughters*
*Naked Paradise* in color
*Jet Fighter*
*Hell Raiders*
See your local American International Exchange!


August 1956-

***It Conquered the World/The She-Creature***
"ALL NEW! MONSTER vs. MONSTER! The Twin Terror Show That Tops Them All!
See: The earth crushed by a nightmare monster! Beauty become a

horrible beast from the unknown! The hideous, terrifying Flying Fingers! The world gripped by terror... panic... death!"

From the pressbook-

AMERICAN is an exhibitor operated company and all of the material shown in this pressbook is tried and PROVEN... USE IT!

BIGGEST DOUBLE HORROR SHOW OF ALL TIME

Not since the days of "Frankenstein," "Dracula," and "Phantom of the Opera" has the screen offered a combination like American International's *It Conquered the World* and *The She-Creature*. Two horrifying monsters- one a visitor from outer space and the other a creation of hypnotism and reincarnation- are seen in these two shockers. Beautiful Marla English leads a double life as a girl under a hypnotic spell in *The She-Creature*, co-starring Chester Morris,

Tom Conway, Cathy Downs, Lance Fuller, Ron Randell, and Frieda Inescort. Science fiction favorite Peter Graves and popular Beverly Garland are teamed in *It Conquered the World* when the universe is conquered by a terrifying creature from Venus.

*It Conquered the World*
Produced and Directed by Roger Corman
Starring Peter Graves, Beverly Garland, Lee Van Cleef

Charles Griffith (Writer): "Lou Rusoff had written a script that was incomprehensible, which was quite strange because he was quite meticulous. Lou's brother was dying at the time, which most likely had something to do with it. Anyway, I had 48 hours to rewrite it. I wrote streams of dialogue. The picture was terrible."

Paul Blaisdell (Special Effects): The script called for a creature that came from Venus. Venus was considered a hot, misty place, given more to the growth of vegetation than animal life. Consequently, intelligent life evolving on such a planet would be more plant-like than mammalian. So I figured we could have a hyper-intelligent mushroom if I could design and build it. I built a miniature version

35

and took it to Jim Nicholson's house. He laughed and said, 'Paul, you've really done it again. I never thought you'd come up with something as far-out as this.'

So I went home and built the full-size, five-foot-high version."

Roger Corman (Producer-Director): Actually, the original idea for that design was mine and I was playing too much back to my early physics classes. It was supposed to have come from a very big planet. Therefore, obviously, it would have a very heavy gravity; any such creature on such a planet would be built low to the ground. I believe it was scientifically correct, except that when the thing was built, I realized that it was very unfrightening because it was so low to the ground."

Beverly Garland (Actress): "I walked up to it and said, '*That* conquered the world?' They were so thrilled with this monster and he was really tiny and looked very plastic to me. Then I kept thinking he wasn't finished. When he's finished, he will *emerge* somehow and be much better. Then when I got into the cave and saw him, they had not done anything. He had not emerged at all."

Film reviews- *It Conquered the World*

*Variety* (September 12, 1956)-

This flying saucer pic is a definite cut above normal and should help pull its weight at the box office despite modest budget. However, militating against this are a number of fairly gruesome sequences which producer-director Roger Corman has injected and which may call down the wrath of groups who oversee kiddie pix fare. But it must be admitted that the packed house of moppets at the show loved the gore and continually shrieked avid appreciation.

The Lou Rusoff screenplay poses some remarkably adult questions amidst the derring-do.

Director Corman does a generally good job of mingling the necessary background setting with fast-paced dialogue to achieve the strongest impact. Only a few patches of abstract discussion fail to hold audience attention.

Producer Corman would have been wiser to merely suggest

the creature rather than construct the awesome-looking and mechanically clumsy rubberized horror. It inspired more titters than terror.

*Los Angeles Examiner*- The picture essays a philosophical inquiry into the danger of bypassing human self-help and our basic nature to improve the race, but other than that, it has little to offer.

*The Hollywood Reporter*- Roger Corman's production is well integrated with science fact and fantasy for enough believability to maintain interest and excitement. There is even a moral to the story that any tyrant, no matter how beneficial he seems, is bad in the end.

*The She-Creature*
Produced by Alex Gordon  Directed by Edward L. Cahn
Starring Chester Morris, Marla English, Tom Conway, Cathy Downs, Lance Fuller, Ron Randell

Alex Gordon (Producer): "Casting the movie was quite an ordeal. [Director] Eddie Cahn was friends with Edward Arnold because they'd worked together on *Main Street After Dark* and he agreed to play the part of the businessman for $3000 for one week's work. I thought it would be terrific if we could get Peter Lorre to play the hypnotist because he and Arnold had been so great together in *Crime and Punishment*. Two days before we were supposed to start the picture, Edward Arnold died. And that's when Lorre decided to read the script. He told his agent that he wouldn't do it and when his agent told him he was already committed, he fired the agent. Then we tried to get John Carradine, but he was on a Shakespearean kick. He said he was through with horror pictures."

Paul Blaisdell (Special Effects): "I made the She-Creature out of block foam because I couldn't afford foam rubber. She wasn't watertight, but she was water resilient. We were shooting at Paradise Cove and I was supposed to slowly stand and come out of the water, which sounds reasonable until you try to do it. She took on a load of ballast and each time I tried to take a step forward, the tide kept pulling me back."

October 1956-

### Shake, Rattle and Rock/Runaway Daughters
"TWIN BOP Rock 'n Sock Show! See (and hear): The top Rock 'n Roll names and dancers! Teenage girls on a speed-crazy thrill hunt! Why parents are to blame for delinquent daughters! The teenagers side of the Rock n Roll question!"

From the pressbook-
ACTION AND THRILLS IN NEW TEENAGE COMBO
*Shake, Rattle and Rock* and *Runaway Daughters*, American International's action-packed new rock 'n roll teenage combination show, is crammed tight with all the popular elements to appeal not only to teenagers, but adults of all ages, too.

Fats Domino, the country's No. 1 exponent of rock 'n roll

songs, is seen on the screen for the first time in *Shake, Rattle and Rock*, featuring his best-selling record hits, "Ain't It a Shame," "I'm in Love Again," and "Honey Chile." Joe Turner and the Choker Campbell Band, Tommy Charles, and Annita Ray provide additional song numbers, while Touch Connors, Lisa Gaye, Sterling Holloway, Raymond Hatton, and Margaret Dumont head the cast. The country's top teenage rock 'n roll dancers also appear prominently.

*Runaway Daughters* is an exciting, thrill-packed action drama of three young girls who try to overcome their teenage and parental problems by running away from home. Marla English, Anna Sten, John Litel, Lance Fuller, and two lovely newcomers, Mary Ellen Kaye and Gloria Castillo, head the cast. Fights, chases, and jazzy music provide popular entertainment for everybody.

ROCK AND ROLL EXPLOITATIONS
Rock 'n roll music has aroused much controversy and interest and is constantly in the headlines in this country and abroad. This picture, with its theme of rock 'n roll and its effect on the youth of today, lends itself admirably to any kind of exploitation in this respect. There is a good moral in the story and at the end, the adults realize that rock 'n roll is no more harmful than the dancing crazes of other eras.

*Shake, Rattle and Rock*
Produced by James H. Nicholson  Directed by Edward L. Cahn
Starring Touch Connors, Lisa Gaye, Sterling Holloway, Raymond Hatton, Douglass Dumbrille

Film Reviews- *Shake, Rattle and Rock*

*Los Angeles Times*- A rather hasty little black and white pudding.

*Variety*- For the rock and roll crowd, this light entry should show good response.

*The Hollywood Reporter-* There are some rock and roll artists involved whose names will aid in the marquee dressing and the picture itself is deftly enough done to please the younger fans.

*Monthly Film Bulletin-* The film's conclusions are arrived at in a singularly unpersuasive manner. The [musical] numbers themselves are surprisingly dull.

*Runaway Daughters*
Produced by Alex Gordon  Directed by Edward L. Cahn
Starring Marla English, Anna Sten, John Litel, Lance Fuller, Adele Jergens, Gloria Castillo

Alex Gordon (Producer): "I got a call at three o'clock in the morning from Wally Middleton. He was Tom Conway's agent and he told me that Tom had suffered a hemorrhage. Now I had to find someone to replace him, which I knew wouldn't be easy because whoever I chose would have to be immediately available at the same salary we'd given Tom Conway without reading the script.

I looked at the Player's Directory and found John Litel. I was waiting in the parking lot when he drove in. Before we finished shaking hands, he asked to see the script. He said, 'Just give me twenty minutes' and went into one of the dressing rooms. Twenty minutes later, he came out with his makeup on and went through the day without once fluffing a line. We were able to finish the picture on schedule and only went two and a half hours into overtime."

October 20, 1956
*Boxoffice Magazine*
AMERICAN INT'L MAKES EXPLOITATION
COMBINATIONS FOR TEENAGE PATRONS
New York- The types of pictures which appeal to the 9-to-24 years of age group are being neglected by the major producers and exhibitors have complained that this type of product is scarce

in today's market, according to James H. Nicholson, president of American International Film Distributing Corp., which has already released two packages of exploitation-type features in July and August and has another package ready for November release.

Nicholson, whose American International has released 15 other features since it was formed approximately 15 months ago, will produce and release six other combination programs of two pictures each from January through July 1957 and will have at least six more combinations for the 1957-58 season, plus four color westerns.

The July 1956 combination, *Girls in Prison*, starring Joan Taylor and Richard Denning, and *Hot-Rod Girl*, with Lori Nelson and John Smith, has been booked to open at 74 RKO Theaters and allied circuit spots in the metropolitan district October 21, Nicholson said. Both pictures are teenage exploitation pictures. Nicholson maintains that this teenage audience, which has not been satisfied by the product issuing from Hollywood, is a faithful movie-going audience despite the competition of TV.

These pictures can be made at a cost of between $100,000 and $200,000 and, because they are made in rented studios and "even converted supermarkets" in about two weeks' shooting time, they can be ready for release within four months of their first planning, according to Nicholson.

"In this way, we select a topical title, have our writers work on it, and have the picture ready while the subject is still hot," he said.

American International's August combination is *It Conquered the World*, with Peter Graves and Beverly Garland, and *The She-Creature*, starring Marla English and Chester Morris. The November combination will be: *Shake, Rattle and Rock*, with Fats Domino and Lisa Gaye, a Rock 'n Roll musical, and *Runaway Daughters*, with Marla English. For January 1957, the combination will be: *Naked Paradise*, American International's first in color, starring Richard Denning and Beverly Garland, and *Flesh and the Spur*, also in color, starring Marla English and John Agar. For February, the combination will be: *The Undead* (a title selected some months ago), with Richard Garland and Pamela Duncan, and *Black Voodoo*, with the cast still to be set.

Other combinations for 1957 release will be built around these titles: *Motorcycle Girls* and *Underwater Girl* for April; *Rock N Roll Girl* and *The Juvenile Delinquent* for May; *Jet Fighter* and *Hell Raiders* for June; *The Nth Man* and *Last Woman on Earth* for July; *Teenage Revolt* and *Dragstrip Girl* for September; and *Island of Prehistoric Girls* and *Gorilla Girl* for November 1957. These pictures will all average 75 minutes in length.

Nicholson believes that too many producers today want to make art instead of merchandise.

"Many of our exploitation combinations outdraw major films in some instances and we have assurances of bookings from top theaters owned by leading circuits," he said. "Our grosses are rarely affected by newspaper reviews," Nicholson commented.

American International is also spending as much to exploit these pictures as "many majors," although the company concentrates on radio and TV trailers instead of magazine advertising, Nicholson said. Exploitation is now costing American International about $20,000 on the national level and from $50,000 to $100,00 on the local level for radio spots, TV trailers, and theatre trailers, which are supplied to exhibitors.

Nicholson came to New York October 2 to talk to exhibitors about new combinations and to discuss bookings with circuits. He was accompanied by Samuel Z. Arkoff, vice-president of American International. The company's financing is flexible, but much of it is secured through Pathe Laboratories, Nicholson said. George Waldman, whose Realart Pictures exchange in New York distributes American International product, attended Nicholson's trade press interview.

October 31, 1956
*Daily Variety 23rd Anniversary Issue*
Trade ad-
Congratulations from the Growing Infant of the Industry
AMERICAN INTERNATIONAL
Coming in 1957-
*The Undead, Black Voodoo, Flesh & the Spur, Naked Paradise, Rock n Roll Kid, The Juvenile Delinquent, Jet Fighter, Hell Raiders, Teenage Revolt, Dragstrip Girl, The Nth Man, Last Woman on Earth, Island*

1956

*of Prehistoric Women, Gorilla Girl, Valley of the Dead, The Wolf Girl, Teenage Werewolf*

Michael Landon in *I Was a Teenage Werewolf*.

# CHAPTER FOUR
# 1957

THIS YEAR WOULD BRING ABOUT WHAT IS WITHOUT A DOUBT THE most famous and controversial title in the AIP canon: *I Was a Teenage Werewolf.* When the film was first announced, it was immediately met with hostility from almost every front, as if the title itself would promote juvenile delinquency. Parent and Teachers organizations, Senators, heads of major Hollywood studios, etc., all decried the film without even having seen it. In his autobiography, Sam Arkoff said that *Teenage Werewolf* "gave plenty of ammunition to the hypercritical nitpickers dedicated to cleaning up America's movie theaters."

January 1957-

*Naked Paradise/Flesh and the Spur*
"GIANT Action-Packed Program in Wide Vision Color."

From the pressbook-
BIGGEST DOUBLE ACTION COLOR THRILL SHOW
   *Naked Paradise*, punch-packed smuggling adventure filmed entirely in Hawaii in beautiful color, and *Flesh and the Spur*, thrill-crammed western hit shot on location in the California Desert and at Gene Autry's famous western movie ranch, form this year's top action combination show from American International.
   Starring popular Richard Denning, science fiction hero of *Day the World Ended* and other hits and the *Mr. and Mrs. North* TV show, with Beverly Garland and Lisa Montell, *Naked Paradise* is a story punctuated with thrills. *Flesh and the Spur* toplines John Agar, Marla English, and Touch Connors in a story of vengeance and Indian warfare in the lawless west.

*Flesh and the Spur*
Produced by Alex Gordon  Directed by Edward L. Cahn
Starring John Agar, Marla English, Touch Connors, Raymond Hatton

   **Mike "Touch" Connors was an Executive Producer on *Flesh and the Spur*. He managed to raise $117,000 from a group of fellow Armenians who were willing to finance him in the film. Conners said that never saw any profit from the picture, blaming Sam Arkoff's "creative bookkeeping."**

*Naked Paradise*
Produced and Directed by Roger Corman
Starring Richard Denning, Beverly Garland, Lisa Montell, Leslie Bradley

   Robert Campbell (Writer): "After *Five Guns West*, I did another picture for Roger [Corman] called *Naked Paradise* and this time I got $400. I also told him I didn't want any credit for it."

46

Charles Griffith (Writer): "I don't know what stopped him, but [the script] was incomplete and I really used Bob's story and wrote a script on top of that."

Dick Miller (Actor): "We were in Coco Palms, which, on Kauai, was the hotel. It was just beautiful. You didn't have single rooms in those days, you had to buddy up, so naturally Jonathan [Haze] and I were buddying up, trying to tear up the island with the little Hawaiian girls. It was nice. We did two pictures back to back there. *She Gods of Shark Reef* was the other one."

Beverly Garland (Actress): "It was the only time I remember going first class on one of Roger's pictures."

Sam Arkoff: "Jim and I both went to Hawaii with our families. I had a part in the picture. One line. I still remember it because it was a key line, 'It's been a good harvest and the money is in the safe.' That was the first and last role. I've never been asked to be in a picture since."

**Beverly Garland (1926-2008) in *Naked Paradise.***

Film Reviews- *Naked Paradise*

*Boxoffice*- Told against the idyllic backgrounds [of Hawaii] is a rough-and-ready crime story that is sufficiently action full to offset what criticism it might generate because of a full dose of brutality. What's more, the cast, under [Roger] Corman's piloting, delivers a bevy of acceptable performances, with emphasis on Richard Denning and Beverly Garland, whose names have some marquee value.

*Variety*- [Roger] Corman helms his characters convincingly and all principals come up with above-average performances. [Richard] Denning is a hardy hero and Miss [Beverly] Garland in particular is a standout, often in dazzling attire.

*The Hollywood Reporter*- *Naked Paradise* is blessed with some magnificent Hawaiian backgrounds that are authentic and well-utilized, good performances, and writing that ingeniously creates individuals and, without overt pretension, probes character and sustains interest.

**AIP reissued *Naked Paradise* in 1960 as *Thunder Over Hawaii*.**

March 1957-

*Voodoo Woman/The Undead*
"The screen's new HIGH in VIOLENT, SHRIEKING, TERROR! See: The girl who lived 1000 years... buried alive! The voodoo blood ceremony! The unholy nowhere of the tortured undead! The hideous creature that was once a beautiful girl!"

From the pressbook-
NEW AND DIFFERENT HORROR THRILL SHOW
Something new in horror pictures is in store for movie fans when

American International's supernatural witchcraft and voodoo combination, *Voodoo Woman* and *The Undead*, comes to the screen.

Lovely pin-up queen Marla English essays the title role in *Voodoo Woman* as a ruthless adventuress who braves headhunters and strange voodoo rites to venture into the deepest jungle for a lost treasure. Tom Conway, demented outlawed scientist, turns her into a monstrous creature which goes on a rampage of murder and destruction in spite of the efforts of Touch Connors, Lance Fuller, and Mary Ellen Kaye.

A man's fight with the devil himself to save the girl he loves from the headman's axe is one of the unusual plot situations in *The Undead*, witchcraft chiller toplining Richard Garland, Allison Hayes, and Pamela Duncan.

Together, *Voodoo Woman* and *The Undead* provide three hours of spine-chilling thrills not equalled since the days of "Frankenstein" and "Dracula."

*The Undead*
Produced and Directed by Roger Corman
Starring Pamela Duncan, Richard Garland, Allison Hayes, Val Dufor, Mel Welles

Mel Welles (Actor): "If you're going to understand *The Undead*, you have to go back to the events that were going on in the world at the time. That picture was based on the Bridey Murphy phenomenon. There was a woman, I don't remember her name, who was hypnotized and under hypnosis described her previous life as a person named Bridey Murphy. It would have been one of the classic films of all time if Roger had shot the script as it was originally written. But Roger lost his nerve."

Charles Griffith (Writer): "I told Roger by the time we got the thing out it would be a dead issue. Then the Paramount movie based on [Morey] Bernstein's book, *The Search for Bridey Murphy*, bombed, so Roger changed the title of the picture from *The Trance of Diana Love* to *The Undead*, which is a zombie title. The whole thing was originally written in iambic pentameter. Roger loved it when he first read it. Then he showed it around and nobody understood it, so he told me to translate it into English a couple of days before we had to shoot. It was a mess then."

Roger Corman (Producer-Director): "It was a very strange film. I haven't seen it for a long, long time. I was maybe a little too ambitious for ten days and seventy or eighty thousand dollars."

*Voodoo Woman*
Produced by Alex Gordon  Directed by Edward L. Cahn
Starring Marla English, Tom Conway, Touch Connors, Lance Fuller, Mary Ellen Kaye

Alex Gordon (Producer): *Voodoo Woman* was a very short schedule picture. We made that in six days for $65,000. We had a sneak preview of the picture at the Cornell Theatre in Burbank. I took my fiancée and afterwards, she gave me back my engagement ring. She said, 'If that's the kind of picture you make, I don't think this marriage is going to work out.'"

Paul Blaisdell (Special Effects): "I was in the middle of designing the monster when I was told that they didn't have enough money to make a new monster. They asked me to take off all of the fins and horns and the head and tail of the She-Creature. Harry Thomas made a mask that Sam Arkoff had got cheap and they stuck that on the She-Creature. So now, instead of an amphibian, I'm a zombie."

March 2, 1957
*Boxoffice Magazine*
NICHOLSON FINDS EXHIBITORS OPTIMISTIC ABOUT BUSINESS ON 30,000-MILE TRIP
New York- "We found tremendous optimism about the film business from exhibitors from the Hawaiian Islands to Canada," according to James H. Nicholson, president of American International Film Distributing Corp. who recently completed a 30,000-mile trip, during which he talked to exhibitors on their product needs.
Nicholson finds that this optimism, the greatest since the end

of World War II, is due to a series of "big pictures" which have brought the public back into the moviegoing habit. Nicholson, who made the trip with Samuel Z. Arkoff, vice-president of American International, also found that almost every former single bill territory in the U.S., with the exception of Atlanta, is now playing double bills except in the case of *War and Peace, Giant,* and other three-hour pictures. A big element in this change is the increase of drive-ins, which always play double bills, Nicholson said.

## TO RELEASE EIGHT DUAL BILLS

For 1957, American International will produce and release at least eight double bill programs composed of exploitation pictures, plus two westerns, compared to five double bill programs released during 1956. The pictures will continue to be "gimmick pictures" with highly exploitable titles, but minus star names, which Nicholson finds have become secondary to the picture's title and theme. "Our type of product, which appeals mainly to the 12-to-25-years age group, doesn't need name stars," Nicholson said. American International is developing a group of young players, including Steve Terrell, Fay Spain, and John Ashley, and plans to use them in several films each season. Another player, Marla English, was featured in *Runaway Daughters* in 1956, then married and retired, but came back to play in *Voodoo Woman,* set for March 1957 release, before retiring again. "We hope she agrees to play in one of our new pictures," Arkoff said.

American International's 1956 pictures, including the combinations of *The She-Creature* and *It Conquered the World* and *Runaway Daughters* and *Shake, Rattle and Rock,* cost little to make, but played 6,000 to 8,000 playdates and will gross between $500,000 to $1,000,000 for each combination, Nicholson said. These pictures are now playing in Oklahoma City, where the new combination of *Naked Paradise* and *Flesh and the Spur* will follow *Cinerama,* he pointed out.

## OTHER COMBINATIONS SET

In addition to this last-named combination, both in Pathe Color, which is a January 1957 release, American International has completed *The Undead* and *Voodoo Woman* as a March 1957 combination and *Dragstrip Girl* and *Rock All Night* for later in the Spring. In March, Nicholson will start filming *I Was a Teenage Werewolf* to be coupled with *Attack of the Saucer Men* for May release. Other combinations will be: *Girls Reform School* and *Motorcycle Girl* for July; *The Cat Girl* and *Colossus* for September; *Jet Squadron* and *Hell Raiders* for October; *Last Woman on Earth* and *The Black Terror* for December release; and *Girl from 2,000,000 A.D.* and *Island of Prehistoric Women*.

"Ninety-five percent of our bookings are for double bills, but the pictures can later be bought singly," Nicholson said. American International uses three San Diego theaters, two of them drive-ins, for test runs before making up the selling campaigns. "Our selling campaigns in our pressbooks are simple and exploitable and are all based on the programs playing as a package."

Nicholson also pointed out that food and other merchandise are now being packaged for the American public- why not pictures? He also mentioned that American International does not have to register its titles except from the morality angle. "We go ahead and pick an exploitable title and then write a story to fit it," he said.


March 1957-

*Motion Picture Herald*
AIP HEADS SET SIGHTS ON TEENAGE PATRON by William R. Weaver
Hollywood- President James H. Nicholson and vice-president Samuel Z. Arkoff of American International Pictures have under consideration the formation of a new producing company, additional to the several they operate, to be called "Teenage Productions." Companies in which the Messrs. Nicholson and Arkoff join their efforts in behalf of product-pressed exhibitors include Carmel, Malibu, Sunset, and Golden Gate, on this side of the Atlantic.

On the other side, where they are currently combining conferences with European distributing executives and the responsibilities of co-producing *The Cat Girl* with Anglo Amalgamated Film Distributors, they are as likely as not to set up some more independent producing companies before returning to these shores sometime next month. They'll have to decide by then whether to launch one under the name of "Teenage Productions," which was in the talking stage when they left.


April 1957-
*Rock All Night/Dragstrip Girl*
"Rockin' Sockin' DOUBLE ACTION SHOW!"

*Rock All Night*
Produced and Directed by Roger Corman
Starring Dick Miller, Russell Johnson, Abby Dalton, The Platters, The Blockbusters

Roger Corman (Producer-Director): "AIP told me that I could have The Platters if I could make a picture with them before they went on tour. I bought a half hour TV show called "The Little Guy" and gave it to Chuck Griffith to rewrite to center around The Platters."

Charles Griffith (Writer): "Then there was a change in their schedule and Roger could only have them for a day, so I had 48 hours to rewrite the script. I took a pair of scissors and cut the script into pieces. I pasted what I could use from the original script on the new pages. The Sir Bob character that Mel Welles played was written for Lord Buckley."

Mel Welles (Actor): "Dick [Lord] Buckley was a guy I used to write for. He was an outrageous comedian that talked in hip talk and yet looked like an English Lord. But Dick was kind of flakey about his movements and disappeared, so I decided to play the part myself."

Dick Miller (Actor): "I had a fight scene at the beginning of the picture where this guy named Burt Nelson carries me out of the place. His girlfriend had given him this gold chain that I completely destroyed. I accidentally put my arm through it and turned it into a two-foot chain."

*Dragstrip Girl*
Produced by Alex Gordon  Directed by Edward L. Cahn
Starring Fay Spain, Steve Terrell, John Ashley, Frank Gorshin

John Ashley (Actor): "I took my girlfriend to the auditions for *Dragstrip Girl* and waited for her in the reception room. Lou Rusoff poked his head out and asked me if I was waiting for an audition. I thought about it for a few seconds and said, 'Sure. Why not?' He asked me to read for a part and I threw in an imitation of Elvis Presley, which I thought was dynamite. I got the part. My girlfriend didn't."

June 1957-

***I Was a Teenage Werewolf/Invasion of the Saucer-Men***
"EXPLOSIVE! AMAZING! TERRIFYING! You won't believe your eyes! See: Teenagers vs. the Saucer-Men! Disembodied hand that crawls! Night the world nearly ended!"

From the pressbook-
TEENAGE    HORROR    VERSUS    FLYING    SAUCER INVASION
The hottest new science fiction horror combination of them all is coming your way-
    *I Was a Teenage Werewolf* and *Invasion of the Saucer-Men* from American International, producers of Hollywood's most unusual science fiction horror hits like *Day the World Ended, It Conquered the World, The She-Creature.*
    Now come two pictures of such punch-packed power that they cannot be compared with any other horror pictures on the screen today. Never before have teenagers been involved in such terrifying adventures- when a brilliant boy becomes a creature of the night and green monsters from outer space invade the earth- starring the new faces exhibitors are asking for- Gloria Castillo, Steve Terrell, Frank Gorshin, Yvonne Lime, and Michael Landon. A shock and shudder show they will remember!

55

*Invasion of the Saucer-Men*
Produced by James H. Nicholson and Robert Gurney, Jr. Directed
by Edward L. Cahn
Starring Steve Terrell, Gloria Costillo, Frank Gorshin

**Lyn Osborn is attacked by an alien during the *Invasion of the
Saucer-Men*.**

Film Review- *Invasion of the Saucer-Men*

*Variety* (July 5, 1957)- *Invasion of the Saucer-Men* is a minor
entry for the science fiction trade. Film suffers from poor use of
attempted comedy and is further handicapped by a haphazard
sort of yarn which makes the film's 69-minute running time seem
twice as long. Steve Terrell and Gloria Costillo co-star, but haven't
much chance other than to look frightened under Edward L.
Cahn's direction. Frank Gorshin, in for comedy relief, has no place

actually in the jagged storyline. Balance of cast don't count for much. Technical credits are stock.

*I Was a Teenage Werewolf*
Produced by Herman Cohen  Directed by Gene Fowler, Jr.
Starring Michael Landon, Yvonne Lime, Whit Bissell, Tony Marshall

Film Reviews- *I Was a Teenage Werewolf*

*Variety* (July 5, 1957)- This latest in the current cycle of regression themes is a combo teenage and science fiction yarn, which should do okay in the exploitation market. There are plenty of story points that are sloughed over in the Ralph Thornton screenplay, but good performances help overcome deficiencies. Michael Landon delivers a first class characterization as the high school boy constantly in trouble and has okay support right down the line. Yvonne Lime is pretty as his girlfriend and Whit Bissell handles doctor part capably, although some of his lines are pretty thick. Gene Fowler, Jr.'s direction is up to standard of the script and Joseph La Shelle's photography leads technical credits.

*Time Magazine* (September 9, 1957)- SHOCK AROUND THE CLOCK
With the eat-'em-ups and the slash-'em-ups proving by good grosses that there is plenty of room at the bottom, the next step in low, lowbrow cinema was a marriage of the undead with the underdone: *I Was a Teenage Werewolf.* Plot synopsis: a mad psychiatrist turns a sensitive adolescent into a hairy, ravening beast. Says 30-year-old Producer [Herman] Cohen: "I heard that 62% of the movie audience was between 15 and 30 and I knew that the movies that were grossing well were horror or rock-n-roll films. So I decided to combine them with an exploitation title. You don't need big names." You don't need a big bankroll, either; *Werewolf* cost less than $150.000 to produce and by last week had taken in a monstrous $1,700,000.

July 1957-

July 20, 1957
*Boxoffice*
MADE-TO-ORDER DOUBLE BILLS ON AN UPSWING
by Frank Leyendecker
New York- The emergence of "exploitation double bills," or two pictures with similar or allied themes, such as science fiction or horror stories, started more than two years ago when American International brought out *Female Jungle* and *Oklahoma Woman,* which played the 42nd Street houses in New York and minor action houses elsewhere to good returns.

American International, headed by James H. Nicholson, has continued to make these double bill exploitation programs with increasing success. Nicholson admits that his organization usually selects a sensational-type title, such as *I Was a Teenage Werewolf,* and then writes a story to fit it. The pictures, which average 60-75 minutes in length, are made for about $100,000 each and usually gross at least $500,000, Nicholson said. No star names are used, but the company has been developing young players, such as Fay Spain, Steve Terrell, Gloria Castillo, and Marla English.

August 1957-

### *Rock Around the World/Reform School Girl*
"Rockin'... Rioting Teenage Fury! See... and hear: 14 new rock & roll tunes! Reformed girls... or teenage tramps! The nightmare jungle of a girls Reform School! Teenage rock' n roll stars from 'round the world!"

*Reform School Girl*
Produced by Robert J. Gurney, Jr., and Samuel Z. Arkoff  Directed by Edward Bernds
Starring Gloria Castillo, Ross Ford, Edward Byrnes

*Rock Around the World*
Produced by Herbert Smith  Directed by Gerard Bryant

Starring Tommy Steele, Nancy Whiskey, Hunter Hancock, Humphrey Lyttelton

**Rock Around the World is the British biopic *The Tommy Steele Story* in which the singer plays himself. At the time of its release, Tommy Steele was relatively unknown in the United States.**

From the pressbook-
*ROCK AROUND THE WORLD* AND *REFORM SCHOOL GIRL* COMING
Something for every teenager and adult moviegoer is presented by American International in its latest action and thrill combination program, *Rock Around the World* and *Reform School Girl*. Worldwide recording favorite Tommy Steele is toplined in the musical part of the show, which includes many fine singers and performers and a total of 14 song hits, including Nancy Wiskey singing "Freight Train." It is the story of Tommy Steele's life, which will be of enormous interest to his millions of fans- his struggle from humble ship's steward to becoming the teenage idol of the Nation. *Reform School Girl* is the inside story of girls behind bars- women without men- fighting the law and each other. Gloria Castillo is a lovely young girl innocently convicted. Edward Byrnes is the psychopathic killer who threatens her life if she talks and Ross Ford appears as the young psychologist who tries to help her. Action, fights, and thrills abound in *Reform School Girl* which, together with *Rock Around the World*, makes for great entertainment.

**White Huntress/Naked Africa**
"DOUBLE DYNAMITE! ACTION! THRILLS!"

*White Huntress*
Produced by C. Ray Stahl  Directed by George Breakston
Starring Susan Stephan, John Bently, Robert Urquhart

*Naked Africa*
Produced by Cedric Worth  Directed by Ray Phoenix

*White Huntress* is a 1954 British color film called *Golden Ivory*, which was bought by AIP, retitled, cut by 17 minutes, and released in black and white. *Naked Africa* is a sensationalistic color documentary which was a precursor to the "Mondo" movies of the Sixties.

September 1957-

*The Amazing Colossal Man/Cat Girl*
"A Savage Giant on a Blood-Mad Rampage!"

From the pressbook-
*AMAZING COLOSSAL MAN* AND *CAT GIRL* BIGGEST HORROR SHOW
From American International, Hollywood's top producer of horror pictures, now comes the most terrifying, most unusual, and the most fantastic horror show of all time! Never before has the screen presented scenes as in *The Amazing Colossal Man*, the story of a man who grows to the size of 70 feet at the rate of 10 feet a day. Starring Glenn Langan, Cathy Downs, and William Hudson, the picture is a breathless experience in science fiction entertainment. Presented on the same program is *Cat Girl*, a chilling mystery of a beautiful girl cursed by a leopard who changes to human form at times. Introducing Barbara Shelley in the title role, the picture was shot entirely on location and is packed with action and thrills.

*Cat Girl*
Produced by Lou Rusoff and Herbert Smith  Directed by Peter Hennessy
Starring Barbara Shelley, Robert Hayes, Kay Kallard

*The Amazing Colossal Man*
Produced and Directed by Bert I. Gordon
Starring Glenn Langan, Cathy Downs, William Hudson

Bert I. Gordon (Producer-Director-Writer): "The burned, near-disintegrated man in the Plutonium Blast was not wearing

60

a rubber suit. It was done solely with makeup- from scratch- with absolutely no appliances. He wore no mask. It was all put on him piece by piece with latex, wrinkling chemicals, grease paint, and about everything else you can think of."

Charles Griffith (Writer): "I spent one day with [Bert Gordon] hanging over my shoulder, telling me what words to write, and I quit. He wanted to dictate, demanding bad dialogue, horrible cliches. I said, 'I'm sorry. I can't work this way.' We both got mad and that was the end of that."

Paul Blaisdell (who created special props for the film): "Bert was very demanding as a director. He also listed himself as the producer, the script writer, the special effects man, the optical effects man- there was *this* by Bert I. Gordon and *that* by Bert I. Gordon, on and on, ad nauseam. And he was rather impatient on the set."

Film Review- *The Amazing Colossal Man*

*Monthly Film Bulletin*- This film has quite a good script, but is let down by poor trick photography.

Trade ad-
Double Boxoffice Blockbuster No. 15
Amazing Colossal Grosses: Milwaukee- Los Angeles.
Next attraction: New York, Paramount.
American International presents *THE AMAZING COLOSSAL MAN*.

**Although trade ads at the time announced this as AIP's "Double Boxoffice Blockbuster No. 15," this was only their 12th pre-packaged double feature. Bert I Gordon's first production for AIP was paired with AIP's first British co-production, *Cat Girl*. This double bill opened in New York City at the Broadway Theatre, making them the first AIP films to play on Broadway. After six months in release, *The Amazing Colossal Man* grossed $848,000.**

September 14, 1957
*Boxoffice*

## J.H. NICHOLSON SAYS YOUTH WANT 'EXCITING' FILMS

St. Louis- Emphasizing the economic need for film productions that appeal to young people, James H. Nicholson, president of American International Pictures, told exhibitors attending the Missouri-Illinois Theatre Owners convention at the Kingsway hotel this week that the young people, from teens through early maturity, are the "regulars" who get out and go to the movies who want "kicks" in everything they do.

Nicholson said he believes that youth want lots of excitement. "We try to package it for them. At the same time, the exhibitor is pleased with any increased supply of the product which turns a profit for them. We feel, furthermore, that our market is inexhaustible: more and more young people come along. We know there will be necessary adjustments in subject matter as tastes change, but we are convinced after three gratifying years that the one priceless ingredient is 'excitement' when the youth market, today's largest moviegoing group, buys its entertainment."

October 1957-

### *Motorcycle Gang/Sorority Girl*
"UNCENSORED... WILD AND WICKED... living with not tomorrow! See: Actual motorcycle chicken race! World's champion stunt riders! Deadly follow-the-leader race!"

From the pressbook-

## GIRLS ON MOTORCYCLES VS. SORORITY GIRLS

A combination of action, stunts, thrills, and laughs is promised when audiences see *Motorcycle Gang* and *Sorority Girl*, American International's latest combination show. Starring Hollywood's popular teenage favorites Steve Terrell, John Ashley, Anne Neyland, Carl Switzer, and Jean Moorhead, *Motorcycle Gang* has all the fun and youthful exuberance of today's young generation plus cycle stunts and thrills never shown before on any screen.

Thrill-crazy kids, roman riding, racing along railway tracks and fighting duels on motorcycles, a gang of cycle hoods terrorizing a small town, vicious fist fights, plus beautiful girls, rock-n-roll, and lots of laughs combine to make *Motorcycle Gang* a "must" for action enthusiasts. *Sorority Girl* is the inside story of the drama and intrigue within a house where young girls from all walks of life are thrown together. Susan Cabot is a scheming girl who shirks at nothing, including blackmail, to get what she wants in this all-new dramatic thunderbolt of thrills.

*Motorcycle Gang*
Produced by Alex Gordon  Directed by Edward L. Cahn
Starring Anne Neyland, Steve Terrell, John Ashley, Carl Switzer, Raymond Hatton, Russ Bender

John Ashley (Actor): "They actually postponed the starting date for *Motorcycle Gang* until I finished my basic training at Fort Ord. They were going to shoot the picture when I got my two-week furlough."

**John Ashley and Steve Terrell in *Motorcycle Gang*.**

*Sorority Girl* (aka **Confessions of a Sorority Girl**)
Produced and Directed by Roger Corman
Starring Susan Cabot, Dick Miller, Barboura O'Neill, June Kenny,
Barbara Crane, Fay Baker

Roger Corman (Producer-Director): "AIP had developed the
script and it had to be rewritten rather hurriedly. Because I was a
partner in the film with AIP, I questioned some of the construction
costs. I decided to rent a house and use it for the sorority house
and saved a great deal of money. The lead in *Sorority Girl* was Susan
Cabot, who was a very dedicated method actress from New York."

November 1957-

**I Was a Teenage Frankenstein/Blood of Dracula**
"FIENDISH, FRENZIED, BLOOD-CHILLING! Nothing
like this in all the history of horror!
Caution: The most gruesome horror ever shown! Not for the
squeamish! Free first aid and smelling salts! Don't come before
dinner! Warning for people who faint easily! See Frankenstein's
monster in COLOR!"

*Hollywood Reporter*- "A surefire exploitation package."

Trade ad-
TOA... Theatre Owners Approve... American International
*I Was a Teenage Frankenstein/Blood of Dracula*
    Opening in 75 theaters in Texas, including Interstate Theaters
Co., Rowley United, and Jefferson Amusement Theaters on
November 28, 1957.
    Opening Warner Theatre, Oklahoma City- plus 50 Video
Independent Theaters, December 12, 1957.
    Opening Paramount and Fenway Theaters, Boston- plus 50
other theaters throughout New England on January 15, 1958.
    Opening Stanley Warner, Alhambra Theatre, Milwaukee on
November 28, 1957.

From the pressbook-
HORROR RUNNING AMUCK ON THE GIANT SCREEN
Not since the days of Lon Chaney has such horror hit the screen as can now be seen in American International's all-new horror combination of *Blood of Dracula* and *I Was a Teenage Frankenstein*. Two monstrous figures- one a schoolgirl who is captured by the hypnotic powers of Dracula and turned into a monster with desire in her eyes and in her veins, the blood of a ferocious beast. The other is a manmade monster that brings terror and destruction to anything that crosses his path. This is a show that will be talked about for a long time to come. *Blood of Dracula* stars Sandra Harrison, Louise Lewis, Gail Ganley, and Jerry Blaine. Starring in *I Was a Teenage Frankenstein* are Whit Bissell, Phyllis Coates, Robert Burton, and Gary Conway.

*I Was a Teenage Frankenstein*
Produced by Herman Cohen  Directed by Herbert L. Strock
Starring Whit Bissell, Phyllis Coates, Robert Burton, Gary Conway

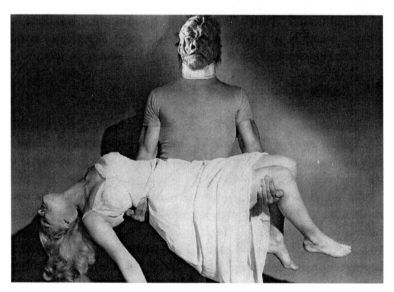

**Gary Conway and Angela Blake in *I Was a Teenage Frankenstein*.**

Sam Arkoff: "Jim and I were having lunch with R. J. O'Donnell, who owned a chain of theaters in Texas. He was complaining about the percentages the major studios were asking for their pictures. 'I hate giving those bastards Thanksgiving week,' he told us. Thanksgiving week was one of the biggest of the year. So Jim, seizing the opportunity, told him we had *Teenage Frankenstein* in the works. O'Donnell told us if he could have it and a second feature, he would give us the Majestic, which was one of his flagship theaters. That was a big day for us because we were not normally getting the flagship theaters."

Herbert L. Strock (Director): "We did a scene where Whit Bissell cuts a leg off with an electric saw. You didn't actually see it. You heard the sound of the blade cutting through the bone and then he picks up this phony leg and holds it in front of the camera with blood all over it. The censors said, 'You can't show him cutting off a leg on camera. You'll have to cut the scene.' I argued that it took place off camera but they insisted they saw him cut into the leg and I had to run the film for them again."

Whit Bissell (Actor): "It wasn't very good really. It was done in a hurry, which is pretty obvious when you see it. If you're an actor, you take the part and you're glad to get it. It's nice to be working."

Film Review- *I Was a Teenage Frankenstein*

*Time Magazine* (March 10, 1958)- THE NEW PICTURES
*I Was a Teenage Frankenstein* (American International). There's this mad scientist, see. He's a descendant of Baron Frankenstein, the mad scientist who invented Boris Karloff, and naturally he wants to keep up the family traditions. So one day, he ups to another scientist and says, sneaky-like: "I plan to assemble a human being." His friend is horrified. "But Professor Frankenstein, you can't!" Oh yes, he can, and what's more, he plans to make a teenage monster. After all, *I Was a Teenage Werewolf* was a howling success at the box office last year. Explains the mad scientist: "Only in youth there is hope." As a sequel to *I Was a Teenage Werewolf*, *IWATF* will probably rank as one of the year's biggest horrors.

*Blood of Dracula*
Produced by Herman Cohen  Directed by Herbert L. Strock
Starring Sandra Harrison, Louise Lewis, Gail Ganley, Jerry Blaine

Herbert L. Strock (Director): "Herman Cohen definitely wanted everything his way. We were shooting in Hancock Park one night and we got into a fight over something and I finally told him to go to hell. I threatened to walk off the picture and everybody in the crew was behind me. He was really hard to get along with. I remember on *Blood of Dracula*, he had Sandra Harrison in tears over something or other."

Film Reviews- *Blood of Dracula*

*The Film Daily*- This is the type of entertainment that should get over in the action houses, especially for audiences who like the shockers.

*Variety*- Slow in takeoff, *Blood of Dracula* nevertheless packs enough interest to hold its audience. Jerry Blaine, one of the victims, is in for a tuneful song number.

November 23, 1957
*Boxoffice*
A group of Embassy Pictures officials greeted Colossal Charlie, a stiltman brought in from New York, in front of the Paramount Theatre in Boston where *The Amazing Colossal Man* opened simultaneously with bookings in more than 600 theaters in New England.

December 1957-

December 7, 1957
*Boxoffice*
THOSE TWO-PICTURE PACKAGES JUST KEEP ROLLING ALONG by Ivan Spear
While it cannot be credited with inventing the paired bookings

idea- the company is too new for that- there is no doubt that the outfit more instrumental than any other in elevating the technique to its present important niche is comparatively newcoming American International Pictures. This is the fast-growing organization founded and masterminded by James H. Nicholson, long a successful exhibitor, and Samuel Z. Arkoff, prominent attorney and business executive. Associated with them is Joseph Moritz and Leon P. Blender, the latter serving as the company's sales manager.

The company's kickoff film was a Roger Corman entry called *The Fast and the Furious*, which can be considered prophetic phraseology to describe the rise of AIP and it was shortly thereafter that the company chieftains recognized the potential market for package deals.

They entered the field of compatible programming with two bundles- *Phantom from 10,000 Leagues* paired with *Day the World Ended* and *Hot Rod Girl*, which was teamed with *Girls in Prison*.

Moreover, Nicholson, Arkoff, and company (including AIP's energetic press agent, Alex Evelove) will have it known that as concerns this business of compatible programming, the industry ain't seen nothing yet. Two other tandem bills are in the works, to wit: *Motorcycle Gang*, with Steve Terrell, Anne Neyland, John Ashley, and Carl Switzer, being produced by Alex Gordon, directed by Edward L. Cahn, and *Sorority Girls*, with Susan Cabot, Dick Miller, Barbara [sic] Morris, with Roger Corman producing and directing; and *The Saga of the Viking Women and Their Voyage to the Waters of the Great Sea Serpent*, with Abby Dalton, Susan Cabot, Brad Jackson, with Corman again producing and directing, and to be packaged with *The Astounding She-Monster*, with Robert Clarke, Kenne Duncan, Marilyn Harvey, producer-director: Ronnie Ashcroft.

Parenthetically, Evelove, et al, contend they aren't kidding about the above-mentioned title of "Viking." If it is permitted to live, there can be no doubt that the picture will hit the market with at least one irrefutable distinction- the longest tag in filmdom's history.

Looking further into the future, there will be the pairing of *Jet Attack*, starring John Agar and Audrey Totter, Gordon and Cahn again serving as the producer-director team, and *Hell Raiders*,

with Michael Connors, John Ashley, Russ Bender, Lou Rusoff producing and, again, Cahn directing.

Then AIP has two that are in the works individually. They might eventually find themselves together in a package or each might be teamed with another feature yet to be selected. They are

*The Cool and the Crazy*, toplining Scott Marlowe and Gigi Perreau, produced by Kansas City's Elmer Rhoden, Jr., directed by William Whitney; and *The Fantastic Puppet People*, with John Agar, John Hoyt, June Kenney, and Russ Bender, on which Bert I. Gordon will be both producer and director.

Perhaps a pair of statistics will illustrate better than anything else the bell-weather position of AIP in the team-'em-up trend. During 1957, the company will have delivered 22 features in 11 packages, which represents better than 10 percent of Hollywood's independent production for the year.

December 14, 1957
*Boxoffice*
EIGHT AIP RELEASES SET JANUARY-MARCH
Hollywood- Eight releases have been set for the first four months of 1958 by American International Pictures, it is announced by company executives James H. Nicholson and Samuel Z. Arkoff. Continuing its policy of fixing its release schedule on the calendar year instead of condensed seasonal periods, AIP will send out at least one program package during each of the first four months of 1958.

**Sam Arkoff and Jim Nicholson.**
**Photo courtesy of Photofest**

# CHAPTER FIVE
# 1958

Flushed with success, Jim and Sam decided to get their own studio. They moved out of their Sunset Boulevard offices and leased the Charlie Chaplin Studios located on Sunset and La Brea in Hollywood. It wasn't long before they realized that having a studio was an unnecessary expenditure, so Jim and Sam sold off their lease to Red Skelton Productions. They moved the company's offices to 8255 Sunset Boulevard on the Sunset Strip. Much of their actual film production at this time would be done at ZIV Studio, located at 7324 Santa Monica Boulevard.

January 1958-

***Viking Women and the Sea Serpent/The Astounding She-Monster***
"DOUBLE SPECTACLE-TERROR! Fabulous! Fantastic! Terrifying! See: Savage blood rituals of a lost empire! Giant sea serpent of the Vortex! Two world of monstrous terror! Superwomen with the courage of giants!"

From the pressbook-
*VIKING WOMEN AND THE SEA SERPENT* AND *ASTOUNDING SHE-MONSTER* COMING
American International Pictures now brings to the screen *Viking Women and the Sea Serpent* and *The Astounding She-Monster*. The screen roars with this all-new action show as the fantastically brave and divinely beautiful Viking Women fight for their lost men in the waters of the great sea serpent. You will also see a beautiful, deadly she-monster prance on her prey and destroy them with a deadly radium. Starring in *Viking Women and the Sea Serpent* are Abby Dalton, Susan Cabot, and Brad Jackson. *The Astounding She-Monster* stars Robert Clarke, Kenne Duncan, and Marilyn Harvey.

*Viking Women and the Sea Serpent*
Produced and Directed by Roger Corman
Starring Abby Dalton, Susan Cabot, Brad Jackson, June Kenney, Richard Devon

Roger Corman (Producer-Director): "Two friends of mine, Jack Rabin and Irving Bloch, brought me a script and some drawings of a sea serpent coming out of the water to attack this boat full of Viking women. They told me they could do all of the special effects for $20,000 plus a piece of the picture. I saw it as an opportunity to make a million-dollar picture on a low budget. That's how the project was sold to me and that's how I sold it to AIP."

**Behind the scenes filming *Viking Women and the Sea Serpent*.**

*The Astounding She-Monster*
Produced and Directed by Ronnie Ashcroft
Starring Robert Clarke, Kenne Duncan, Marilyn Harvey, Jeanne
Tatum, Shirley Kilpatrick

Robert Clarke (Actor): "When we made the picture, it was called *The Naked Invader*. It was kind of a piece of junk. Certainly I couldn't be very proud of having been in it. Ronnie Ashcroft was the director. He owned an editing service. He was a nice guy. I made a couple of thousand bucks on that picture because it made quite a lot of money and in addition to my salary, which I think was something like $500, Ronnie promised me four percent of his producer's share. He wasn't a particularly good filmmaker, but he was an honest man."

Film Reviews- *The Astounding She-Monster*

*Monthly Film Bulletin-* The Feminine monster shimmers and wobbles and oscillates on each of her many sinister appearances, but unfortunately, the rest of the picture behaves accordingly and it is only the absence of the monster that allows the image to remain static.

*Motion Picture Herald- The Astounding She-Monster* should be welcomed by those patrons who dote on the far-from-conventional behavior of mere earthlings when confronted by visitors from outer space.

January 27, 1958
*Boxoffice*
25,000 THEATERS BY '70, AIP PRESIDENT PREDICTS
Dallas- Instead of decreasing, the number of indoor and drive-in theaters in the United States will rise in the next 12 years and, by 1970, there should be approximately 25,000 motion pictures theaters. This was the cheerful prediction of James H. Nicholson, president of American International Pictures, in a talk before the Texas Drive-In Theatre Owners Ass'n convention here this week. At present, there are approximately 18,5000 theaters, of which about 4,500 are drive-ins.

Nicholson appealed to the drive-in operators for "showmanship that goes beyond tacking up a one-sheet" and reiterated AIP's recently announced pledge of increased production, with no sales to television for a minimum of at least ten years after release.

February 1958-

**Jet Attack/Suicide Battalion**
"THUNDERING DOUBLE-ACTION from Heaven to Hell and Back!"

*Jet Attack*
Produced by Alex Gordon  Directed by Edward L. Cahn
Starring John Agar, Audrey Totter, Gregory Wallcott, James Dobson

*Suicide Battalion*
Produced by Lou Rusoff  Directed by Edward L. Cahn
Starring Michael Connors, John Ashley, Russ Bender, Jewell Lain, Bing Russell, Scott Peters

From the pressbook-
*JET ATTACK* AND *SUICIDE BATTALION* NEW ACTION COMBO
*Jet Attack* and *Suicide Battalion* is the latest thrill-packed action combination from American International, the company that specializes in high-powered action programs aimed at audiences of all ages. *Jet Attack* is the thrilling story of three jet aces who parachute behind enemy lines in Korea on a daring rescue mission. Starring John Agar and Audrey Totter, the picture presents authentic U.S. Air Force films of jest in action, flying air cover and roaring destruction at the Reds. A helicopter rescue, which fails, fights with guerillas, and suspense-filled truck and car chases punctuate this picture, which is the story of the Hell's Angels of the Korean war. On the second half of this all-action combination is *Suicide Battalion*, which stars Michael Connors, John Ashley, and Jewell Lain and shows a relentless fight to demolish enemy installations during the second World War. Action at its best is presented in this story as five men fight through the jungles of the Philippines on a one-way road to death. On the lighter side of this action feature, Hilo Hattie provides much laughter doing a Hawaiian Hula. This is an all-new, thrilling and exciting action combination that is aimed at both adult and teenage audiences.

February 10, 1958
*Boxoffice*
Producer Roger Corman welcomed his brother Gene on the set of *Machine Gun Kelly*, American International production on which Gene will be Roger's associate.

February 17, 1958
*Boxoffice*
AIP ADS, PROMOTION TO CARRY TV PLEDGE
Louisville- American International Pictures will insert notices in posters, trade paper, and general advertising and promotional material that its pictures will not be shown on television for at least ten years, if ever. James H. Nicholson, AIP president, told the Allied convention here this week. This is being done because both exhibitor and the public require assurance that new motion pictures will not be available on home screens, he said.

February 17, 1958
*Boxoffice*
Street ballyhoo was set up by Manager R.A. Bergeron of the Central Theatre, Biddenford, ME for the showing of *I Was a Teenage Frankenstein* and *Blood of Dracula*. A "body" was paraded up and down the business district during the busiest hours of the day by an "undertaker" and was followed by two girls wearing horror masks. Result on opening day was the largest gross in 18 months, Bergeron said.

March 1958-

***Dragstrip Riot/The Cool and the Crazy***
"TWIN ROCK N RIOT SHOW!"

*Dragstrip Riot*
Produced by O. Dale Ireland  Directed by David Bradley
Starring Yvonne Lime, Gary Clarke, Fay Wray, Bob Turnball, Connie Stevens

*The Cool and the Crazy*
Produced by E. C. Rhoden, Jr.  Directed by William Witney
Starring Scott Marlowe, Gigi Perreau, Richard Bakalyan, Dick Jones

March 17, 1958
*Boxoffice*
NEW WIDESCREEN PROCESS IS ANNOUNCED BY AIP

Kansas City- American International Pictures, which began production and distribution of features with a pair of double bills three years ago, is ready to step up both the quantity and the quality of its product, James H. Nicholson, president of the up-and-coming company, revealed at the Show-A-Rama held here this week by Kansas-Missouri Theatre Ass'n and Allied Independent Theatre Owners of the Kansas and Missouri area.

Nicholson announced a new anamorphic widescreen process, Superama, in which all AIP pictures will eventually be produced. He did not reveal further details about the process, but he said that as the widescreen system is expanded, more and more of the company's features will be in color.

March 24, 1958
Trade ad-
James H. Nicholson and Samuel Z. Arkoff... of AMERICAN INTERNATIONAL PICTURES welcomes their worldwide distribution organization to its 3rd Anniversary Convention in session at Hollywood, March 24-26, 1958.

To follow up our current box office showmanship packages of *Jet Attack* and *Suicide Battalion*... *Viking Women and the Serpent* and *The Astounding She-Monster*... *Dragstrip Riot* and *The Cool and the Crazy*... you will see...

*Machine Gun Kelly* and *The Bonnie Parker Story*... *The Fantastic Puppet People* and *The Girl from 5,000,000 A.D.*... *Hot Rod Gang* and *High School Hellcats*... *How to Make a Monster* and

*The Colossal Beast*... *Submarine X-2* and *Ram-Jet*... *The Spider* and *Beast Without a Body*...

and introducing anamorphic SUPERAMA.

*Boxoffice*
March 24, 1958
FIRST FILMS IN SUPERAMA

A pair of gangster films, *Machine Gun Kelly* and *The Bonnie Parker*

*Story,* will be the first AIP features to reach the nation's screens in the company's new 2-to-1 ratio Superama process.

These features, as well as future releases in the added dimensions, will be provided to exhibitors at no increase in cost. It is expected that by midsummer, all AIP releases will be in the new widescreen system.

Superama is achieved through a reversal of the "print-down" methods used to reduce CinemaScope, Todd-AO, and other wide film techniques to 35mm prints. The AIP method of standard photography offers production, setting, lighting, and editing savings while eliminating focus problems common in the shooting of many widescreen processes, according to James Nicholson and Samuel Z. Arkoff, AIP toppers.

*Boxoffice*
March 24, 1958
30 FILMS TO GO BEFORE AIP CAMERAS IN 1958
American International Pictures to Reveal Plans at Its First National Sales Meeting- by Ivan Spear

Hollywood- When on Monday (March 24) the film capitol hands out its welcome signs for attendants to American International Pictures' first national distributors meeting, a sizable percentage of the nation's theater operators will voice a sincere and enthusiastic "Amen" to the greetings.

For here assembled for the initiator of such conclaves will be the men and women whose activities in bringing to the celluloid marketplace the product of the company founded and being operated by James H. Nicholson and Samuel Z. Arkoff have played such an important part in keeping open the doors of thousands of showcases which, confronted by product shortage, might otherwise have found themselves in serious trouble.

The founding fathers of AIP has a single objective- the production and acquisition of features which would offer exhibitors entertainment to draw profitable patronage. They foreswore so-called artistic ventures from the start in favor of marketable product. They have a mutual pact to watch out for threatening artistic signs in each other. But in their avoidance of art subjects in favor of tried-and-true entertainment, they have not lost sight of quality. They predicate quality on pocketbook. Their aim is what they call "high EQ," short for entertainment quality.

March 24, 1958
*Boxoffice*
A student from the physics laboratory of Butler University was happy to help Leonard Barrow, student assistant manager at the Indian Theater in Indianapolis, rig up a "lab" in the lobby prior and during the run of *I Was a Teenage Frankenstein* and *Blood of Dracula*. Barrow mixed up the chemicals for a few eerie demonstrations, including the "severing" of his hand. To increase the horror effect, the lobby lights were damped and a green spot was thrown over the whole display. The teenagers love it!

March 31, 1958
*Boxoffice*
AIP TO SPEND $3 MILLION ON YEAR'S PRODUCTION
Hollywood- American International Pictures will make or acquire for distribution 24 to 30 feature films during the company's fiscal year beginning April. These pictures will cost approximately $3,000,000 and the average budget of each will be about $150,000. This compares   with an average cost of approximately $120,000 per film in the past and a release slate of 18 films during the year just drawing to a close. Six of the 24 to 30 photoplays are already in the can or are in the process of production. While many of the others have been blueprinted, nothing unalterably binding has been determined as concerns them.

May 1958-

***Machine Gun Kelly/The Bonnie Parker Story***
*Variety*- "One of the best exploitation duos of the year."

*The Bonnie Parker Story*
Produced by Stan Shpeter  Directed by William Witney
Starring Dorothy Provine, Jack Hogan, Richard Bakalyan

*Machine Gun Kelly*
Produced and Directed by Roger Corman
Starring Charles Bronson, Susan Cabot, Morey Amsterdam, Richard Devon, Jack Lambert

Dick Miller (Actor): "I was supposed to play Machine Gun Kelly. Bobby [R. Wright] Campbell wanted his brother William to get the part. He made phone calls and sent telegrams saying that I was all wrong for the role and only his brother could play it, that he was tailoring the script for him. Jim, Sam, and Roger got tired of it all, so they gave the part to Charles Bronson. I walked away from a lot of parts, but this one walked away from me and I really wanted it."

**Charles Bronson as *Machine Gun Kelly*.**

Film Reviews- *Machine Gun Kelly*

*Boxoffice*- Convincing, accurate, rapidly-paced action-laden biography of one of the hardest hombres of his hectic era. For the film's authenticity of atmosphere as well as its many other superior qualities, much of the credit is due to energetic Roger Corman, who both produced and directed the feature.

*Variety*- A first-rate little picture. Script is remarkable for the crisp flavor of the dialogue and takes the trouble to sketch briefly, but effectively, minor characters and incidents that give weight and meaning to the otherwise sordid story.

May 5, 1958
*Boxoffice*
AIP SETS 12 RELEASES FOR MAY, JUNE, JULY
Los Angeles- Leon Blender, general sales manager for American International Pictures, has announced 12 releases for May-June-July, setting a record release for the company.

For May release are AIP's first Superama productions, *Machine Gun Kelly* and *The Bonnie Parker Story*, slated for national showing May 28. In June, *Attack of the Puppet People, Terror from the Year 5000, Hot Rod Gang*, and *High School Hellcats* will be released. *How to Make a Monster* and *War of the Colossal Beast* will be released July 2 and July 23 will see *Tank Battalion* and *Hell Squad* in release.

June 1958-

**High School Hellcats/Hot Rod Gang**
"The Truth About High School Sororities!"

*High School Hellcats*
Produced by Charles Buddy Rogers  Directed by Edward Bernds
Starring Yvonne Lime, Brett Halsey, Jana Lund

Edward Bernds (Director): "I can't say I was aware of breaking any new ground. I merely tried to give a representation of what was going on at the time."

Film review- *High School Hellcats*

*The Hollywood Reporter* by Jack Moffitt
Contrary to the current Hollywood dogma that young people demand a film diet of youthful criminal violence, I found this teenaged audience so enthusiastically and vociferously on the side of virtue that I left the theatre comfortably reassured concerning the next generation and more than a little inspired. *High School Hellcats* has strong appeal for young audiences and it pleases them.

*Hot Rod Gang*
Produced by Lou Rusoff  Directed by Lew Landers
Starring John Ashley, Jody Fair, Gene Vincent

John Ashley (Actor): "I was offered a part on *Matinee Theatre*. It was a good, dramatic part and Janis Paige was the star. AIP wanted me to do *Hot Rod Gang* and I asked for a postponement because I really wanted to do the show. I thought it might help pull me out of the B movies. Sam Arkoff wouldn't let me do it. He had me under contract and that was that as far as he was concerned. I was going to do the show anyway and Sam got an injunction to stop me. I never really forgave him for that."

June 23, 1958
*Boxoffice*
AIP IN RECORD OUTPUT; 10 RELEASES IN JULY
Albuquerque- Continuing to express confidence in the motion picture industry, American International Pictures will release ten features in July, a record output, James H. Nicholson, president, announced at the convention of the New Mexico Theatre Owners Ass'n here Tuesday (17).
The company will release a package of two pictures on each of the five Wednesdays in the month, he said.

**John Ashley (1934-1997) in *Hot Rod Gang*.**

Nicholson declared that fear had become too powerful a factor in determining the channels in which both production and exhibition should move.

"AIP" definitely does not fear the future. Our own experience tells us there is still a growth factor remaining in exhibition and production. It is possible to fight fear, the opiate of the industry, in many ways. Production of marketable entertainment for the exhibitor is the best way.

"Instead of doing as much of that as we can," he declared, "many filmmakers and exhibitors dull their creative ability with fears- fear there is a shrinking audience, fear there won't be enough product, fear of subject matter, fear of expenditure for exploitation, fear of continuing constriction of the industry and its market, fear of television, fear of a dozen other straw men.

"If," he commented, "the motion picture industry in and out of Hollywood doesn't check its fears quickly, we will see a return to the chaos of the mid-30s. That period alone should give us confidence in the ability of our industry not only to survive, but to expand after a time of crisis.

The situation then was met by positive action after a period of quaking and shaking. The old heads of the industry woke up finally and saw where fear had taken them. They reversed their psychology and by tremendous effort brought the industry to its high peak of prosperity.

"The same kind of reverse psychology is necessary today," he declared. "It is all in the point of view. We should think like the optimistic brother in the story- somewhere at the bottom of all this stuff there is gold. It's just a matter of eliminating the stuff that surrounds it."

AIP's contribution to the campaign against fear, he said, is a ten-picture schedule for July.

The release dates for the features are: July 2, *Hot Rod Gang* and *High School Hellcats*; July 9, *How to Make a Monster* and *Teenage Caveman*; July 16, *Tank Battalion* and *Hell Squad*; July 23, *Screaming Skull* and *Terror from the Year 2,000* [sic]; and July 30, *Night of the Blood Beast* and *The She-Gods of Shark Reef*. They will come as combos.

**As with many of Nicholson's rousing speeches, some of AIP's plans were altered or did not come to pass. One of these combos was released in June, two were released in July, and two more in August.**

July 1958-

*Attack of the Puppet People/War of the Colossal Beast*
"INCREDIBLY FANTASTIC! You won't believe your eyes! See: The wild Rock & Roll dance of the doll dwarfs! The Beast crush giant buildings! The Colossal Beast destroyed... in COLOR!"

From the pressbook-
FANTASTIC HUMAN PUPPETS AND A HUMAN GIANT
*The Attack of the Puppet People* and *War of the Colossal Beast*, American International Pictures' latest thrill combination.

*The Attack of the Puppet People*, starring John Agar and June Kenny, tells the story of a famous European dollmaker who takes up residence in a large American city. He becomes so desperately lonely that his mind twists to the point where he develops a machine for reducing humans to puppets. He can animate these doll dwarfs at will for his own amusement... thereby never again being lonely. In the world of these little people, cars are wheeled monsters, dogs are voracious killers, and a razor blade is a guillotine!

*War of the Colossal Beast* stars Sally Fraser and Dean Parkin in a sequel to A.I.'s *Amazing Colossal Man*. The savage giant of the original picture survives a fall from Boulder Dam, but in a horribly mutilated condition. He escapes to the wilds of Mexico, where he ravages the land. His sister organizes an expedition which goes south of the border, drugs the towering monstrosity, and brings him back to the United States, where he creates havoc.

*Attack of the Puppet People* (aka **The Fantastic Puppet People**)
Produced and Directed by Bert I. Gordon
Starring John Agar, John Hoyt, June Kenney

Bert I. Gordon (Producer-Director): "We needed a rat for a scene in *Attack of the Puppet People*. We got one and were ready to shoot. The rat took one look at the camera, got scared, had a heart attack, and dropped dead!"

John Hoyt (Actor): "I thought the movie as a whole was excellent, especially when you consider the comparatively small budget we had to work with."

Film Reviews- *Attack of the Puppet People*

*Los Angeles Times*- A well-done minor-key science fiction film.

*Monthly Film Bulletin*- Some ruthless cutting and a brisker pace would have helped the film.

*War of the Colossal Beast* (aka ***Revenge of the Colossal Man***)
Produced and Directed by Bert I. Gordon
Starring Sally Fraser, Roger Pace, Dean Parkin

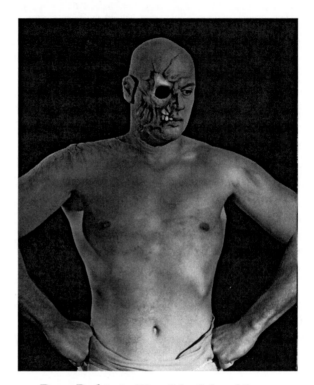

**Dean Parkin in *War of the Colossal Beast*.**
**Photo courtesy of Mark McGee**

Film Review- *War of the Colossal Beast*

*Monthly Film Bulletin*- The trick photography of these Further Adventures of the Amazing Colossal Man is ludicrously unconvincing and in any case, the idea has lost its pristine impact. The dialogue strikes an oddly hieratic note; the charm school heroine reacts to every plot development with a winsome smile while the rest of the players apparently prefer not to react at all.

A full page July 1958 trade ad featured a picture of Arkoff on the left, Nicholson on the right, and a skull in between them. The text reads as follows:

LET'S TALK ABOUT THE FELLOW IN THE MIDDLE...
He's not really dead... He's the livest thing in show business right now! Treat him right and you'll find he's the best friend you've had in years!

The aim of the founders of American International Pictures, Jim Nicholson (he's the fellow on the right), and Sam Arkoff (he's the fellow on the left), is to turn out well-planned exploitation pictures that will turn a profit for showmen. Wherever the Hollywood-originated "do it yourself" advertising has been thoroughly used, the results have been uniformly tremendous. The highly acclaimed *Machine Gun Kelly* and *The Bonnie Parker Story* rolled up sensational record-breaking grosses in an eighty-theatre saturation booking in the Cincinnati territory; *Attack of the Puppet People* and *War of the Colossal Beast* topped all "big" company grosses in a Los Angeles multiple first run; *Hot Rod Gang* and *High School Hellcats* produced the best AIP results to date in the Kansas City territory. Impressive first engagements are coming in on three more combinations just starting into distribution: *Tank Battalion* and *Hell Squad*; *How to Make a Monster* and *Teenage Caveman*; *She-Gods of Shark Reef* and *Night of the Blood Beast*. Next come two of the absolutely greatest horror shows ever produced by these specialists in the field. First, the "gimmick"-loaded shocker *The Screaming Skull* (he's the fellow in the middle) and then shortly afterwards, the never-to-be-forgotten thriller of a lifetime, *The Spider!*

### Tank Battalion/Hell Squad
"Raging Inferno of War! Where Kids Learned to Kill or Be Killed! The Guts and Gore of Desert War! Terrible in War... Tender in Love!"

### Tank Battalion
Produced by Richard Bernstein  Directed by Sherman A. Rose
Starring Don Kelly, Marjorie Hellen, Edward G. Robinson, Jr.

*Hell Squad*
Produced and Directed by Burt Topper
Starring Wally Campo, Brandon Carroll, Frederic Gavlin

**How to Make a Monster/Teenage Caveman**
"It will SCARE the living yell out of you! See: The madman's gruesome chamber of horrors! The savage attack of the monster at midnight! The Teenage Werewolf vs. the Teenage Frankenstein! A man turned into a monster before your very eyes!"

From the pressbook-
YOUNG PEOPLE STAR IN MOVIES OF MODERN AND PREHISTORIC WORLDS

*How to Make a Monster* and *Teenage Caveman,* two new motion pictures from American International which are heralded as super-thrillers, commence their first local showing today.

*How to Make a Monster* shows Robert H. Harris in the role of Hollywood makeup expert who goes berserk when his job is threatened by his studio's new owners. At the time he is given notice, he is working on a picture which involves his two most famous monsters, the TEENAGE WEREWOLF and the TEENAGE FRANKENSTEIN. He works a secret formula makeup cream in with the monster makeup, which enables him to control the actions of these actors. Under his spell, his monster creations go on a wild killing orgy, which has been filmed in flaming color.

*Teenage Caveman* details the life of a prehistoric rebel who flees to the highlands with his blond lady love, where he fights off giant dinosaurs to protect his home.

*How to Make A Monster*
Produced by Herman Cohen  Directed by Herbert L. Strock
Starring Robert H. Harris, Paul Brinegar, Gary Conway, Gary Clarke, John Ashley

**Gary Conway (born 1936) appeared in AIP's *I Was a Teenage Frankenstein, Viking Women and the Sea Serpent,* and *How to Make a Monster.***

Herman Cohen (Producer): "*How to Make a Monster* was an idea I came up with when I was leaving the studio late one night. We shot it at ZIV Studios. For the picture, we put up a sign that said American International Pictures. It was there for weeks and Jim and Sam would drive by and tell people it was their studio."

Herbert L. Strock (Director): "We had this special effects man named Charlie Duncan. 'Drunkin' Duncan,' we used to call him. He was a good special effects man if you could keep him sober. We were between scenes for the fire at end of the film when Charlie decided to rehearse the gas jets. Before we knew it, the whole place was on fire. So I shoved the actors onto the set, grabbed the cameraman and pushed him behind the camera and we hurried through the scene before the set burned to the ground."

Sam Arkoff: "Herman Cohen really wanted to be a part of AIP. He resented the fact that Roger [Corman] seemed to get the deals. There was every reason in the world why because Roger could move. It didn't take him forever and he wasn't pompous. The word for Herman is pompous. We kept up what you might call a forced cordiality."

Film Reviews- *How to Make a Monster*

*Variety*- The Script has some sharp dialogue and occasionally pungent Hollywood Talk ("That's the way the footage cuts"), although these aspects will be largely lost on the audiences this picture will attract.

*The Hollywood Reporter*- The massed small fry in the audience expressed its preference, but a sort of scattered acclamation, for real monsters rather than made up ones.

*Los Angeles Examiner*- It is not a do-it-yourself treatise on how to fashion your own household eyesores. Rather, it's a torpid tale without even the so-called horror which is supposed to attract adolescents.

*Teenage Caveman* (aka **Prehistoric World**)
Produced and Directed by Roger Corman
Starring Robert Vaughn, Darrah Marshall, Leslie Bradley

Roger Corman (Producer-Director): "Robert Vaughn was supposed to kill a bear and carry it back to camp. The prop man provided us with a stuffed bear and I knew it would look ridiculous because this bear was stiff as a board. But it was the end of the day and I knew we wouldn't be able to come back to the location, so I put the camera behind some trees and filmed it in a long shot. At the sneak preview, the audience laughed when that scene came on, so I cut it out of the picture."

Film Reviews- *Teenage Caveman*

*Motion Picture Herald-* The title role is played with sincerity by Robert Vaughn. A similar approach to the original story and screenplay by R. Wright Campbell is made by producer-director Roger Corman, creating a modest budget film with some stature.

*Variety-* This is obviously a low budget picture and in theatrical terms, it doesn't always sustain, but the message is handled with restraint and good taste and gives substance to the production.

*Los Angeles Times-* Without the epilogue, *Teenage Caveman* would have closed with an impact unusual in a low-budget production. However, the ten cent title notwithstanding, this is an interesting motion picture and judged within the context of its intent, remarkably good.

August 1958-

**Night of the Blood Beast/She Gods of Shark Reef**
"From towering wild adventure... to the depths of hellish horror!"

From the pressbook-
SKY AND SEA MONSTERS IN NEW FEATURES
*She Gods of Shark Reef* and *Night of the Blood Beast,* two new American International Pictures.
　　*She Gods of Shark Reef* was filmed entirely in magnificent color in the Hawaiian Islands. It stars Don Durant and Lisa Montell in a story of high adventure. The story tells of a young man who, in order to finance his easy way of life, commits a murder during an attempted robbery. He flees to a nearby town and enlists the aid of his brother who lives there to help him escape. They put out for a distant island in an outrigger canoe. They are caught in a hurricane and their craft overturns. They are rescued by a tribe of beautiful native maidens, who take them to their lush tropical island paradise peopled only by women.
　　*Night of the Blood Beast* tells the fascinating story of a stowaway

monster from another planet who returns to earth in a space ship. The monster wreaks havoc amongst the populace until a way is found to control him. Michael Emmett and Angela Greene are starred.

Michael Emmet confronts the title creature in *Night of the Blood Beast.*

*Night of the Blood Beast*
Produced by Gene Corman  Directed by Bernard L. Kowalski
Starring Michael Emmet, Angela Greene, John Baer

**Writer Martin Varno had been paid $900 for his script *The Creature from Galaxy 27,* but after having to do several rewrites, he asked to be paid more money. Producers Roger and Gene Corman refused.  Varno's agent, Forrest J. Ackerman,  went to the Writer's Guild for arbitration and Varno was eventually paid another $600.**

Film Reviews- *Night of the Blood Beast*

*Boxoffice*- The screenplay by Martin Varno is no more imaginative and unbelievable than others of its ilk. While the cast boasts no names that will over-weight the marquee, under the play-it-for-spine-tingling direction of Bernard L. Kowalski, performances are sincere and enthusiastic with a mite of special credit due the trio of topliners.

*The Hollywood Reporter*- Production has been given adequate mounting in a restricted interior set and several location areas for chases. Director Bernard L. Kowalski took every advantage to generate suspense, even though it is formula.

*Variety*- A suspenseful picture that is the better half of the new American International package. Although the screenplay does fall into expected pitfalls, it is strong enough to sustain interest all the way.

*Monthly Film Bulletin*- A routine science fiction thriller despite the picturesque title.

*She Gods of Shark Reef*
Produced by Ludwig H. Gerber  Directed by Roger Corman
Starring Don Durant, Lisa Montell, Bill Cord

Roger Corman (Director): "I was approached by a lawyer named Ludwig Gerber, who had this script he wanted to make in Hawaii. I mentioned the project to Jim and Sam and they suggested that I make a film [*Naked Paradise*] for them while I was there and they'd pay half the transportation and equipment costs, effectively cutting the cost of each production in half."

Film Reviews- *She Gods of Shark Reef*

*Motion Picture Herald*- Roger Corman is responsible for this intriguing attraction, embellished considerably through adroit use of Pathecolor and peopled with relative unknowns who display considerable spirit.

*Variety*- Completed a year and a half ago and just now released, *She Gods of Shark Reef* boasts fine color, rich red blood, capable underwater photography, and very little story.

*The Hollywood Reporter*- There's little novelty to the boy-meets-girl story, but director Corman maintains an interesting pace throughout.

*Monthly Film Bulletin*- Some lush, bizarre exteriors, beautifully shot in Eastman color, have been thrown away on a poor script, indifferently performed.

### *The Screaming Skull/Terror from the Year 5,000*
"TWIN GHOST STORIES to haunt you forever!"

From the pressbook-
THE GHOST OF EARTH PAST AND EARTH FUTURE
*The Screaming Skull* and *Terror from the Year 5,000*, American International's thrilling new program.

*The Screaming Skull*, starring Alex Nicol, Peggy Webber, and John Hudson, begins with Hudson bringing his new bride, Peggy, to his palatial home. Shortly after they take up residence, strange and occult happenings ensue. At first, they consider the frightening occurrences the work of the caretaker, Alex Nicol, who was devoted to Hudson's first wife, recently deceased. Events become truly blood chilling when the reality of the situation proves that the disturbances are being caused by the ghost of Hudson's first wife. This becomes known when she appears in a ghastly and frightening form to the newlyweds.

*Terror from the Year 5,000* stars Joyce Holden and Ward Costello. In a lonely swampland in central Florida, a young scientist conducts experiments with a "time machine." The machine materializes weird creatures from the future, such as a cat with two foreheads and six eyes. The machine also produces a fierce female who become madly enamored with the scientist.

*The Screaming Skull*
Produced by John Kneubuhl  Directed by Alex Nicol
Starring John Hudson, Peggy Webber, Alex Nicol

*Terror from the Year 5000*
Produced and Directed by Robert J. Gurney, Jr.
Starring Joyce Holden, Ward Costello, Frederic Downs

Film Reviews- *Terror from the Year 5000*

*The Hollywood Reporter*- The film is fairly interesting because of the far-fetched novelty.

*Monthly Film Bulletin*- The woman from the future is an unimaginative creation and whatever horrific possibilities she has are soon expended... a sad little creature in a tight set of black woolies. The film is crudely photographed with no noticeable interest in continuity and little attempt at convincing setting.

*Variety*- A weakie for even the small exploitation field.

October 1958-

**The Spider/The Brain Eaters**
"50 TONS of Creeping Black Horror!"

**Although *The Spider* and *The Brain Eaters* were released together, it was not an "equal billing" combination as the other AIP double feature programs had been. *The Spider* was the main feature and *The Brain Eaters* was the support and given far less substantial billing. Unlike previous AIP pressbooks, there is only a two-page sheet in *The Spider* pressbook for the double feature campaign.**

From the Double Campaign sheet in the pressbook-
A MASSIVE SPIDER AND BRAIN EATING PARASITES
THRILL LOCAL AUDIENCES

*The Spider,* the story of a marauding massive spider, and *The Brain Eaters* are currently showing on the same program.

*The Spider* recounts the story of one of nature's most hideous mistakes. An ordinary bird spider continues his growth until it becomes a 50-ton monstrosity, bigger than a house. Bullets can't hurt it, flames can't burn it, nothing can destroy it as it forages throughout the land seeking humans to feed upon. It is a constant threat to the continued existence of the populace. The science teacher in a nearby high school marshals all available forces to bring *The Spider* under control. The eventual solution to the problem forms a most thrilling climax.

*The Brain Eaters,* which features a cast of rapidly rising young players including Ed Nelson, Joanna Lee, and Jody Fair, tells what happens when a community is invaded by strangers from another world. These strangers bring with them parasites that prey upon human brains and dictate the actions of their victims. *The Brain Eaters* was produced for American International Pictures by its star, Ed Nelson.

*The Spider* (aka ***Earth vs. the Spider***)
Produced and Directed by Bert I. Gordon
Starring Edward Kemmer, June Kenney, Gene Persson

**After *The Spider,* Bert I. Gordon severed his relations with AIP for several years, claiming that they owed him more money on his pictures. Gordon would return to AIP to make *The Food of the Gods* (1976) and *Empire of the Ants* (1977).**

Sam Arkoff: "What ultimately happened with Bert is that he got more piggish as he went along. A common thing. His pictures were modestly successful. They were cheap pictures and they made money. But there was nothing that was an incredible blast out. And after the first couple of pictures, his wife started in on him because she worked with him. She was what I'd call a ball-buster type. So after a couple of pictures he came in and started wanting this and wanting that. And we went around and around and finally his demands were just too goddamn great. And that's why we finally split."

*The Brain Eaters*
Produced by Edwin Nelson  Directed by Bruno VeSota
Starring Edwin Nelson, Joanna Lee, Alan Frost

**The Brain Eaters was an uncredited adaptation of Robert Heinlein's novel *The Puppet Masters*. Bruno VeSota wanted to direct the picture. He brought the script to Roger Corman, who gave him $28,000 to make it. With that size budget, the movie would be a non-union shoot, so Corman hired Ed Nelson as producer.**

Roger Corman (uncredited Executive Producer): "Then I got this letter from Robert Heinlein's lawyer. I called Bruno and asked what it was all about. He said it was absolute nonsense, so I told my secretary to get me a copy of *The Puppet Masters*. I read it. Now Heinlein was, and is, one of the most respected science fiction writers in the world and they were denying they stole his story. They changed a few things so it wasn't exactly the same, but it was really obvious that they took it. So I had a meeting with Heinlein and his lawyer. We settled for a $5,000 amount because it was such a low budget picture."

October 6, 1958
*Boxoffice*
(Excerpts from a lengthy article by Ivan Spear charting AIP's development as a company.)
AIP STARTS FOURTH YEAR WITH STRONGEST LINEUP- Average of 7,000 Playdates Per Picture Achieved by Fast-Growing Company
Four years old and nearly as many accounts as many so-called major companies accumulate during three generations of motion picture making and distribution. That's the proud and praiseworthy story of American International Pictures.
With 56 features already produced in its short, happy life, American International Pictures is upping its production sights. It plans more and will range the world to make them. Three other continents are the sites of further productions. Australia, for instance, will be the location for *She*, the H. Rider Haggard

novel. Nicholson and Arkoff will entrust it to their bright young producer-director Roger Corman, who even now is scouting "down under" locations. *Eve and the Dragon,* entrusted to another of AIP's bright young men, Stanley Shpetner, is planned for South American shooting. *Horrors of the Black Museum* is being shot in England now and will be followed there by *The Headless Ghost,* with both being produced by AIP's chill-dispenser Herman Cohen.

The healthy confidence of youth which exemplifies the company is neatly summed up in the slogan chosen for American International Week, October 31 through November 6. It simply exhorts the exhibitor to "Laugh All the Way to the Bank- Book American."

October 1958
Trade ad-
Western Union telegram from Nat Fellman of Stanley-Warner Theaters to Leon Blender, Sales Manager of AIP says:

"Congratulations on AIP fourth anniversary. We are happy to co-operate with your playdate drive Oct. 31 to Nov. 6th with an American International picture on every screen. We look forward to breaking all records with your biggest and best picture to date... *The Spider,* opening Oct. 29th in our top theaters. Regards.

October 20, 1958
*Boxoffice*
30 AIP FEATURES IN '59; BUDGETS ALSO INCREASED
Hollywood- American International Pictures, during 1959, plans to put an experimental toe into the waters of more costly production. Four of the burgeoning company's forthcoming pictures will be budgeted between $500,000 and $1,000,000 each, figures materially more than anything heretofore undertaken in AIP's four years of rapid growth. Moreover, the regular pictures on the organization's forthcoming slate will be allocated budgets of $250,000 to $500,00, which is from two to four times the average cost of AIP features.

AIP will deliver 30 feature films during the coming year, including the quartet of high budgeters, as compared to 24 pictures made this year. The four specials will be filmed in CinemaScope and color. All will be co-productions. They are:

*Horrors of the Black Museum,* to start October 20 in England, with an Aben Kandel screenplay to be produced by Herman Cohen.

*She,* from H. Rider Haggard's novel, to be shot in Australia, Roger Corman producing and directing.

*Eve and the Dragon,* to be shot in South America with Stanley Shpetner producing from his own screenplay.

*Take Me to Your Leader,* the screenplay of which is now being developed as a combination of animated cartoon and live action.

The 26 other AIP features for 1959 delivery will include *Paratroop Command* and *Submarine X2,* the first of the company's extended budget films and both scheduled for January release.

*Tank Destroyer,* written, directed, and produced by Burt Topper, starts October 20 for February release with another feature as yet untitled.

March releases will be *Machine Gun Lady,* to be written and produced by Stanley Shpetner, and *Jailbreakers.*

*Horrors of the Black Museum* and *The Headless Ghost,* both produced by Herman Cohen, are scheduled for April delivery.

*The Dragracers,* a Lou Rusoff production in color, and *High School Bride* are calendared for May.

*Insect Woman,* to be produced and directed by Roger Corman, and *Attack of the Giant Leeches,* to be produced by Gene Corman, will be June releases.

July will be the release month for *Eve and the Dragon.*

*She* and *Take Me to Your Leader* also will be released in the last half of 1959 with the rest of the year's schedule now being formulated.

**Many of AIP's more ambitious plans never came to fruition. *Insect Woman* became *The Wasp Woman* and was produced and released in 1959 by Roger Corman's own company, The Filmgroup, independent of AIP.**

# CHAPTER SIX
# 1959

AIP decided to expand the range of their product with films made overseas. *Horrors of the Black Museum* and *The Headless Ghost* were made in England in conjunction with Nat Cohen's Anglo Amalgamated Pictures. Herman Cohen went to England to oversee these productions. In an attempt to take advantage of the current trend in epic movies, AIP acquired the Italian-made films *The Sign of Rome* and *Terror of the Barbarians*. These pictures were retitled and released with a considerable amount of fanfare.

January 1959-

January 7, 1959
*Variety*
Trade ad-
AMERICAN INTERNATIONAL PICTURES
The YOUNG company with YOUNG executives presents its YOUNG producers and their coming attractions:

Producer Herman Cohen- *Horrors of the Black Museum*- color and CinemaScope In release: *How to Make a Monster*

Producer Roger Corman- *SHE*- color and CinemaScope- In release: *Night of the Blood Beast*

Producer Lou Rusoff- *Submarine Seahawk*- In release: *Hot Rod Gang*

Producer Stanley Shpetner- *Paratroop Command*- In release: *The Bonnie Parker Story*

Producer Burt Topper- *Blood and Steel*- In release: *Hell Squad*

February 1959-
**Submarine Seahawk/Paratroop Command**
"The BIGGEST WAR SPECTACLES of the YEAR!"

From the pressbook-
NEW FILMS FEATURE SAILORS AND PARATROOPERS
*Submarine Seahawk* and *Paratroop Command*, two outstanding new war films from American International Pictures.

*Submarine Seahawk* stars ruggedly handsome John Bentley in the role of the sub's captain. He is torn between his devoted wife's advice to stretch regulations and be friendly with his men and his stern, rigid devotion to command by the book. The men do not understand his refusal to engage the enemy in action. Actually, his secret orders are to seek out the main body of the Japanese fleet. When he does locate their hidden warships, he radios to the nearby land and carrier-based planes of the U.S. and they move in for the kill. The ensuing sky, surface, and sea battle is a vast panorama of violent war action unlike anything ever before filmed.

*Paratroop Command* is a brilliant study of a group of our sky commandos marooned behind enemy lines. Furious combat is interspersed with the romances of the men with peasant girls of the Italian underground. Richard Bakalyan and Carolyn Hughes are starred.

AIP is building its own stable of multiple threat young producers; *Submarine Seahawk* is largely the work of Lou Rusoff, who wrote and produced. *Paratroop Command* was written and produced by Stanley Shpetner.

*Paratroop Command*
Produced by Stanley Shpetner  Directed by William Witney
Starring Richard Bakalyan, Ken Lynch, Jack Hogan, Jimmy Murphy

*Submarine Seahawk*
Produced by Alex Gordon  Directed by Spencer G. Bennet
Starring John Bentley, Brett Halsey

**Submarine Seahawk would be the last movie produced by Alex Gordon for AIP. Alex, like Bert I. Gordon, claimed that he was never given monies owed him for his films. This seems to have been a constant refrain from people who worked for AIP and had profit participation deals. Jack Rabin, Edward Bernds, Herman Cohen, Richard Matheson, Sid Pink, and Shelley Winters all made similar claims about AIP's "creative bookkeeping."**

Alex Gordon: "After four years, I was still trying to live on deferred salaries. When I got married, I wanted to take my wife on a honeymoon. I told Sam I needed money. He gave me $2000 and called it an *advance*, which was only a fraction of what they owed me. I realized the only way I'd ever get the money was to sell my interest in the company."

Sam Arkoff: "The problem was, Alex got to taking himself seriously. And I suppose it was aided and abetted by his wife, who kept saying, 'You should be more important. You should go in and stand up and tell them.' Ultimately he came in and said, in his own gentle way, 'If I can't call the tune then I'd like to sell out my share.' I tried to prevail on him not to do it. I told him he was going to regret it. So we bought him out."

February 2, 1959
*Boxoffice*
AIP ENGAGES AD AGENCY TO ASSIST EXHIBITORS
Los Angeles- American International Pictures will increase its promotional aids to exhibition with the appointment of the Goodman Organizations as its national ad agency, effective with the *Daddy-O* and *Road Racers* program.

AIP's first national agency, for which Mort Goodman, president, will serve as account executive, will work with Richard McKay, company advertising director, on national campaigns.

James H. Nicholson, AIP topper, said that the appointment of the Goodman Organization is in line with his company's policy of stepping up point-of-purchase effort on behalf of the exhibitor who pays AIP product.

March 1959-

**Roadracers/Daddy-O**
"The BIG 2... Roaring! Rocketing! Relentless!"

*Roadracers*
Produced by Stanley Kallis  Directed by Arthur Sweroloff
Starring Sally Fraser, Alan Dinehart, Jr., Skip Ward, Joel Lawrence

*Daddy-O*
Produced by Elmer Rhoden, Jr.  Directed by Lou Place
Starring Dick Contino, Sandra Giles, Bruno VeSota

From the pressbook-
HARD DRIVING KIDS FEATURED IN NEW FILMS
*Roadracers* and *Daddy-O,* twin movies about today's sensation-seeking kids, will have their first local showing commencing today.

*Roadracers* cast Joel Lawrence as a race driver who is banned from American tracks for two years because of his reckless driving, which caused the death of another driver. He leaves the country for Europe and the top road events there. His girlfriend, played by Marian Collier, promises to wait for him. After becoming a star overseas, he returns to American competition.

In the meantime, Miss Collier has fallen in love with driver Skip Ward. Skip and Joel become hot rivals on and off the track. The climax occurs during the thrilling running of the American Grand Prix.

*Daddy-O* casts famed accordionist Dick Contino as a singer in a club frequented by the younger set. He owns a sport car, which he is goaded into drag racing against beautiful Sandra Gile's Thunderbird. The race has tragic consequences and Dick is forced to collaborate with the underworld. Sandra and Dick eventually become involved in one of the most thrilling finishes ever filmed.

*Daddy-O* was produced by Elmer C. Rhoden, Jr. *Roadracers* was produced by Stanley Kallis; it is a James H. Nicholson and Samual Z. Arkoff Production for American International Pictures.

### Tank Commandos/Operation Dames
"Battle Born Passions of Defiant Men at War!"

*Tank Commandos*
Produced and Directed by Burt Topper
Starring Wally Campo, Maggie Lawrence, Robert Barron, Donato Farretta

*Operation Dames*
Produced by Stanley Kallis  Directed by Louis Stoumen
Starring Eve Meyer, Chuck Henderson, Don Devlin


April 1959-

### Horrors of the Black Museum/The Headless Ghost
"Modern science has perfected an ancient art to put you in the picture!"

Michael Gough (1916-2011) appeared in AIP's *Horrors of the Black Museum, Konga,* and *The Crimson Cult.*

Herman Cohen went to London to produce *Horrors of the Black Museum,* which was a joint venture between AIP and Anglo Amalgamated Pictures. It was the first AIP movie to be filmed in both color and CinemaScope. Although *Horrors of the Black Museum* would be the most lurid and graphic movie AIP had released to date, Sam and Jim felt that the U.S. release needed an extra something to promote it. This "extra something" turned out to be Hypno-Vista, which consisted of tacking a 13-minute prologue onto the film featuring Emile Franchel ("Registered Psychologist, State of California, Specialty- Hypnotism").

106

Franchel attempts to explain the powers of hypnosis to the theatre audience in the dullest and most unconvincing terms, proving that the power of suggestion wasn't necessary to produce yawns. Herman Cohen was also given the responsibility of producing a second feature to accompany *Horrors of the Black Museum* and this became the inexpensive black and white horror-comedy *The Headless Ghost.*

*The Headless Ghost*
Produced by Herman Cohen  Directed by Peter Graham Scott
Starring Richard Lyon, Lilian Sottane, David Rose, Clive Revill

*Horrors of the Black Museum*
Produced by Herman Cohen  Directed by Arthur Crabtree
Starring Michael Gough, June Cunningham, Graham Curnow, Shirley Anne Field

Reviews- *Horrors of the Black Museum*

*New York Times* (April 30, 1959) by Richard W. Nason
*Horrors of the Black Museum* has more significance as a promotional stunt than as a motion picture. Its arrival was emblazoned with a broad advertising campaign. It is decked out in wide screen and florid color. It flamboyantly claims for itself the introduction of a new film technique called Hypno-Vista.

The attraction itself, however, makes an embarrassing mockery of such advance billing. In virtually every category of craftsmanship, this picture bears evidence of only an ounce of thought for every pound of CinemaScope footage. The Gothic promise of the title finds little support in what unfolds on the screen.

Herman Cohen produced the film and also helped with the script, whose dialogue shows a convenient disregard for motivation and dramatic technique. The acting and directing seem designed more for quick production than for entertainment effects. As we say, the premeditation in this kind of showmanship is funneled into the promotion rather than the picture.

On the same bill is a pale and protracted bit of miscast whimsy entitled *The Headless Ghost.*

Both pictures were made in England by American International.

*Variety-* The producers have relied on sensationalism without subtlety of characterization, situation, or dialogue. As a result, this rather distasteful item is likely to gather more misplaced laughs than shudders among discriminating audiences.

April 13, 1959
*Boxoffice*
## AIP PRODUCTION SHIFT; MORE SINGLE FEATURES
Las Vegas- A radical revision in its production policy to emphasize quality single-bill features, increase use of color and CinemaScope, and fully diversify its product will be made by American International Pictures, according to company toppers James H. Nicholson and Samuel Z. Arkoff.
## SEE A SHIFT IN TASTES-
Reporting to the distributors present at the company's first international convention, the company heads said that while standard double-bill packages will not be ignored in future production plans, there will be fewer of them and they will be designed to meet the changed tastes of the public, which is not buying the horror and teenage films in double doses anymore.

According to recent AIP tabulations, Nicholson and Arkoff stated that only major horror films do profitable business. Therefore, the company will release only two horror-category features, both for single-bill sale, in the next year- *Horrors of the Black Museum* and *The House of Usher.*

Each film will feature AIP's new gimmick, Hypnovista, which, according to its sponsors, gives the audience full feeling of integration with the picture for more personal enjoyment. *Museum* will get saturation booking treatment in a record 100 New York RKO theaters starting May 1.

Diversification of product will see AIP features spreading into comedy, war, adventure, fantasy, teenage, and spectacle categories in addition to the two mentioned horror biggies. Of next year's features, seven will be in color and widescreen with two more both in color and Hypnovista.

Nicholson also set at rest rumors that AIP was negotiating for major releasing arrangement for its production arm, affirming that the company would continue with its present releasing pattern via independent distributors.

Among productions detailed to the delegates were *Take Me to Your Leader,* live-action cartoon comedy, *Diary of a High School Bride, Bombs Away, Blood Hill, She, Eve and the Dragon,* and Jules Verne's *In the Year 2998.*

ACQUIRE ITALIAN FILMS-

The first Italian-made feature to be released by AIP is *The Last Days of Rome,* starring Anita Ekberg, in which AIP was associated with Italy's Galatea Films. The second Italian film, *The Barbarians,* will be a co-production with Standard Productions of Rome and will star Steve Reeves and Bruce Cabot. Three other AIP co-production deals in Italy will add two Biblical spectacles and one based on Greek mythology to the company's schedule.

April 20, 1959
*Boxoffice*
AIP ANNOUNCES FORMATION OF RECORD COMPANY
Hollywood- American International toppers James Nicholson and Samuel Arkoff have announced the formation of American International Records for the manufacture, sale, and distribution of records of songs and soundtracks from AIP features. AIR will also record other than AIP film songs, with emphasis on new vocal and band talent.

The first AIR records already made are *Horrors of the Black Museum* backed with *Headless Ghost,* both titled for upcoming AIP film releases; *Roadracers,* the title song from the AIP feature, backed with *Leadfoot;* and *Girls, Girls, Girls,* from AIP's *Operation Dames,* backed with *Campus Rage.*

Donald E. Leon, assistant general counsel for AIP, is general manager of AIR.

**American International Records incorporated on March 19, 1959. Among their early 45 rpm records were "Oooh, I'm Scared of the Horrors of the Black Museum" with a flip side of "The Headless Ghost" by Nightmares; The Jimmie Maddin Orchestra, "Bucket of Blood" with a flip side of "The Leeches" by Bill Anson; and "Geronimo" with a flip side of "Charge" by The Renegades.**

May 3, 1959
*Boxoffice*
AIP's VALUE TO INDUSTRY AFFIRMED BY PRODUCER
New York- "The motion picture industry needs American International" according to Herman Cohen, producer of the company's biggest picture to date, *Horrors of the Black Museum*, which opened in more than 100 theaters in the New York metropolitan area Wednesday, April 29.

"AIP is a young, fresh company which gives a producer a feeling of life," Cohen said in stressing the fact that the firm will spend $250,000 in advertising and promoting *Horrors*, which is in color and CinemaScope, the company's biggest promotion budget.

Cohen produced five previous features for AIP, starting with *I Was a Teenage Werewolf*, which cost $150,000 and grossed over $2,000,000 in the first 12 months of release. This picture was credited with starting the cycle of teenage horror films and was followed by Cohen's *I Was a Teenage Frankenstein*, *Blood of Dracula*, and *How to Make a Monster*.

May 11, 1959
*Boxoffice*
"MEDUSA" ON AIP SLATE: EIGHT RELEASES RESET
Hollywood- American International Pictures toppers James H. Nicholson and Samuel Z. Arkoff have announced *Medusa*, based on the maiden of mythology, as a forthcoming feature.

At the same time, AIP disclosed it has rescheduled released dates for eight 1959 features and set dates for three 1960 pictures. New dates for the eight rescheduled films are:

July 8- *Diary of a High School Bride*; July 29- *The Haunted House of Usher*; August 19- *Sheba and the Gladiator*; September 23- *The*

*Girl on Death Row*; September 23- *The Jailbreakers*;
November 18- *Colossus and the Golden Horde*; and December
23- *Take Me to Your Leader.*

The three AIP features scheduled so far for 1960 are:
January 13- *Bombs Away*; January 13- *Foxhole*; and February
3- *Eve and the Dragon.*

June 1, 1959
*Boxoffice*
"SHEBA AND THE GLADIATOR" TO BE AIP
ROADSHOW
Los Angeles- American International Pictures has announced
*Sheba and the Gladiator,*

color spectacle starring Anita Ekberg, George Marshall [sic],
and Jacques Sernas, as its first release to be shown on an advanced
admission, extended run roadshow basis.

Simultaneous pre-release premieres of *Sheba* will be set
for August 5 in 30 key city hard-ticket houses on AIP's most
expensive feature release to date. All engagements, according to
Leon Blender, AIP general sales manager, will be accompanied
by special, heavy-budgeted promotional campaigns and will be set
and supervised by him.

July 1959-

**Diary of a High School Bride/Ghost of Dragstrip Hollow**
"The bold motion picture that dares to speak for teenage lovers!"

*Diary of a High School Bride*
Produced and Directed by Burt Topper
Starring Anita Sands, Ronald Fraser, Chris Robinson

*Ghost of Dragstrip Hollow*
Produced by Lou Rusoff Directed by William Hole, Jr.
Starring Jody Fair, Martin Braddock, Russ Bender

**Sanita Pelkey wears a bizarre costume in *Ghost of Dragstrip Hollow*.**

From the pressbook-
TEENAGERS FEATURED IN TWO NEW HITS
*Diary of a High School Bride* and *Ghost of Dragstrip Hollow* is the
latest combination from American International Pictures dealing
with the problems of young Americans.

*Diary of a High School Bride* tells the story of Judy, a high
school senior, who marries Ron, a law student. The young couple
desperately tries to make a go of their marriage against tremendous

112

odds. One of the great difficulties they encounter is from a former boyfriend of Judy's, Chris. He is young and handsome and refuses to accept the fact that any girl would prefer another young man than himself. Consequently, he makes desperate attempts to dissolve the union. The climax is reached when Chris attempts to attack Judy on a catwalk high above a Hollywood movie stage.

*The Ghost of Dragstrip Hollow* is a sequel to the highly successful laugh riot of last year, *Hot Rod Gang*. It features a haunted house, a talking hot rod, and a wisecracking parrot.

July 27, 1959
*Boxoffice*
AIP- FROM COMBOS TO SPECTACLES IN 5 YEARS by Ivan Spear
American International Observing Fifth Anniversary by Adding Top-Budget Pictures.

*Sign of the Gladiator* will be introduced to the public by the largest campaign in AIP's history, using all possible point-of-sale media: newspapers, radio, television, outdoor advertising, and three special trailers. The picture will premiere September 9 in a huge Los Angeles area saturation of hardtops and drive-ins with a campaign running over a period of 45 days. Similar saturation plans with 100 theaters in New York will be followed through the country. A first print order of 300 has been placed by AIP.

*Diary of a High School Bride,* starring AIP discovery Anita Sands, is the company's current release, presold to millions in the title's age group by a heavy national magazine campaign.

With *Bucket of Blood* as the Halloween release, the nation's showmen are assured of an audience draw appropriate to the season. Its own special campaign, conceived in the spirit of Halloween legend and fun, will tip the consumer to *Bucket of Blood.*

The November-December release from AIP is another spectacle, *Colossus and the Golden Horde*, starring Steve Reeves of *Hercules* fame, in color and the Dyaliscope process. *Colossus,*

like *Sign of the Gladiator,* was made abroad utilizing Italian and Yugoslavian locations. The two color spectacles represent further progress in AIP's coproduction efforts abroad. Subsequent foreign coproduction will see the company engaged in England again with *Aladdin and the Giant,* which will be produced by Herman Cohen. Nat Cohen's Anglo Amalgamated Film Distributors of London will be the cooperating company on *Aladdin.* AIP will also coproduce Jules Verne's *In the Year 2889* in Japan and will coproduce *David and Goliath* in Italy and several other European countries early next year.

July 1959
Trade ad-
THE INFANT OF THE INDUSTRY GROWS UP! Following the smash success of *Horrors of the Black Museum,* American International proudly announces a program of six more box office blockbusters.

July- *Diary of a High School Bride* and The Hot Rod Gang meet the *Ghost of Dragstrip Hollow*

September- A Violent, Sweeping Spectacle of Pagan Rome! *Sign of the Gladiator*

October- Special Showmen's Halloween Package combining the most unique ad campaign with the surprise picture of the year! *A Bucket of Blood*

November- A Titanic Man versus 50,000 Blood Barbarians! *Colossus and the Golden Horde*

January- *Take Me To Your Leader* The Out-of-This-World Comedy in Live Action and Animation

February- A Towering Tale of Horror! Edgar Allen Poe's *Mysterious House of Usher*

September 21, 1959
*Boxoffice*
NICHOLSON PROPOSES ONE-YEAR TRUCE BETWEEN EXHIBITORS AND DISTRIBUTORS
Cincinnati- A one-year "truce" between exhibition and distribution as a first step to end the "cold war" between buyer and seller elements in the motion picture industry was proposed at the Allied convention here this week by James H. Nicholson, president of American International Pictures.

The truce, he declared, would prove to be "the salvation" of the industry. "The cold war between exhibitor and producer cannot end until there is understanding that each arm of our industry is helpless without the other."

Nicholson said that honest effort on the part of each side can make the producing-selling job work smoothly and profitably. "It will take some sincere soul-searching under the light of reason, but it can be done."

October 1959-
*Sign of the Gladiator*
"Wondrous Spectacle Bigger Than Anything You Have Ever Seen! See: 10,000 horsemen charge the Valley of Blood! The amazing fire throwing catapults of war! The barbarian torture catacombs of horror! The destruction of a mighty pagan empire!"

Produced by Vittorio Musy-Glory  Directed by Guido Brignone Starring Anita Ekberg, Lorella De Luca, Georges Marchal, Jacques Sernas

Sam Arkoff: "We had a foreign department in New York with a guy in charge named Bill Wright. We went to Italy and that's where I met Fulvio Lucisano because Bill Wright knew him. Fulvio was a young producer and he served as a liaison for us. On that particular trip, we picked up two pictures, one of which became *Sign of the Gladiator* and the other which was a Hercules picture. We made that *Goliath and the Barbarians*. And those two pictures revitalized the whole company."

From the pressbook-
SIGN OF THE GLADIATOR MIGHTY SPECTACULAR
American International's *Sign of the Gladiator* stars Anita Ekberg in one of her finest performances to date as the beautiful Zenobia, who led her troops into battle against the Roman Legions.

*Sign of the Gladiator* is the biographical sketch of that most horrible era when Aurelian became Emperor of Rome and thought it would be advisable to have Zenobia become an ally of the Roman people. General Marus Valerius was sent to the borders to bring about a peace between the Syrians and Romans, but instead was taken prisoner by Zenobia, which eventually led to her downfall.

*Sign of the Gladiator* is in magnificent Colorscope and uses the actual location of its story as the background.

## AMERICAN INTERNATIONAL RECORDS IS YOUR PARTNER IN SELLING *SIGN OF THE GLADIATOR*

American International Records had produced a new song, Xnobia [sic], the title song from the motion picture *Sign of the Gladiator*. This record is available on 45rpm. It is a modern ballad and is sung by Bill Lee. "Zenobia" is backed with a very clever instrumental titled "Slave Dance." The song "Zenobia" was written by Dominic Frontiere and the lyrics by Milton Raksin. "Slave Dance" was written by Dominic Frontiere. Both songs were produced for American International Records by Al Simms, general manager of the record company.

October 3, 1959
*Motion Picture Herald*

## AIP LAUNCHES BIG PUSH FOR "SIGN OF THE GLADIATOR"

American International has devised the biggest selling campaign in its history for *Sign of the Gladiator*.

With the release set this month of *Sign of the Gladiator*, American International Pictures, under the guidance of president James H. Nicholson and vice president Samuel Z. Arkoff, reaches another milestone in its phenomenal growth as one of the most aggressive and successful of the new production-distribution companies in America. For AIP, which got its start just a few years ago with comparatively inexpensive program packages carefully tailored to teenage tastes, *Sign of the Gladiator* now marks the company's entry into the big budget, single feature field.

Here is a multi-million-dollar spectacle starring Anita Ekberg, George Marshall [sic], and a huge international cast, filmed in Colorscope in Italy and Yugoslavia in cooperation with Italian film interests.

Poster art for *Sign of the Gladiator*.

Despite the ballyhoo, *Sign of the Gladiator* was in reality a mediocre and modestly budgeted Sword and Sandal movie which was picked up inexpensively by AIP. Jim and Sam didn't care for the original title, *The Sign of Rome*, so Jim suggested changing it to *Sign of the Gladiator*. Arkoff approved of the title change, but mentioned that there was no gladiator in the movie. In his autobiography, Sam Arkoff says, "Jim and I pondered the problem for a few minutes and realized that since we were going to have to redub the picture anyway, we could take care of a change in the plot when we dubbed it in English." And that's exactly what they did in addition to trimming eighteen minutes from the original running time.

AIP also added an end title song called "Xenobia" sung by Bill Lee. This song was released on an AIP Records 45rpm single backed with "Slave Dance" by Al Simms Sextet.

October 19, 1959
*Boxoffice*

## AIP PLANS 16-18 IN 1960; NINE HIGH-BUDGETERS SET

New York- American International, which started producing low-budget exploitation pictures in 1955, will graduate from double-bill programs to blockbusters in 1960, according to James H. Nicholson, president. The company has completed or planned five CinemaScope and color features for the first nine months of 1960, starting with *Goliath and the Barbarians*, filmed in Italy starring Steve Reeves, for January; *Horror of the House of Usher*, from the Edgar Allen Poe classic, starring Vincent Price, for March; *Aladdin and the Giant*, for May; *Circus of Horrors*, for July; and *in the Year 2889*, from the Jules Verne classic, for September. In addition, AIP will have lower budget exploitation films, including *Take Me to Your Leader*, a science-fiction comedy, and *The Talking Dog*, to total 16-18 pictures for the year, Nicholson said.

This total compares to four pictures in 1955, eight in 1956, twelve in 1957, twenty-two in 1958, and eighteen in 1959, most of those being modest-budget exploitation films. The switch to high-budget pictures is to help the product shortage, especially in films which can play a week or more.

AIP, which grossed 20 percent higher in film rentals in 1958 than in the preceding year, will also expand its field staff by adding division managers for the west coast, the central states, and the southwest, plus an exploitation man in each territory.

October 26, 1959

## AIP BILLINGS ABROAD ARE 35% OF DOMESTIC

New York- Foreign billings of American International Pictures for the current fiscal year will equal 35 percent of the domestic income and are expected to equal 50 percent of the domestic billings by 1961, according to William G. Reich, general sales manager of American International Export Corp., foreign distribution unit of the company.

Less than one year old, the export company this year has released 16 AIP pictures abroad, finding ready acceptance of its product in Latin America and Europe. Recently, it has been making some headway in South Africa. Remi Crasto, AIP far eastern supervisor, is now arranging distribution deals in the east.

*A Bucket of Blood/The Giant Leeches* double feature is released for Halloween.
"You'll be sick, sick, sick- from LAUGHING!"

From the pressbook-
*A BUCKET OF BLOOD* NEW COMEDY TERROR SHOW
The new spoof comedy feature from American International Pictures is *A Bucket of Blood*, starring Dick Miller, Barboura Morris, and Antony Carbone. All the beatnik and coffee house-type glamour is featured in this satire-type horror comedy.

Dick Miller portrays a poor, sympathetic soul who seeks the popularity of his fellow companions, but is steadfastly brushed off due to his creative inability. Killing a cat accidentally, Walter tries to hide the dead cat, but is unable to think of a place where it would not be detected. In frustration, he covers the cat with a coating of clay. Much to his amazement, the clay-covered body is accepted as an astonishing piece of sculpture, unknowingly to his admirers of the substance beneath the clay. Additional such incidents occur throughout *A Bucket of Blood*, which will certainly claim this comedy spoof as one of the most different motion pictures to come from Hollywood in some time.

Also on the same bill is the new terror feature *The Giant Leeches*, starring Ken Clark and Yvette Vickers. Out of the swamps come the horrifying mysterious creatures, thirsting for the blood of humans, sending a whole countryside on an endless reign of terror in American International's newest horror film, *The Giant Leeches*.

*A Bucket of Blood*
Produced and Directed by Roger Corman
Starring Dick Miller, Barboura Morris, Anthony Carbone

Charles Griffith (Writer): "Roger [Corman] took me to the studio where the sets were still standing for *Diary of a High School Bride*. 'You see these sets?' he said. "They're going to be standing for another week. Write a horror picture with these sets,' which consisted of a beatnik coffee house, a jail, and an apartment. I wrote something called *The Yellow Door* and when I handed him the first twenty pages, he was furious because it was a comedy."

Dick Miller (Actor): "*A Bucket of Blood* is still my favorite picture. None of these are great pictures understand, but I always thought if *A Bucket of Blood* had another chunk of money in production, it would have ranked with any of the top horror films. It's the best script Chuck Griffith ever wrote."

*The Giant Leeches* (aka ***Attack of the Giant Leeches***)
Produced by Gene Corman  Directed by Bernard L. Kowalski
Starring Ken Clark, Yvette Vickers, Jan Shepard, Michael Emmet

Bruno VeSota (Actor): "*The Giant Leeches* as a picture wasn't bad at all. The only thing I found fault with was the monsters. If you took one close look, you'd laugh your head off. During the shooting of the underground cave, where the leeches bring their victims, we were standing around watching the leeches and their crummy suits were coming apart."

Yvette Vickers (Actress): "We were in a tank, on the set, and they had this plaster barrier, an enclosure to contain water. We were doing our final death scene and all of a sudden, out of nowhere, the thing broke. It looked like a typhoon. You never realized that the tank held *that* much water. Some electrician fortunately had the presence of mind to pull the plugs or we could have all been electrocuted."

Gene Corman (Producer): "We had to mount a camera on a raft and somebody had to move it. The Union wanted extra money for that- a water rate. I didn't want to pay it, so I did it myself."

November 2, 1959
*Boxoffice*
HERMAN COHEN STICKING WITH AIP; TO MAKE A
SECOND MAJOR FEATURE

**Tyler McVey, Ken Clark, and Jan Shepard in *The Giant Leeches*.**

New York- Herman Cohen, the 32-year-old producer who made *Horrors of the Black Museum*, American International's biggest grosser for 1959 to date, is sticking with AIP because this company is expanding into the international market, for which he is slanting his pictures.

Cohen's *Black Museum*, which was in CinemaScope and color, was nationally released in May 1959 and has already grossed close to $3,000,000- this on a budget of $400,000, he admitted.

As his next picture for AIP, Cohen will produce *Aladdin and the Giant*, which also will be filmed abroad with locations in Majorca and interiors at the Merton Park and Shepperton Studios in London in association with Anglo Amalgamated of Great Britain, which also co-produced *Black Museum*.

The picture, which will also be in CinemaScope and color, deals with three American teenagers on a tour of Europe who "go back to yesterday" after being wrecked off Majorca and meet Aladdin and other fantastic characters. Cohen plans to cast American players in the teenage roles and British actors in other parts. *Aladdin* will have a budget of $1,000,000 and will be in production for three months, starting November 25.

November 9, 1959
*Boxoffice*
LONDON REPORT by Anthony Gruner
According to Nat Cohen, managing director of Anglo Amalgamated, by December, his company will have five major British features costing more than a million pounds in production. This is a record for any independent distributor. First subject is *Circus of Horrors,* part of a program in the recent deal with Julian Wintle and Leslie Parkyn's company, Independent Artists.

This production is directed by Sydney Hayers and Norman Priggen is associate producer. The cast is headed by Anton Diffring, Erika Remberg, German Actress, and Yvonne Monlaur, French star.

December 1959-

***Goliath and the Barbarians*** (aka ***Terror of the Barbarians***)
"10,000 Barbarians feared his strength and called him GOLIATH! See: The savage attack of the barbarians! Goliath and the test of strength! The orgy of the exotic sword dance! The night monster from the hills! Goliath and the test of 20 spears!"

Produced by Emimmo Salvi
Directed by Carlo Campogalliani
Starring Steve Reeves, Chelo Alonso, Bruce Cabot

**The film has its world premiere at the Roosevelt Theatre in Chicago and set a new house record for mid-week holiday attendance.**

From the pressbook-
STRONG MEN THROUGH THE AGES
Steve Reeves, starring in American International's *Goliath and the Barbarians,* is no exception to the rule that strong men through t

**Steve Reeves in** *Goliath and the Barbarians.*

the ages have been lauded, admired, imitated, and heaped with praise and honor.

In this stirring Color and Totalscope picture, which co-stars exotic discovery Chelo Alonso as the barbarian girl he loves and Bruce Cabot as the king of the barbarians and includes a thundering cast of thousands, Reeves receives admiration for his acting and personality as well as for his physical handsomeness and prowess.

Mythology, fable, folklore, and history are full of stories of heroic men who have been able to do the almost impossible by reason of superior strength.

From the American International Records soundtrack album liner notes-
The music of this album tells a story... half fact and half fancy... set in the year 568 A.D. in northern Italy. It tells of the savage invasion of the barbarians, composed of many races and united only by the desire for conquest. It tells of a single man among the conquered who rose up against them and because of his feats of strength gained the name "Goliath."

To this Les Baxter tells a story in music, once again proving that he is the great talent of today in relating passion, fury, and mood in terms of music. It is a big new sound.

Technical Data: This American International record has been produced under our own special patented process for hi-fidelity... on three separate tracks called... TRI-SONIC SOUND.

December 14, 1959
*Boxoffice*
AIP SEEKS DEALS ABROAD; 18 FEATURES DUE IN '60
New York- The possibility of a Hollywood strike over television residuals as well as certain financial advantages has led American International Pictures to seek more foreign coproduction deals, Samuel Arkoff, vice president, told the trade press Monday at the Hotel Astor.

James Nicholson, president, and he will go to Italy in January to finalize plans for *Goliath and the Dragon*, coproduction and follow-up to *Goliath and the Barbarians*, which scored heavily at the Roosevelt Theatre in Chicago. The new film will be a Christmas 1960 release.

Camera work on *Aladdin and the Giants*, to be co-produced with the British, will start in March at Jamaica, work on miniatures for *In the Year 28*, Jules Verne story to be made with the Japanese, has already begun, and other coproduction deals are in prospect, Arkoff said.

American International plans to release 18 features during the present fiscal year compared with 22 the preceding fiscal year, according to Arkoff. They will be bigger pictures and four will be in color against only one last year. They will be aimed at a slightly more mature, but still youthful audience and have exploitation values. One of them will be *The Angry Red Planet*, produced by Sid Pink in Cinemagic and color. American International will start production next month in Hollywood of Edgar Allan Poe's *Fall of the House of Usher*, starring Vincent Price.

March production is planned for *Take Me to Your Leader*, a comedy.

December 1959
Trade ad-
The Big "G"- Gigantic GOLIATH Grosses Everywhere!
"*Goliath and the Barbarians* opened in Dallas, Houston, San Antonio, Fort Worth, and Galveston on Friday, December 18th to the biggest grosses of any picture in the history of our company pre-Christmas playing time."- Raymond Willie, vice president and general manager, Interstate Circuit, Inc.

"Christmas Day at Palms Theatre with *Goliath* scored biggest single day's gross in five years."- Woody Praught, United Detroit Theaters.

"*Goliath and the Barbarians* opened in fifteen of our towns to block-buster grosses. This engagement in all situations extending through Christmas should set records everywhere." - Duncan R. Kennedy, vice president, Publix Great States Theaters, Inc.

**Unlike *Sign of the Gladiator* and many of their subsequent foreign pickups, AIP actually had money invested in the production of *Goliath and the Barbarians*. The Italian producer, Emimmo Salvi, had run out of money and the picture was in danger of not being completed. Sam and Jim viewed the rushes, decided it was worth taking a chance on, and invested $20,000 to finish the picture. The investment paid off and *Goliath and the Barbarians* went on to become one of the company's biggest grossers to date, thereby ending the Fifties with a bang for AIP.**

**AIP's sand and surf sweethearts Annette Funicello and Frankie Avalon in *Beach Party*.**

# PART TWO

**THE SIXTIES- Beach Parties and Edgar Allan Poe**

"Enter the Domain of THE DAMNED
and THE DEMENTED!"

**Color, Widescreen, Vincent Price, Frankie and Annette: With classic horror stories and crazy comedies, AIP hits on two major formulas which bring them great box office success.**

# CHAPTER SEVEN
# 1960

Trade ad-
THE TEST OF TRUTH
As in *Goliath and the Barbarians,* American International has
"Muscles" at the Box Office.

In 1959, we promised you top Product... we delivered! This
was our first test of truth.

Here are six more box office Giants... coming to you in 1960.
This is our second test of truth... and we WILL deliver again!

March '60- Cinemagic. An adventure into the 4th dimension
that takes you on man's first invasion of *THE ANGRY RED
PLANET.*

April '60- A tower of terror... a spectacle of fun! *CIRCUS OF HORRORS*

May '60- Terry Moore and Debra Paget in *I WAS ON DEATH ROW.* The true story of the guilty and the innocent!

June '60- From the pen of the genius of terror... Edgar Allan Poe's *THE FALL OF THE HOUSE OF USHER*, starring Vincent Price. In CinemaScope and Color.

Coming in '60- In Colorscope *KONGA*... as big as "King Kong."

Coming in '60- In the tradition of "Goliath"- Adventure-Spectacle-Action! *GOLIATH AND THE DRAGON* in Colorscope.


March 1960-

### *The Angry Red Planet*

"Spectacular Adventure Beyond Time and Space... in magnificent color and CINEMAGIC"

Produced by Sid Pink and Norman Maurer   Directed by Ib Melchior

Starring Gerald Mohr, Nora Hayden, Les Tremayne, Jack Kruschen

Sid Pink (Writer-Producer): "The idea of Cinemagic was to render the backgrounds as cartoon illustrations. We could then project whatever we wanted behind the actors and Cinemagic would blend them right into these backgrounds. We could use drawings, puppets, miniatures, whatever, and everything would blend perfectly."

Ib Melchior (Writer-Director): "Even though I'd directed over 500 TV shows in New York, I was told that the only way I'd be able to get a job in Hollywood was if some producer said I was the only one who could do a particular job. Then I could get into the guild and work. So I agreed to write the script for scale if Sid would let me direct the picture."

130

Les Tremayne (Actor): "Whenever we were outside of the spaceship on Mars, we were covered with white makeup. We all looked like ghosts. We wore helmets, of course, but they didn't have visors because they were using a lot of lights and didn't want any reflections. There was a scene where Nora [Hayden] found some Martian flower and she put it through the helmet to sniff it. We all laughed."

**Gerald Mohr and Nora Hayden in *The Angry Red Planet.***

Film Reviews- *The Angry Red Planet*

*Los Angeles Examiner*- The spectacle of the thing gets you even as you find the dialogue among the space travelers somewhat inane.

*Monthly Film Bulletin*- A juvenile piece of science fiction. The Martian landscape looks like a risible collection of cardboard cutouts, photographed in a kind of infrared light against which the human figures blur like ink on a blotting paper.

*Los Angeles Times*- Simply embarrassing. [Ib] Melchior's direction is not too imaginative and the potentially clever effects process is rendered useless by producer [Sidney] Pink's use of cheap, clearly unreal backdrops.

*Variety*- While it may take considerable ingenuity to produce the [Cinemagic] effect, the result isn't really worth it.

**Although it was almost unanimously panned by critics, *The Angry Red Planet* did good business for AIP, playing first run hold-over engagements for three weeks in the Los Angeles area alone.**

March 28, 1960
*Boxoffice*
A PAIR OF FORTHCOMING FEATURES
Shooting simultaneously at the Amco Studios, home of American International Pictures, were
   *Girl on Death Row*, being produced by Richard Bernstein, and *Fall of the House of Usher*, which Roger Corman is producing-directing. Both films are scheduled for June release through AIP.

April 18, 1960
*Boxoffice*
NICHOLSON SEES 6TH YEAR AS THE BIGGEST FOR AIP
Hollywood- American International Pictures' sixth year, which

starts in July, has every promise of being the biggest in the company's history, AIP's president James H. Nicholson confidently informed the Hollywood trade press at a luncheon-conference held at Amco studio on Friday. Several factors should enter into AIP's continued growth, said Nicholson, principally a general upgrading of the type of pictures it has on its distribution docket under the AIP label and the product shortage, which will be increased by the actor's strike.

Nicholson admitted that the walkout of troupers exerted somewhat of a hardship on his company inasmuch as it eliminated virtually all rental activities at its recently acquired Amco studio, but the loss of revenue entailed therein has been or will be more than compensated by a larger market for AIP pictures, current and those to come.

Nicholson and AIP's vice president, Samuel Z. Arkoff, while in Europe recently acquired a rough story draft of *Ali Baba and the 7 Wonders of the World,* which will be the company's most ambitious undertaking to date. A combination story and travelog, it will be filmed in Technicolor and SuperTechnirama 70.

AIP's future lineup already set for 1960 release include: *Circus of Horrors,* May; *Jailbreakers,* June; *Why Must I Die?,* June; *House of Usher,* July; *Konga,* August; *Male and Female,* September; *Journey to the 7th Planet,* October; *Gateway to Gaza,* October; and for 1961, *The Talking Dog,* Easter; *Ali Baba and the 7 Wonders of the World,* Thanksgiving.

Additionally, the company has determined on two reissues, *Naked Paradise,* retitled *Thunder Over Hawaii,* and *Apache Woman,* retitled *The Apaches.*

**While on their European junket, Jim and Sam viewed an Italian horror movie directed by Mario Bava called *The Mask of Satan.* Sam later said, "It was one of the best horror pictures I had ever seen." They immediately bought the U.S. distribution rights, re-dubbed it, re-scored it, and retitled it *Black Sunday.***

May 1960-

### *Circus of Horrors*
"SPECTACULAR TOWERING TERROR! The strange thrills... the beauty and blood of the most bizarre circus in the world!"

Produced by Julian Wintle and Leslie Parkyn  Directed by Sidney Hayers
Starring Anton Diffring, Erika Remberg, Yvonne Monlaur

From the Imperial Records soundtrack album liner notes-
American International's *Circus of Horrors* sounds like a horror story, but it isn't!
It is a lavishly mounted, richly produced, dramatically directed, exquisitely colored film high in excitement and menace, which contrasts for brilliant effect with circus life and a bevy of scantily-clad European charmers who star in the picture and are beautiful and provocative from whichever angle you view them.
The American International film offers top entertainment, covering and including the thrills of a real circus in the actual circus scenes of performing acts. As background for the clown, wild animals, horses, bears, chimpanzees, and specialty numbers is the story of the brilliant surgeon who surrounds himself with beautiful girls who, unfortunately, do not live long once a new headliner arrives at the "Jinx Circus."

Film Review- *Circus of Horrors*

*New York Times* (September 1, 1960) by Howard Thompson
STYLISH SHOCKER
With a text that might scare the horns off a billy goat, *Circus of Horrors* turns out to be the crispest, handsomest, and most stylish movie shocker in a long time. As still another frankly melodramatic variation on the mad surgeon theme, it's very well handled indeed. Much better, in fact, than most.
This is a British picture, first of all. And Julian Wintle and Leslie Parkyn, the producers, are the team responsible for *Tiger*

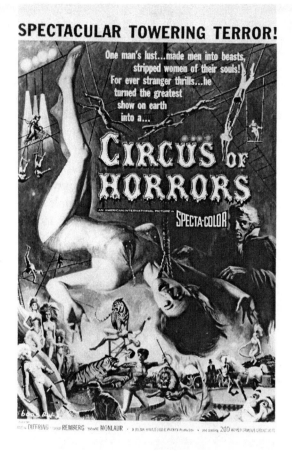

**Poster art for *Circus of Horrors*.**

*Bay-* a clue, at least, as to why the "circus" isn't the qualitative horror it might have been. For that matter, and perhaps best of all, the beguiling color photography superbly captures the big top glitter and atmosphere.

The ending, enfolding two murders, a half-crazed woman, a standard chase, and the phoniest-looking gorilla we've ever laid eyes on, nearly collapses the tent and the movie. But for a hair-raiser that could have wallowed in primeval absurdities, *Circus of Horrors* is surprisingly civilized.

May 2, 1960
*Boxoffice*
## $3.5 MILLION AD BUDGET TO BACK AIP PRODUCT
Hollywood- Embarking on its most ambitious production program, American International Pictures will back its release of the pictures with a minimum expenditure of $3,500,000 in all forms of advertising, it was announced last week at AIP's national sales and advertising conference. The three-day meeting was held Thursday, Friday (21, 22), and Monday (25) at the Amco Studios.

At present, the company is using full page, four-color advertisements in Hearst's Pictorial Living Sunday supplement to reach 10 major markets. This is being supplemented by fan magazine advertising on a regular basis. However, to promote such pictures as *Why Must I Die?*, *House of Usher*, *The Rough and the Smooth*, *Konga*, and *Goliath and the Dragon*, AIP is considering such publications as *Look*, *Life*, and *Saturday Evening Post*.


June 1960-

### *Why Must I Die?/Jailbreakers*
"Only the motion picture screen would dare to tell this shocking story!"

*Why Must I Die?*
Produced by Richard Bernstein  Directed by Roy Del Ruth
Starring Terry Moore, Debra Paget, Bert Freed

*Jailbreakers*
Produced and Directed by Alexander Grasshoff
Starring Robert Hutton, Mary Castle

Film Review- *Jailbreakers*

*New York Times* (January 5, 1961) by Howard Thompson
*Jailbreakers* is a one-man effort, written, directed, and produced by Alexander Grasshoff with a tiny cast headed by Robert Hutton and Mary Castle, set almost entirely in a ghost town, also tiny.

The same applies to the entertainment value of this feeble, static, and trumped-up clinker about escaped convicts menacing a young couple.


July 1960-

*House of Usher*
"Edgar Allan Poe's classic tale of THE UNGODLY... THE EVIL... *HOUSE OF USHER!*"

Produced and Directed by Roger Corman
Starring Vincent Price, Mark Damon, Myrna Fahey

**AIP took their biggest gamble to date with the production of *House of Usher*. A fifteen-day shooting schedule and $50,000 salary for name star Vincent Price contributed to an elevated budget of almost $300,000. Fortunately, the gamble paid off and this became the first in AIP's long-running and highly profitable series of movies based on the writings of Edgar Allan Poe.**

***House of Usher* had its world premiere at the Paramount Theatre in Atlanta, Georgia on June 22, 1960, and went into general release in July.**

Roger Corman (Producer-Director): "It was my idea to make *House of Usher*. It was something I'd wanted to do for a long time. I had been making low budget, black and white films and I felt the time had come for a change. So at a lunch meeting with Jim and Sam, I said, 'Look, instead of making two ten day, black and white films for $100,000 each, why don't we make one movie in fifteen days for $300,000?' They agreed."

Vincent Price (Actor): "I believed that the works of Edgar Allan Poe had never really been properly done on the screen. I thought that Richard Matheson had captured the essence of Poe. Not Poe necessarily, because it's very difficult to turn a short story into a long picture. But somehow he caught the essence of it and

Sam Arkoff and Jim Nicholson seemed dedicated to letting Roger have his head."

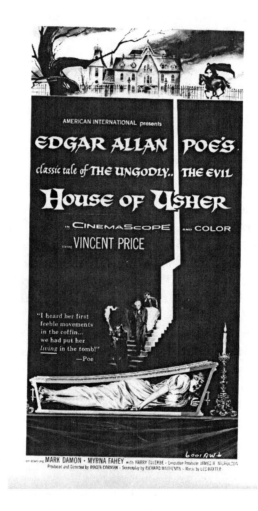

Letter from Milton Moritz to AIP's distributors:

Dear Mr. Exhibitor:

    I am happy to enclose a proof of the newspaper campaign that has been prepared for the Edgar Allan Poe Classic *HOUSE OF USHER* in CinemaScope and Color starring Vincent Price.

As you will note from these proofs, we have included a little of everything to reach the largest possible audience.

At this time, I would also like to advise you that the radio campaign for *HOUSE OF USHER* was prepared by Gordon McLendon, who has a reputation for turning out some of the most powerful radio campaigns ever heard. The radio spots on *HOUSE OF USHER* are among the most impressive he has ever done.

We are sure with the quality of the advertising material that will be made available to you in addition to the national promotion of this feature, *HOUSE OF USHER* will be one of the top grossers this year.

Film Reviews- *House of Usher*

*The Hollywood Reporter* (viewed at a press screening June 22, 1960)- *House of Usher* has the same visual elegance and attempt at story depth as the superior horror films made in recent years by Hammer. It is in the grand tradition of the horror film, with rich and lavish settings, a great horror of a house slowly disintegrating, guttering candles flickering in the wind, murky secret passageways, and cobwebbed burial crypts.

*New York Times* (September 15, 1960) by Eugene Archer
The 'fall' has been omitted from the film version of *The House of Usher*, but not the pitfalls.

American International, with good intentions of presenting a faithful adaptation of Edgar Allan Poe's classic tale of the macabre, blithely ignored the author's style and fell right in.

*The New York Herald Tribune- House of Usher* walks conscientiously in Poe's stylistic steps. The mood is set by the artwork, the music, the direction, and the acting of [Vincent] Price, whose intellectual grasp of this bizarrerie is fine to see. The film is a restoration of finesse and craftsmanship to the genre of dread.

*Variety*- It is a film that should attract mature tastes as well as those who come to the cinema for sheer thrills. All things considered, pro and con, the fall of the *House of Usher* seems to herald the rise of the house of AIP.

*Los Angeles Examiner*- A film that kids will love that never once insults adult intelligence.

*Los Angeles Times*- A better than average horror film, if that's saying much.

**The Amazing Transparent Man/Beyond the Time Barrier**
"See the world of tomorrow!"

**The Amazing Transparent Man and Beyond the Time Barrier were two movies made by Miller-Consolidated Pictures (MPC) in 1959 and given a limited release by that company the same year. Both films were directed by Edgar G. Ulmer. In 1960, AIP acquired the rights to these movies and gave them a wider release as one of their double feature programs.**

*The Amazing Transparent Man*
Produced by Lester D. Guthrie  Directed by Edgar G. Ulmer
Starring Marguerite Chapman, Douglas Kennedy, James Griffith, Ivan Triesault

Film Review- *The Amazing Transparent Man*

*Monthly Film Bulletin*- Gim-crack science fiction-cum-crime melodrama, lacking in personality and invention. Acting, staging, and script are all consistently abysmal.

*Beyond the Time Barrier*
Produced by Robert Clarke  Directed by Edgar G. Ulmer
Starring Robert Clarke, Darlene Tompkins

Film Reviews- *Beyond the Time Barrier*

*Variety*- The only ingredient that distinguishes this effort from its many predecessors is the presence of a timely moral message.

*Monthly Film Bulletin-* Uninspired science-fiction melodrama with a crudely expressed political message. Director Edgar G. Ulmer is happy enough, in a routine way, when the action is set in 1960, but his conception of 2024 behavior is pretty absurd.

August 1960-

August 22, 1960
*Boxoffice*
Distributor showmanship directed at the exhibitor was a highlight of the world premiere of *House of Usher* held at the Paramount Theatre in Atlanta. American International Pictures and Capitol Releasing, the latter of Atlanta, set up chiller-type selling displays at a *House of Usher* luncheon wake held for exhibitors and newspaper and radio folk. One display consisted of a coffin with a "hand" extending from underneath a closed lid and a sign, "Bury the Blues... *House of Usher* Brings Boxoffice Grosses to Life." A comely gal in bathing suit paraded around with a sash-type banner designating her as "Miss Get in the Swim with *House of Usher* Grosses."

**At this luncheon wake, there was also a tombstone which read "Here Lies Mr. ? Exhibitor, who didn't book Capitol's *House of Usher.*" A merry time was had by all.**

September 1960-
Trade ad-
Presenting the seven wonders of American-International... who said there was a shortage of <u>good</u> product?
    October 1960- *Journey to the Lost City* in Colorscope
    November 1960- *Goliath and the Dragon* in Colorscope
    January 1961- Cinemagic, Inc. presents *Reptilicus* in Color
    February 1961- *Konga* in Color and SpectaMation
    Coming 1961- Jules Verne's *Master of the World* in Color and Dynamagic starring Vincent Price
    Coming 1961- Edgar Allan Poe's *The Pit and the Pendulum* to be filmed in CinemaScope and color

Coming 1961- *Ali Baba and the Seven Wonders of the World* to be filmed in Technirama 70 and Technicolor

October 1960-

**Journey to the Lost City**
"She challenged a savage empire... Lost a thousand years in time!"

Produced by Louis de Masure and Eberhard Meichsner
Directed by Fritz Lang
Starring Debra Paget, Paul Christian, Walter Reyer, Claus Holm

**Journey to the Lost City is a combination of two German films directed by Fritz Lang in 1959. The first, *The Tiger of Eschnapur*, ran 101 minutes and the second, *The Indian Tomb*, ran 102 minutes. AIP edited them together into one fairly incoherent 95-minute movie.**

Film review- *Journey to the Lost City*

*New York Times* (December 8, 1960) by Eugene Archer
*Journey to the Lost City* should have genuine appeal for children under 12 years and for the most esoteric connoisseurs of cinematic technique. Viewing the new import yesterday at its neighborhood theatre opening, a more reasonable majority of filmgoers found it merely ridiculous.

This exhilarating nonsense, astonishingly set in a remote province of contemporary India, is played in appropriate deadpan style by its cast, particularly Miss [Debra] Paget, who at one point performs a temple dance with all the bumptious flair of a latter-day Sally Rand. Mr. [Fritz] Lang, with an apparently limitless budget, lavish color, and staggeringly opulent sets, has filmed it all with obvious relish and an unparalleled eye for visual decor.

His film may or may not be art, but no one will deny that it is unusual.

142

November 1960-

***Goliath and the Dragon***
"The mightiest adventure of them all! See Goliath <u>BATTLE</u> the mammoth dragon in the seven caves of Moloch! <u>CONQUER</u> the killer elephants! <u>DARE</u> the black pit of terror!"

Produced by Achille Piazzi and Gianni Fuchs
Directed by Vittorio Cottafavi
Starring Mark Forest, Broderick Crawford, Eleonora Ruffo

**Mark Forest flexes his muscles on the set of *Goliath and the Dragon*.**

**After the success of *Goliath and the Barbarians*, Lou Rusoff wrote a script called *Goliath and the Dragon* that Sam and Jim planned to film in Italy with Debra Paget. These plans fell through and AIP ended up buying an Italian movie called *The Vengeance of Hercules* and reworking it to fit their title by adding scenes with a dragon.**

From the pressbook-
ANCIENT GREECE PRODUCES A NEW AND MIGHTY HERO- GOLIATH!
The ancient land of Thebes in Greece, which had provided the world with many legendary heroes- Hercules, Jason who found the Golden Fleece, Theseus who slew the Minotaur- brings forth a new and fascinating figure: Emilius the Mighty, known to his followers as Goliath.

American International brings some of this man's remarkable feats of strength and bravery to the screen in their color production *Goliath and the Dragon* starring Mark Forest as Goliath,

Academy Award winner Broderick Crawford as the villainous King Eurystheus, and lovely Eleonora Ruffo as Goliath's wife. To save his kingdom, home, and family, Goliath faces worldly beasts- a killer elephant, a giant bear, and horrors from another world: a three-headed dragon dog, a giant bat, and a fire-breathing, flesh-eating dragon.

Film Review- *Goliath and the Dragon*

*New York Times* (January 5, 1961) by Howard Thompson
Very loosely, *Goliath* follows the pattern of those Steve Reeves adventure fantasies from Italy, in dubbed English, with the hero performing superhuman feats, filching a lovely maiden from an evil ruler, and finally leading a victorious army against the enemy.

There are two exceptions here. Mark Forest, another American athlete, is no Steve Reeves by a long shot. Almost lopsided with biceps, Mr. Forest substitutes grinning and grimacing for the other's noble profile.

Furthermore, the plot, the acting, and the very animals are more cardboard than any of Mr. Reeves' set-'em-up exercises. The dragon is an inflated fugitive from "Kukla, Burr and Ollie."

Mr. Reeves and Ollie are still ahead.

November 14, 1960
*Boxoffice*
## AIP's AD CHIEF URGES BROADER HORIZONS
Chicago- Exhibitors were urged to identify themselves as being in the "entertainment business" rather than a more limited "in the motion picture business" in an Allied convention address by Milton Moritz, director of advertising and publicity for American International Pictures.

Speaking at a luncheon meeting at which AIP was host, Moritz declared, "There is a vastly different meaning between these two phrases... and the difference is obvious. When one is in the entertainment business, one is constantly alert to the changing demands of the audience. When one is in the motion picture business, he is hanging on to that non-existent movie habit."

Moritz said that, at AIP, they have long observed "that audiences had determined that there are no longer major motion picture companies, only major pictures."

## AIP PLANNING TO RELEASE BLOCKBUSTER A MONTH
New York- American International Pictures will release one blockbuster a month in 1961 plus eight additional features, an increase of 30 percent over the 14 films released in 1960, James H. Nicholson, president, announced this week. This year, AIP concentrated on four blockbusters and ten other releases.

*Konga*, produced in England in association with Anglo Amalgamated, will be AIP's release for February 1961; *Fright*, a horror film created for adult patronage, will be released in March; *Reptilicus* will be released in April; and *Master of the World*, just completed with Vincent Price starred, will be released in May.

American International will produce Edgar Allan Poe's *The Pit and the Pendulum* with the same team responsible for the company's 1960 blockbuster, *House of Usher*, for release in June 1961 with Roger Corman as producer-director, Richard Matheson doing the screenplay, and Vincent Price to star. Nicholson said that *Usher* will be the company's biggest grosser to date.

AIP is currently negotiating with Roger Corman's Filmgroup to handle the foreign distribution of its U.S. releases, Nicholson said.

November 21, 1960
*Boxoffice*
Hollywood Report by Ivan Spear
MANY JULES VERNE STORIES ON FUTURE SCHEDULES
Hollywood apparently has discovered or rediscovered Jules Verne. Resultantly, the theatrical screen during the next several months will exhibit a noteworthy number of photoplays based on the 50-odd-years-old writing of the granddaddy of science-fiction.

AIP's contribution begins with *Master of the World*, a Vincent Price starrer which just finished shooting in Hollywood under the production aegis of James Nicholson. William Witney directed with Charles Bronson and Henry Hull filling other top roles. Now they are looking at blueprints for Verne's *In the Year 2889* and *The Floating City*.

# CHAPTER EIGHT
# 1961

January 1961-

January 23, 1961
*Boxoffice*
AIP ADDS FOUR FEATURES AIMED AT ART THEATERS
New York- American International Pictures is setting up a special sales department under the supervision of Leon P. Blender for special product designed for the art houses and expects to release three to four pictures in this category each year. The first will be Peter Rogers' comedy, *Beware of Children*, recently acquired from Anglo Amalgamated Productions in England.

These new AIP pictures will increase the 1961 program from 16 to 10 pictures, according to James Nicholson, president.

Blender, AIP sales distribution vice president, also said that most of the regular AIP releases can also play art houses, starting with the company's February release, *Portrait of a Sinner,* starring Nadja Tiller and William Bendix, to be followed by *Black Sunday,* also a British picture, starring Barbara Steele and John Richardson.

Other releases in what Nicholson described as "the strongest lineup of top product our company has had to date" will be: *Konga,* in color and SpectaMation, and *The Hand,* a British-made supporting feature, both for March release; *Two Faces of Dr. Jekyll,* in color and Megascope, starring Paul Massie and Dawn Addams, made by Hammer, for April release; and Jules Verne's *Master of the World* in color and Dynamagic, starring Vincent Price, Henry Hull, and Charles Bronson, to be released in June. The last named was produced under Nicholson's personal supervision. *The Pit and the Pendulum,* starring Vincent Price, John Kerr, and Barbara Steele, is currently being produced and directed by Roger Corman.

Nicholson mentioned that *House of Usher,* starring Vincent Price, was AIP's "biggest grosser to date."

February 1961-

### *Black Sunday* (aka *The Mask of Satan*)
"Once every 100 years... the undead demons of hell terrorize the world in an orgy of stark horror!"

Produced by Massimo de Rita  Directed by Mario Bava
Starring Barbara Steele, John Richardson, Ivo Garrani, Andrea Checchi

From the pressbook-
## WITCHCRAFT DATES BACK TO MAN'S BEGINNING
American International's *Black Sunday* is an experience in the supernatural and one that takes the viewer into the black day when an ancient curse is revived with devastating results.

*Black Sunday* shows how the evil forces are vanquished by the powers of good. Helping in that fight are John Richardson as Dr. Gorobec and Barbara Steele as Katia. The screenplay by Ennio de Concini and Mario Serandrei is based on a story by celebrated

novelist Nikolai Gogol. The film was directed by Mario Bava, who also served as art director. Exteriors of the picture were filmed at one of the famed Massimo castles outside Rome.

SEAT SELLING SLANTS-
Place a coffin in front of your theatre with a microphone inside of the coffin, whereby a person in a strategic point can see the coffin and hold conversations with those persons walking by. This has been used on many occasions and was found to be very effective.

Film Reviews- *Black Sunday*

*Time Magazine* (September 1, 1961)- *Black Sunday* (Galatea-Jolly; AI) is a piece of fine Italian handiwork that atones for its ludicrous lapses with brilliant intuitions of the spectral. Director Mario Bava makes subtle uses of a Gothic setting- much of the film was shot in a medieval Italian castle- to enhance the Gothic mood.

*Motion Picture Herald*- A classic quality permeates this gruesome, shocking, horrifying story of a vengeful, bloodthirsty vampire. Effectively photographed in low key black and white against rich settings of macabre design, *Black Sunday* achieves frightful elements of surprise through clever makeup and performances.

*Hollywood News Citizen*- The technicians and artisans are to be highly commended for creating moods and illusions with skilled sets, props, costumes, cinematography, musical score, and particularly the editing.

*Variety*- There is sufficient cinematographic ingenuity and production flair to keep an audience pleasantly unnerved.

February 18, 1961
*Motion Picture Herald*
PIT AND THE PENDULUM IS AIP's LATEST EXCURSION INTO THE WONDERFUL REALM OF EDGAR ALLEN [sic] POE by Samuel D. Berns, Hollywood
On the premise that "nothing succeeds like success," American International Pictures is parlaying the healthy grosses earned on Edgar Allen Poe's *The House of Usher* to another Poe classic, *The Pit and the Pendulum*.

AIP's masterminds, James Nicholson and Samuel Arkoff, have almost doubled the budget used on *Usher* and are banking on producer-director Roger Corman to see that the *Pendulum* swings the company's grosses to a new high.

We visited several of the sets occupying a number of stages

at California Studios and were immediately impressed with the production values, lavish settings, and costumes authenticated for the period piece. A vast amount of hand-carved antique furniture, authentic coats of arms, rugs, and bric-a-brac has been gathered by the property master to enrich the color film in Panavision.

We had the "harrowing" experience of walking through spiked passageways, cobwebbed dungeons, and burial tombs and watched the testing of the huge, eerie pendulum with a knifed edge, a powerful weapon for any torture chamber.

We watched Roger Corman direct two lengthy scenes with the film's stars, Vincent Price, John Kerr, Barbara Steele, and Luana Anders, finishing each in one take and the happy command, "Print it!"

The visit gave further credence to AIP's aim to build its importance as a source of money-making product.

March 1961-

### Konga
"Not since KING KONG... has the screen exploded with such mighty fury and spectacle!"

Produced by Herman Cohen  Directed by John Lemont
Starring Michael Gough, Margo Johns, Jess Conrad, Claire Gordon

From the pressbook-
"KONGA" NO MECHANIZED MONSTER
American International's mighty *Konga* will be a revolution as well as a revelation to movie audiences everywhere, for it presents a new screen technique called SpectaMation. No mechanized monster is used. Instead, a live chimpanzee, through 'tricks' performed inside the camera, will grow into a monstrous gorilla standing over 100 feet tall to threaten the city of London and many of its famous landmarks, including Big Ben.

*Konga* stars Michael Gough, Margo Johns, Jess Conrad, and Claire Gordon. The Color film was directed by John Lemont from

151

a screenplay by Aben Kandel and Herman Cohen. Cohen also produced the picture.

SEAT SELLING SLANTS-
Schedule special screening of *Konga* for chimpanzees and monkeys in your local Zoo. If you do not have a zoo, switch to local pet stores with monkeys and chimps. Invite the press to cover the animal's reactions to *Konga*, with an almost guaranteed top feature story the result.

***Konga* has Michael Gough in his clutches.**

Film Reviews- *Konga*

*Monthly Film Bulletin-* Slow development and ludicrously inadequate dialogue... and the trick work is deplorable. Though good for a laugh, the film is in every other respect a wasted opportunity.

*Variety*- The script is burdened with verbose repetitious scientific gobbledegook.

### The Hand
"From War-Torn Burma to the Asphalt Jungles of the Big City- His Revenge was The Crime of the Century!"

Produced by Bill Luckwell  Directed by Henry Cass
Starring Derek Bond, Ronald Leigh Hunt, Reed de Rouen, Ray Cooney

March 13, 1961
*Boxoffice*
VAMPIRES, TALKING CORPSE, WILD FRONT MAKE HOT 'SUNDAY'
*Black Sunday*, which was world-premiered at the Allen Theatre in Cleveland and has been showing frequently to SRO business, almost had to get off on a bat's wing and a magic sign in lieu of the usual promotion and the wildly colorful front put up just before the opening.

Due to fast booking arrangements, Milt Moritz, American International advertising-publicity executive, arrived in town with ten days to arrange for the world premiere ballyhoo. Alerting of potential theatergoers was accomplished via radio, television, the newspapers, and drugstores.

The No.1 promotion was the Ten Best Ghouls competition, a zany affair planted with the *Cleveland Plain Dealer*.

To multiply the impact of the [theatre] front, a coffin was placed in the outer lobby with a ghoulish-looking dummy inside. Concealed under the lid was a microphone and loudspeaker wired to another speaker and mike in the lobby. Operating the latter was a girl who could see the coffin, but could not be seen. Hundreds "talked" with the corpse.

Last, but not least, Barbara Steele came in for a press luncheon, radio, and television appearances. She was taped with Dick Wright, Stanley-Warner zone manager, for the half-hour

"Lights, Camera... Questions!", a WJW-TV Sunday show, and judged the horror contest prior to the premiere at 2 p.m. Wednesday afternoon.


April 1961-

***Beware of Children*** (aka ***No Kidding***)
"Parents of the World Unite! From the producers of 'Carry on Nurse' another 'Daffodil' to shock your funny bone!"

Produced by Peter Rogers  Directed by Gerald Thomas
Starring Leslie Phillips, Geraldine McEwan, Julia Lockwood, Noel Purcell

April 3, 1961
*Boxoffice*
ONE BLOCKBUSTER A MONTH SET AS '61 GOAL OF AIP
Hollywood- Seven years of phenomenal growth and unshakable confidence in the future are the principal factors in the determination by American International Pictures to make 1961 the biggest year in its history.

To implement the attainment of such goal, AIP has embraced a policy of releasing one picture of outstanding proportions each month for the next 12 months. [James] Nicholson termed his company's plans "New Horizon's Project '61." The program starts with *Black Sunday,* just going into release.

Details of the "project" are set forth in a 23-page brochure outlining campaigns for upcoming pictures. In addition to *Sunday,* among these are *Konga, Jekyll's Inferno, Master of the World,*
*The Pit and the Pendulum, Reptilicus,* and *Ali Baba and the Seven Miracles of the World.*

Nicholson will leave soon for a tour of the nation's ten principal market areas to screen *Master of the World,* the company's most ambitious and most expensive venture to date, for exhibitors and special test audiences.

May 1961-

*House of Fright*
"Like nothing you have ever seen! A completely new version of
the classic story... a new Dr. Jekyll... a handsome, evil Mr. Hyde!
A SHOCK ENDING THAT YOU DARE NOT REVEAL!"

Produced by Michael Carreras  Directed by Terence Fisher
Starring Paul Massie, Dawn Addams, Christopher Lee

**House of Fright was actually *The Two Faces of Dr. Jekyll*,
a Hammer Film production made in 1960 as part of a multi-
picture deal with Columbia Pictures. Columbia declined to
release the film in the U.S. and sold the rights to American
International, who changed the title to *Jekyll's Inferno*. Shortly
before its release, the title was again changed to *House of Fright*.**

From the pressbook-
*HOUSE OF FRIGHT*
Few tales of the macabre have so successfully captured the
imagination of successive generations as Robert Lewis Stevenson's
Victorian classic, *The Strange Case of Dr. Jekyll and Mr. Hyde*.
      Now this eerie thriller, one of the world's most gripping horror
stories, comes to the screen again, more exciting than ever before
with the aid of several ingenious new twists guaranteed to make
your hair stand on end.
      This latest filmization of the macabre drama is American
International's *House of Fright*, starring Paul Massie, Dawn
Addams, and Christopher Lee.
      Screenplay writer Wolf Mankowitz has injected some startling
and original new material, such as an unfaithful wife for Dr. Jekyll
and the degenerate Mr. Hyde as a young, handsome, debonair
gentleman with a fatal fascination for women!

SEAT SELLING SLANTS-
Borrow a small aquarium from a tropical fish store. Place it on
a stand in your lobby. On the floor of the aquarium, place a pair
of well-worn men's shoes. On one wall of the aquarium, place a

155

sign: Who's the owner? This man jumped out of his shoes while watching *House of Fright*.

Film Review- *House of Fright*

*Variety*- There is little to horrify audiences of whatever age. There is, however, abundant flouting of the moral code- adultery, two rapes, and the standard genre violence- that make this anything but a kiddie's matinee film.

June 1961-

### Master of the World

"ROBUR THE CONQUEROR and his amazing flying warship... destroyer of the armies of the world... the fabulous adventures of the man who conquered the earth to save it!"

Produced by James H. Nicholson  Directed by William Witney Starring Vincent Price, Charles Bronson, Henry Hull, Mary Webster, David Frankham

**Although *Master of the World* had the biggest budget of any AIP film thus far, it was still basically an A movie concept made with a B movie budget. The all-too-obvious use of stock footage for some of the large-scale action sequences helps to betray its B movie origins. This was the first AIP movie to have several merchandise tie-ins: an Ace paperback novel, which included both the Jules Verne novels *Master of the World* and *Robur the Conqueror*, a Dell four color Movie Classic comic book adaptation of the film, and a soundtrack recording of Les Baxter's score on VeeJay Records.**

From the VeeJay Records soundtrack album liner notes-
Just as the name Jules Verne in storytelling means excitement, thrills, and high adventure, so the name Les Baxter in music means haunting mood music, exciting rhythms, and singable and danceable melodies.

156

Add to this combination one of Jules Verne's most unusual and thrilling stories, *Master of the World*, made into a memorable motion picture with songs and music by the same Les Baxter, and you have the ingredients that made the music for *Around the World in 80 Days* the most popular film score in many a year.

Film Reviews- *Master of the World*

*Time Magazine* (September 22, 1961)- SUBTEEN SPECIAL *Master of the World* (American International). The Albatross is the name of the flying machine and its master is Robur (Vincent Price), a mysterious neo-Nemo who calls himself "a citizen of the world" and grandly declares "war against war." In short order, he destroys the British fleet and breaks up a battle in North Africa, but in the end, of course, Robur suffers the fate that Hollywood perennially reserves for those whose means are evil though their ends be good and the world goes happily back to war. The paper-airplane crowd may find the ethics of the film a bit confusing, but they are bound to get a band out of The Albatross, which is indeed a gorgeous gadget.

**James Nicholson poses with the model of "The Albatross" from *Master of the World*.**

*The New York Herald Tribune*- It's not so much the inevitable grotesquerie of the picture's mechanical marvels, but the drabness of the characterization and dialogue that keeps it well below the level of interest adult moviegoers would expect.

*Variety*- Watered-down Jules Verne, diluted by modern, dramatic agents foreign to the nature of the author's original fantasy. Also, there is a certain element of monotony and repetition about the long ride in the air, a suspended lethargy that director William Witney has not been able to disturb too frequently.

*New York Times* (September 16, 1961) by Eugene Archer
TWIN BILL: "KONGA" AND "MASTER OF THE WORLD" ARRIVE

The children attending yesterday's new double bill greeted *Konga* with misplaced guffaws, but accorded *Master of the World* a smattering of applause.

For a 10-year-old age group, both evaluations were appropriate. While the British *Konga* is nothing more than an overblown *King Kong*, hammily played by Michael Gough and an improbable-looking ape, *Master of the World*, taken from a pair of Jules Verne novels, has pleasantly nostalgic qualities.

For one thing, the hero, quietly acted by Charles Bronson, is a likable type, homely, modest, and altogether noble. The villain, too, is the good old-fashioned kind in the surprisingly restrained hands of Vincent Price.

Adults dragged in to watch the American International release will find it devoid of artistic pretensions, but a lot more sufferable than they would suppose.

**Richard Harrison (born 1936) played Alistair, the navigator of the Albatross, in *Master of the World*. During the filming, he met Jim Nicholson's daughter, Loretta, and married her shortly thereafter. In a 1990 interview, Mr. Harrison told me that rather than accept an AIP contract from his father-in-law, he chose to go to Europe to try and make it on his own. He succeeded admirably as he had a lengthy career in Europe, appearing in**

every type of Italian genre movie, from Sword and Sandal films
to Spaghetti Westerns and beyond.

June 5, 1961
*Boxoffice*
AIP FILM IS HONORED
Parents Magazine Special Merit Award for July has been awarded
to American International Pictures' *Master of the World*. Leo Dan,
advertising director of the magazine, presented the award to
president James H. Nicholson, who also produced the Jules Verne
classic. *Master of the World*, which stars Vincent Price, Henry Hull,
Charles Bronson, Mary Webster, and David Frankham, is in color
and StereoSonic sound.

'MARKET FOR LOW-BUDGET FILMS IS DEAD',
CONTENDS PRODUCER ROGER CORMAN
New York- "The little picture (meaning low-budget) is dead
in today's market," in the opinion of Roger Corman, one of
Hollywood's youngest producers, who has been making this type of
film for his own Filmgroup, but has recently switched to American
International, for which he has made two CinemaScope-color
features, *The House of Usher* and *The Pit and the Pendulum*.

Corman, who started producing six years ago, about the same
time as American International started up, said that James H.
Nicholson and Samuel Z. Arkoff of AIP also saw that the market
for their low-budget pictures was drying up and had concentrated
on fewer and bigger pictures in the last two seasons.

Corman has just signed a new three-feature production deal
with Nicholson and Arkoff and will start off with *The Haunted
Village*, which will be scripted by Charles Beaumont from a short
story by H.P. Lovecraft. Corman's other two properties are *X*, a
story by Ray Russell, a former editor of Playboy Magazine, and
H.G. Wells' *When the Sleeper Wakes*, all three being in the horror-
science fiction vein.

June 12, 1961
*Boxoffice*
DISCUSS AIP RELEASE
Roger Corman, producer of *The Pit and the Pendulum* for American International Pictures, held a trade press luncheon at New York's Absinthe House to discuss the September release of the film and forthcoming pictures for AIP. *The Pit and the Pendulum* is in color and Panavision and stars Vincent Price, John Kerr, Barbara Steele, and Luana Anders.

July 1961-

*Alakazam the Great* (aka *The Magic Land of Alakazam*)
"American International's funtastic full-length cartoon feature in COLOR and MAGISCOPE"

Produced by Lou Rusoff and Hideyuki Takahashi   Directed by Daisaku Shirkawa
Featuring the voices of Frankie Avalon, Dodie Stevens, Jonathan Winters, Sterling Holloway

*Alakazam the Great* **was the 1960 Japanese animated feature** *Journey to the West,* **which was produced by Toei Company and picked up by AIP for U.S. release. The film marked the beginning of a long association between teen idol Frankie Avalon and AIP. Avalon supplied the singing voice of Alakazam in the AIP dubbed version.**

July 3, 1961
*Boxoffice*
AIP BUDGETS $10 MILLION FOR 13 FILMS JUNE-DECEMBER
Hollywood- Adhering with all possible closeness to the "New Horizons 1961" credo declared at the year's beginning, James H. Nicholson and Samuel Z. Arkoff, respectively president and vice president of American International Pictures, now emphasize that

13 films with a total budget of $10,000,000 will go into release or production during the last six months of the year.

Details of the schedule were revealed prior to Nicholson's departure for New York, where he was to set exhibitor screenings for AIP's July release, the full-length cartoon *Alakazam the Great*. The color and MagiScope cartoon stars the voices of Frankie Avalon, Dodie Stevens, Jonathan Winters, Sterling Holloway, and Arnold Stang, with music by Les Baxter.

Ready for release is the Edgar Allan Poe story, *The Pit and the Pendulum*, in color and Panavision, starring Vincent Price, John Kerr, and Barbara Steele, and now in early distribution is Jules Verne's *Master of the World* in color, also starring Vincent Price.

Further on the 1961 schedule and at present being cut are *Lost Battalion*, starring Diane Jergens; *Journey to the 7th Planet*, in color, starring John Agar and Greta Thyssen; and *Black Mutiny*, in color and scope, starring Don McGowan and Silvana Pampanini.

Two others currently in production are both full-length cartoon features being co-produced in Japan with Toei Productions. One is titled *The 7th Wonder of Sinbad* and the other is as yet untitled.

Five others are set to go before the cameras during the next six months, starting in August with the science fiction thriller *X*, in color. It is the story of a man with X-ray vision, with screenplay by Ray Russell and to be produced and directed by Roger Corman.

Also set for production this year are H.G. Wells' *When the Sleeper Wakes*, also in color; *Conjure Wife* (tentative title), to be filmed in England as a coproduction with Anglo Amalgamated; an as yet untitled war film, which will be a coproduction with Herman Cohen; and a remake, in color and scope, of the silent film classic *Metropolis*.

July 10, 1961
*Boxoffice*
AIP's 'ALAKAZAM' HAS MANY TIEUPS
New York- James H. Nicholson, president of American International Pictures, was host for exhibitors at Sardi's Restaurant Monday, July 3, to outline the advertising-publicity campaign stressing the theatrical merchandising on the full-length cartoon feature *Alakazam the Great*, a first for AIP.

Nicholson said that AIP is so high on the box office prospects of *Alakazam*, which was made in MagiScope and color in Japan, that the company is entering into negotiations for future deals with Toei Company. Jonathan Winters was present at the luncheon, as were Lou Rusoff, producer of *Alakazam*, and Salvatore Billiteri, AIP east coast production head.

August 1961-

### The Pit and the Pendulum
"Until now no one has dared to film this... the most diabolical classic of all time!"

Produced and Directed by Roger Corman
Starring Vincent Price, John Kerr, Barbara Steele, Luana Anders

From the pressbook-
## PRODUCER-DIRECTOR CORMAN BECOMING TERROR EXPERT
Director-producer Roger Corman, with *The Pit and the Pendulum* as his second Edgar Allan Poe film, both made for American International Pictures, is rapidly becoming Hollywood's newest terror authority.

His previous Poe story, *The House of Usher*, won acclaim when it was released in this country and currently receiving critical and audience praise in Japan and throughout Europe.

Corman is one of the youngest and ablest producer-directors in the motion picture industry. He now heads his own company, The Filmgroup, and produces and directs many of his own films.

## SEAT SELLING SLANTS-
Here's a wonderful "gimmick" for extra publicity: The mystery atmosphere of the picture can be heightened by keeping the theatre dark before *The Pit and the Pendulum* is screened and having the ushers seat the audience by flashlight. Additional atmosphere can be added by having the ushers wear black hooded capes. This will

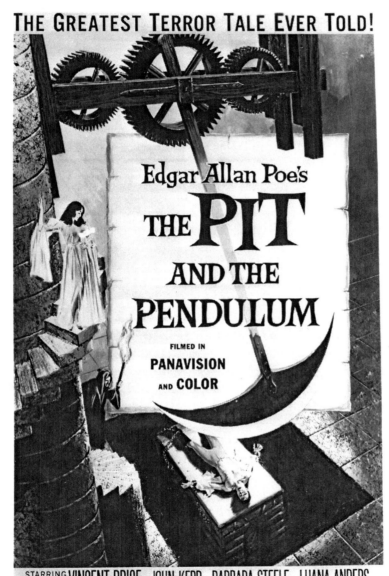

mean extra publicity as newspapers will surely go for a story about this novelty situation in a theatre.

Film Reviews- *The Pit and the Pendulum*

*Time Magazine* (September 1, 1961)- BLOOD PUDDING
*The Pit and the Pendulum* and *House of Usher* (AI) are a couple of literary hair-raisers that are cleverly if self-consciously Edgar Allen [sic] Poetic. Both pictures are filmed in redolent colors, both feature Vincent Price, a sort of sissified Bela Lugosi, and both are crowded with what the press agents call "torturous passageways."

*Films in Review*- The script utilizes a lot of non-Poe stussel-bussel and omits the Inquisition (to spare Catholic sensibilities, apparently). But Roger Corman is as inventive as he was on *Usher* and effectively employs all the stock shocks and a few new ones.

*Los Angeles Examiner*- One of the best "scare" movies to come along in a long time. Skillfully directed by [Roger] Corman with Vincent Price turning in the acting job of his career.

*Los Angeles Times*- Price mugs, rolls his eyes continuously, and delivers his lines in such an unctuous tone that he comes near to burlesquing the role. [John] Kerr seemed to be trying to balance things by hacking out his lines so stiffly and disjointedly that he might have been a driller working on a block of concrete.

*The Hollywood Reporter*- A class suspense-horror film of the caliber of the excellent ones done by Hammer.

*Hollywood Citizen News*- When the dramatic histrionics evoke laughter rather than edge-of-your-seat suspense, then it must be admitted that this new American International release is not up to very much.

*Motion Picture Herald*- The mood throughout combines reality with the dreamlike ornateness and dark imagery of the original, resulting in a resounding good screen story and a remarkably accurate transliteration of Poe's mood and purpose.

*Variety*- While [Richard] Matheson's script takes a good

deal of time, including three extended flashbacks, to get to the denouement, it's almost worth it. The last portion of the film builds with genuine excitement to a reverse-twist ending that might well have pleased Poe himself.

*The New York Times*- Atmospherically, at least- there is a striking fusion of rich colors, plushy decor, and eerie music- this is probably Hollywood's most effective Poe-style horror flavoring to date.

### Operation Camel
"The Cold War Turns Hot... when the desert legions surrender to the desirable damsels of
the Nile!"

Produced by Henrik Sandberg  Directed by Sven Methling
Starring Nora Hayden, Louis Renard, Carl Ottosen

August 28, 1961
*Boxoffice*
AIP TO MAKE EIGHT FILMS OF ITS OWN NEXT YEAR
New York- American International will produce at least eight pictures of its own in Hollywood next year in addition to participating in coproduction deals abroad, James Nicholson said here Tuesday, August 22, upon his arrival from Europe.

Nicholson arranged for the Western Hemisphere distribution of a British picture while in London. The film has a temporary title of *Witch Wife* and will be produced by Independent Artists, Ltd. starting on September 18. He also arranged for the coproduction of a picture in Spain under the title of *The Sea Fighters*, which will have an American director and cast.

Nicholson said work had started on the script of *Alababa* [sic] *and the Seven Miracles of the World*, which will be a feature-length animated cartoon to be made in Japan. More than two years of work will be required for the production, which is slated for release at Christmas 1963.

AIP will start a Vincent Price picture titled *X* in November and *Tales of Terror*, based on a series of Edgar Allan Poe stories, will go into production in January. In March, two pictures will start, *The Haunted Village* and an untitled war picture. Four other properties have not been selected.

September 1961-

***The Lost Battalion***
"200 MEN and ONE GIRL...TRAPPED in a RING of STEEL!"

Produced and Directed by Eddie Romero
Starring Leopold Salcedo, Diane Jergens, Johnny Monteiro

September 18, 1961
SAMUEL SEIDELMAN TO AIP AS FOREIGN DEPT. CHIEF
New York- Samuel L. Seidelman has succeeded William G. Reich as vice president in charge of foreign distribution of American International Export Corp., subsidiary of American International Pictures. Reich, who recently resigned, will remain with AIP in an advisory capacity. Seidelman will take over his new duties immediately.

September 20, 1961
*Motion Picture Herald*
MASTER DRIVE AIDS *"MASTER OF THE WORLD"* PLAYDATE AT SINGAPORE'S CATHAY
A very extensive promotion campaign was employed by the Cathay cinema, Singapore, in putting over American International's release of James H. Nicholson's production of Jules
Verne's *Master of the World* at this house. Highlights of the campaign included:
 1. Contest: A "Master Brain of Singapore" competition with contestants called upon to answer questions ranging from mathematics to politics.
 2. Fashion Show: A "World of Fashions" show was held on stage of the theatre.

3. Float: A very striking lorry float toured the city and suburbs a fortnight in advance of opening day.

4. Lobby: Unusual theatre displays *featured* an 18-foot balloon with gondola which was suspended from the ceiling of the cinema lobby for an amazing effect.

November 1961-

Trade ad-

In the box office tradition of *House of Usher* and *The Pit and the Pendulum,* American International Pictures now takes pride in presenting Vincent Price, Peter Lorre, Basil Rathbone, and Patricia Medina in Edgar Allan Poe's *Tales of Terror* in Panavision and color. Production starts November 28, 1961.

**Patricia Medina would be replaced by Debra Paget in the finished film.**

December 1961-

*Portrait of a Sinner* (previously titled *The Rough and the Smooth)*
"I am the image of evil...only when you are with me...can you feel alive."

Produced by George Minter  Directed by Robert Siodmak
Starring Nadja Tiller, Tony Britton, William Bendix, Natasha Parry

December 6, 1961
*The Hollywood Reporter*
98 AIP PRODUCTIONS IN 7 YEARS GROSSED OVER $230 MILLION
Miami- Over the last seven years, the 98 films produced and released by American International Pictures have realized a domestic box office gross of $230,706,207, Milton Moritz, national ad-pub director, told a luncheon hosted yesterday by AIP for the Allied States Assn. convention.

167

Moritz made the disclosure in pointing out that major companies were "sacrificing show business to the false idol of money by cutting production schedules, eliminating sales offices, and cutting advertising and exploitation budgets to the bone" during the same period.

# CHAPTER SEVEN
# 1962

From an AIP promotional brochure for 1962:

AIP- Always In Profit
In the year 1962, American International will take pride in presenting a program of diversified and important motion pictures... new and fresh in concept... solid in selling angles... superior in quality and production values... you will note an increase in star power as well as "behind the camera" talent... each succeeding season we have moved ahead... in 1962, AIP takes the GIANT STEP!

*Burn Witch, Burn-* Terror... Surprise... Shock... an adventure in suspense unlike anything ever brought to the screen!

*Journey to the 7th Planet-* A Cinemagic Production in color
Four who dared the invasion of a planet lost in the stars... a weird world beyond imagination!

*Guns of the Black Witch-* An American International Picture in ColorScope
What was the terrible secret of this hell ship?

Alexandre Dumas' immortal classic *The Iron Mask* in ColorScope

Edgar Allen [sic] Poe's *Tales of Terror* in Panavision and color
A trilogy of shock and horror based on three stories of the macabre by the great master of shock- a new concept in motion pictures!

*Warriors Three-* An incredible true saga of World War II filmed where it actually happened. In color, starring Jack Palance.

*The Seafighters-* Death was their destiny! In ColorScope.

The man with the X-ray eyes... the man called *"X."*

*The Maid and the Martian-* He came to conquer the earth... but didn't plan on our secret weapon... the blonde in the black negligee!

*Ali Baba and the Seven Miracles of the World-* The most fabulous entertainment ever brought to the screen. In Super Technirama 70mm color by Technicolor.

*The Haunted Village-* Where a new dimension in unspeakable horror began! Starring Vincent Price.

*Survival-* The most astounding motion picture made. In ColorScope... all star cast.

*When the Sleeper Wakes-* H.G. Wells' fantastic tale of the future

170

The preceding lineup of distinguished and important motion pictures represents thirteen more steps in the growth of American International. Today, we are proud that AIP is recognized by exhibitors all over the world as an important source of product. This carries an obligation we fully appreciate... a continuing supply of better pictures for better box office!

January 1962-

January 4, 1962
*The Hollywood Reporter*
AMERICAN INTERNATIONAL
*Survival* will star Ray Milland, who also directs, with Frankie Avalon and Jean Hagen, rolling Feb. 21. *Warriors Five* has been completed with Jack Palance starred and also set for early summer release is *Poe's Tales of Terror* with Vincent Price, Peter Lorre, and Basil Rathbone, produced and directed by Roger Corman with screenplay by Richard Matheson and photography by Floyd Crosby- the team that turned out *Pit and the Pendulum.*

Coming along later will be *The Haunted Village*, starring Vincent Price, produced and directed by Corman; *End of the World*, another from the Wintle-Parkyn team; *The Seafighters,* super war film to be shot overseas; *The Man with the X-Ray Eyes*, a science fiction film; *The Mutineers*, an action-packed sea story; *When the Sleeper Wakes*, based on the H.G. Wells novel; and, in a different category, an untitled teenage musical extravaganza to be filmed in Palm Springs.

January 11, 1962
*The Hollywood Reporter*
AIP FAVORS POLICY OF 'SMALL AND SAFE'
New York- Declaring American International Pictures is made up of "young people who make it a point to explore every possibility in picture-making and exploitation," president James H. Nicholson yesterday told the annual franchise and branch convention here that it "would rather be small and safe than big and wobbly."

He told the session, "We haven't let a few hits go to our heads.

The motion picture graveyard is full of producing and distributing companies whose biggest disaster was a hit picture which couldn't be followed up."

February 1962-

**At this time, AIP moved their offices to 7165 Sunset Blvd. in Hollywood near Formosa Ave.**

*Guns of the Black Witch*
"Unconquerable Barbarians of the Sea- What was the Secret of this Phantom Ship?"

Produced and Directed by Domenico Paolella
Starring Don Megowan, Emma Danieli, Silvana Pampanini

March 1962-

*The Premature Burial*
"He suffered the worst horror the human mind can imagine-LIVING DEATH!"

Produced and Directed by Roger Corman
Starring Ray Milland, Hazel Court, Richard Ney, Heather Angel

From the pressbook-
POE TERROR CLASSIC STARS RAY MILLAND
From the pen of Edgar Allan Poe, the acknowledged master of the macabre... from American International Pictures, the company which has brought Poe's most chilling works to life on the screen... from the directorial genius of Roger Corman, who was responsible for *House of Usher* and *The Pit and the Pendulum,* now comes the newest and most bloodcurdling motion picture of the year, Poe's *The Premature Burial.*

A cast of master thespians headed by Ray Milland, Hazel Court, Heather Angel, and Richard Ney brings to life one of Poe's

172

most nightmarish themes- burial alive. While Poe has used this theme in other stories, it is only in *The Premature Burial* that he weaves his whole tale about this horrible death. It is the obsessive dread of the main character, portrayed by Ray Milland, that he might be buried alive that forms the powerful basis of this unusual story of fear.

SEAT SELLING SLANTS-
Key exploitation stung for *The Premature Burial,* which will result in top space in all newspapers and on TV, is an actual "burial alive" demonstration by a man or pretty girl. Should you have difficulty in contacting a stuntman or woman in your area for this purpose, get in touch with publicity dept. American International Pictures, 7165 Sunset Blvd. Hollywood, Calif.

**Roger Corman had originally intended to make this film for Pathe, away from the auspices of AIP. A threat from Sam Arkoff to Pathe owner William Zeckendorf- "If you make this new movie, I'll cancel all our lab work with you. That's several million dollars of business a year!"- and the project was turned over to AIP.**

Roger Corman (Producer-Director): "Pathe was the company that did all of the lab work for AIP and they wanted to get into film production. Since I'd had quite a bit of success with the Edgar Allan Poe pictures, I proposed that we make *The Premature Burial.* Now, Vincent Price had a deal with AIP not to make any Poe movies for any other company, so we hired Ray Milland to star in the film. I was surprised to see Jim and Sam walk onto the set the first day of shooting. I thought it was nice that they'd come to wish me luck."

Sam Arkoff: "I shook Roger's hand and said, 'Welcome back to AIP.'"

Film Reviews- *The Premature Burial*

*Motion Picture Herald*- Roger Corman has produced and directed this handsomely mounted film with his usual expert attention to eerie suspense.

*Boxoffice*- While this is not quite as bloodcurdling as Corman's *House of Usher* of 1960 or *The Pit and the Pendulum* of 1961, it is a strong box office contender, made-to-order for the horror-cation devotees.

*Variety*- Not only is the plotting discouragingly predictable, but its gloomy and cavernous interior setting is peculiarly similar to those in the first two pix. By this time, many film fans (and at least one reviewer) are as familiar with Corman's downstairs dungeon as they are with their own basement hobby shops.

### Journey to the 7th Planet
"What is this monstrous THING? With the power of mind over matter! There beyond the stars, your unspeakable fears... deepest desires... come alive... and you are trapped in a spectacle of terror-your secret fears pitted against you!"

Produced and Directed by Sidney Pink
Starring John Agar, Greta Thyssen, Ann Smyrner, Mimi Heinrich

From the pressbook-
"JOURNEY TO THE 7TH PLANET" TAKES YOU ON FIRST TRIP TO MYSTERIOUS URANUS
Is there any life on other planets?
For centuries the world has wondered about Mars and the other worlds of our Solar System.
Now, for the first time, through the magic of American International's *Journey to the 7th Planet* you will see the wonders of a faroff neighbor planet, Uranus, one of the most mysterious and least known of the worlds of our Sun.
You will explore Uranus and its horrors with an intrepid crew of Earthmen in this exciting science fiction thirller. Starring in

the space adventure are John Agar, Greta Thyssen, Ann Smyrner, and Mimi Heinrich, who combine to give you the screen thrill of a lifetime.

SEAT SELLING SLANTS-
Contact your local Air Force public information office or nearby missle manufacturing industry for use of space equipment- missle models, space suits, etc.- in lobby exhibit to tie-in with *Journey to the 7th Planet*. This equipment can also be used for shopping center exhibit or tie-in.

John Agar (Actor): "Greta Thyssen kept trying to upstage me. We would do a two shot and she'd back up slightly so that I'd have to turn my back to the camera. One afternoon, I backed her to the edge of the backdrop so that she had nowhere to go. 'Let's play it 50/50,' I told her."

Jim Danforth (Special Effects): "We did a sequence with a furry monster that AIP approved, but when they saw it, they thought it looked like a giant teddy bear and wanted something different.
I had to work around the clock, on the weekend, to meet the deadline. I was miffed because as far as I was concerned, we'd done it right the first time."

Film Review- *Journey to the 7th Planet*

*New York Times* (May 25, 1962)-
A chap named Sidney Pink rates the ripest raspberry of the season for *Journey to the 7th Planet,* a science fiction item at neighborhood theaters.
For some remote reason, Mr. Pink directed, produced, and helped write this terrible little film, which has a quartet of poker-faced earthlings clumping around a seedy-looking planet (No. 7, it says here), pawing a handful of mysteriously materializing girls (real or unreal, they're real lookers) and colliding with some rubbery-shaped monsters.

*Twist All Night*
"Dig the PLAYGIRL Sensation of the Nation!"

Produced by Maurice Duke and Alan David  Directed by William Hole, Jr.

**Twist All Night was a 1961 independent film, originally called *The Continental Twist*, which was picked up by AIP. The musical comedy starred Louis Prima and June Wilkinson and was directed by William Hole. Jr., who was also responsible for *Ghost of Dragstrip Hollow*.**

March 26, 1962
*Boxoffice*
AIP PREVIEWS NEW PRODUCT TRAILER AND '*BURN WITCH*'
New York- James H. Nicholson, president of American International, and Samuel Z. Arkoff, executive vice president, screen a 30-minute product trailer, including clips of *Tales of Terror,*

*Survival*, and *Premature Burial*, for circuit heads and trade press Friday, March 16, preceding a sneak preview of *Burn Witch, Burn* at the RKO 86th Street Theatre. The screening marked the first in a series scheduled over the next three weeks in 16 cities.

Nicholson pointed out that AIP now has 11 pictures completed out of 21 planned for release in 1962, the first year with this total number scheduled for release. He emphasized that AIP "will become and now is a source of steady product for exhibitors all over the world."

In addition to *Prisoner of the Iron Mask, Premature Burial,* and *Twist All Night*, released during the first three months of 1962, and *Burn Witch, Burn* for late March-early April release, the completed 1962 productions are *The Brain That Wouldn't Die* and *Invasion of the Star Creatures*, a double-bill program for April; *Warriors 5* for May; *Survival* for June, *The Adventures of Marco Polo* for June, *Tales of Terror* for July and *Wild Cargo* for August release.

*Goliath and the Golden City*, starring Gordon Scott and Yoko Tani, will be released in September.

April 1962-

**Burn Witch, Burn**
"Once in 1000 years, the blackness of night is pierced by the shriek of the stone eagle's bloodlust cry... ARISE... ARISE!"

Produced by Albert Fennell  Directed by Sidney Hayers
Starring Janet Blair, Peter Wyngarde, Margaret Johnson

**Janet Blair and Peter Wyngarde in *Burn Witch, Burn*.**

From the pressbook-
*BURN WITCH, BURN* PROLOGUE PERFORMS ANCIENT RITES TO PROTECT AUDIENCES FROM EVIL
Motion picture history will be made before each performance of American International's modern-day tale of witchcraft, *Burn*

*Witch, Burn,* when ancient rites for casting out black magic are performed for audiences in a special prologue to the film.

The unique prologue informs the audience at every showing that *Burn Witch, Burn* contains a centuries-old spell used by practitioners of witchcraft. To relieve the management of the theatre and producers of the film from any responsibility of the consequences of this black magic, an ancient rite is performed before the beginning of the picture so that the film may be shown with safety for everyone in the theatre.

**Burn Witch, Burn was the British-produced horror movie Night of the Eagle. The spoken prologue was added by AIP when they distributed the movie in the United States. There is no indication that unprotected British audiences suffered any consequences of black magic during the viewing of Night of the Eagle.**

Film Review- *Burn Witch Burn*

*New York Times* (July 5, 1962)-
This low-budget British import with Janet Blair and a small cast is quite the most effective "supernatural" thriller since *Village of the Damned* several seasons ago.

Simply as a suspense yarn blending lurid conjecture and brisk reality, growing chillier by the minute, and finally whipping up an ice-cold crescendo of fright, the result is admirable. Excellently photographed (not a single "frame" is wasted) and cunningly directed by Sidney Hayers, the incidents gather a pounding, graphic drive that is diabolically teasing.

Count on seeing a good, unholy brew, seasoned by professional hands and rising to a boil.

May 1962-

May 24, 1962
*The Film Daily*
AIP STRENGTHENS EUROPE OPERATION

New York- American International Pictures will be increasing its continental European operations, President James H. Nicholson and Vice President Samuel Z. Arkoff told *The Film Daily* yesterday.

The strengthening of the continental European situation would leave AIP with a top international organization which is efficient and economical, Nicholson and Arkoff indicated. The pair recently returned from Europe, leaving their AIP foreign distribution head, Samuel L. Seidelman, to hire the Paris representative. The Paris office, once established, will be run on a similar basis to the one currently maintained in Hong Kong for Far East operations.

Foreign grosses last year represented 25 percent of AIP's total income and eight years ago, when the company began, some 10 to 15 percent. Today, it represents 35 percent.

May 28, 1962
*Boxoffice*
CITIES GROWTH OF AIP IN LAST EIGHT YEARS
New York- From a humble beginning eight years ago with four employees, American International Pictures has grown in stature and is continuing to grow, James Nicholson, president, reported at a breakfast meeting with the trade press here Wednesday, May 23.

Nicholson and Sam Arkoff, executive vice president, had returned earlier in the week from Europe where they, along with Sam Seidelman, AIP's foreign sales manager, set plans for European expansion of operations.

The company now has 250 persons on its payroll, compared with about 160 a year ago. It operates nine branches of its own and distributes its product through 19 other exchanges on a franchise basis.

AIP now makes pictures for the foreign as well as the domestic market and has several co-production deals in work. Camera work is being completed on *Warriors 5*, a French-Italian co-production picture.

**Warriors 5 was a 1960 film titled *The War Continues* which was picked up for U.S. distribution by AIP.**

June 1962-

*The Prisoner of the Iron Mask*
"MONSTER or MAN?... WHAT WAS BEHIND THIS HIDEOUS MASK? The madness of thirst... the horror of his own growing beard strangling him alive! The victim screams for mercy of a quick death!"

Produced by Francesco Thellung  Directed by Francesco de Feo Starring Michel Lemoine, Wandisa Guida, Andrea Bosic

From the pressbook-
REVENGE, LOVE, LUST AND HATE MARK EXCITING ADVENTURE CLASSIC FILM
All the ingredients of top thrills and excitement, blended in a classic setting of bygone days, are featured in American International's exciting adventure film, *The Prisoner of the Iron Mask*.

Set in Eighteenth Century Italy and France, the tale of revenge, love, lust, and hate literally forces you to hold your breath. The sweep of Techniscope and the breathtaking beauty of natural color transport you to a time of men of action, beautiful women, and beautiful scenery and costumes amid scenes of passion, fighting, blood, and violence.

June 8, 1962
*The Film Daily*
AIP FAVORS H'WOOD; SETS FOUR
Nicholson and Arkoff Plan 12-a-Year Schedule of 'Big Picture, Big Star'
Hollywood- Four new top-budget, big name-starring films will be produced in Hollywood by American International Pictures during the next six months of 1962, it was announced yesterday by AIP chiefs James H. Nicholson and Samuel Z. Arkoff at a luncheon-press conference here.

Scheduled to start here as part of an AIP master plan to move entirely into big "A" production are:

*The Raven*, based on the famed Edgar Allan Poe poem, starring Vincent Price and, if current negotiation is successful, Peter Lorre, with Roger Corman producing and directing;

*The Haunted Village*, based on a story by Charles Beaumont, produced and directed by Corman;

*The Seafighter* to be directed by Anthony Carreras; and *X-the Man with the X-Ray Eyes*, to be produced by Lou Rusoff from a Ray Russell story.

The four new "Made in Hollywood" productions announced by Nicholson and Arkoff are in addition to *The Young Racers*, currently being filmed by AIP in Europe with Corman producing and directing. Two other important upcoming releases also are Hollywood-made: *Poe's Tales of Terror*, starring Vincent Price, Peter Lorre, and Basil Rathbone, and *Panic in Year Zero*, starring Ray Milland, Jean Hagen, and Frankie Avalon.

Also announced for AIP's 1962 production schedule by Nicholson and Arkoff are two co-productions, one with English producers Julian Wintle and Leslie Parkyn and one with Italian International Films. The English co-production will be *The Children*, a tentative title, from a story by Sidney Hayers; and the Italian production is the previously scheduled *Anzio Express*, with screenplay by Luciano Vincenzioni.

"In the can" and scheduled for release this year are *Marco Polo*, starring Rory Calhoun and Yoko Tani; *Warriors 5*, starring Jack Palance and Anna Ralli; *Goliath and the Warriors of Genghis Khan*, starring Gordon Scott and Yoko Tani; and *The Mutineers*, starring Edmund Purdom and Pier Angeli.

June 27, 1962
*The Hollywood Reporter*
MAYOR INVITED TO 'PANIC'
Mayor Samuel Yorty and members of the L.A. City Council and the L.A. County Board of Supervisors have been invited to tonight's preview of American International's *Panic in Year Zero* at the Academy Award Theatre. The atomic background story stars Ray Milland, Jean Hagen, and Frankie Avalon. Milland also directed with Lou Russoff and Arnold Houghland producing.

July 1962-

### Duel of Fire

"Brutal Murder... Barbaric Reprisals... Savage Love... One man's lust for vengeance explodes in violence!!"

Produced by Fortunato Misiano  Directed by Umberto Lenzi
Starring Fernando Lamas, Liana Orfei, Armand Mestral, Lisa Gastoni

**This Italian film was given a limited regional theatrical release by AIP and later showed up as part of a 1965 AIP TV package.**

### Tales of Terror

"A Trilogy of Shock and Horror!"

Produced and Directed by Roger Corman
Starring Vincent Price, Peter Lorre, Basil Rathbone, Debra Paget

**Vincent Price and Peter Lorre in "The Black Cat" episode of *Tales of Terror*.**

Film Reviews- *Tales of Terror*

*Variety*- Producer [Roger] Corman has played his latest entry for all it's worth and has assembled some tasty ghoulish acting talent which have marquee strength.

*New York Times* (July 5, 1962)- *Tales of Terror* is a dull, absurd, and trashy adaptation of three Edgar Allan Poe stories, broadly draped around the shoulders of such people as Vincent Price, Peter Lorre, and Basil Rathbone (who at least bothers to act). Skip it.

*The Hollywood Reporter*- Roger Corman has subtly mixed ghoul and gag for the kind of entertainment that will titillate fans of the eerie and may draw beyond that group.

*Films and Filming*- Fiendish fun done to a turn. Gore galore and much murder, horrible haunting, and shrill screaming. Just the thing for a night out at the local flea-pit.

*Cue Magazine*- The writing is ordinary and the direction occasionally awkward, but the spine-chilling cinema combination provides plenty of Poe-like shivers and is the perfect cooler-offer in this warm weather.

### Panic in Year Zero
"An orgy of looting and lust... A Day when civilization came to an end!"

Produced by Lou Rusoff and Arnold Houghland    Directed by Ray Milland
Starring Ray Milland, Jean Hagen, Frankie Avalon

**Panic in Year Zero underwent a series of title changes prior to release. Filmed as *Survival*, the title was later changed to *End of the World* before AIP eventually settled on *Panic in Year Zero*. In September 2005, Michael Atkinson of *The Village Voice* said of the film: "This forgotten, saber-toothed 1962 AIP cheapie might be the most expressive on-the-ground nightmare of**

the Cold War era, providing a template not only for countless social-breakdown genre flicks but also for authentic crisis."

Film Reviews- *Panic in Year Zero*

*Boxoffice*- The film is well produced on a modest budget.

*The Hollywood Reporter*- A good sound melodrama.

*Los Angeles Herald-Examiner:* This very unhappy and demoralizing picture is told with all the stops out. It wasn't too expensive to make, but the story is a blockbuster.


August 1962-

*The Brain That Wouldn't Die/Invasion of the Star Creatures*
"FANTASTIC! WEIRD! HORRIFYING!"

This was the first black and white pre-packaged horror double feature that AIP had released since 1959. In quality, the films really harkened back to their earlier efforts of the Fifties. *The Brain That Wouldn't Die* was an independent movie called *The Head That Wouldn't Die*, produced by Rex Carlton in 1959. *Invasion of the Star Creatures* was an "in joke" written and directed respectively by AIP alumnus Jonathan Haze and Bruno VeSota. The film was shot in six days for $25,000.

*The Brain That Wouldn't Die*
Produced by Rex Carlton  Directed Joseph Green
Starring Herb Evers, Virginia Leith, Leslie Daniel

*Invasion of the Star Creatures*
Produced by Berj Hagopian  Directed by Bruno VeSota
Starring Bob Ball, Frankie Ray

Jonathan Haze (Writer): "I wanted to write a comedy for me and Dick Miller to star in, using the names of the people who worked for AIP as the characters and places in the story. My title was *The Monsters of Nicholson Mesa*. They changed everything and it was really crappy then."

Dick Miller (Writer): "I told Jonathan fine, but I wanted to be involved with the writing of it. We worked on it for a little while, but I didn't like the way it was going and I finally gave up on it."

Bruno VeSota (from an interview with Barry Brown): "The original screenplay for *Invasion of the Star Creatures* was by Jonathan Haze and Dick Miller. They tried to sell it to Roger Corman. Mel Welles bought the script from them. When [producer] Berj Hagopian dissociated himself from Welles, it became Hagopian's property. They turned the script over to me. It took us about two weeks to rewrite the script."

### Marco Polo

"Mightiest Adventurer of Them All! Conqueror... of the barbarian hordes of the Orient! Lover... of a thousand exotic women!"

Produced by Luigi Carpentieri and Ermanno Donati  Directed by Hugo Fregonese
Starring Rory Calhoun, Yoko Tani

From the pressbook-
*MARCO POLO* RECALLS CAST OF 1938 MOVIE
American International's new color and CinemaScope adventure spectacle, *Marco Polo*, brings back memories of the famous 1938 black and white film, *Adventures of Marco Polo*, which starred the late Gary Cooper in the title role.

Rory Calhoun portrays the famed traveler and adventurer in the 1962 motion picture, while the lovely Japanese actress Yoko Tani stars in the princess role, originally enacted by Sigrid Gurie.

The new *Marco Polo* is directed by the noted spectacle specialist, Hugo Fregonese, while the old film was directed by Archie Mayo.

SEAT SELLING SLANTS
Chinese restaurants are a focal point for selling tie-ins with *Marco Polo*. Most owners will be happy to set up table tents which you can furnish at very little cost to  plus the picture and an exotic special tropical drink called "The Marco Polo." In turn, you can plug the restaurant in your lobby.

Film Review- *Marco Polo*

*New York Times* (September 20, 1962)-
Rory Calhoun, playing the title role of *Marco Polo* in doublet and tights, is as dauntlessly American as Gary Cooper, who acted the role in an equally foolish Hollywood version a couple of decades ago. Under Hugo Fregoneses's passable direction, the swashbuckling saga from American International is predictably juvenile, colorful, and harmless. As usual, any resemblance between the dubbed soundtrack and the events pictured on the screen is purely coincidental.

August 6, 1962
*Boxoffice*
AIP FILM AWARDED
James H. Nicholson, president of American International Pictures, accepted a *Famous Monsters of Filmland* magazine award from James Warren, publisher. The award went to AIP's *Pit and the Pendulum* after a vote among the magazine readers for the best horror picture of the year.

August 15, 1962
*The Film Daily*
AIP ANNIVERSARY ISSUE

**The AIP tribute begins with the one page article "AIP Showmanship..." by Jim Nicholson, which is followed by a one-page article from Sam Arkoff called "...And Growthmanship."**

Quote from "AIP Showmanship..." by James H. Nicholson: "Showmanship and Imagination are synonymous. The industry must do everything possible to make full use of both."

Quote from "...And Growthmanship" by Samuel Z. Arkoff: "American International has shown a steady growth since the company was organized in 1954. Much of its success can be attributed to manpower, which I think is too often neglected in this business."

**Other articles are "AIP: A Company with a Plan," "Two Men With But One Purpose," "Nick and Sam: 8 Years of Growth," and "The Never Ending Quest." There are also profiles of Leon Blender and Samuel Seidelman. Below is a rundown of AIP's key staff members at this time:**

James H. Nicholson- President
Samuel Z. Arkoff- Executive vice president
David J. Melamed- Financial vice president
Al Simms- Director of music and personnel
Mickey Zide- Assistant sales manager
Milton Moritz- National director of advertising and publicity
Leon P. Blender- Vice president in charge of distribution
Lou Rusoff- Vice president in charge of production
Barney Shapiro- AIP legal counsel
Ruth Rologe- Eastern publicity manager
Louis Lagalante- AIP export controller
Salvatore Billitteri- Head of East Coast production
Samuel L. Seidelman- Vice president in charge of foreign distribution
Mort Golden- Service department manager
Richard Guardian- Latin American supervisor
Keith Goldsmith- Foreign administrative manager

August 27, 1962
*Boxoffice*
RECORD TOTAL OF 16 FILMS SET BY AIP FOR 1963
Hollywood- A record total of 16 new films has been set for 1963 by American International Pictures in the eight-year-old company's biggest and most ambitious schedule, it was announced

by James H. Nicholson and Samuel Z. Arkoff, AIP heads, at a press conference here on Thursday, August 23.

Six new large-scale productions were announced in addition to ten pictures previously reported. The company toppers also disclosed the signing of Frankie Avalon to star in four pictures during the next year, making a total of four big-name stars now under contract to AIP. Recently signed to multi-picture contracts were Vincent Price, Peter Lorre, and Boris Karloff.

Nicholson and Arkoff also said that their multi-million roadshow production of *Genghis Khan*, to be made both abroad and in Hollywood, will be sold in advance of production on a country-by-country distributor basis, following the pattern used by Samuel Bronston with *El Cid* and *55 Days at Peking*.

The six new productions announced are:

*The Pit*, British coproduction now being filmed in London, starring Dirk Bogarde and Mary Ure, a psychological science fiction thriller, produced and directed by Michael Relph and Basil Dearden.

*Schizo*, Italian coproduction starring John Saxon and Leticia Roman, a horror film, produced and directed by Mario Bava.

*War of the Planets*, a super-science fiction thriller in color, now being scripted for Hollywood production.

*Masque of the Red Death*, another Edgar Allan Poe thriller, to be produced in color and Panavision in Hollywood, starring Vincent Price and directed by Roger Corman.

*The Great Deluge*, to be produced in color and Scope in Hollywood, a modern story of a great flood with a parallel to the Biblical Noah and the Ark.

*Costa Brave*, a Spanish coproduction to be filmed on the Spanish Riviera, the story of Gypsies and witchcraft set against the Queen of the Gypsies Festival.

Previously announced for 1963 production were *The Raven*, starring Vincent Price, Peter Lorre, and Boris Karloff; *Beach Party*, starring Frankie Avalon; *The Seafighters*, *The Haunted Village*, *X-The Man With the X-Ray Eyes*, *Genghis Khan*, *Bikini Beach*, *Dunwich Horror*, *The Children*, and *Anzio Express*.

September 1962-

**White Slave Ship**
"CAGED in a BLACK PIT of HORROR... 13 women journeying
to a living hell!"

Produced by Giorgio Agliani  Directed by Silvio Amadio
Starring Pier Angeli, Edmund Purdom, Armand Mestral, Ivan
Desny

September Trade ad-
Solid box office insurance for '63 from American International
    October- *Warriors Five*
    November- *Reptilicus*
    December- *Samson and the 7 Miracles of the World*
    January- *The Pit*
    February- Edgar Allan Poe's *The Raven*
    March- *The Young Racers*
    ...And more to come!

September 11, 1962
Letter from Jim Nicholson and Sam Arkoff to Frankie Avalon

Dear Frankie:

Our thanks to a great young showman--fine actor as well as
singer--for helping to make the Los Angeles area engagement of
"Panic in Year Zero" a smashing success.

We of American International Pictures appreciate your
cooperation and hard work in making possible your record-
breaking and back-breaking (total of thirty in five days) personal
appearances in behalf of "Panic in Year Zero," which once more
demonstrated your continued great mass appeal and popularity.

We look forward to a continued successful relationship with
"Beach Party" and the other three films which you have signed to
do for American International.

**Frankie Avalon (born 1939) lent his talents to fifteen
AIP features.**

September 17, 1962
*Boxoffice*
NICHOLSON SAYS FOREIGN COPRODUCTION
HELPS THE AMERICAN FILM INDUSTRY
New York- The motion picture industry as a business brings back
more dollars from overseas than any other industry in its sum total
business capacity, according to James H. Nicholson, president

of American International Pictures. In defending American production abroad, Nicholson said that his company actually was bringing back more dollars to the United States than were being expended.

"For example," Nicholson said, "if our share of a foreign coproduction runs $200,000, we add $100,000 for new music tracks, editing, etc. here in the states. Based on past performance, this same production will bring back to this country $500,000 to $1,000,000 in overseas income."

Samuel Z. Arkoff, executive vice president, and Nicholson recently returned from Europe, where they probed coproduction in Spain, England, Italy, and Yugoslavia, resulting, Nicholson said, in confirmed confidence in the superiority of American know-how in production.

Nicholson added that AIP had six pictures scheduled for production in Hollywood, starting with *The Raven* on September 20.

October 1962-

*Warriors Five*
"You fight war with your weapons... I fight with mine!"

Produced by Fulvio Lucisano  Directed by Leopoldo Savona
Starring Jack Palance, Anna Ralli, Folco Lulli, Serge Reggiani

October 4, 1962
*The Hollywood Reporter*
$2 MILLION BUDGET FOR AIP 'WAR OF THE PLANETS'
*War of the Planets*, $2,000,000 science fiction film, will be made in color and in Hollywood, personally produced by James H. Nicholson for American International Pictures release, according to Nicholson and Samuel Z. Arkoff, AIP heads. Projects Unlimited, which did the special effects for George Pal's *Wonderful World of the Brothers Grimm*, has been signed to do the same chore on *War* starting in January.

Production on the Vincent Price-Boris Karloff vehicle will begin in March. Harlan Ellison is adapting his own original.

November 1962-

*Reptilicus*
"INVINCIBLE... INDESTRUCTIBLE! What was this BEAST born fifty million years out of time? See: Missiles and atom bombs powerless! Civilization rioting with fear! A mighty city trampled to destruction!"

Produced and Directed by Sidney Pink
Starring Carl Ottosen, Ann Smyrner

From the pressbook-
*REPTILICUS* FEATURES PEOPLES, ARMIES OF DEMARK IN CAST
A total of over 900,000 persons, the entire population of Copenhagen, capital of Denmark, and the Scandinavian nation's army, navy, and air force are featured in American International's science fiction thriller, *Reptilicus*.

The huge populace of the famed Danish city are seen in the picture as the nation's armed forces battle a rampaging prehistoric monster which threatens to destroy the country and the world.

*Reptilicus*, which stars Carl Ottosen and Ann Smyner, tells the tale of an incredible beast, seemingly indestructible and invincible, which runs amok in Northern Europe.

**AIP invested $100,000 to help Sidney Pink make *Reptilicus*. After viewing a rough cut, Sam Arkoff insisted that, although the Danish actors were speaking English, Pink re-dub the picture with American voices; otherwise, AIP would not release the film. Pink retaliated by filing a lawsuit against AIP for breach of contract. An industry screening of *Reptilicus* was arranged, after which Pink dropped the lawsuit and re-dubbed the film. Sid Pink also attempted to sue Monarch Publishing over the sexed-up paperback novelization of the movie.**

Film Reviews- *Reptilicus*

*Hollywood Citizen News*- I suppose it would be supercilious to say that *Reptilicus* is ridiculous. But in critical essence, it ranks far below most films of the nature, failing even in the technical department to register any appreciable degree of surprise or horrifying suspense.

*Monthly Film Bulletin*- A disappointing addition to the abnormal zoology cycle. The lame and plodding narrative is made worse by singularly bad acting. The thin story is padded out by superfluous material, including a contribution by a cabaret singer and some travelogue views of Copenhagen.

November 26, 1962
*Boxoffice*
AMERICAN INTERNATIONAL SETS 24 FEATURES FOR 1963 RELEASE
New York- American International will make great strides in 1963, both in a total number of releases, which will double the company's schedule, and by installing a complete IBM system of digital computers, which will reduce the company's releasing operation overhead, according to James H. Nicholson, president.

AIP's 1963 release schedule will include 24 features, double the number released in 1962, mainly by handling the U.S. distribution of all forthcoming Filmgroup product. The deal was made by Nicholson and Samuel Z. Arkoff of AIP with Roger Corman and Harvey Jacobson, president and executive vice president, respectively, of Filmgroup.

The new distribution agreement will start with Filmgroup's *Battle Beyond the Sun*, a science fiction thriller in color and VistaScope, while the second production will be *The Terror*, in color and VistaScope, starring Boris Karloff, now being produced in Hollywood.

Corman and Jacobson plan to produce 15 features budgeted at a total of $12,000,000 over the next two years, with 12 of these to be made in Hollywood. Among the titles slated for Filmgroup production are *The Man Who Sold the Earth, Robert E. Lee, Women in War, Haunted Dream,* and *Juliet.*

Corman produced the first film for AIP release, *The Fast and the Furious,* eight years ago. His current film for AIP release is Edgar Allan Poe's *The Raven,* which will be released in January 1963, following *Tales of Terror,* which he produced for AIP release in July 1962.

"In order to cope with our expanding release schedule, we are installing this new IBM system, which will revolutionize branch operations as we know it today," Nicholson said. Nicholson, who made the two AIP announcements at a luncheon at the Tower Suites Hemisphere Club Tuesday, November 20, then introduced David J. Melamed, financial vice president of the company, who explained the new AIP digital computer system in detail.


December 1962-

### Samson and the 7 Miracles of the World
"The Wonder Film of the Year! See the miracles of the Golden Tiger, the Tree of Mystery, the Chariot of Death, the Rock of Freedom, the Living Dead, the Bell of Truth, the Man Made Earthquake!"

Produced by Ermanno Donati and Luigi Carpentieri  Directed by Riccardo Freda
Starring Gordon Scott, Yoko Tani


*Samson and the 7 Miracles of the World* was the Italian movie *Maciste at the Court of the Grand Khan.*

From the pressbook-
SCREEN'S "TARZAN" MOVES UP TO GREATER FEATS AS "SAMSON"
From the King of the Jungle to the strongest man of all time!
After five successful portrayals of Tarzan of the Apes, Gordon Scott moves on to bigger things and wider vistas with his most exciting and challenging role- that of the title role in American

International's wonder film of the year, *Samson and the 7 Miracles of the World.*

The broad-shouldered, handsome, and virile Scott co-stars with lovely Yoko Tani in the ColorScope adventure spectacle.

SEAT SELLING SLANTS
Set up a float cruising the city streets prior to opening with local strong men demonstrating muscles. The float should be adorned with pretty girls and "Samson" posters to make an impressive "seat selling" ballyhoo promotion.

December 5, 1962
*Boxoffice*
Hollywood Report by Chris Dutra
Tab Hunter and Frankie Avalon signed contracts to star in *The Seafighters* for American International. Production for the thriller started in Hollywood on November 26.

# CHAPTER TEN
# 1963

Despite a proposed accelerated production schedule for 1963, the year saw an actual reduction of AIP Hollywood-produced pictures. Half of their releases were pickups and, even with this, they did not have a new film in release every month as they had in prior years.

January 1963-

***The Raven***
"The Terror Began at Midnight!"

Produced and Directed by Roger Corman
Starring Vincent Price, Peter Lorre, Boris Karloff, Hazel Court, Olive Sturgess, Jack Nicholson

For his fifth Edgar Allan Poe film, Roger Corman decided to take a lighthearted approach, combining comedy with horror. Although some critics may not have approved, *The Raven* was another big box office winner for AIP and Corman.

Hazel Court and Boris Karloff gleefully torture Olive Sturgess in *The Raven.*

Film Reviews- *The Raven*

*New York Times* (January 26, 1963) by Bosley Crowther
Edgar Allan Poe's Raven might well say "Nevermore" to appearing in Hollywood films after taking a look at the movie called *The Raven* that is allegedly based on the poem by Poe. Strictly a picture for kiddies and the bird-brained, quote the critic.

*Time Magazine* (February 1, 1963)- UGLY CONTEST
This is just a sappy little parody of a horror picture cutely calculated to make the children scream with terror while their parents scream with glee. It does seem a shame that three grown

men- Price is 51, Lorre is 58, Karloff is 75- can find nothing better to do with their time and talents. But on the other hand, it's fun to see the old horrors all together- sort of like watching an Ugly Contest. Karloff plays an admirable King Lear; Price wears a hairline mustache that looks like a third lip; Lorre at his loveliest suggests a contented tarantula. The real star is Scenarist Richard Matheson, who has written three or four of the hairiest lines of the year.

*Variety*- Edgar Allan Poe might turn over in his crypt at this nonsensical adaptation of his immortal poem, but audiences will find the spooky goings-on of a flock of 15th century English sorcerers a cornpop of considerable comedic dimensions.

*Motion Picture Herald*- [Roger Corman] has extracted a deal of suspense, excitement, and general fun from the lively screenplay by Richard Matheson, while the men who handled the special effects are entitled to a deep bow for the magic they impart.

*Boxoffice*- It should make more money in a week at one first-run house than Edgar Allan Poe made in his lifetime.

### The Young Racers
"A Little Death Each Day... A Lot of Love Every Night!"

Produced and Directed by Roger Corman
Starring Mark Damon, William Campbell, Luana Anders

Film Reviews- *The Young Racers*

*Films and Filming*- I've seen a microphone dangle into a shot before now, but I've never seen, as here, an entire technician calmly pulling at cables during a location tracking shot. I was quite startled to notice that [Roger] Corman's technicians don't always wear skates. Indeed, one sometimes wishes he could get his scenarios to move as fast as his production teams do.

*Variety-* The dialogue is incredibly stilted and artificial and there is just too much of it.

January 2, 1963
*The Film Daily*
**An article entitled "Outlook for the New Year: Leaders Speak" offers comments by industry figures Harry Brandt, Arthur B. Krim, W.J. Turnbull, and James H. Nicholson.**
Nicholson says: "While the onset of a new year always helps create an optimistic outlook, it is with a practical and realistic appraisal of the facts that I predict a definite upswing, indeed a revival of 'made in Hollywood' production for 1963, along with a parallel upswing in employment and product."

January 21, 1963
*Boxoffice*
Hollywood Report by Chris Dutra
Honored- James H. Nicholson, president of American International Pictures, received the Los Angeles Film Row Club's annual Outstanding Achievement Award from Alan Mowbray, veteran actor, at the group's yearly dance at the Ambassador Hotel. Nicholson was cited for his personal contributions and those of AIP to the film industry.

February 1963-

February 1, 1963
*Boxoffice*
United Theatre Owners of the Heart of America have chosen James H. Nicholson and Samuel Z. Arkoff, president and executive vice president respectively, of American International Pictures to receive the organization's Producer of the Year Award. The presentation will be made at UTOHA's annual Show-A-Rama VIII event, to be held March 1-4 at the Continental Hotel in Kansas City, Mo.

February 4, 1963
*The Hollywood Reporter*
AIP RELEASING 10 IN FEBRUARY-MAY
New York- In the February through May period, where there usually is a paucity of new releases, American International Pictures will distribute 10 films, president James H. Nicholson told an exhibitor-press luncheon meeting here Friday.

Following the current *The Raven*, AIP will put out *Battle Beyond the Sun, Night Tide*, and *California.* The company closed a deal with Edwin Tabolowsky, representing Larry Buchanan, for *A Question of Consent*, produced at PSI Studios in Dallas, and is dickering for more films from this Dallas organization. Other upcoming releases include: *The Mind Benders*, Anglo Amalgamated Production starring Dirk Bogard and Mary Ure; *Miracle of the Vikings* and *Nightmare*, first of nine or more pictures coming from Galatea over the next three years; and three teenage musical comedies, *Beach Party, Bikini Beach*, and *Under 21*, all to be filmed in Hollywood.

AIP also has a co-production deal with Julian Wintle and Leslie Parkyn covering several films to be made in England, but the company is swinging more of its production to Hollywood.

*A Question of Consent* **would be retitled** *Free, White and 21* **and marked the beginning of AIP's association with Texas-based producer-director Larry Buchanan (1923-2004). Between 1965-1967, AIP would employ Buchanan to make eight movies for AIP Television:** *The Eye Creatures, Zontar the Thing from Venus, In the Year 2889, Creature of Destruction, Hell Raiders, Curse of the Swamp Creature, It's Alive,* **and** *Mars Needs Women.*

*Free, White and 21*
"CRIME OR PASSION... Was she pure and innocent or was she an irresistible tease? A man's life depended on proving it a question of consent. SHOCK after SHOCK... bold beyond belief!!"

Produced and Directed by Larry Buchanan
Starring Frederick O'Neal, Annalena Lund

March 1963-

*Operation Bikini*
"On a BEACHHEAD or in a BEACH HOUSE... these are the men that never fail!"

Produced by James H. Nicholson and Lou Rusoff  Directed by Anthony Carras
Starring Tab Hunter, Frankie Avalon, Scott Brady, Jim Backus, Jody McCrea, Gary Crosby

From the *Operation Bikini* pressbook-
*OPERATION BIKINI* OPENING TODAY, STARS TAB HUNTER FRANKIE AVALON
An all-star cast headed by Tab Hunter, Frankie Avalon, Scott Brady, Jim Backus, Gary Crosby, Michael Dante, and Jody McCrea is featured in *Operation Bikini*, acclaimed as "THE war action adventure film of the year."
   *Operation Bikini* also introduces the voluptuous Eva Six, Hungarian sex-sation, in her first American film role. She portrays a native guerrilla fighter who falls in love with Tab Hunter, but loses her life so that he might live.

SEAT SELLING SLANTS-
Offer free admission to *Operation Bikini* to all females who show up at the box office wearing a bikini. The appearance of a group of girls, who might be members of Frankie Avalon or Tab Hunter fan clubs, all clad in brief bikinis will make a sure-fire publicity photo for your local newspaper or a TV newsreel film clip.

**At some point, the oft-mentioned title *The Seafighters* became *Operation Bikini*. In his autobiography, Tab Hunter says of the film: "Despite the title, the suggestive ads featuring the producer's buxom girlfriend in a skimpy swimsuit, and Frankie Avalon as one of the costars, *Operation Bikini* was *not* a beach party movie. Oh no, It was yet another war movie... Frankie sings about going home, surrounded by warheads. Only AIP would have the chutzpah to advertise a story about the development**

of the atomic bomb with the tagline TEMPTATION IN PARADISE... NEITHER HELL NOR HIGH HEELS COULD STOP THEM!"

Jody McCrea, Jim Backus, Frankie Avalon, and Gary Crosby in *Operation Bikini.*

*California*
"Fearless Frontiersmen Led by a Danger-Loving Soldier of Fortune!"

Produced and Directed by Hamil Petroff
Starring Jock Mahoney, Faith Domergue

March 22, 1963
*The Film Daily*
'NO TV' CLAUSE ADOPTED BY AIP
Company in Pledge to Keep Its Films Off TV for 5 Years- by

Louis Pelegrine
A breakthrough in exhibition's battle against the showing of new-vintage films on TV came to light yesterday with the disclosure that American International Pictures is putting into immediate effect a policy providing for a "no television" clause on all AIP-produced films.

The new policy was announced jointly by President James H. Nicholson and Executive Vice President Samuel Z. Arkoff at a press conference at the Americana Hotel at which representatives of exhibition were present.

The policy will go into effect with *The Raven* and *Operation Bikini*. Nicholson pledged that "these films and those to follow will not be seen on TV sooner than five years from national release, subject only to bank foreclosures or financial loss."

"Cannibalism of the worst sort" was the way Nicholson characterized "the current rash of pictures hardly out of the sub-runs and now showing on television."

**AIP's "No TV" clause generated a great deal of publicity for the company with lengthy articles also appearing in the March 25 issue of *Boxoffice* and the April 3 issue of *Motion Picture Herald*.**

April 1963-

*Battle Beyond the Sun/Night Tide*
"BILLIONS OF LIGHT YEARS AWAY... out in space beyond the sizzling sun... in TERRIFYING UNKNOWN WORLDS!"

**These were the first two features to be released by AIP in their new deal with Roger Corman to distribute movies made by his Filmgroup company. *Battle Beyond the Sun* was a 1959 Russian movie called *Niebo Zowiet* (*The Sky is Calling*), which was re-edited and re-dubbed by Filmgroup. *Night Tide* was the 1961 feature film debut by director Curtis Harrington (1926-2007).**

*Battle Beyond the Sun*
Produced by Francis Coppola  Directed by Thomas Colchart
Starring Edd Perry, Arla Powell, Andy Steward, Bruce Hunter

From the *Battle Beyond the Sun* pressbook-
FROM FOOTBALL HERO TO MOVIE STAR IN ONE
EASY JUMP INTO SPACE
Ask Edd Perry how to get to be a movie star and he'll tell you:
"Simple! Just volunteer for space duty!" And that's just about the
way it happened. Edd, a former student at East High School in a
small town in Iowa, decided he'd like to join the space program.
When a news story about his volunteering reached Filmgroup
Productions, they decided he might be interested in seeing outer
space from the inside... that is, as star of their upcoming color
feature *Battle Beyond the Sun*.

**Edd Perry's involvement with *Battle Beyond the Sun*
consisted of re-dubbing one of the voices.**

*Night Tide*
Produced by Aram Kantarian  Directed by Curtis Harrington
Starring Dennis Hopper, Linda Lawson, Luana Anders, Gavin
Muir

Film Review- *Night Tide*

*Time Magazine* (December 6, 1963)- POE WITH A
MEGAPHONE
Fact and fantasy interweave in this first feature by Writer-
Director Curtis Harrington. Shot along the Southern California
beach front on a $75,000 budget, the film emits an uncommon
glow of freshness and imagination. Harrington daringly chose to
unfold his realistic tale of suspense as if he were Edgar Allan Poe
with a megaphone and most of the time, the experiment succeeds.
He heightens reality, giving a nightmare quality to commonplace
events. *Night Tide* ebbs when it tries to be too logical, for a legend
tends to slacken under close scrutiny down at police headquarters.
But solid professionalism is evident everywhere.

May 1963-

*The Mind Benders*
"PERVERTED... SOULLESS! The sound of the trapped Monkey... the wasp beating against the glass... eight hours of hell in THE TANK- and his memory of her warm, loving body turned to repulsive clay!"

Produced by Michael Relph  Directed by Basil Dearden
Starring Dirk Bogarde, Mary Ure, John Clements

**Previously announced by AIP as *The Pit*, *The Mind Benders* is an excellent British thriller from the producing-directing team of Michael Relph and Basil Dearden. Although originally planned for a wider release, AIP relegated the movie to mostly co-feature status.**

June 1963-

*Erik the Conqueror* (aka *The Invaders* )
"HE LUSTED FOR WAR and WOMEN! In his blood path of conquest there stood only one temptation... Rama, Queen of the Vestal Virgins!"

Produced by Massimo de Rita  Directed by Mario Bava
Starring Cameron Mitchell, Alice and Ellen Kessler, Giorgio Ardisson

From the pressbook-
*ERIK THE CONQUEROR* ADVENTURE EPIC, STARS CAST OF THOUSANDS
Thousands of extras back up an all-star cast in making the lust and glory of the mighty Viking hordes come alive again in American International's Colorscope adventure epic, *Erik the Conqueror.*
Cameron Mitchell and the beautiful twin acting sisters recently featured on the cover of *Life Magazine*, Alice and Ellen Kessler, star in *Erik the Conqueror.*

Featuring adventure and excitement comparable to any of Cecil B. DeMille's classic thrillers, with the scope of *El Cid* and *Goliath and the Barbarians, Erik the Conqueror* brings to the screen the breathtaking thrills and action of the mighty Northmen who plundered the Coasts of Europe in the 8th Century A.D.

**Despite AIP's comparisons to DeMille and *El Cid*, *Erik the Conqueror* is yet another modestly budgeted Italian import. Also known by the titles *The Invaders* and *Fury of the Vikings*, this above average Euro-epic was inventively directed by Mario Bava. For once, AIP did not replace the original score by Roberto Nicolosi with one by Les Baxter, which had become standard practice for their imports by this time.**

June 7, 1963
*The Hollywood Reporter*
AMERICAN INTERNATIONAL SETS 24-PICTURE SLATE FOR 1963-64
American International Pictures' program for fiscal year 1963-64 calls for a $20 million production and release program, including 24 films and enlargement of the company's roster of name stars and production talent, it is announced by AIP toppers James H. Nicholson and Samuel Z. Arkoff. A minimum of nine pictures will be made here with more to be added before year-end, they said. Detailing the company's rapid growth and expansion plans, Nicholson and Arkoff listed:

Addition of Elsa Lanchester and Ray Milliand to AIP star lineup under contract for two or more films in the coming year; signing of William Asher and Daniel Haller to direct; signing of Richard Matheson, Charles Beaumont, and Ray Russell on multi-picture writing assignments, joining writer-producer-director Robert Dillon; extension of Roger Corman's pact to produce-direct, with Edgar Allan Poe's *Masque of the Red Death* as his probable next.

To finance its expanded operations, the AIP heads said TV rights to certain American Releasing Corp. films will be offered for licensing soon. This does not conflict with AIP's recent announcement of a five-year TV ban on all new productions by the company, they said.

Films slated for shooting here in the next 12 months include *It's Alive,* with Peter Lorre and Elsa Lanchester; *Comedy of Terror,* with Vincent Price, Lorre, and Boris Karloff; *Muscle Beach,*

teenage musical; *Under 21, The Dunwich Horror, Bikini Beach, War of the Planets, Something in the Walls,* and *Genghis Khan.*

Several co-productions abroad were finalized by Nicholson and Arkoff during their recent trip to Europe, including *The Magnificent Leonardi,* with Milland; *When the Sleeper Wakes* and *Masque of the Red Death,* with Price; and *Sins of Babylon.* Also on AIP's schedule are one or more exploitation specials on the order of current *Free, White & 21.*

Ten completed pictures are set for release in next three months.


July 1963-

Trade ad-

*BEACH PARTY-* American International Pictures color and Panavision trade screened for exhibitors and members of the press, radio, and television in New York, Boston, Chicago, and Los Angeles.

President James H. Nicholson, Vice President and General Sales Manager Leon P. Blender, and Milton I. Moritz, Director of Advertising Publicity, start a rousing tour of key cities with lovely

Annette Funicello, one of the brightest stars in the *Beach Party* galaxy of star performers.

A high-flying swinging musical guaranteed to abolish those mid-summer blues excited the trade and press, who turned out in force to see the film and attended the live "Beach Parties" locally.

### Beach Party

"The inside story of what goes on when the sun's gone down... the moon's come up... and the water's too cold for surfin'."

Produced by James H. Nicholson and Lou Rusoff  Directed by William Asher

Starring Bob Cummings, Dorothy Malone, Frankie Avalon, Annette Funicello, Harvey Lembeck

William Asher (Director): "We were committed to *Beach Party* and we didn't even have a cast. Well, we did have a cast. We had, hopefully, Frankie and Annette, but Annette was the property of Disney. And we had thirty pages of script. Disney had to approve it. Not having all the material, he was concerned about Annette's image. I told him that there wouldn't be anything that would offend, that it wasn't that type of a picture. They were a little wary because it was AIP."

Jim Nicholson: "Our position as regards to complaints from the self-appointed guardians of public morals is that there are no overtly sexy sequences and no sex talk among the kids. In fact, the stars of AIP's beach pictures are always talking about getting married. And that, to us, is the epitome of morality."

John Ashley (Actor): "We all had to wear body makeup because nobody had a tan. One day Frankie and I had some dialogue to do on our way to the water with our surfboards. It was colder than hell that day and the water was freezing. We had our backs to the camera and Frankie said, 'Man, can you believe us? Two thirty-year-old guys in body makeup playing teenagers.'"

Sam Arkoff: "At least 200 newspapers throughout the country brushed out all of the belly buttons on the ads for *Beach Party* as though some evil lurked in the belly button."

From AIP: A CONFIDENTIAL MESSAGE TO PARENTS
(who sometimes must wonder)
Every summer, when the sun is hot and the surf is up, the younger generation, like a horde of lemmings, wends its way seaward. Once on the beach, they pair off on blankets to participate in a pagan rite common to all societies, both civilized and savage. This is known to sociologists as the "post adolescent beach party" and to parents

**Jody McCrea (1934-2009), son of actor Joel McCrea, was
featured in eight AIP productions.**

as "Oh, Horrors!" If you don't know just what happens on a beach
party (or why it's so much fun), here's your chance. We dare you
to take it.

You may be shocked to death... but you'll die laughing!

Film Reviews- *Beach Party*

*Time Magazine* (August 16, 1963)- *Beach Party* is an
anthropological documentary with songs.

The beach resembles Seal Rock in mating season. Frankie
Avalon, with his pack of gold-necked surf jockeys, and Annette
Funicello, with her bevy of busty beach bunnies, are- in the words
of one of their tribal hymns- "just asurfin' all day and swingin' all
night." As a study of primitive behavior patterns, *Beach Party* is
more unoriginal than aboriginal.

*Variety*- William Asher has carefully directed the picture with an eye on his potential market. It moves quickly and easily and has been dressed with handsome production values, including spankingly clean camera work by Kay Norton.

*New York Times*- The real trouble is that almost the entire cast emerges as the dullest bunch of meatballs ever, with the old folks even sillier than the kids. Jody McCrea, Harvey Lembeck, and Morey Amsterdam, as sideline comics, are downright embarrassing. Mr. [Robert] Cummings has to be seen to be believed and Miss [Dorothy] Malone had better hold tight to that Academy Award.

Trade ad-
*BEACH PARTY* "Smash"- "Torrid"- "Sockeroo" nationally in the United States and on its way to you. Put up the red ropes and then get ready for the CROWDS!!! Presenting America's newest dancing and singing craze!

July 10, 1963
*The Hollywood Reporter*
AIP PACTS FUNICELLO IN MULTIPLE-FILM DEAL
Annette Funicello, who made her first film away from Walt Disney as star of American International's *Beach Party*, has signed to a seven-year multiple-picture deal by AIP toppers James H. Nicholson and Samuel Z. Arkoff. Her next will be *Rumble* and co-starring with her will be Frankie Avalon, also of the *Beach Party* starring cast, whose pact with AIP has been extended four years.

In its "turn to youth" policy, AIP has also signed two other *Beach Party* stars- John Ashley, for at least two more films, and Harvey Lembeck to co-star with Peter Lorre and Elsa Lanchester next month in *It's Alive* and for another musical, *Muscle Beach*, next spring.

July 22, 1963
*The Hollywood Reporter*
*BEACH PARTY* STARS HITTING THE ROAD
Seven members of the cast of American International's *Beach Party* will be hitting the road on behalf of the musical comedy during

the next two months. Annette Funicello, Frankie Avalon, Dorothy Malone, John Ashley, Morey Amsterdam, Harvey Lembeck, and Eva Six will participate in the extensive p.a. activity covering all parts of the country.

## WILLIAM ASHER TO DIRECT SECOND AIP 'BEACH' FILM

William Asher, who directed *Beach Party*, signed a second directorial contract with AIP over the weekend and will helm either *Muscle Beach* or *Bikini Beach*- whichever goes first. Robert Dillon is pencilled in to write both films. Annette Funicello and Frankie Avalon co-star.

August 1963-
### *The Haunted Palace*
"What was the terrifying thing in the PIT that wanted women?"

Produced and Directed by Roger Corman
Starring Vincent Price, Debra Paget, Lon Chaney

From the pressbook-
## POE'S *THE HAUNTED PALACE,* DUE TO TERRORIZE HERE SOON, STARS PRICE, PAGET, CHANEY

Edgar Allan Poe's chilling terror, with an added element of fear and suspense, that of black magic, is due to entertain and thrill local audiences again when American International's latest filmization of the famed writer's work, *The Haunted Palace*, opens here soon.

Based on a Poe poem of the same name, *The Haunted Palace* was filmed in Panavision and Pathecolor and stars Vincent Price, Debra Paget, and Lon Chaney.

The same top production team which brought AIP's five previous Poe hits to the screen is again responsible for the new terror film. Producing and directing is Roger Corman with Academy Award-winning Floyd Crosby as director of photography and Daniel Haller as art director.

Vincent Price stars in a challenging dual role, giving him another chance to display his amazing acting versatility and his ability to make the unbelievable believable. Miss Paget plays the

212

beautiful Ann Ward while Lon Chaney enacts the type of key character role which made both him and his father famous.

The result is *The Haunted Palace* and it's pulse-throbbing thrills and chills- motion picture terror entertainment at its best.

SEAT SELLING SLANTS-

Just about every community has an old, deserted house or mansion that has accumulated a reputation among the younger set as being "haunted." The history of this house "palace" can be traced or even guessed at by a local newspaper or used as the basis of a contest by a radio or TV personality to promote Edgar Allan Poe's *The Haunted Palace*.

**Debra Paget (born 1933) had her final film role in *The Haunted Palace*. She appeared in four AIP releases.**

Film Reviews- *The Haunted Palace*

*San Diego Evening Tribune* by Dave McIntyre

Edgar Allan Poe, who has been almost as important to Vincent Price's career as Sears & Roebuck, supports him again in *The Haunted Palace*. This is the sixth Poe tale Price has done for American International in recent times. And with all that experience, you rightfully expect him to be accomplished in the role. He is. There is the usual assortment of creaky stairs, cobwebbed corridors, misty graveyards, and rotting coffins, plus enough witches, warlocks, and evil curses to give the kiddies nightmares for a full week. They'll love it.

*New York Times* (January 30, 1964) by Eugene Archer

Roger Corman is an old hand at turning out lurid horror melodramas in low budget color, such as *The Haunted Palace*. It has the director's usual star (Vincent Price), his obvious shock devices (sudden cuts to close-up emphasizing fantastic make-up), and his usual inane dialogue. Nothing about it calls for comment, except perhaps the proficient color photography by another old professional, Floyd Crosby.

*New York Herald Tribune*- The moral is that you can't keep a keen warlock down- and who would want to when he's so debonair a chap as [Vincent] Price, telling an unwilling but admiring visitor to his torture chamber, "Ah yes, Torquemada spent many a happy hour here, a few centuries ago." The Torquemada line is almost worth the price of admission- but not quite.

*Films and Filming*- Roger Corman has risen above the limitations of his medium to create a powerful and unified surrealist fantasy.

*Newsweek*- A well-made horror film, weirdly enough, a healthy specimen with black blood coursing through its veins. The perverse yet persistent interest of the public in necromancy does not merely support a shoddy effort, but raises a competent work to inadvertent moments of lyricism.

Coinciding with the release of *The Haunted Palace* and accompanied by a photo from the film, newspaper Sunday supplement *Parade Magazine* published the following article:

EFFECT OF HORROR FILMS
What is the effect of horror films on children? Dr. Frederick Wertham, psychiatrist and author, believe that violence on TV and in motion pictures has made the average U.S. child indifferent to human suffering and has contributed to the rise of crime by the young.

"Thirty years ago," Dr. Wertham says, "a person who committed murder was at least 17 or 18. Today, it is not uncommon to see murderers of 12 and 13, while children 8 and 9 are found torturing each other and committing acts of sadism."

In refutation, Herman Cohen, Hollywood producer of horror films, says, "I'm performing a public service because my horror films provide a healthy way of releasing fear and tension." Cohen, who produces such films as *I Was a Teenage Frankenstein, How to Make a Monster, Werewolf,* and others of that type, explains that by participating vicariously in on-screen violence, children rid themselves of their own violent and hostile impulses.

August 7, 1963
*The Hollywood Reporter*
AIP, RANSOHOFF IN 'MUSCLE BEACH' RACE
American International Pictures and Martin Ransohoff's Filmways, Inc. are going to tangle on *Muscle Beach*, both companies claiming the title. Because of excellent exhibitor reactions to its *Beach Party*, AIP has decided to rush *Muscle Beach* as a sequel with Frankie Avalon, Annette Funicello, John Ashely, and Harvey Lembeck starred. Picture will be made on a $1,000,000 budget in color and Panavision.

Ransohoff has scheduled *Muscle Beach*, from the Ira Wallach satirical novel, for release through MGM. Wallach will do the screenplay of his book. Shooting will take place on the California beach site and MGM studios.

James Nicholson and Robert Dillon will produce the AIP

picture from a script by Dillon. Shooting will be done in Hollywood and Malibu.

Additionally, AIP is delaying the start of *It's a Lie* [sic], due to go this month, in order to concentrate on the sequel.

**The Martin Ransohoff movie eventually became *Don't Make Waves* (1967) starring Tony Curtis and Claudia Cardinale.**
**It's a Lie is actually AIP's often mentioned project, *It's Alive*.**

August 9, 1963
*The Hollywood Reporter*
AIP HONORED BY MUSICIANS UNION
Musicians Local 47 has honored American International Pictures with a Certificate of Appreciation for "enrichment of musical life and furthering the presentation of live music" for reversing the "runaway" trend by using live American music in pictures filmed here as well as for dubbing American music into foreign films distributed by the company.

August 19, 1963
*Boxoffice*
NICHOLSON ACCUSES FILM INDUSTRY OF 'BEING STINGY WITH ITS WARES'
Hollywood- The motion picture industry "has become stingy with its wares despite the pleadings of exhibitors for more films," declared James H. Nicholson, president of American International Pictures, here Wednesday, August 14, adding, "This is in complete contradiction to the one factor which has sustained America's vital economy and the success of its major industries, the recognition by the automakers and other such manufacturers of the validity of the law of supply and demand."

Acknowledging that production in Hollywood is far below what it was 20 years ago, or even ten years ago, the AIP executive said, "We, at American International, recognize no excuse for ignoring the law of supply and demand, nor do we choose to omit a single tenet of good business in the handling of our products.

"We will produce pictures in greater volume than ever before in future months and we, personally, will continue to crisscross the country and the world, like a politician conducting a grassroots campaign with his heart set on the White House, to keep our fingers on the pulse of public demand."

August 23, 1963
*The Hollywood Reporter*
NICHOLSON AND FUNICELLO IN 142 P.A.s FOR 'PARTY'
James H. Nicholson, president of American International, and Annette Funicello, star of AIP's *Beach Party*, returned last night from a whirlwind week-long tour, during which they made a total of 142 personal appearances in two cities. They visited Dallas and Miami for gala premiers of *Beach Party* and chalked up a total of 58 record store autograph parties, 40 radio appearances, 19 TV appearances, 17 theatre personal appearances, and eight newspaper interview sessions.

September 1963-
*X the Man with the X-Ray Eyes*
"He stripped souls as bare as bodies!"

Produced and Directed by Roger Corman
Starring Ray Milland, Diana van der Vlis, Harold J. Stone, John Hoyt, Don Rickles

Roger Corman (Producer-Director): "I feel it was an opportunity that was slightly missed. The original idea to do a picture about a man who could see through objects was Jim Nicholson's and then the development of the basic idea was mine and Ray Russell's. I almost didn't do the picture for two reasons. One, I felt the script had not turned out as well as I had expected and two, the more I got into it, the more I felt we were going to be heavily dependent on the special effects. The picture was shot in three weeks on a medium low budget and I felt we were not going to be able to photograph what Xavier could see and that the audience would be cheated."

Film Reviews- *X the Man with the X-Ray Eyes*

*New York Times* (October 24, 1963)- Alertly directed and produced in color by Roger Corman, it shapes up as a modern parable about a dedicated doctor done in by humanity after he tampers with the unknown. As written by Robert Dillon and Ray Russell, the concept is original and the tone is thoughtful. An odd little movie that aims for sensible novelty and to some extent succeeds.

*Films and Filming*- The overall conception of the film is poised uneasily between science fiction and horror and only the occasional humorous touches and gory details are likely to appeal to [Roger] Corman followers and/or horror addicts.

### *The Terror/Dementia 13*
"From the depths of an evil mind came a diabolical plan of torture... inconceivable... unbelievable!"

**With *The Terror* and *Dementia 13*, AIP released another double feature from Roger Corman's Filmgroup company. *The Terror* was a movie conceived primarily because Boris Karloff still owed Corman a few days' work when *The Raven* wrapped ahead of schedule. With a script by Leo Gordon and Jack Hill, Corman, along with disciples Francis Ford Coppola, Dennis Jakob, Monte Hellman, and Jack Nicholson, concocted a motion picture built around scenes that Karloff filmed over one weekend on sets left over from *The Raven*.**

*The Terror*
Produced and Directed by Roger Corman
Starring Boris Karloff, Jack Nicholson, Sandra Knight

Leo Gordon (Writer): "Corman called me up and told me he needed scenes for Boris Karloff. He didn't have a story, just Karloff, a couple of actors, and the damn castle. He paid me $1600."

Boris Karloff (Actor): "I was in every shot, of course. Sometimes I was walking though and then I would change my jacket and walk back."

Film Reviews- *The Terror*

*Hollywood Citizen News*- [*The Terror*] manages to project a goodly number of thrills and chills and presents an interesting, well-plotted story as well.

*Films and Filming*- No one believes in what they are doing and it comes all too obviously across. Still, three days... I wonder how other directors would have responded to such a challenge... I also wonder what would have happened had Corman been turned loose on *Cleopatra!* Probably would have finished it in a week!

*The Hollywood Reporter*- An imaginative horror picture, done with sound production values that make it a class item in its field.

*Dementia 13*
Produced by Roger Corman  Directed by Francis Coppola
Starring William Campbell, Luana Anders, Bart Patton, Mary Mitchell, Patrick Magee

Roger Corman (Producer): "I was making *The Young Racers* in Europe. I had three assistants on the film. One was Francis Coppola. Francis said, 'I'd like to make a film.' I said, 'All right, Francis. We're going to be finishing the picture at the English Grand Prix in Liverpool. If you can come up with a low budget horror film in Dublin, I will back you.' Which he did and that was *Dementia 13*, which was his first film."

Film Reviews- *Dementia 13*

*New York Times* (October 24, 1963)- Don't ask what the title means- or whatever happened to the first 12 dementias. One is enough. Under the stolid direction of Francis Coppola, who also wrote the script, the picture stresses gore rather than atmosphere and all but buries a fairly workable plot. William Campbell and Luana Anders head the unlucky cast.

*Films in Review* (March 1965) by Allen Eyles
(Reviewed under the British title: ***The Haunted and the Hunted.***)

The horror story is heavily red-herringed and none too credible and the film doesn't escape looking a bit of a quickie. But the director, Francis Coppola, has confidently assembled the film and given it a sharp sense of atmosphere. It lacks polish, but its ideas are right.

September 3, 1963
*The Hollywood Reporter*
AIP IS GOING ALL-AMERICAN

The company plans to release between 18 and 24 features in the year ahead. Of these, 14 will be higher-budget productions. It has only two remaining commitments for foreign pictures, one in Italy and one in England. A British co-production, *The Sleeper Wakes,* H.G. Wells story with Vincent Price starred, is scheduled as an AIP project. Although the company is not ruling out all foreign filming, if the story locale makes it advisable, [James] Nicholson said the rise in production costs abroad now has reached the point where, all other things being equal, pictures can be made here more economically- besides the other advantages.

September 6, 1963
*The Hollywood Reporter*
*MUSCLE BEACH PARTY* GETS 200 THEATRE DATES BEFORE IT ROLLS

*Muscle Beach Party,* American International's *Beach Party* sequel, though not set for production here until December, already has been booked for over 200 playdates during Easter week 1964, according to AIP toppers James H. Nicholson and Samuel Z. Arkoff.

The amazing pre-production exhibitor response to *Muscle Beach Party* is based on the record-breaking grosses hit by *Beach*

*Party* this summer, according to Nicholson and Arkoff. The sequel will feature the same stars that were such a hit in the original musical comedy- Frankie Avalon, Annette Funicello, Harvey Lembeck, John Ashley, and Jody McCrea.

September 16, 1963
*Boxoffice*
Hollywood Report by Syd Cassyd
ALL-STAR *COMEDY OF TERRORS* CAST FETED
James H. Nicholson, American International Pictures president, was host to the all-star cast of AIP's *Comedy of Terrors* prior to start of production in Hollywood on September 4. Nicholson is also co-producer of the film. In attendance were director Jacques Tourneur, Peter Lorre, Vincent Price, Joyce Jameson, Basil Rathbone, and Boris Karloff. This marks the first time that Price, Lorre, Karloff, and Rathebone have starred together in a motion picture. Samuel Z. Arkoff, AIP executive vice president, coproduces with Nicholson.

**Vincent Price, Jacques Tourneur, Boris Karloff, and Peter Lorre on the set of *Comedy of Terrors*.**

October 1963-

October 7, 1963
*Boxoffice*
## NICHOLSON AND ARKOFF TO SPONSOR ALLIED LUNCHEON ON OCTOBER 23
New York- American International again will sponsor a luncheon Wednesday (23) at Allied States convention. James H. Nicholson and Samuel Z. Arkoff, AIP heads, have taken an active part in Allied States convention activities and will receive the "1963 Producer of the Year" award on the final day of the meet.

October 14, 1963
*Boxoffice*
Hollywood Report by Syd Cassyd
Producer Bill Redlin has signed veteran actor John Hoyt for the starring role in *Time Trap*, written by Ib Melchior. The feature will be released by American International Pictures, for whom Hoyt costarred with Ray Milland in the soon-to-be released *X*.

## AIP IS HONORED
James H. Nicholson and Samuel Z. Arkoff, American International Picture heads, were presented an award by Melvin L. Gold, Associated Motion Picture Advertisers president, at Ampa's luncheon October 3 in New York. The award was a salute to AIP, which Ampa judged had made the most progress in 1963 with important film product.

October 18, 1963
*The Hollywood Reporter*
## AIP FINALIZING 2 ITALIAN DEALS
Fulvio Lucisano, Italian International Films president, has arrived here to meet with American International Pictures toppers James H. Nicholson and Samuel Z. Arkoff to finalize co-production plans on two major film projects. First deal is for the filming of *The Dunwich Horror* in Rome starting in January. Second project to be set up will be the co-production of a one-hour TV documentary,

*The Life and Art of Michelangelo,* with Vincent Price as narrator and star.

**Less than a month after AIP stated that "if a story locale makes it advisable," a picture would be made in the United States, they announced that H.P. Lovecraft's New England set horror story, *The Dunwich Horror,* will be made in Italy. Go figure.**

October 28, 1963
*Boxoffice*
Convention Sidelights by Al Steen
American International's luncheon, held Wednesday (23) at the Allied States Ass'n convention at the Americana Hotel in New York, topped all previous affairs of its kind. Scenes from *The Comedy of Terrors* were presented, after which two beautiful gals opened a wooden box in front of the dais and out popped Morey Amsterdam, whose line of gags kept the hundreds of guest in an uproar. And Candy Johnson wowed the guests with exotic dancing.

AIP also took over the front page of the *New York Daily News* with a three-line streamer headline reading: "Allied Ain't Seen Nothing Yet, Says AIP." The luncheon show proved that they were right.

**The following article in the same issue of *Boxoffice* provides even more details of this madcap affair.**

AIP HEADS POINT TO INDUSTRY PROGRESS
New York- In reply to those who have been wisecracking that the movie industry is all washed up, James H. Nicholson, American International president, stressed there is "a current boom of new movie houses and an increase of production activity in Hollywood."

Nicholson and Samuel Z. Arkoff, AIP executive vice president, sponsored a luncheon at the Allied States Ass'n convention held in the Georgian Room of the Americana hotel. Arkoff emphasized the future growth of the industry, saying, "Ours is a thriving, growing business and should be reverently spoken of as such."

AIP's forthcoming musical, *Muscle Beach Party,* was the motif for the luncheon, which also included a 15-minute film starring Vincent Price with a surprise ending- Morey Amsterdam, master-of-ceremonies, popping out of a coffin carried by six Gaslight girls and carrying on a conversation with the on-celluloid Price. Fred Astaire dance teachers were on hand to introduce the "Mau Mau," new dance choreographed for *Muscle Beach*, and Jerry Jerome and his orchestra provided music for the luncheon.

November 1963-
*Summer Holiday*
"...a fabulous summer affair in Technicolor and CinemaScope. From first KISS (in PARIS)... to last BLUSH (in GREECE), it's the craziest Four-Way love affair that ever shook up the folks back home! Starring CLIFF RICHARD, the nation's hottest new swinger, singing, "Les Girls," "Summer Affair," "Bachelor Boy"... and many more!"

Produced by Kenneth Harper  Directed by Peter Yates
Starring Cliff Richard, Lauri Peters, David Kossoff, Ron Moody, The Shadows

Film Review- *Summer Holiday*

*New York Times* (August 6, 1964) by Bosley Crowther
*Summer Holiday* is a tinny British teenage musical which would have looked feeble and imitative back in the years when Betty Grable was making college musical comedies for Paramount.

**Unfortunately, in my hometown of San Diego, *Summer Holiday* opened Thanksgiving week 1963, two days after JFK was assassinated. A frothy British musical was definitely not in keeping with the temperament of that time.**

November 4, 1963
*Boxoffice*
HONORED AS PRODUCERS OF THE YEAR
James H. Nicholson, American International Pictures president, and Samuel Z. Arkoff, executive vice president, were honored as

San Diego newspaper ad for *Summer Holiday.*

Producers of the Year and presented silver bowls by Jack Armstrong, Allied States president, and Irving Dollinger, convention chairman, at the Allied States Ass'n convention October 25 at the Americana Hotel in New York.

**For the 33rd Anniversary issue of *The Hollywood Reporter* (November 19, 1963), Jim Nicholson contributed the following article, reproduced here in its entirety.**

LIGHTER AND BRIGHTER HORROR by James H. Nicholson

The best Wall Street advice on "how to succeed in business" is that every organization should know at the outset where it is going and the best Hollywood psychiatrists contend that the safest and sanest way to get there is to have fun en route.

We confess to having fun at American International and we do not deny a certain amount of success, but it may come as something of a surprise to some to learn that what we set out to do is a thing which a number of acquaintances often suggested we do and that is "go to the Devil."

What? The Devil?

Well, why not the Devil?

It has been said with reasonable wisdom that there are only two subjects which are of basic concern to people: good and bad.

Love, money, and fun, and variations thereof, fall into the category of things good. Hate, poverty, and misery, with attendant variations, are at the opposite end of the pole.

Somewhere between the two is that devilish area of fear and fantasy in which most persons dwell. It is Old Satan's stomping ground and that is where we feed, sometimes on fear, sometimes on both fear and fantasy, occasionally on fantasy alone.

The churches attracting millions to their pews each Sunday, the Billy Grahams converting hundreds of thousands during a Hollywood crusade, and the high cost of the Biblical spectaculars indicated to us that the good end of the pole of human experience was territory too tough to tackle.

A bit of self-appraisal revealed that we were afraid. And a

quick look around suggested that we had plenty of company in that state of existence. We were in the midst of the masses.

It was then that we did a devilishly sneaky thing.

We went to a movie and sat through two showings of the same picture, watching the people rather than the picture the second time around.

Since the prime purpose of movies is to entertain, to permit theatre patrons to slip into the anonymity of a darkened room and escape problems faced in the glare of the sun, every laugh, every knowing look, and every shriek was of infinite importance to us.

We discovered that the human animal, for some inhuman reason, is happiest when something more fearsome is added to his normal everyday fears. He finds something gleeful in being taken by surprise. A man with hatchet in hand or a ghoul on a movie screen makes him titter in anticipation of a frightful act.

When the inordinate occurs, he is tranquilized by the story's return to the ordinary. When the terrifying and unfamiliar is thrust upon him, he finds security in the belief that "it's all impossible."

When the monster on the screen makes his girl shudder and snuggle close to him, he is happy to let her do it and she is delighted to have an excuse for doing it.

Our devilish little session of peeking and spying seemed to have thrown us into a cauldron of devilish carryings-on where both the Devil and the masses were apparently having a whale of a time.

There was just one other thing to consider: Is the science fiction, horror, chill-thrill motion picture on sound dramatic footing?

We took a third look at our sample film and found that such film fare fits well against the yardstick of what experts say are the 10 vital ingredients for film hits.

There is universality. People around the globe understand and like them for what they are-sheer escapism.

The stakes are high. Life and death are pivotal in the horror drama.

Visuality and action are built in. The makeup man's monster involves the audience in the dramatic action the moment he appears on the screen.

Sex and love are incorporated in the struggle of the hero and the heroine against the assaults of the villainous beast.

Ambition and achievement are found in the missions of both the protagonist and the antagonist and the mission of the hero is a noble one.

These and other qualities necessary to the successful motion picture are actually a restatement of the tenets of classical drama. Each time Vincent Price gets his comeuppance after having tried to throw the beauty into a bottomless pit, he has enacted a modern version of "Everyman," the classical medieval morality play which depicted the eternal struggle between good and evil, the Devil struggling for possession of Man's soul.

But it seemed to us that in a national climate fraught with threat of cataclysm, the blatant preachments of the moralistic play would be anathema. And thus we decided to insert tongue in cheek.

The result has been a highly successful combination of the classic Poe stories with the comedic, though straight-faced histrionics of such powerful performers as Price, Peter Lorre, Boris Karloff, and Basil Rathbone, among others, who have brought us so much fun and financial glee at American International.

Significantly, we have never pretended in making our shockers that the audience isn't in on the secret. We feel they like to be. They nudge each other and say, "See, I knew that was the way it was going to turn out," and they go away happy.

Of equal significance is a determination on our part always to send 'em away happy.

We have never taken audiences' reactions lightly. And our long experience as well as our continuing surveys among exhibitors proves that it is the picture which sends the moviegoer home with a happy feeling, which brings him back to the ticket windows.

We believe the average modern man has so many problems outside the theatre that he has no stomach for having the traumatic experiences of the world's Freudian misfits vomited from the screen into his popcorn.

Our philosophy of motion picture production is to deal at all times with the lighter and brighter side of life. Our pictures are intended to shock, but never to be lewd, lascivious, or obscene.

Of the people who line up for seats at the movie, three-quarters of them are young people- members of a new generation which has come of age. To them, the ghost story, the fairy tale, the mystery story, and that story which tells of great scientific adventure is just as popular as it was with their grandparents.

It is all rather fantastic, but the spell of fantasy is utterly dateless, for it is an unforgettable part of every man's journey through life.

That is how we have come to what we call our "turn to youth" policy typified by the highly successful, topical musical comedy *Beach Party*, which will augment our horror and science fiction productions hereafter.

*Beach Party*, as conceived by the late Lou Rusoff, is a light, frothy, sometimes spicy, and occasionally slapstick story of life among today's young people and its impact upon the generation which preceded it. It has the evidences of ingenuity and artistry modern motion picture making requires.

It was fun to make. It is fun to see. Audiences go waltzing out whistling the tunes.

We believe at American International that if you're having fun, you should let your friends in on it.

Certainly there is a great good fun in making the horror film, especially when it is done for chuckles as well as chills. There is also great fun in making the light, music-filled fun picture which sends the audience home happy. We try at all times to share our picture-making fun with our picture-viewing audience. Things are sticky enough all around and we feel a little fun never hurt anybody.

There simply isn't enough laughter in the world today. Laughter is a contagious thing and, what the Devil, only in the incongruous fantasy of the horror film do men kill with a smile on their faces.

December 1963-
Trade ad-
YOUR FAVORITE CREEPS... TOGETHER AGAIN! Every shroud has a silver lining when old friends get together for a real swinging blast of murder... grave robbery and multiple mayhem!

American International presents COMEDY OF TERRORS in color and Panavision set to come your way JANUARY 1964.

December 9, 1963
*The Hollywood Reporter*
TOURNEUR TO DIRECT AIP's *GENGHIS KHAN*
Jacques Tourneur, who recently directed American International's *Comedy of Terrors,* has been set by company toppers, James H. Nicholson and Samuel Z. Arkoff, to repeat on the action spectacle *Genghis Khan,* for which AIP announces the biggest budget in its history- $4,500,000.
Filming in 70mm and Technirama is slated for summer in Italy and Spain.

December 25, 1963
*Motion Picture Herald*
American International Pictures held a cocktail reception in New York following a preview of its new picture, *The Comedy of Terrors.*

# CHAPTER ELEVEN
# 1964

January 1964-
*The Comedy of Terrors*
"Your favorite creeps together again!"

Produced by James H. Nicholson and Samuel Z. Arkoff  Directed
by Jacques Tourneur
Starring Vincent Price, Peter Lorre, Boris Karloff, Basil Rathbone,
Joyce Jameson, Joe E. Brown

From the pressbook-
VINCENT PRICE EMERGES AS TOP COMEDY STAR AS
CAREER TAKES A NEW TURN AFTER TERROR REIGN
In the glittering world of motion pictures, the amazing acting
versatility of Vincent Price has been overshadowed by those

231

glamour stars who stay in one performing mold for their entire career.

Price's overwhelming dramatic talents are further emphasized by an entirely new development in his long and honored career, which has seen him score as both romantic leading man and heavy in every type of motion picture and stage role, from Shakespeare to Edgar Allan Poe.

The newest Vincent Price image in motion pictures, after his most recent decade as a terror film monarch, is as a deft and clever comedian in American International's *The Comedy of Terrors*. Co-starring in the fright comedy romp are Peter Lorre, Boris Karloff, and Joyce Jameson with Joe E. Brown and Basil Rathbone as guest stars.

The new comic Vincent Price does not, by any means, indicate that he is abdicating his title as Hollywood's King of Horrors. His hilarious role in *The Comedy of Terrors* just means that he has added another and just about final dimension to his acting career.

## SEAT SELLING SLANTS-

Unusual preview screenings can be set up for *The Comedy of Terrors*, restricting audiences to newspaper obituary editors and to owners and employees of local funeral parlors. These can be tied in to current nationwide controversy on funeral costs, etc. Opening day showings of *The Comedy of Terrors* can feature free admission to all gravediggers and morticians who identify themselves as such at the box office.

Film Reviews- *The Comedy of Terrors*

*New York Times* (January 23, 1964) by Howard Thompson
A musty, rag bag of tricks rigged as a horror farce. American International, which has been mining the spook vein for laughs lately, is billing this color exercise as a "horroromp." Make that "chillerdiller"- dill as in pickle.

*San Diego Evening Tribune* by Dave McIntyre- Vincent Price, Peter Lorre, and company frisk it with caskets in *Comedy of Terrors*. There's ample comedy here, stretching the meaning of the term to its broadest, most farcical limits. But any fright will be only for the most cloistered. In spite of the variety of talent, the film essentially is restricted to one thin, somewhat grisly joke.

Humor about corpses does have its limitations.

*Los Angeles Times*- The undiscriminating may find this labored nonsense funny or scary now and then, but I am inclined to echo one [Basil] Rathbone comment as a summation of the whole situation: "What jiggery and pokery is this?"

*Time Magazine* (May 15, 1964)- *Comedy of Terrors* is a lushly produced little parody of Hollywood scream fare, hopefully labeled a "horroromp." Vincent Price and the late Peter Lorre* play a team of New England undertakers. Basil Rathbone gets buried alive, while Boris Karloff eyes his former gloom-mates and a dose of poison with equal distaste. "When I was young," Karloff grumbles, "we knew how to live." They also knew how to die- back in the days when a tongue in the cheek was soon pickled in brine.

**\*Peter Lorre died March 23, 1964.**

January 2, 1964
*The Hollywood Reporter*
$25 MILLION AIP BUDGET FOR '64- 36% INCREASE IN OUTLAY IS SCHEDULED FOR PROGRAM OF 25 RELEASES THIS YEAR
American International Pictures' program of 25 films for 1964 will involve a total budget of $25,000,000, a 36% increase in cost and 28% in the number of features over the 1963 period, it was announced in a year-end press conference by AIP toppers James H. Nicholson and Samuel Z. Arkoff. Last year, the company distributed 18 features costing $16,000,000.

Because of the success of *The Comedy of Terrors*, AIP has moved up the production of *The Graveside Story*, Nicholson said. He also announced title changes of *Evil Eye* for *House of Terror* and *Commando* for *Twelve Guns East*.

Besides *Comedy of Terrors*, already showing, the 1964 releases include: *Commando* with Stewart Granger, Dorian Gray; *Torpedo*

*Bay*, James Mason, Lili Palmer; *Under Age*, Anne MacAdams, Judy Adler; *Some People*, Kenneth More, Ray Brooks, Annika Wills; *Black Sabbath*, Boris Karloff, Mark Damon; *Evil Eye*, Leticia Roman, John Saxon; *Muscle Beach Party*, Frankie Avalon, Annette Funicello, Luciana Paluzzi, John Ashley, Don Rickles; *Last Man on Earth*, Vincent Price; *Unearthly Stranger*, John Neville, Philip Stone; *Goliath and the Island of Vampires*, Gordon Scott; *Time Travelers*, Preston Foster, Philip Carey.

Also *Warlords of Space*; *Captive City*, David Niven, Ben Gazzara; *Masque of the Red Death*, Vincent Price; *Bikini Beach*, Frankie Avalon, Annette Funicello, John Ashley, Don Rickles, Harvey Lembeck; *It's a Wonderful Life*, Cliff Richard, Walter Slezak; *Graveside Story*, Vincent Price, Peter Lorre, Boris Karloff, Basil Rathbone, Elsa Lanchester; *Moontrap; Dunwich Horror,* Boris Karloff; *Rumble*, Frankie Avalon, Annette Funicello, John Ashley, Harvey Lembeck; *She,* from the H. Rider Haggard story; *The Gold Bug,* Vincent Price, Peter Lorre, Elsa Lanchester; *Genghis Khan; It's Alive* starring Peter Lorre, Elsa Lanchester, and Harvey Lembeck; *Color Out of Space; City in the Sea;* and *When the Sleeper Wakes.*

**The proposed Edgar Allan Poe picture, *The Gold Bug,* is announced here for the first time. It would not be the last. Although it was mentioned often in lists of forthcoming AIP projects, the film never did get produced. Perhaps Charles Griffith's description of the story explains why.**

Charles Griffith (Writer): "I did a Poe picture that never got made, *The Gold Bug,* which was one of the funniest scripts I ever wrote. Completely zany. It was very long and AIP was furious. Vincent Price was a Southern planter whose mansion was burned out. Basil Rathbone was an English carpetbagger who was trying to kick everybody out. And Peter Lorre was the servant in the house. The Gold Bug was a little bug that lived in a snuff box that Lorre had and it would dance on the keys of the harpsichord at night, doing the Gold Bug Rag. When it bit people, it turned them into gold. Price tries to melt them down and they turn back into flesh."

January 20, 1964
*The Hollywood Reporter*
FOREIGN 'LIQUIDATION' HELPS U.S.- CRISIS ABROAD FORCING SALE OF LIBRARIES; AIP'S ARKOFF SEE BETTER O'SEAS SETUPS
The recent and current crisis in major foreign film-producing countries abroad, resulting from overproduction, rising cost, and low percentage of output having sufficient quality for the world market, has touched off extensive liquidation of film libraries, thereby presenting some unusual opportunities for American companies with foreign distribution facilities, according to Samuel Z. Arkoff, executive v-p of American International Pictures.

As a result of the film crisis in Italy, Arkoff and AIP president James H. Nicholson recently were able to make some "advantageous arrangements" for 17 Italian features and negotiations

now are under way for a considerable number of additional films. Some of the pictures are being handled only in a certain number of countries, including a few for South America, and only a small number may get much if any playing time in the U.S., Arkoff noted.

February 1964-
*Goliath and the Sins of Babylon/Samson and the Slave Queen*
"All New SAMSON vs. GOLIATH Never Seen! See: The orgy of the seven Tortures! The parade of the Doomed Virgins! The battle of the Slave Galleons!"

From the pressbook-
News copy in this pressbook is intentionally different. It is the result of AIP surveys among motion picture editors of leading newspapers, who asked for releases with a gimmick upon which they can hang an unusual picture and a catchy headline. Art and stories in this pressbook have been written and selected with this in mind. Be sure to call them to the attention of the motion picture editor in your city.

## MIGHTIEST OF MUSCLE MEN COMING TO LOCAL THEATRE

Mirror, mirror, on the wall, who's the mightiest man of all?

The prodigious feats of strength performed by the legendary heroes of old have run a gamut from slaying of a thousand Philistines with nothing more than a mule jaw for a weapon to the singlehanded destruction of massive temples and yet neither Goliath, Samson, Hercules, Ajax, nor Atlas holds the undisputed world championship.

So now come Samson and Goliath to match muscles in an American International double spectacular bill of *Samson and the Slave Queen* and *Goliath and the Sins of Babylon.*

Of course, the championship will remain unsettled by these two new AIP sagas, but movie fans were never exposed to more awe-inspiring scenes, rich in color and lush in costume from the times when men were mighty and their numbers were many.

*Goliath and the Sins of Babylon* (aka **Maciste, the Greatest Hero in the World**)
Produced by Elio Scardamaglia  Directed by Michele Lupo
Starring Mark Forest, Jose Greci, Guliano Gemma

*Samson and the Slave Queen* (aka **Maciste vs. Zorro**)
Produced by Fortunato Misiano  Directed by Umberto Lenzi
Starring Pierre Brice, Alan Steel, Moira Orfei

February 19, 1964
*The Hollywood Reporter*

## AIP TO ENTER TV WITH TWO SERIES; AFTER THEATERS TOO

New York- American International Pictures, embarking on diversification, is entering TV production with two series, president James H. Nicholson and executive v-p Samuel Z. Arkoff disclosed at a trade press conference yesterday. First will be *Beach Party,* based on the AIP hit; the other, *It's Alive,* from film to be released within a year. Company also plans to build or acquire drive-ins and shopping center theaters where AIP product is not getting satisfactory release.

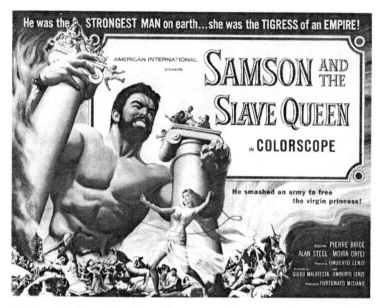

**Although from the artwork one would anticipate a movie set in ancient times, *Samson and the Slave Queen* is actually set in Spain and has Samson meeting Zorro.**

At the same time, the executives announced AIP worldwide revenue had risen 40% in fiscal 1964 over prior year, and The Reporter learned that income thus far this year is 100% above corresponding 1963 period.

AIP will release in coming year a minimum of 22 pictures. Roger Corman and Buddy Hackett took part in the conference.

February 19, 1964
*Variety*
AMERICAN INT'L DIVERSIFYING- Will Venture Into Video Production- Also Acquire Some Theaters
American International Pictures, which in its 10-year history to date has concentrated exclusively on theatrical productions, is now about to make two important moves toward diversification. Prez James H. Nicholson reported in New York yesterday (Tues.) that (1) the company will start production of its first two television

series sometime this fall and (2) is about to close a deal for the acquisition of its first theaters, which will be located both in the U.S. and abroad.

The TV series will be 'spin-offs"- that is, based on two of the company's theatrical releases, *Beach Party*, a 1963 release for which theatrical sequel has already been completed and another planned, and *It's Alive*, a comedy-horror pic which is being made this spring. Nicholson emphasized that both series will be for the 1965-66 season and will in no way conflict with the theatrical pix which will have played off by that time. No network or syndicator tie-ups have yet been made, but prez says he is confident deals will have been concluded by this fall. The feature pix themselves are serving, in effect, as the show's pilots.

March 1964-
*Muscle Beach Party*
"When 10,000 Biceps go around 5,000 Bikinis... you KNOW what's gonna happen!"

Produced by James H. Nicholson and Robert Dillon  Directed by William Asher
Starring Frankie Avalon, Annette Funicello, Luciana Paluzzi, John Ashley, Don Rickles

William Asher (Director): "We met Jim [Nicholson] in Miami, Bob Dillon and I, and we concocted another story that weekend. The first inclination was to grow with the characters and I said, 'What are we going to grow with? This is comic strip. They don't have to be a year older. They don't have to be in jobs now. It can be the longest summer on record.' There was some discomfort with that, but they agreed."

Film Review- *Muscle Beach Party*

*New York Times* (May 28, 1964) by Bosley Crowther
(playing on a double bill with the Warner Bros. western *A Distant Trumpet*)

**Mary Hughes (1944-2007) appeared in a dozen AIP
productions from 1964 to 1967. Her first film was
*Muscle Beach Party*.**

The second feature on the program is a twitch-and-twist musical film entitled *Muscle Beach Party*, which stars Frankie Avalon and a tangle of vigorous young people with beautiful bodies and empty heads. If you can last through *A Distant Trumpet* and then this, you're a double-dyed stoic.

*The Last Man on Earth/Unearthly Stranger*
"How much horror can you face?"

From *The Last Man on Earth* pressbook-
TERROR FILM FORECASTS RESULTS OF GERM WARFARE
When an unknown disease causes an epidemic that wipes out the entire population of the United States, it is scientist Vincent Price who survives as *The Last Man on Earth* in the new American International science fiction drama.

And in a terrifying twist of poetic justice, it is Price's best friend, a fellow scientist who foresaw the epidemic as an enemy germ attack, who leads a horde of the undead who wish to kill the last surviving man.

Photographed in scope in the stark silence and emptiness of a deserted and devastated American city, *The Last Man on Earth* gives movie fans an insight into what might occur in the event of a true nuclear or germ attack while also providing spine-tingling entertainment.

**Based on Richard Matheson's 1954 novel *I Am Legend*, *The Last Man on Earth* was an Italian-American co-production filmed entirely in Italy.**

*The Last Man on Earth*
Produced by Robert L. Lippert  Directed by Sidney Salkow
Starring Vincent Price, Franca Bettoia, Emma Danieli, Giacamo Rossi-Stuart

Film Review- *The Last Man on Earth*

*Los Angeles Times* (May 9, 1964)-Vincent Price continues his macabre film adventures as the star of a shocker called *The Last Man on Earth*. His portrayal almost becomes a one-man show and this versatile actor makes the most of it.

*Unearthly Stranger*
Produced by Albert Fennell  Directed by John Krish

240

Starring John Neville, Gabriella Licudi, Philip Stone

From *Unearthly Stranger* pressbook-
UNEARTHLY STRANGER IS SCIENCE FICTION
THRILLER OF OUT-OF-THIS-WORLD FOE
An incredible and terrifying story of a power beyond space and
time makes for suspense almost beyond endurance in American
International's *Unearthly Stranger.*

The astonishing new science fiction thriller stars John Neville,
Gabriella Lucidi, and Philip Stone.

*Unearthly Stranger* is the tale of a newly-married scientist who
tries to unravel the mysterious death of a friend, who was working
on an experiment which would have enabled man to project
himself through time and space. When he investigates the death
and tries to continue the experiments, his life with his new bride
becomes a nightmare.

March 2, 1964
*Boxoffice*
AIP SPONSORS BREAKFAST
Comedian Buddy Hackett and producer-director Roger Corman
flanked American International Pictures president James H.
Nicholson at an AIP-sponsored trade press breakfast at the
Warwick Hotel in New York. Nicholson spoke about AIP's future
TV plans and forthcoming product, one of which is *Muscle Beach
Party* starring Hackett, Frankie Avalon, Annette Funicello, and
Luciana Paluzzi.

March 6, 1964
*The Hollywood Reporter*
TV DISTRIBUTION AS WELL AS PRODUCTION IS
PLANNED BY AMERICAN INTERNATIONAL
In addition to entering production of TV series, as already
announced, American International Pictures also will go into the
distribution end of telefilm product, it was disclosed yesterday as
notices were issued for a press meeting to be held on Monday at
which time full details will be announced. The press luncheon will
take place in the Lanai Terrace of the Beverly Hills Hotel.

March 10, 1964
*The Hollywood Reporter*
40 FILMS IN FIRST PACKAGE FOR RELEASE BY AIP
TO TV
American International Pictures toppers Samuel Z. Arkoff and
James H. Nicholson yesterday confirmed *The Hollywood Reporter*
story of last Friday that the company was forming a TV distribution
as well as a production arm on a national and international basis.
At a press conference, Arkoff and Nicholson said the company,
which now has more than 150 features in release, would hold to
its promise to exhibitors that not one of its features would be given
over to TV until a five-year period has passed.

AIP-TV's initial offering is a 40-feature package which
includes the Italian-made *Prisoner of the Iron Mask, Sign of the
Gladiator, Goliath and the Dragon, Journey to the Lost City,* and
*Goliath and the Barbarians* along with other adventure spectacles
which were acquired especially for TV.

At the same time, Nicholson and Arkoff announced the
appointment of Stanley Dudelson as v-p and general manager
of AIP-TV. Dudelson is a veteran of TV sales and formerly was
national sales manager for Screen Gems. Nicholson and Arkoff
said the new TV company would have offices in Los Angeles,
Chicago, and New York to distribute one or two packages of
features per year.

March 12, 1964
*The Hollywood Reporter*
8 AIP STARS TREK FOR 'MUSCLE BEACH'
Eight of the stars of American International Picture's *Muscle Beach
Party* will tour the U.S. and Canada to make personal appearances
for premieres of the musical comedy, according to AIP ad-pub
chief Milton I. Moritz.

Definitely set to hit the road are Frankie Avalon, Annette
Funicello, John Ashley, Jody McCrea, Morey Amsterdam, Amedee
Chabot, Alberta Nelson, and Dolores Wells.

Avalon goes to San Francisco and Miami. Miss Funicello,
who returns today from European tour for *Beach Party* and *Muscle
Beach Party,* will accompany Avalon to San Francisco.

Ashley will appear in the Detroit area, then to Toronto. McCrea will appear at San Francisco opening, then tour the Northern California and Bay area.

Miss Chabot will tour Omaha area, Miss Nelson goes to Seattle for Northwest openings, and Miss Wells flies east for openings in Baltimore and Washington areas.

April 1964-

*Pyro*

Produced by Sidney W. Pink and Richard C. Meyer  Directed by Julio Coll
Starring Barry Sullivan, Martha Hyer, Sherry Moreland, Soledad Miranda, Luis Prendes

**Pyro was another European-made movie from producer Sid Pink. AIP decided to approach the movie in two ways. Part of the advertising campaign presents the film as a horror movie, featuring ads showing a close-up of a disfigured face and the ad copy "LOOK AT THIS 'MAN' and BEWARE... there is nothing human about him... except his desires! PYRO... The Thing Without a Face!" The other part of the campaign stresses the erotic aspects of the film. These ads show a sexy close up of star Martha Hyer accompanied by the ad copy "Meet 'LAURA'... what is her strange desire that man's love cannot quench? What deadly promise lies in her scorching lips?"**

Film Reviews- *Pyro*

*Time Magazine* (May 15, 1964)
*Pyro* glosses over its terror with a sort of Hitchcock-and-bull story photographed in Spain in flamenco hues and laved in bucketfuls of blue butane gas. The film casts Barry Sullivan as a philanderer who becomes a firebug when castoff Playmate Martha Hyer sends his house up in flame. His wife and daughter dead, Barry survives, a hideously deformed monster with a "carbonized"

brain. Crazed, hunted, vowing fiery vengeance, he hides behind a mask that inexplicably looks just like his old self. To keep the movie's audience from straying out for a smoke, there are some stunning pyrotechnics, views of the rugged Spanish landscape and- at last- the ghastly terrain of Sullivan's singed face, done to a turn by a mad makeup artist.

*San Diego Evening Tribune* by Dave McIntyre
Fire breaks out frequently on screen in *Pyro*, but it fails to generate much heat. As entertainment, this contrived melodrama is strictly cold turkey. Barry Sullivan and Martha Hyer, both of who deserve better, are defeated by the unlikely leading roles. Filmed in Spain, the picture has the saving grace of some interesting backgrounds. The story drags desultorily, however, and after the first half-hour or so, turns into formula fare which is completely predictable.

### *Commando*
"With DANGER or a DAME, they go where the action is HOTTEST!"

Produced by Willy Zeyn  Directed by Frank Wisbar
Starring Stewart Granger, Dorian Grey, Fausto Tozzi, Riccardo Garrone

April 2, 1964
*The Hollywood Reporter*
AIP OFFERING 40-FILM PACKAGE AT TV MEET
American International Pictures, participating in its first TV convention at the NAB meet starting Sunday in Chicago, will unveil its 40-feature "Epicolor '64" package in the television film exhibit at Pick-Congress Hotel with a continuous trailer projection and distribution of a full color program book.

April 6, 1964
*The Hollywood Reporter*
STAR TOURS HYPO 'MUSCLE BEACH' BIZ
Weekend box office reports from most of the 40 cities visited by

nine stars and five American International Pictures executives to promote *Muscle Beach Party* indicated that business was running more than 30% ahead of the predecessor *Beach Party*, according to sales chief Leon P. Blender.

Hitting the road for the film were Frankie Avalon, Annette Funicello, John Ashley, Jody McCrea, Morey Amsterdam, Darlene Lucht, Amedee Chabot, and Dolores Wells, all in the cast, and AIP's James H. Nicholson, Samuel Z. Arkoff, David J. Melamed, Milton Moritz, and Blender.

They chalked up 286 radio interviews, 215 TV appearances, and 197 newspaper interviews, plus participating in luncheons, fashion shows, yacht parties, dinners, theatre openings, and other events.

April 8, 1964
*The Hollywood Reporter*
AIP BANS SMOKING IN ITS PICTURES
American International Pictures has clamped a ban on cigarette smoking by characters in all its productions, according to AIP top executives James H. Nicholson and Samuel Z. Arkoff. The edict goes into effect with the musical comedy *Bikini Beach*, rolling April 20.

Among reasons behind this new policy, the AIP executives stated, is that "the majority of moviegoers today are aged 15 to 25 years" and "our motion picture stories for young Americans can set an example to all who see them by showing that smoking need not be a part of everyday life."

**Frankie Avalon does smoke a cigarette in *Muscle Beach Party*, but not in any of the "Party" films thereafter.**

April 13, 1964
*The Hollywood Reporter*
ACKERMAN IN 'BIKINI'
Forrest J. Ackerman, editor of *Famous Monsters of Filmland* magazine, has parlayed his cameo role in AIP's *Time Travelers* into a guest stint in the company's *Bikini Beach Party*.

April 20, 1964
*Boxoffice*- London Report by Anthony Gruner
ARKOFF IN ENGLAND- Vincent Price joked with Samuel Z. Arkoff, American International Pictures' executive vice president, while on the set of *The Masque of the Red Death* in England.

The color and Panavision release also stars Hazel Court and was directed by Roger Corman.

April 27, 1964
*Boxoffice Showmandiser*
LOTS OF TWIST, MUSCLES, SQUEALS AND GLAMOR AT 'MUSCLE BEACH' PREMIERE
American International Pictures concentrated its management, star, and promotion brigades in San Francisco for the world premier of *Muscle Beach Party* at the big Fox Warfield Theatre and Mission Drive-In. With James H. Nicholson and Samuel Z. Arkoff on hand to provide top generalship, the premiere was proclaimed on numerous fronts and in all media.

Star Annette Funicello greeted a crowd of teenagers, estimated at 5,000, who gathered at the Hillsdale Shopping Center. Jody McCrea and Frankie Avalon also were there with Morey Amsterdam, the comedian who appears in the picture, doing emcee chores.

From an AIP promotional brochure for 1964 -
AIP 10th ANNIVERSARY- "A Decade of Progress"
Congratulations Jim Nicholson and Sam Arkoff

AMERICAN INTERNATIONAL PROUDLY PRESENTS ITS 10TH ANNIVERSARY JUBILEE OF HITS!

May 1964- *Black Sabbath* in Color
Starring Boris Karloff, Mark Damon, Michele Mercier
Eerie, shocking melodrama, with Boris Karloff more wicked and fearsome than ever as a "wurdalak"- a vampire of medieval times who thrives only on the blood of loved ones.
From the same producer who brought us *Black Sunday*.

June 1964- Edgar Allen [sic] Poe's *The Masque of the Red Death* in Color-Scope
Starring Vincent Price, Hazel Court, Jane Asher
The master of the macabre plays the role of a depraved, lustful medieval baron who ignores the cries of the oppressed, but whose Bacchanalian orgies attract a strange, crimson-clad visitor to his castle.
Filmed in London on the most magnificent and lavish scale ever seen in an AIP production.

July 1964- *Bikini Beach* in Pathecolor and Panavision
Starring Frankie Avalon, Annette Funicello, Martha Hyer, Harvey Lembeck, Don Rickles, John Ashley, Jody McCrea, Candy Johnson, Little Stevie Wonder, The Pyramids, The Exciters, and Special Guest Star Keenan Wynn
The same "Beach Party Gang" shifting momentarily to the danger and excitement of a drag strip with the roar of powerful motors and some of the world's fanciest hot rods.
A delightful glimpse of the new breed of American Youth... with one hand on his girl's waist and the other on his surfboard.

August 1964- *The Time Travelers* in Color
Starring Preston Foster, Philip Carey, John Hoyt, Merry Anders
Filmed utilizing $2,000,000 worth of equipment used to send an astronaut into space, this futuristic exploration of unknown worlds boasts a unique ending never before seen and not likely to be seen again.
Highlighted with spine-tingling surprises and startling photographic effects, some of Hollywood's finest actors make this unbelievable tale of tomorrow terrifyingly believable.

September 1964- *Conquered City*
Starring David Niven, Ben Gazzara, Martin Balsam
An action drama of wartime heroics played against a background of idyllic romance and petrifying terror.

David Niven heads an exciting international cast as he portrays a British agent betrayed by a spy in the midst of an underground cell.

September 1964- *Operation War Head*
Starring Sean Connery (star of *Dr. No* and *From Russia With Love*), Stanley Holloway, Alfred Lynch, Wilfred Hyde-White, Alan King
A hilarious comedy production featuring a pair of military malingerers a la Sergeant Bilko with British accents. Funnier than Abbott and Costello, a cockney and a gypsy, with the brawn servicing the brain, go free-wheeling through several unorthodox business enterprises in the midst of war for a screamingly funny, merry carnival of fun.

December 1964- *The Maid and the Martian* in Color-Scope
Starring Tommy Kirk, Annette Funicello
A pair of America's most popular young stars involved in a series of terrifying experiences with unwelcome visitors from outer space, interrupted by an occasional romantic song and dance to bring the audience from under the seats.

Coming 1965- *Pajama Party* in Color-Scope
Starring Hollywood's Young New Stars
A rollicking, nerve-tingling new AIP dramatic innovation in which a pair of teenaged pretties host a pajama party in a haunted palace.
More frightening than Halloween night and more fun than a beach party, this festival of fun combines teen interest and introduces dozens of new Hollywood faces and figures supported by a hand-picked cast of veteran terror masters.

Easter 1965- *Beach Blanket Bingo* in Color & Scope
Starring Frankie Avalon, Annette Funicello
Old enough to know better, but young enough not to care, the beachnik gang gets together again for another romp in the sea and sand.

Sequel to the record-breaking hits *Beach Party, Muscle Beach Party, Bikini Beach,* the girls alone are worth the price of admission.

Coming 1965- H.G. Wells' *2164 A.D.- When the Sleeper Wakes* in Color & Scope

Starring Vincent Price, Martha Hyer

Top quality science fiction based on an original story by H.G. Wells, the man who accurately forecast the world in which we live and the world of the uncharted future.

Features appearing on the preceding pages are merely a sample of what is to come.

Shortly to go into production will be the first multi-million dollar production in AIP history, *Genghis Khan,* to be filmed in 70mm color in Hollywood and on actual locations. Another in the highly successful series of Edgar Allen (sic) Poe classics will be *City in the Sea,* to be filmed in Color and Scope with another of AIP's star-studded casts.

In addition to H.G. Wells' *2165 A.D.- When the Sleeper Wakes,* another classic from the pen of this master forecaster of the world of tomorrow will be *The Porroh Man,* which promises to be an even more startling science fiction melodrama than unforgettable *Things to Come.*

Other features starting production shortly are *Malibu Madness, Color Out of Space, The Haunted Planet,* and *Seven Footprints to Satan.*

All of this, we believe, is the beginning of another decade of progress for American International and for the exhibitors of the world, who have learned to look to the company that has and always will be their friend.

**It's amazing that, after all the money they made off of him, AIP couldn't seem to spell Edgar Allan Poe's middle name correctly.**

May 1964-

*Goliath and the Vampires* (aka *Maciste Against the Vampire*)
"MONSTER vs. GOLIATH... All New... The Mightiest Battle of Them All! See: The revolt of the faceless humanoids! The torture chamber of the blue men! The virgin-harem of the vampire god! The lost island of the vampires!"

Produced by Paolo Moffa  Directed by Giacomo Gentilomo
Starring Gordon Scott, Gianna Maria Canale, Jacques Sernas

From the pressbook- *Goliath and the Vampires*
GOLIATH AND THE VAMPIRES  PITS STRONG MAN AGAINST A TERRIFYING, NON-HUMAN EVIL
Spectacular adventure action with a weird science fiction twist provides exciting thrills in American International's *Goliath and the Vampires*.
　　Filmed in wide screen Colorscope, the adventure film stars Gordon Scott, Gianna Maria Canale, Jacques Sernas, and a cast of thousands of extras.
　　*Goliath and the Vampires* pits one of the strongest men of all time against an inhuman monster and his army of faceless, robot-like henchmen in a story of treachery, adventure, and hand-to-hand battles against overwhelming odds.
　　The action spectacular offers the most unusual thrills ever seen for the most exciting of all Goliath adventures.

SEAT SELLING SLANTS-
Your local ice cream parlor or chain of ice cream stores should go for a special "Goliath Sundae" ... or offer prizes to the local "Goliath ice cream eating champ"... the local youngster who can pack away the most ice cream eating at one sitting.

Film Review- *Goliath and the Vampires*

　　*Time Magazine* (May 15, 1964)- *Goliath and the Vampires* improbably combines a routing fang film with a beefcake B. Goliath (Gordon Scott), the hero, is a fellow who has obviously spent more time in Malibu than in Gath. According to a studio release, he stands 6 ft. 3 in., weighs 212 lbs. and sports a 50-in. bust- bigger than Jayne Mansfield's and, strange to say, almost as voluptuously formed. What's more, even though he plays a country boy, Gordon's nails are exquisitely manicured, his teeth are expensively capped, and his wardrobe apparently includes a loincloth by Balenciaga.

***Black Sabbath*** (aka *Three Faces of Fear*)
"Not since FRANKENSTEIN have you seen such horror!"

Produced by Paolo Mercuri  Directed by Mario Bava
Starring Boris Karloff, Mark Damon, Michele Mercier

From the pressbook-
*BLACK SABBATH*, STARRING BORIS KARLOFF AS TERROR VAMPIRE, OPENS HERE TODAY
Boris Karloff stars in the type of terrifying role that made him famous in American International's frightening new tale of vampires and ghosts, *Black Sabbath*.

The terror thriller, filmed in chillingly realistic color and widescreen scope, opens here tomorrow. Also starring in *Black Sabbath* are Mark Damon and Michele Mercier, with Mario Bava of *Black Sunday* fame the director.

Karloff plays a new kind of vampire in his latest thriller- a "wurdalak!" Wurdalaks differ from the conventional "Dracula" type of vampire in that they only drink the blood of those they love. Otherwise, they lose their souls, come back from death, have no reflections in mirrors, and have all the other deadly vampire characteristics.

Damon and Miss Mercier play doomed lovers in this tale of terror and the supernatural. The seeing is the classic lair of vampires- the same eerie Balkan mountain regions of Eastern Europe which spawned Dracula and Frankenstein.

SEAT SELLING SLANTS-
A surefire publicity stunt is to advertise for or, via publicity stories, call for volunteers to sit alone in the theatre through a screening of *Black Sabbath* as a test for bravery.

Film Review- *Black Sabbath*

*Time Magazine* (May 15, 1964)- *Black Sabbath* is a three-part demonthology. The Wurdalak, longest and scariest episode in the picture, represents that hoary old horror, Boris Karloff, as an East European vampire who carries somebody's head around in a canvas sack and one dark night, while everybody is sleeping, tears the throat out of his four-year-old grandson. Silly stuff, of course, but it's nice to know that a monster emeritus can somehow manage to eeeeeek out a living.

*The Evil Eye* (aka *The Girl Who Knew Too Much* )
"Look deep into THE EVIL EYE to the twilight world of the Supernatural... where horror waits for you!"

Produced by Massimo de Rita  Directed by Mario Bava
Starring John Saxon, Leticia Roman, Valentina Cortesa

1964

From the pressbook- *The Evil Eye*
*EVIL EYE* SUSPENSE TALE OF GIRL'S NIGHTMARE OF TERROR, FEAR AND MURDER
Imagining witnessing a murder and finding out that the fearful crime actually occurred more than ten years earlier!

That's the beginning of the plot of American International's *Evil Eye*. Directed by Italy's Hitchcock, Mario Bava, the suspense thriller stars John Saxon, Leticia Roman, and Valentina Cortesa.

Miss Roman portrays the terrified young woman, who is witness to a crime out of the past, while Saxon plays the handsome young doctor who befriends her and tries to help unravel the mystery.

*Evil Eye* is a thriller after the fashion of *Psycho* and other suspense masterpieces complete with a terrifying succession of fearful events, murders, and a shock surprise ending.

SEAT SELLING SLANTS-
A potent box office stimulant is a front-of-theatre display featuring a huge "Evil Eye," which can have a light that flashes on and off. The display can be made even more effective with a loudspeaker hidden inside, which will blare out the exciting radio spots made for *Evil Eye*.

May 18, 1964
*Boxoffice*
TWO AIP MEETINGS HELD; OTHERS SET THIS WEEK
New York- The first of four regional sales meetings conducted by American International Pictures got under way here Monday (11), with exchange heads, franchise dealers, and exhibitors of the company's Eastern region attending the sessions.

Other meetings were held at Chicago's Blackstone Hotel May 14-16 and will be held in New Orleans May 18-19 and in Hollywood May 21-22.

A highlight of the conventions was discussions of the AIP 10th Anniversary Sales Drive set for July 22 through August 4, with the objective of "an AIP release on every screen in the U.S.A." during the period. Product reels were shown, including *The Masque of the Red Death, Bikini Beach, Captive City, Operation*

253

24, *rhead,* and *The Time Travelers.* Prizes up to $1,000 are being offered exchange personnel as well as exhibitors.

**I have included the following article in its entirety as I feel it is an important document in tracing the history and impact of AIP as a company.**

May 27, 1964
*Motion Picture Herald*
HOLLYWOOD HORIZON by Raymond Levy, Hollywood Editor

A Tenth Anniversary of a successful business- in particular such a one as the company now named American International Pictures, which has advanced to a status that is extraordinary by contrast with its modest beginnings- is a time for at least a quick look back to note the how or the why of that accomplishment.

After all, ten years is a relatively short span of time for a business to be hoisted by its own bootstraps from a staff of four and a total capital of $3,000 to a flourishing operation requiring a payroll of some 300 regular employees. It is estimated that the 150 feature films released by the company during this decade have grossed an aggregate of more than $225 million. Each of the ten years has been a period of new growth.

Basically, the reason is simple. It is simple because it stems from following the maxim which has been fundamental in creating and developing an endless number of business successes: "find a real need, and fill it."

That there was a need for product in the motion picture field certainly has been no secret throughout all of this decade and before then. But most emphatically, it was a hue and cry for pictures of important calibre and most of all for those which could be described as "block-busters," big budget films to lure the public away from home television.

That was not the kind of need that the then little company could hope to fill, either in product they could obtain to distribute or films they could hope to produce. They decided to ignore all the current edicts about the market. They selected a niche for themselves, convinced that therein lay the "need" they could and would seek to fill.

That niche comprised, or sometimes combined, two categories: teenagers and terror. Obviously, the Messrs. Nicholson and Arkoff, who founded the company they still head most actively today, were not aiming for Oscars. Their object then, as it continues to be now, was to provide exploitable pictures- in short, films which could be made to sell tickets, films to satisfy the audience they were created to attract, films that would yield a profit for all concerned.

To James H. Nicholson and Samuel Z. Arkoff, motion pictures means business and business requires profit to re-invest in more and greater business. And so they have proceeded from that completely realistic basis throughout the decade to date.

To the categories of teenager and terror films (both comic and dramatic), they soon added science fiction thriller. Look over their schedule for this year of 1964, stated to be for a total production budget investment of some $20 million spread over 24 features, and it can be seen again to consist largely of teenage and terror and science fiction categories.

The main difference now is that production values of AIP-produced films have steadily improved through reinvestment of earnings via higher budgets, through expanding status in the bank line of credit to finance films, and through constantly improving know-how in picture- making, importantly, stepped up consumer promotion for greater results per picture has kept pace with the company's expanded status in all of the free markets of the world.

The policy to now does not mean that AIP will continue to confine itself to the teenage and chiller-diller fields. These two men, who need consult nobody else in order to decide on films to produce (or to be co-produced here or abroad or to acquire for distribution) are still governed only by the same main tenet for determining the coming need and seeking to fill it.

One of the points of being able to make quick decision whenever it may be advisable to do so, Jim Nicholson and Sam Arkoff derive a special kind of pleasure by revealing now the fact that many deals that seemed to be made by one of them in his office were actually agreed upon by the pair in quick consultation. Between the office of president Nicholson and the office of executive vice president

Arkoff is a private washroom; when both men have visitors and a fast decision may be advantageous, the washroom serves as a place for all the "conference" they need. There could be significance in their philosophy that "too many cooks spoil the broth" in decision-making.

They stress the point that not only are they always open to consider original story properties, requiring only their own decision, but that such decision is subject only to their own judgment as to potential box office value.

While AIP can be expected to continue to mine the fields in which they have successfully specialized during their first ten years, it should not be surprising if they move also into additional categories of feature filming whenever they see indications of a need that can be filled profitably. For that, in essence, is the policy in their watchful look to the horizons ahead: "find a real need and fill it."

June 1964-
*The Masque of the Red Death*
"BEHIND A BLACK DOOR, BENEATH A BLOOD RED WINDOW OF A HORROR HAUNTED CASTLE... Half-madman, half-monster... It waits for those whose turn has come!"

Produced and Directed by Roger Corman
Starring Vincent Price, Hazel Court, Jane Asher

From the pressbook- *The Masque of the Red Death*
MASTERS OF SCREEN TERROR JOIN FORCES TO MAKE POE's *THE MASQUE OF THE RED DEATH*
Vincent Price and director Roger Corman, the masters of screen terror, joined forces to make their first film in England... Edgar Allan Poe's *The Masque of the Red Death*.

An American International Pictures production, it is set in 12th century Italy, where Prince Prospero, a tyrannical power in the land and a devout worshipper of Satan- whom he believes to be the real master of the world- practices his corrupted philosophy.

**Jane Asher and Hazel Court in *The Masque of the Red Death*.**

Hazel Court filmed her third role in the successful Edgar Allan Poe series as Juliana, Prospero's beautiful companion in the pursuit of evil.

Roger Corman, 37-year-old American director who has made all seven films in the series, had directed some of the most visually exciting scenes to be seen yet in his current thriller, one of the high spots of which is the Masque Ball, at which Death is the uninvited guest.

SEAT SELLING SLANTS-
Since the "masque" of the title of *The Masque of the Red Death* refers to a ball or dance and the affair is a masked one in the film, the sponsorship of a teenage "Masque of the Red Death Ball," with all who come required to be masked and dread in menacing costumes, would stir up great advance interest in the film.

Film Reviews- *The Masque of the Red Death*

*New York Times* (September 17, 1964) by Eugene Archer
Hollywood's most prolific director, Roger Corman, boasts more than 50 films in the last 10 years. *The Masque of the Red Death* represents the dauntless young filmmaker at the top of his form. The film is vulgar, naive, and highly amusing, and it is played with gusto by Mr. [Vincent]
Price, Hazel Court, and Jane Asher. On its level, it is astonishingly good.

*Time Magazine* (May 15, 1964)- *The Masque of the Red Death* dusts off a trifling Poe classic and adapts it to fit the collected smirks of Vincent Price. Poe's original described a masked ball at which the vulgar Prince Prospero and all his company succumb when Death appears disguised as a plague victim. In the elegant, elongated movie version, Prospero is a Satanist who scourges the entire 12th century countryside. He tortures peasants, tries to corrupt a village maid, and lets his pet dwarf barbecue a guest. Fortunately, by the time Death get to the party, most of the nicer people have fled.

*New York Herald Tribune*- The film is beautifully costumed, the sets are lavish, the props exquisite.

**Some People**
"From the land of the 'Beatles' come the young rebels... wild and explosive! All bad? You never can tell about... *Some People*"

Produced by James Archibald  Directed by Clive Donner
Starring Kenneth More, Ray Brooks, Annika Wills

June 4, 1964
*The Hollywood Reporter*
Travel Logs-
NICHOLSON TO KEYNOTE CATHOLIC
FILM MEETING
James H. Nicholson, president of American International Pictures,

will deliver the keynote address during the International Catholic Film Office Study Days in Venice, June 20-24. Nicholson, whose firm now is celebrating its 10th Anniversary, will speak on "The Moral Responsibilities of the Film Maker." He will be accompanied to Venice by AIP music coordinator Al Simms.

June 15, 1964
*Boxoffice*
BIGGEST RELEASE SCHEDULE IN ITS HISTORY MARKS AIP's "DECADE OF PROGRESS"
The most ambitious production and release schedule in its history marks the tenth anniversary "decade of progress" year for American International Pictures, according to James H. Nicholson, president, and Samuel Z. Arkoff, executive vice president. At midyear, the company already had 11 productions in release with another 13 ready and nine others scheduled for production, making a total of 33 major releases for the 12-month period.

While the company continues to follow its highly successful formula of diversified releases with action drama, suspense action, straight terror, and science-fiction films, it simultaneously remains on the lookout for new formats, such as the most recent chill-chuckle-terror features and musical comedies geared for teenage audiences.

Trade ad-
AIP 10th Anniversary- A Decade of Progress

American International Pictures marks a decade of progress with this lineup of product which is set to light up box offices everywhere.

*The Masque of the Red Death, Bikini Beach, Godzilla vs. the Thing, Taboo* (successor to *Mondo Cane*), *Pajama Party, Voyage to the End of the Universe, Diary of a Bachelor, The Time Travelers, Hercules Against the Barbarian, Tomb of Ligeia*

Features appearing above are merely a sample of what is to come.

259

June 29, 1964
*Boxoffice*
AIP LAUNCHES 'LIGEIA'
American International Pictures conducted a press reception in London to launch the new Edgar Allan Poe film *Ligeia*. Samuel Z. Arkoff, AIP's executive vice president, attended along with Macgregor Scott, managing director of Warner-Pathe Distributors Ltd., and Nat Cohen and Stuart Levy, heads of Britain's Anglo Amalgamated Productions, Ltd., with whom AIP has had an association for ten years. Vincent Price stars in the film, which starts at Shepperton Studios on June 29.

July 1964-

**Bikini Beach**
"IT'S WHERE THE BOYS MEET THE GIRLS... and everyone can SEE what they're gonna be up against! See the Beach Party Gang Go DragStrip!"

Produced by James H. Nicholson and Samuel Z. Arkoff  Directed by William Asher
Starring Frankie Avalon, Annette Funicello, Martha Hyer, Harvey Lembeck, John Ashley

July 13, 1964
*Boxoffice*
AIP CELEBRATES 10TH YEAR AT N.Y. WORLD'S FAIR
New York- American International Pictures and its president James H. Nicholson and executive vice president Samuel Z. Arkoff celebrated the company's tenth anniversary with day-long festivities at the New York World's Fair, July 4, which included the first showing of *Bikini Beach*, the company's summer musical release. The 250 guests of AIP, including exhibitors, members of the newspaper and trade press, and AIP executives, also attended the Hollywood Pavilion, where Frankie Avalon, Annette Funicello, and Harvey Lembeck, stars of *Bikini Beach*, and Buddy Hackett,

another AIP comedy star, placed their hand and foot prints in the cement walk, a lunch at the Better Living Center, and cocktails and buffet supper at the Hilton International Cafe, followed by the Fair's display of Fourth of July fireworks.

July 13, 1964
*The Hollywood Reporter*
SUSAN HART SIGNS MULTIPLE AIP DEAL
Producer James Nicholson has signed Susan Hart for a three-picture deal with American International Pictures. The young actress, currently co-starring in Columbia's yet to be released *Ride the Wild Surf,* will be co-starred in each of these pictures to be made within a year.

She reports to director Don Weiss tomorrow for script meetings on the first film, entitled *Pajama Party.* The second feature, as yet untitled, will roll in November in which she will co-star with Frankie Avalon and Annette Funicello. Briskin-Levee Agency, who represents Miss Hart, negotiated.

July 30, 1964
*The Hollywood Reporter*
AIP WILL CONTINUE MAKING 'BEACH' FILMS, SIGNING PACTS
New York- AIP will continue making "Beach" pictures because they attract family audiences as well as the younger element and are ideal vehicles to build your players to stardom, James H. Nicholson, company president, so stated yesterday at a press luncheon honoring Susan Hart, newest addition to AIP's contract roster.

AIP is signing young talent to 52-week contracts, either using them in pictures or keeping them on publicity tours, and plans to extend personality tours overseas as well as here, Nicholson said. Company currently has 20 players under various contracts, five writers, and five directors.

Releasing 18 pictures this year, AIP for 1965 plans 12 top features in color, each costing $1,000,000 or more, plus others, Nicholson revealed.

He said *Beach Party* had 11,000 domestic playdates plus

repeats for over $3,000,000 film rentals and *Muscle Beach Party* is also whopping.

*Genghis Khan*, AIP's upcoming biggie, has been switched from a spectacular (because there have been so many) to more romantic treatment. Originally announced as a multi-million dollar production, the cost has been pared down and decision has been made not to roadshow it. Samuel Z. Arkoff leaves Hollywood tomorrow for Italy to get preparation started.

July 30, 1964
*The Film Daily*
ROOM FOR EXPANSION AIP TOPPERS HOLD
Hollywood- "There is much room for expansion in the motion picture industry," American International Pictures President James H. Nicholson and Executive Vice President Samuel Z. Arkoff told *The Film Daily*.

Nicholson pointed to recent estimates that the number of theaters in the U.S. has risen to a total of some 17,000, the highest figure since TV first began to make a dent in the movie going public. Furthermore, both AIP toppers pointed out, because of drive-ins and new types of theaters, there is actually more of an attendance capacity today than there was right after World War II.

"250 to 300 prints," it was pointed out, "used to be plenty for a saturation booking. We had 450 prints for *Bikini Beach* and it still wasn't enough."

AIP is going to lean much more toward science fiction in next year's production slate as well as continue its teenage pictures in the *Bikini Beach* tradition, although a number of the films will be "off the beach." Among forthcoming teenage pictures will be *Pajama Party, Beach Blanket Bingo, Jet Set,* and *Malibu Madness.*

August 1964-

August 10, 1964
*Boxoffice*
AIP EXPECTS TO HAVE 21 RELEASES IN '65
New York- American International Pictures, currently celebrating

its tenth year in the industry, will have a "Golden Dozen" of major releases during 1965 in addition to lesser pictures which will bring the year's total to approximately the 20-21 released in 1964, according to James H. Nicholson, who, at a luncheon at Sardi's Restaurant, introduced the company's first long-term contract player, Susan Hart.

Miss Hart, a dark-eyed beauty of 23 who previously appeared in *For Those Who Think Young* and the current Columbia release *Ride the Wild Surf*, will be featured in AIP's *Pajama Party*, which will go into production in Hollywood August 10 with Tommy Kirk, Annette Funicello, William Bendix, and Elsa Lanchester heading the cast. Later, Miss Hart will be cast in other youthful pictures, including *Jet Set Party*, under her 52-weeks-a-year contract. But Nicholson said she will be available for loan to other studios.

AIP also has Vincent Price, Boris Karloff, Annette Funicello, Frankie Avalon, Candy Johnson, John Ashley, and Harvey Lembeck under non-exclusive contracts for certain pictures yearly, but Miss Hart and another newcomer, Bobbi Shaw, are the first to receive long-term deals.

September 1964-

### Voyage to the End of the Universe
"Dare you take the incredible adventure into the 25th Century? See: Life aboard the might rocket-city as it hurtles through space! The horrible secret of the rocket ship lost 9 million years!"

Produced by Rudolph Wohl  Directed by Jack Pollack
Starring Dennis Stephens, Francis Smolen, Dana Meredith, Irene Kova, Rodney Lucas

From the pressbook-
*VOYAGE TO THE END OF THE UNIVERSE* DEPICTS HAZARD, THRILLS OF YEARS-LONG TRAVEL THROUGH VASTNESS OF SPACE TO STARS
What will it be like to travel across space for five, ten, twenty years to reach another world, another sun? What will be the hazards, the

mysterious things that would be encountered on such a trip, and how would you eat, drink, and live on an epic journey?

All the thriller answers, based on current scientific fact, are found in American International's

*Voyage to the End of the Universe.* Starring in the widescreen scope fiction thriller are Dennis Stephens and Francis Smolen, plus some of the most amazing special effects and "out-of-this-world" sets ever seen in a motion picture.

The story tells of a dedicated group of fifty men and women, mostly scientists, and their fight against unknown terror and the sheer boredom of a long trip confined aboard a gigantic spaceship.

**Voyage to the End of the Universe was a 1963 Czech film titled Ikarie XB-1, which AIP imported, dubbed into English, and cut from 81 to 65 minutes. The names of the stars are actually Zdenek Stepanek and Frantisek Smolik.**

September 21, 1964
*Boxoffice*
AIP SIGNS CHERYL SWEETEN AS 'STAR OF THE FUTURE'
New York- As part of its tenth anniversary policy of signing "stars of the future," American International Pictures has added 20-year-old Cheryl Sweeten as its third such contractee destined for an all-out star buildup campaign. Miss Sweeten, who makes her AIP debut in the recently completed *Pajama Party*, has been signed to a seven-year exclusive term contract calling for extensive personal appearance and publicity-promotion tours.

Cheryl, a five-foot-six-inch hazel-eyed blonde, was Miss Colorado of 1963 and before that Miss Teenage Colorado. She also was finalist in the Miss American pageant and won the talent award in the Miss Teenage America competition of 1962. She is a native of Denver and now resides with her parents in the San Fernando Valley of Los Angeles. Her only previous experience in Hollywood was in the TV series "Saints and Sinners" while she also appeared in stage productions of the Arvada (a Denver suburb) Civic Theatre.

October 1964-

*Godzilla vs. The Thing*
"Nothing like this EVER on the screen! What is IT? How much terror can you stand? See: The war of the GIANTS! The BIRTH of the world's most terrifying monster! Armies of the world destroyed by THE THING!"

Produced by Tomoyuki Tanaka  Directed by Ishiro Honda
Starring Akira Takrada, Yuriko Hoshi, Hiroshi Koizumi

**_Godzilla vs. The Thing_ is _Godzilla vs. Mothra_, the fourth film in Toho Studios' long-running Godzilla franchise and the first of many Toho films released by AIP.**

**Poster art for _Godzilla vs. The Thing_ concealed the fact that The Thing was actually Mothra.**

From the pressbook-
SPECIAL EFFECTS PLUS TRICK PHOTOGRAPHY GIVE REALITY TO *GODZILLA VS. THE THING*

New dimensions of science fiction realism with resultant new peaks of thrills and new vistas of spectacle are achieved in American International's *Godzilla vs. The Thing.*

The color and scope science fiction thriller features devastating effects through startling new Japanese techniques in trick photography. The new photographic effects feature four layer composition filming and large, motor-driven miniatures for greater realism.

The amazing human expressions on Godzilla's face is achieved by new ultra-slow motion photography, while the hide of the monsters is made realistically frightening with plastic and foam rubber. Many models of the monsters, both Godzilla and the mysterious Thing, were used in the productions according to the size of the sets in use.

Add beautiful and realistic color and wide screen scope and the result is terrifying, exciting, and realistic entertainment.

SEAT SELLING SLANTS-
Spot all places where buildings have been wrecked or razed in your area or where pre-construction digging is going on and post signs on surrounding fences reading "Godzilla fought The Thing here!"- another effective attention-getter.

Film Review- *Godzilla vs. The Thing*

*New York Times* (November 26, 1964) by Eugene Archer
A title such as *Godzilla vs. The Thing* poses only one real question. What sort of thing is it, anyway?

Well, there are three Things, not counting the movie. One has wings and green eyes and looks like a big bee. The other two are hatched from the first Thing's egg after quite a bit of worshipful kootch dancing from a pair of foot-tall native goddesses.

This Thing's progeny are big worms. They squirt juice all over Godzilla and it turns into a spider web. Godzilla himself is still breathing fire and swatting his tail upon the Japanese landscape, exactly as he did the last time out.

*Diary of a Bachelor*
"This Picture is dedicated to LIFE... LOVE... and the pursuit of anything worth chasing!"

Produced and Directed by Sandy Howard
Starring Joe Silver, Dom De Luise, Arlene Golonka, Paula Stewart, William Traylor

*The Time Travelers*
"YOU are in the FUTURE before it happens!"

Produced by William Redlin  Directed by Ib Melchior
Starring Preston Foster, Philip Carey, Merry Anders, John Hoyt, Dennis Patrick

October 5, 1964
*The Film Daily*
AIP GOING FOR YOUTH "THEATRE OWNERS OF AMERICA" MEETING IS TOLD
Chicago- In addition to the continuing expansion of AIP's "turn to youth" policy through the production of more films for the 15-25 group, James H. Nicholson and Samuel Z. Arkoff pledged AIP to the continuing introduction of "new faces" stars and expanded personal appearance tours and the utilization of a new "think tank" to keep abreast of audience needs.

Nicholson told some 1,000 persons at the Hotel Hilton luncheon that "we feel that the exhibitor should be as hopped up, as enthusiastic and as active as we are in putting every ounce of showmanship into the promotion of a new picture."

"We feel also," he said, "that the exhibitor has an obligation to join in the making of a star."

The presentation of a product reel with scenes from three major upcoming attractions- *Pajama Party, The House at the End of the World,* and *Atragon*- was a high spot of the luncheon.

A special feature of the luncheon was a "Starburst of Youth for the World's Young at Heart" presentation, which turned out to be a musical skit in which these AIP players appeared: Vincent Price, Frankie Avalon, Annette Funicello, Susan Hart, Donna

Loren, Bobbi Shaw, and Cheryl Sweeten. Don Rickles was master of ceremonies.

October 5, 1964
*Boxoffice*
AIP DISTRIBUTION OFFICE IS OPENED IN ITALY
New York- American International has opened an office in Italy as a first step toward a new formula for improving its distribution abroad and getting a better box office potential for its new pictures, according to David D. Horne, vice president in charge of foreign distribution, who returned from a trip to Italy, Spain, Portugal, and England in mid-September.

Horne predicts that 1964 will bring in "300-400 per cent more revenue" from Italy than it did in the previous year. With the United Kingdom the leader in revenue for AIP abroad, he said that the revenue for the month of September "was 100 per cent over the same month last year."

October 8, 1964
*The Hollywood Reporter*
AIP SHOWING BEST FOOT TO ALLIED
Four young American International Pictures actresses, representative of AIP's new "A Starburst of Youth for the World's Young at Heart" policy, will travel to Detroit for the Allied States Theater Owners convention to enable delegates to meet them in person.

The new stars going to the Motor City are Susan Hart, Bobbi Shaw, Donna Loren, and Cheryl Sweeten. Another American International top star joining them will be comedian Don Rickles.

October 13, 1964
*The Hollywood Reporter*
AIP TO CONTINUE TO COPYRIGHT PRESS BOOK
American International Pictures has and will continue to fully copyright its pressbooks and all their content after several instances of pirating of ad art and other pictures by exhibitors, it was announced yesterday by Barnett Shapiro, AIP general counsel.

At the same time, he said that AIP has dropped plans for legal action against an east coast theatre chain for unauthorized use of American International advertising material for *Black Sabbath* for another film.

The film and distribution company's general counsel further stated that, despite suspension of legal action in this instance, "American International Pictures will not tolerate such practices in the future."

October 19, 1964
*Boxoffice*
## HONORS TO AIP TOPPERS
Plaques declaring them "Master Showmen of the Decade" were presented by Theatre Owners of America to James H. Nicholson and Samuel Z. Arkoff with TOA president John H. Rowley officiating while AIP star Annette Funicello looked on.

The award was made at the president's banquet climaxing the recent TOA convention held in Chicago. It saluted the AIP executives on the tenth anniversary of the company "in grateful appreciation for their confidence in the future of motion picture exhibition and outstanding efforts to alleviate the product shortage by producing quality box office attractions for the screen of the theaters of the United States."

November 1964-
### Pajama Party
"The Party Picture that takes off (way off) where the others stopped!"

Produced by James H. Nicholson and Samuel Z. Arkoff  Directed by Don Weis
Starring Annette Funicello, Tommy Kirk, Elsa Lanchester, Harvey Lembeck, Jesse White

**Pajama Party was the project originally announced by AIP as *The Maid and the Martian*. This was the first of the "Party" pictures that didn't star Frankie Avalon opposite Annette Funicello (although he does make a cameo appearance). Tommy Kirk and Annette had just appeared together in *The***

*Misadventures of Merlin Jones,* which was a considerable box office hit for Walt Disney. By re-teaming Tommy and Annette, AIP hoped to duplicate that success. This film was AIP's first association with Louis M. "Deke" Heyward (1920-2002), who wrote the script. Heyward would eventually work his way up in the company to become vice president in charge of production for AIP's European branch.

November 16, 1964
*The Film Daily*
AMER-INT'L HAS VIDEO PRODUCTION AMBITION
Seven-month-old American International Television, reports President James H. Nicholson, is at work in Hollywood on *The Adventures of Sinbad, Jr.,* a series consisting of 130 five-minute full color, full animation cartoons.

Nicholson, noting that all of AI-TV's product to date has consisted of outright film acquisitions and overseas co-production, told a press luncheon at Sardi's West that he is intensely interested in TV production in the U.S. He divulged that plans for the co-production of a musical special in the "very near future" are under discussion with "a major New York TV network."

Stanley E. Dudelson, the company's vice president in charge of distribution, reported the first sale of *The Adventures of Sinbad, Jr.* had been made to Metro Media for viewing on its seven stations March 5, 1965.

Dudelson also told of the acquisition by AI-TV and Richard G. Yates of the company's fourth package, *Thrillers from Another World,* a series of 20 suspense dramas.

Dudelson said that "AI-TV with its sound commercially entertaining films will also build stars for television," adding that "these new stars will make personal appearances in territories sold to build up public interest and curiosity." Currently, the company is developing Rock Stevens, muscleman who appeared in *Muscle Beach Party.* He is working in Rome in his first TV production *Challenge of the Gladiators,* which will be released here shortly.

**In 1964, Rock Stevens made three theatrical Sword and Sandal pictures in Italy: *Challenge of the Gladiator, Goliath at the***

*Conquest of Damascus,* and *Hercules and the Tyrants of Babylon.* All three were given limited regional theatrical releases by AIP in the U.S. prior to being released by AI-TV as part of their TV movie packages. Rock Stevens would later find TV fame on *Mission: Impossible* using his real name, Peter Lupus.

Rock Stevens, aka Peter Lupus.

### Challenge of the Gladiator
"Infamy and cruelty sweep the Roman Empire as a madman turns the country into a bloody arena!"

Produced by Ferdinando Felicioni  Directed by Domenico Paolella
Starring Rock Stevens, Gloria Milland, Massimo Serato

From the pressbook-
MUSCLEMAN STARS IN *CHALLENGE OF THE GLADIATOR*
When you have the build and the physique of the strongest man in the world, it's almost impossible to avoid type-casting as a strong man. Such an actor is Rock Stevens, star of American International Pictures' *Challenge of the Gladiator.*

Muscleman Stevens was born in Indianapolis, Indiana, and attracted national attention when he won the "Mr. Indianapolis" title soon after he graduated from high school and entered Butler University. Later, after being cast in several local theatre plays, he went to Hollywood and appeared on several TV shows, including the Jack Benny Show. He was picked out of hundreds of musclemen for a key role in AIP's *Muscle Beach Party.*

*Challenge of the Gladiator* gives Rock a chance to prove his acting ability in addition to displaying his fantastic strength. As Spartacus, the Thracian gladiator, Rock leads an oppressed country in the struggle for freedom.

The color spectacle also stars Gloria Milland and Massimo Serato.

### Goliath at the Conquest of Damascus
"GOLITAH... THE AVENGER... his invincible might pitted against the armies of corrupt Damascus."

Produced by Fortunato Misiano  Directed by Domenico Paolella
Starring Rock Stevens, Helga Line, Mario Petri

### Hercules and the Tyrants of Babylon
"Against the thundering attack of the might Babylonian cavalry stands HERCULES... his only weapon his superhuman strength!"

Produced by Fortunato Misiano Directed by Domenico Paolella
Starring Rock Stevens, Mario Petri, Helga Line, Arturo Domenici,
Anna Maria Polani

November 17, 1964
*The Hollywood Reporter*
FRANKIE, ANNETTE RE-TEAM IN AIP's *BEACH BLANKET*
Frankie Avalon and Annette Funicello have been signed by
American International Pictures producer-executives James H.
Nicholson and Samuel Z. Arkoff to co-star in AIP's *Beach Blanket
Bingo*, their fourth such joint appearance. Production begins in
Hollywood November 30.

Also signed for starring roles in the color and Panavision
musical comedy were Deborah Walley and John Ashley. William
Asher, who directed the three previous beach films, also will helm
*Beach Blanket Bingo*.

November 19, 1964
*The Hollywood Reporter*
LEMBECK IS SIGNED TO REPRISE AIP CHARACTER
Harvey Lembeck has been signed to portray his zany Eric
Von Zipper characterization for the fourth time in American
International's *Beach Blanket Bingo*, it was announced yesterday
by James H. Nicholson and Samuel Z. Arkoff, AIP toppers and
producers.

Lembeck's Von Zipper character was first introduced in AIP's
*Beach Party*. It was repeated in *Bikini Beach* and again in *Pajama
Party*.

December 1964-
*Navajo Run*
" Two Giants of the plains... meet in DEADLY COMBAT! A
Navajo warrior... captive of a vengeful killer so maddened by hate-
his greatest pleasure is MAN-KILLING!"

**Harvey Lembeck (center) as Eric Von Zipper is surrounded by his Rat Pack.**

Produced and Directed by Johnny Seven
Starring Johnny Seven, Warren Kemmerling, Virginia Vincent, Ron Soble

December 14, 1964
*Boxoffice*
The London Report by Anthony Gruner
Boris Karloff plays a "monster" in the new American International Pictures science fiction horror film *House at the End of the World*, which goes into production at Shepperton Studios on February 15. The picture is based on a story, "Color Out of Space," by H.P. Lovecraft and will mark the debut as a director of Daniel Haller, the young Hollywood artist and motion picture designer.

AIP HEAD IN LONDON- On the set of *City in the Sea*, the Anglo Amalgamated/American International coproduction starring Vincent Price, Tab Hunter, and Susan Hart, the film's director, Jacques Tourneur, greeted James H. Nicholson, president of American International Pictures, at Pinewood Studios in London.

December 29, 1964
*The T.A.M.I. Show*- Special one night showing of a live stage concert featuring The Beach Boys, Chuck Berry, James Brown, The Rolling Stones, Lesley Gore, Jan and Dean, The Supremes, and others. The film went into general release in January 1965.

**1964 ended on a sour note for AIP. Sylvia Nicholson filed for divorce from Jim on the grounds of adultery. Susan Hart was named as correspondent. As part of her divorce settlement, Sylvia received a portion of Jim's stock in AIP, thereby giving Sam Arkoff controlling interest in the company.**

# CHAPTER TWELVE
# 1965

January 1965-
***Tomb of Ligeia***
"CAT or WOMAN or a thing too evil to mention? Listen for the SCREAM in the night! Look into the eyes of the creature who rules the land of the living dead!"

Produced and Directed by Roger Corman
Starring Vincent Price, Elizabeth Shepherd

From the pressbook-
PRICE CALLS *TOMB OF LIGEIA* MOST TERRIFYING OF POE FILMS
"It is the most terrifying Poe film ever made," actor Vincent

Price says of *The Tomb of Ligeia*, the new American International Pictures terror production based on the works of Edgar Allan Poe.

And if anyone should know whereof he speaks, it is Price, who has starred in seven previous AIP films based upon Poe's works.

Brilliantly and imaginatively directed by Roger Corman, the new cinema version of the Maryland poet's terror tales introduces English actress Elizabeth Shepherd in the title role of a beautiful, voluptuous woman whose will is so powerful, so evil, that it survives her own death.

Filmed in Color and Scope largely on location in and around a sinister, 1000-year-old abbey in Norfolk, England, the supporting cast of *Tomb of Ligeia* includes John Westbrook, Derek Francis, Oliver Johnston, and Robert Adam.

Film Reviews- *Tomb of Ligeia*

*New York Times* (May 6, 1965) by Howard Thompson
Mr. Corman at least cares about putting Mr. Poe- or at least some of the master's original ideas- on the screen. If they are frankly made to be screamed at, they are not to be sneezed at. The picture is not nearly as finished as *Masque of the Red Death* and *The Pit and the Pendulum* remains our favorite of all. But the Corman climate of evil is as unhealthy and contagious as ever.

*Time* (May 21, 1965)- THE SIMPLE ANNALS OF POE
If Producer-Director Roger Corman had anything on his mind more substantial than cobwebs and curdled blood, he might easily extend to others the excitement he creates among a small but thrill-thirsty band of followers who await each Corman film as though it contained fresh plasma.

Opulently photographed in and around a crumbling English abbey, *Ligeia*, like its predecessors, offers meticulous decor, shrewd shock techniques, and an atmosphere of mounting terror that fails to deliver on its promise.

*Los Angeles Times*- Roger Corman, who has been called the Orson Welles of the Grade Z movies, his writer Robert Towne, and Vincent Price know just how far to go with their bravura style.

They continually teeter on the brink of the ludicrous, but never quite fall off.

*Newsweek-* It is as if Roger Corman were no longer in control, but being manipulated by his material, driven to a kind of poetic madness by the horror he has made his business.

*Films and Filming* (March 1965) by Robin Bean
Devoid of the gadgetry of *Pit and the Pendulum* or, to a lesser extent, *Masque of the Red Death,* [Roger] Corman concentrates on a more subjective treatment of a man's struggle which superficially is against the supernatural, but basically is against the fears of being dominated by a stronger-willed person, of being forced down, controlled, and eventually submerged. Very impressive.

**Conquered City**
"SPY and COUNTER SPY live the supreme adventure of suspense!"

Produced by Lux Film  Directed by Joseph Anthony
Starring David Niven, Ben Gazzara, Martin Balsam, Lea Massari, Michael Craig

**Conquered City is a 1962 Italian World War II movie starring David Niven which AIP attempted to pass off as a spy thriller.**

February 1965-

**Operation Snafu**
"WARM LIPS OR HOT LEAD... he's after action not medals!"

Produced by S. Benjamin Fisz  Directed by Cyril Frankel
Starring Sean Connery, Alfred Lynch, Cecil Parker, Wilfred Hyde-White, Stanley Holloway

*Operation Snafu* is the 1961 British World War II comedy *On the Fiddle*, starring a pre-James Bond Sean Connery. AIP's advertising features buxom, pistol-packing babes and ad copy to make it appear to be a spy film. When this ploy failed, AIP brought the film out again in May 1965 as *Operation War Head*.

Film Review- *Operation Snafu*

*New York Times* (May 22, 1965) by Howard Thompson
*Operation Snafu* is a friendly little wartime comedy from England. This American International release was made four or five years ago, before Sean Connery, a struggling young actor, hit the big time as James Bond, and its appearance now is an obvious cash-in on his popularity.

The wonder is that a picture with a story already done, gag by gag, a hundred times is so easy to take. It is, though- flip, friendly, brisk, and a wee bit cynical in its take-it-or-leave-it jauntiness.

Even the final switch to heroics clicks into place as deftly played by Alfred Lynch and Mr. Connery. The film is familiar and trifling, but it's perky.

March 1965-

### Atragon
"THE MOST FANTASTIC SCIENCE SHOCKER EVER FILMED! You will ride the SUPER-SUBMARINE... from the outer limits of space to the evil EMPIRE at the bottom of the Seven Seas!"

Produced by Tomoyuki Tanaka  Directed by Ishiro Honda
Starring Tadao Takashima, Yoko Fujiyama, Kenji Sahara, Jun Tazaki

### The Lost World of Sinbad/War of the Zombies
"New HIGHS in ADVENTURE! See: The blood dance of the Zombies! The undead cross swords with the living! The goddess of the Night Star, whose gaze mummifies men!"

Touted as "The Double Shock Show of the Year," this is one of AIP's most duplicitous double bills. *The Lost World of Sinbad* is the Japanese movie *Samurai Pirate* and *War of the Zombies* is the Italian Sword and Sandal film *Rome Against Rome*.

*The Lost World of Sinbad*
Produced by Tomoyuki Tanaka  Directed by Senkichi Taniguchi
Starring Toshiro Mifune, Tadao Nakamura, Mie Hama

*War of the Zombies*
Produced by Ferruccio de Martino and Massimo de Rita  Directed by Giuseppe Vari
Starring John Drew Barrymore, Susi Andersen, Ettori Manni

From the pressbook-
SINBAD, ZOMBIES BRING CHILLS TO LOCAL SCREENS
Fantasy adventure film fans will get a large double dose of their favorite diet when American International's *War of the Zombies* and *The Lost World of Sinbad* open.

Filmed in exciting Colorscope, both thrillers feature large casts, lavish production, and pulse-throbbing action tales, heroes battling against fearful out-of-this-world and supernatural enemies.

Together, they make for unparalleled adventure entertainment film fare with an added mixture of fantasy to heighten the excitement.

March 29, 1965
*Boxoffice*
AIP WINS FEDERAL SUIT ON CORPORATE NAME USE
Dallas- American International Pictures has won a federal district court permanent injunction against use of its corporate name by a Dallas motion picture film calling itself Eagle-American

International Films, according to Samuel Z. Arkoff, AIP executive vice president.

March 31, 1965
*The Film Daily*
AIP OFFERING FOUR TV PACKAGES THIS YEAR
American International Television has assembled four new packages of films for showing on TV in 1965. These include "Thrillers from Another World," "Adventure '66," "Amazing '66," and "Operation Snafoo- The Zany World of International Espionage." Each package is made up of 20 films.

AIP, which entered the TV programming field last May 1, has a total of more than 160 feature films plus 130 five-minute full color, animation cartoons and a full-length feature cartoon in release. Company's own films are released to TV no sooner than five years after theatrical release.

April 1965-

**Beach Blanket Bingo**
"It's the game that separates the girls and the boys... into groups of two!"

Produced by James H. Nicholson and Samuel Z. Arkoff Directed by William Asher
Starring Frankie Avalon, Annette Funicello, Deborah Walley, Harvey Lembeck, John Ashley

**Taboos of the World**
"It's the picture that OUT-MONDO'S them all!"
Produced by Guido Giambartolomei    Directed by Romolo Marcellini
With comments by Vincent Price

From the pressbook-
VINCENT PRICE NARRATES *TABOOS OF THE WORLD*
Actor Vincent Price, world traveled as an art connoisseur, brings the convincing quality of his Stentorian stage voice as well as the wisdom of his avocation to the commentary upon American

International's probing study of secret societies and exotic rituals in *Taboos of the World*.

Couching his remarks in flowing Elizabethan phrases and spiced with modern humor, Price describes such sights as the intimacies of Japanese baths, the simple, 3-word Pakistani divorce proceedings, and the inside of a Leprosarium.

The color production is made up of many other spine-tingling, informative, and sometime shocking camera's-eye views of man's jealously guarded secret rites which strangely form the foundation of civilized society.

Film Review- *Taboos of the World*

*Los Angeles Times* (July 30, 1965)- Once again, human suffering and ignorance are exploited and exotic customs patronized to make a fast buck. As usual, the result is a large dose of grisly and pointless trash. Horror film star Vincent Price serves as narrator. He tries to bring wit, compassion, and taste to this shapeless, shoddy footage, but it is a task doomed from the outset.

April 26, 1965
*Boxoffice*
SKOURAS NAMED AIP's EUROPEAN SALES SUPERVISOR
New York- Daniel P. Skouras has been appointed European sales supervisor for American International Pictures, announces David D. Horne, vice president in charge of foreign distribution for the company. He fills the post vacated by Jeffry Sion, who resigned.

In July, Skouras and his family will move to London, where he will make his headquarters.

April 29, 1965
*The Film Daily*
WORTHY CAUSE
James H. Nicholson, president of American International Pictures, practiced his newspaper selling technique after signing up as a volunteer "old newspaper boy" for the New York Variety Club's Special Edition, to be printed by the New York Journal American

on June 29. It's part of a campaign to raise $250,000 for the establishment of a Children's Heart Center at the N.Y. Medical College Flower and Fifth Avenue Hospital. Nicholson himself is chief barker of the Los Angeles Variety Club.

Trade ad-
AMERICAN INTERNATIONAL GETS THEM OFF THE BEACHES AND TO THE BOXOFFICE

> May 26, 1965- *War-Gods of the Deep*
> June 16, 1965- *Ski Party*
> July 7, 1965- *How to Stuff a Wild Bikini*
> August 11, 1965- *Sergeant Deadhead*

May 1965-

**War-Gods of the Deep** (aka *City Under the Sea* )
"A fantastic journey to a lost empire one thousand fathoms beneath the sea!"

Produced by Daniel Haller  Directed by Jacques Tourneur
Starring Vincent Price, Tab Hunter, Susan Hart, David Tomlinson

From the pressbook-
LEGENDARY LAND SCENE OF STORY OF NEW THRILLER
Lyonesse, the lost undersea land of the story of American International's *War-Gods of the Deep*, actually is mentioned in early English chronicles and also was the scene of the famed Arthurian romances.

The old English histories mention Lyonesse as a flourishing part of what is now the coast of the province of Cornwall until its sudden and mysterious disappearance beneath the waves.

It also was the scene of "the last great battle of the West"- the final conflict between King Arthur and his lifelong foe, Sir Modred.

**Susan Hart (born 1941) appeared in five AIP productions.**

In the color and scope thriller, Lyonesse is ruled by Vincent Price. Also starring in the film are Tab Hunter, David Tomlinson, and Susan Hart.

Film Reviews- *War-Gods of the Deep*

*The Hollywood Reporter* (June 2, 1965)- *War-Gods of the Deep* is not up to the other AIPers in this field. Dialogue is fumbling and, except for the last half hour, there isn't enough menace or suspense. Vincent Price seems a little subdued, playing with less

285

than his customary flamboyance. The picture needs that kind of color.

*New York Times* (June 3, 1965) by Howard Thompson
What a cast! What a plot! Call it submerged science fiction, naturally in color. This briny safari was directed by Jacques Tourneur, who made *The Cat People*. We'll take those other cats any day.

### Swinger's Paradise
"Live the WILD NIGHTS and the WAY OUT DAYS!"

Produced by Kenneth Harper  Directed by Sidney J. Furie
Starring Cliff Richard, Walter Slezak, Susan Hampshire, The Shadows

**Swinger's Paradise is a British musical originally titled *Wonderful Life*.**

### Go Go Mania
"16 TOP ACTS with the NEW INTERNATIONAL BEAT that's ROCKIN' the WORLD!"

Produced by Harry Field  Directed by Fred Goode

**Go Go Mania is the British film *Pop Gear*, a musical compilation showing the "British Invasion." It is hosted by U.K. TV personality Jimmy Savile and the acts featured include The Animals, Herman's Hermits, Matt Monro, Peter and Gordon, The Spencer Davis Group, and The Beatles.**

May 17, 1965
*Boxoffice*
AIP  SURVEY  OF  MOVIE  EDITORS  SHOWS
PREFERENCES IN PUBLICITY MATERIAL
Hollywood- American International Pictures, as a result of a spot survey of entertainment editors in 50 daily newspapers, henceforth "will lean toward carefully prepared press kits with a different

style of news release," Milton Moritz, AIP national director of advertising and publicity, revealed this week.

The survey found that entertainment editors rarely use a story from a motion picture press book, Moritz said, adding, "They think pressbooks are old tea bags returned too often to the pot."

The majority of editors, the survey shows, prefer short news stories and behind-the-scenes features with action or off-stage photographs. Interview-type stories with good quotes from actors are also sought.

June 1965-

### Ski Party
"When the SKI'NICKS meet the SKI'CHICKS it's called SNOW A GO-GO with BIKINIS, yet!"

Produced by Gene Corman  Directed by Alan Rafkin
Starring Frankie Avalon, Dwayne Hickman, Deborah Walley, Yvonne Craig, Robert Q. Lewis

July 1965-

### How to Stuff a Wild Bikini
"IT'S THE BARE OUTLINE... of a beginners' course in BOY-GIRLSMANSHIP with a special emphasis on figures! Thrills and spills in a first time view of the wildest MOTORCYCLE RACE ever run!"

Produced by James H. Nicholson and Samuel Z. Arkoff  Directed by William Asher
Starring Annette Funicello, Dwayne Hickman, Brian Donlevy, Harvey Lembeck, John Ashley

July 5, 1965
*Boxoffice*

# AIP TO DISCONTINUE SECOND FEATURES; TO CONCENTRATE ON QUALITY FILMS

New York- "The second feature no longer has a place in today's market," James H. Nicholson, president of American International, told the trade press and magazine representatives at a luncheon at the Hemisphere Club on Thursday to introduce AIP's "Starburst of Youth" players to New York.

"Too many exhibitors are more inclined to book the top hits of the previous season as supporting fare instead of new 'B' product," he emphasized.

In addition to *How to Stuff a Wild Bikini*, for July 14 release, and *Sergeant Deadhead* for mid-August, the AIP product for the balance of 1965 will be *Die Monster Die*, starring Boris Karloff and Nick Adams, and *Planet of Terror*, starring Barry Sullivan, a science fiction horror bill for late September or October. *Dr. Goldfoot and the Girl Machine*, in Panavision and color, starring Vincent Price, Frankie Avalon, and Dwayne Hickman, will start production July 21 under Norman Taurog's direction to be released at Thanksgiving time. *Bang! You're Dead*, in color, starring Dana Andrews, Brett Halsey, and Pier Angeli for Christmas. The latter, filmed in Italy, was formerly titled *Epitaph for a Spy*.

Nicholson pointed out that *Frankenstein meets the Giant Devil Fish* is currently filming in Tokyo for a February 16 release and *War- Italian Style* will start filming in Rome on August 2 for a March 16 release date. AIP's first 1966 release will be *Mondo Taboo*, a documentary sequel to *Taboos of the World*, which will also be narrated by Vincent Price and is now shooting around the world for January showing with Salvatore Billitteri producing. The first Hollywood-based feature for 1966 release will be *Pajama Party in a Haunted House*, another teenage musical set to go before the cameras September 8 for an April 6 release date. *Trunk to Cairo* starring AudieMurphy is now shooting in Israel and Berlin for a May 4 release date.

A total of 13 features will be released during 1966, seven to be filmed in Hollywood and six to be shot abroad. In addition to the five mentioned above, they will include *Robinhood Jones*, which will begin shooting in Hollywood on January 12 for a June 22 release, with Vincent Price, Frankie Avalon, Susan Hart, and Annette Funicello starred in a costume spoof to be directed by William Asher. *Girl in the Glass Bikini* will roll in Hollywood and Palm Springs on March 9 for a July 13 release date with Annette Funicello, Dwayne Hickman, Paul Peterson, and Buster Keaton starred in the musical comedy romp. *Sergeant Deadhead Goes to Mars*, the sequel to the August 1965 release, will start April 13 for a national release August 3, again starring Frankie Avalon. *Dr. Goldfoot for President*, again starring Vincent Price, will start May 18 for a September 14 release.

Rounding out the 1966 schedule are the following: *2066 A.D.- When the Sleeper Wakes*, based on the H.G. Wells classic, an AIP-Italian coproduction to be made in Rome; *Cruise Party*, a musical to be filmed abroad with Frankie Avalon and Dwayne Hickman; *The Big Chase*, to be filmed in Hollywood starting August of 1966 with Buster Keaton in the first silent to come out of the movie capitol in many years; and *Jet Set Party*, the final project on the 1966 slate, to roll in Hollywood in September 1966 with Frankie Avalon and Annette Funicello starred and William Asher directing.

July 19, 1965
*Boxoffice*
AIP YOUTHFUL STARS CONTINUE P.A. TOURS
Hollywood- A second wave of American International Pictures stars embarked on a 14-20 day personal appearance tour last week, continuing heavy in-person plugging of company summer product- *Ski Party, How to Stuff a Wild Bikini*, and *Sergeant Deadhead*. James H. Nicholson was host to a number of the nation's top exhibitors at a party held at New York's Gaslight Club to introduce nine of AIP's bright young stars and starlets: Aron Kincaid, Ed Garner, Bobbi Shaw, Susan Hart, Jo Collins, Mary Hughes, Sue Hamilton, Patti Chandler, and Salli Sachse.

July 26, 1965
*Boxoffice*
AIP INFORMS EXHIBITORS OF LIFE MAGAZINE PLUG

**Aron Kincaid (1940-2011) appeared in five AIP productions.**

Hollywood- American International Pictures has made special purchase of some 5,000 copies of the current *Life Magazine* for special mailing to top exhibitors across the country to call attention to Alan Levy's laudatory article on the young film production distribution company, according to Milton I. Moritz, AIP advertising-publicity director.

Principally an editorial feature with photos of only AIP toppers James H. Nicholson and Samuel Z. Arkoff and AIP stars Annette Funicello, Frankie Avalon, and Buster Keaton, the article is entitled "Peek-a-Boo Sex- or How to Fill a Drive-In." It runs for six pages and tells the story of AIP's success as a Hollywood filmmaking newcomer with its pace-setting terror films, surfing musicals, and constant search for new gimmicks.

*The Film Daily*
July 29, 1965
7-DAY AIP FILM FESTIVAL TO BE STAGED IN MEXICO CITY
Mexico City- Mexico's Producciones Sotomayor will stage a seven-day American International Pictures film festival here starting today. During the festival, AIP President James H. Nicholson and Executive Vice President Samuel Z. Arkoff will be cited as producers having had the greatest impact on international teenage audiences during the past decade.

August 1965-

**Sergeant Deadhead**
"The Funniest Foul Up of the Space Age!"

Produced by James H.Nicholson and Samuel Z. Arkoff  Directed by Norman Taurog
Starring Frankie Avalon, Deborah Walley, Cesar Romero, Fred Clark, Eve Arden, John Ashley

Film Review- *Sergeant Deadhead and Ski Party*

*New York Times* (October 23, 1965) by Harry Gilroy-
AVALON DOUBLE BILL
Tapioca pudding is nice, but three hours of it as served in two Frankie Avalon pictures is faintly horrifying. In the deep-dish of this pair of American International pictures, Mr. Avalon keeps a missile base on Red Alert while he is on the alert for a redhead, played by a natural-born kisser, Deborah Walley. This work is *Sergeant Deadhead* and Mr. Avalon plays both that sergeant and another who is ordered to impersonate him.
In *Ski Party*, along come Frankie and Deborah again. The

**Frankie Avalon, Harvey Lembeck, and John Ashley
in *Sergeant Deadhead*.**

scenery of the Sawtooth National Forest is gorgeous and a busload of girls who agitate their bikinis and ski pants at the camera are willowy. When will this couple play Romeo and Juliet? It seems awfully inevitable.

September 1965-

September 20, 1965
*Boxoffice*
SPECIAL COLOR FEATURETTE ON PRODUCT READY BY AIP
Hollywood- A special color product featurette, highlighted by sequences from the spoof comedy *Dr. Goldfoot and the Bikini Machine*, currently in production, has been completed by American International Picture heads James H. Nicholson and Samuel Z. Arkoff for showing at the company's annual luncheon honoring delegates to the Allied States convention at the Penn-Shearton

Hotel, Pittsburgh, October 13.

The theme of the AIP luncheon this year is The Golden Magic of Showmanship. The special featurette will also be shown on October 28 in the Coconut Grove of the Ambassador Hotel during a similar luncheon for delegates attending the Theatre Owners Ass'n convention in Los Angeles.

## WORLD PROMOTION TOUR SET FOR AIP ACTORS

Los Angeles- American International Pictures executives James H. Nicholson and Samuel Z. Arkoff this week announced a worldwide tour of young Hollywood talent to promote a motion picture, the film industry, and goodwill on behalf of the U.S. The globe-girding trip will send stars Frankie Avalon, Susan Hart, and three AIP starlets on a 30-day tour of 18 cities in 13 countries starting from here November 1.

They will promote *Dr. Goldfoot and the Bikini Machine* through public appearances and meetings with local press and exhibitors. Nicholson, AIP president, will accompany the group. The starlets making the tour are Bobbi Shaw, Salli Sachse, and Mary Hughes.

October 1965-

### *Die Monster Die/Planet of the Vampires*
"The FANTASTIC vs. the FRIGHTENING! Two unearthly, spine tingling adventures!"

*Die Monster Die* (aka *Monster of Terror*)
Produced by Pat Green  Directed by Daniel Haller
Starring Boris Karloff, Nick Adams, Susan Farmer

*Planet of the Vampires* (aka *Terror in Space*)
Produced by Fulvio Lucisano  Directed by Mario Bava
Starring Barry Sullivan, Norma Bengell, Angel Aranda, Evi Marandi

From the pressbook-

## KARLOFF RETURNS AS MONSTER, BARRY SULLIVAN STAR IN NEW COLOR AND SCOPE THRILLER

Boris Karloff returns as a monster for the first time in thirty years and his first non-Frankenstein creature role while Barry Sullivan stars as leader of spacemen exploring a mysterious planet in a faraway galaxy in two terrifying science fiction thrillers from American International.

Karloff stars in *Die Monster Die,* chilling color and scope tale of a mysterious monster-breeding object from outer space which terrifies a quiet country family. Nick Adams and Suzan Farmer also star in the fantastic adventure film, which blends science fiction with old-fashioned terror suspense.

Sullivan stars with Norma Bengell in the companion color and scope feature, *Planet of the Vampires,* which takes place on a mysterious Earth-like planet of a distant sun. What happens when Sullivan and his fellow space explorers try to do battle with an intelligent but unseen foe with human-like qualities makes for spine-chilling science fiction action.

*Die Monster Die* and *Planet of the Vampires* make for one of the most unusual and most imaginative film combinations ever paired on theatre screens. It's a double dose of nightmare-producing, terror thrill-paced motion pictures.

## PROMOTION

Issue WARNINGS to patrons that the combination of *Die Monster Die* and *Planet of the Vampires* is "not for the weak of heart," "the scared," or "the nervous." Warn them via snipes posted on all display paper, in your newspaper ads, and herald it via radio and TV.

November 1965-

### Dr. Goldfoot and the Bikini Machine
"It has a KISS-BUTTON and a KILL-BUTTON. You have to know which button to push!"

Produced by James H. Nicholson and Samuel Z. Arkoff  Directed

by Norman Taurog
Starring Vincent Price, Frankie Avalon, Dwayne Hickman, Susan Hart, Jack Mullaney

Film Reviews- *Dr. Goldfoot and the Bikini Machine*

*Hollywood Citizen News* (November 12, 1965)
Highly imaginative from start to finish, *Dr. Goldfoot and the Bikini Machine* cleverly combines elements of sci-fi, horror, and beach films with a spoof on James Bond. This is certain to make it a hit with teenagers. And surprisingly enough, adults will enjoy it, too. All players performed well, but Vincent Price, as always, stole the show.

**Dwayne Hickman, Frankie Avalon, Vincent Price, and Jack Mullaney in *Dr. Goldfoot and the Bikini Machine*.**

*New York Times* (February 17, 1966) by Howard Thompson

Occasionally, it's diverting to see just how bad or unfunny a supposed laugh-package of a movie can be. Meet *Dr. Goldfoot and the Bikini Machine*. Is there anything at all funny about it? Yes-

Fred Clark. Otherwise, this new American International goody is pure, dull junk. The withering sarcasm of Mr. Clark is welcome, as usual, from the bald veteran. But, brother, the picture! What a mess and what a waste!

November 2, 1965

*The Hollywood Reporter*

ABC-TV AIRING AIP DOCUMENTARY

American International Pictures is the key subject for an ABC-TV News documentary, "The New Hollywood," to be aired on "Scope" Nov. 13 at 10:30 pm. Francis X. Bushman, Patsy Kelly, director Norman Taurog, writer Louis "Deke" Heyward, actor Aron Kincaid, a brace of AIP beach beauties, and company bosses James H. Nicholson and Samuel Z. Arkoff comment on movies for the multi-million dollar youth market.

November 15, 1965

*Boxoffice*

AIP HONORS SUSAN HART AT 'GOLDFOOT' RECEPTION

New York- Susan Hart, American International contract player and star of *Dr. Goldfoot and the Bikini Machine*, was guest of honor at a "Goldfoot" party in the Gold Room of the Tower Suites on Thursday, November 4, prior to a sneak preview of the AIP November release at the RKO 86th Street Theatre.

James H. Nicholson, AIP president, and Samuel Z. Arkoff, executive vice president, and Leon J. Blender, vice president in charge of sales and distribution, were hosts at the party and screening.

The "Gold" motif dominated the cocktail party as gold favors and door prizes were distributed, including gold-covered gifts from Barracini Candies, Harriet Hubbard Ayer, Faberge, Dorothy Gray, Germaine Monteil, and Lanvin.

Miss Hart had previously starred for American International in *Pajama Party* and *War-Gods of the Deep.*

November 22, 1965
*Boxoffice*
## SUSAN HART IN LONDON FOR 'GOLDFOOT' PROMOTION
New York- Susan Hart, American International star, left for London last week on the first leg of a worldwide promotional tour for *Dr. Goldfoot and the Bikini Machine.* She made a two-day stopover here to plug the film on radio, television, and in press interviews. She had previously participated in premiers of the film in Wenatchee, Wash. and in San Francisco and Los Angeles.

In London, Miss Hart was joined by co-star Frankie Avalon for the tour of principal cities on four continents.

November 29, 1965
*Boxoffice*
## AIP SETS 18 FILMS FOR '66; FORMS FOREIGN SUBSIDIARY
New York- American International will release 16 to 18 pictures in 1966 and will set up another subsidiary, Trans American Films, to distribute art and specialty films which James H. Nicholson, president, and Samuel Z. Arkoff, executive vice president, will obtain from foreign sources, Nicholson told the trade press at a luncheon at Sardi's Restaurant Friday, November 19.

The new subsidiary, which will release about five films a year, is similar to other major company subsidiaries for foreign product.

American International will start off the New Year with a special one-shot showing of *The T.N.T. Show,* a live show to be filmed before a live audience in Los Angeles by Henry Saperstein November 29 with 12 acts of the musical variety, including Joan Baez, Petula Clark, Bo Didly, The Byrds, Ray Charles, Nina Simone, Roger Miller, Donovan (the English Bob Dylan), Lovin' Spoonful, and David McCallum performing in the Electrofilm presentation.

*The T.N.T. Show* will be a special New Year's Eve feature in over 400 theaters in the U.S. and will be nationally released January 26.

During the first six months of 1966, three pictures are scheduled to be filmed in Hollywood, one of them starring Fabian, who has been signed to a multiple-picture, five-year contract by AIP. His first picture, *Fireball 500*, with Annette Funicello co-starring, will be released next June.

Among the other big 1966 releases, *Bikini Party in a Haunted House*, in Pathecolor and Panavision, starring Tommy Kirk, Deborah Walley, Aron Kincaid, Nancy Sinatra, and Claudia Martin, with established stars Patsy Kelly, Basil Rathbone, and Francis X. Bushman, is to be released at Easter; *War Italian Style*, in color, starring Buster Keaton, Martha Hyer and Fred Clark, is to be released in May; *The Girl in the Glass Bikini*, a science fiction comedy with music, to be made in Pathecolor and Panavision, starring Frankie Avalon, Annette Funicello, and Aron Kincaid, is for July release.

In the works is *Dr. Goldfoot and the 'S' Bomb*, a sequel to the current 'Goldfoot' feature, which will star Vincent Price, Avalon, and Miss Hart, to be released next August, *Frankenstein Conquers the World*, starring Nick Adams, *Invasion of the Night Things, File 77*, and *Trunk to Cairo*. The latter, being filmed in Europe with Audie Murphy, Marianne Koch, and George Sanders starred, is one of three to be co-produced in England or Italy. All these will be released later in 1966.

*The Wild, Weird World of Dr. Goldfoot*, inspired by the AIP 'Goldfoot' feature, was telecast November 18 by ABC-TV as AI-TV's debut in feature TV production and several other television "specials" will be produced within the next six months under the direction of Louis Heyward, now head of AI-TV production.

December 1965-

December 30, 1965
*The Big T.N.T. Show*

**This was a special one night showing of a filmed stage concert featuring Joan Baez, The Byrds, Ray Charles, Petula Clark,**

Donovan, The Lovin' Spoonful, and others. The film went into general release in January 1966.

# CHAPTER TWELVE
# 1966

January 1966-

*Secret Agent Fireball/Spy in Your Eye*

*Secret Agent Fireball*
Produced by Mino Loy   Directed by Martin Donan (Luciano Martino)
Starring Richard Harrison, Dominique Boschero, Wandisa Guida

*Spy in Your Eye*
Produced by Fulvio Lucisano and Lucio Marcuzzo   Directed by Vittorio Sala
Starring Brett Halsey, Pier Angeli, Dana Andrews

These were two Italian films picked up by AIP. The original titles are, respectively, *The Spies Kill in Beirut* and *Berlin, Appointment for the Spies*. *Berlin, Appointment for the Spies* underwent a number of title changes by AIP before they finally settled on *Spy in Your Eye*. It had previously been called *Epitaph for a Spy* and *Bang! You're Dead*.

January 3, 1966
*Boxoffice*
LONDON REPORT by Anthony Gruner
James H. Nicholson, president of American International Pictures, was guest of honor at a press reception in London, England, hosted by Nat Cohen and Stuart Levy of Anglo Amalgamated in the Pinafore Room at the Savoy Hilton Hotel for the global launching of AIP's release *Dr. Goldfoot and the Bikini Machine.* The mystery-suspense comedy stars Vincent Price, Susan Hart, Frankie Avalon, and Dwayne Hickman.

Guests at the Savoy reception included Miss Hart and a number of Warner-Pathe, ABC, and Anglo Amalgamated executives. Also present were representatives of the British and American trade press as well as Fleet Street personalities.

At this press reception, Jim Nicholson and Susan Hart also announced their plans to marry, which they did shortly thereafter.

January 17, 1966
*Boxoffice*
TO PROMOTE AIP FILMS WITH LIVE SHOW UNITS
Hollywood- American International Pictures has finalized arrangements with the John F. Dugan Agency to develop and produce variety show entertainment units keyed to the theme of AIP's "beach and bikini" theatrical films, which Dugan will book for "live" appearances throughout the United States. The deal is another facet of company showmanship designed to increase theatre attendance, according to AIP heads James H. Nicholson and Samuel Z. Arkoff.

**This wedding photo of Susan Hart was distributed by the AIP publicity department.**

The new traveling Beach Gang Variety Show units will feature personalities who have appeared in AIP's popular beach films, bolstered by other well-known stars who have worked in AIP pictures.

Dugan emphasized that while each season brings out numerous touring companies and concert attractions, this is believed to be the first time a major motion picture company has developed and produced a stage attraction featuring its contract players "live" on a nationwide show tour.

January 31, 1966
*Boxoffice*
## AIP DEAL CONCLUDED WITH LANDAU-UNGER
Hollywood- American International Pictures executives James H. Nicholson and Samuel Z. Arkoff this week confirmed the conclusion of negotiations between AIP and the Ely Landau-

Oliver Unger Co. for distribution of the latter company's films. The agreement includes 20 Landau-Unger films and covers television rights to the pictures acquired for theatrical distribution. TV sales will be through AIP's subsidiary, AI-TV.

The 20 pictures to be distributed by AIP are: *The Pawnbroker; File 777;* the English-language version of *La Dolce Vita; Bang You're Dead,* formerly *I Spy, You Spy, We All Spy; The Umbrellas of Cherbourg; The Servant; The Eleanor Roosevelt Story; King and Country; The Fool Killer; The Girl Getters; Love Life of the Teenager; Life Upside Down; 90 Degrees in the Shade; The Sands of Beersheba; The Trial; Rope Around His Neck; Three Sisters; Rocco and His Brothers; The Swindle;* and *Long Day's Journey Into Night.*


February 1966-

February 7, 1966
*Boxoffice*
## AIP LISTS ITS PEAK LINEUP OF 19 FILMS FOR RELEASE
Hollywood- American International Pictures, just two films less from finalizing a 19-feature release schedule, announces the most extensive and diversified product lineup in its 12-year history. Ten films are in the cans (including four acquired from the Ely Landau-Oliver Unger group), a new record in the AIP backlog- and not a single beach picture is on the list.

The lineup will be AIP-labeled in contrast to the Trans American art subsidiary separate release schedule.

AIP's releases for September and October are not yet revealed due to incomplete negotiations for two important motion pictures. A list of AIP's "Big 19" and national release dates follow:

January 26: *The Big T.N.T. Show,* folk and rock music variety show.

February 23: *The Pawnbroker,* Rod Steiger, Brock Peters, Geraldine Fitzgerald.

March 2: Horror Combination, *Queen of Blood* in color, John Saxon, Basil Rathbone, Judi Meredith, and *Blood Bath,* William Campbell, Lori Saunders, Marissa Mathis.

March 16: *File 777,* Vittorio Gassman, Robert Ryan, Henry Fonda.

April 6: *Ghost in the Invisible Bikini,* color and Panavision, Tommy Kirk, Deborah Walley, Basil Rathbone, Harvey Lembeck, Jesse White, Aron Kincaid, Nancy Sinatra, Quinn O'Hara, Patsy Kelly, Boris Karloff, and Susan Hart.

April 27: *La Dolce Vita,* Marcello Mastroianni, Anita Ekberg, Anouk Aimee, Nadia Grey, and Yvonne Furneaux; new English-language version.

May 4: Woody Allen's *What's Up Tiger Lily?* in color-'Scope.

May 11: *The Great Spy Chase* in 'Scope, Lino Ventura, Bernard Blair.

June 29: *Fireball 500,* in color, Frankie Avalon, Annette Funicello, Fabian (Southern U.S. pre-release on June 8).

June 15: *Bang You're Dead,* in color and 'Scope, Tony Randall, Terry-Thomas, Senta Berger, Herbert Lom.

July 20: *Hell's Angels on Wheels,* color- 'Scope, cast not yet set.

August 10: *War Italian Style,* color, Buster Keaton, Fred Clark, Martha Hyer.

August 17: *Trunk to Cairo,* color, Audie Murphy, George Sanders, Marianne Koch.

September: to be announced.

October: to be announced.

November 23: *Dr. Goldfoot and the S-Bomb,* color and 'Scope, Vincent Price and Frankie Avalon.

December: *Land of Prehistoric Women,* color, cast to be set.

March 1966-

## *Queen of Blood/Blood Bath*
"A New High in BLOOD CHILLING HORROR!"

*Blood Bath* (aka *Track of the Vampire*)
Produced by Jack Hill   Directed by John Hill and Stephanie Rothman
Starring William Campbell, Marrisa Mathes, Linda Saunders

*Queen of Blood* (aka *Planet of Blood*)
Produced by George Edwards   Directed by Curtis Harrington
Starring John Saxon, Basil Rathbone, Judi Meredith, Florence Marly, Dennis Hopper

Film Review- *Queen of Blood* (See *Three in the Attic* review)

**Queen of Blood is one of three films that AIP concocted using footage from a 1962 Russian science fiction movie they had acquired called *Planeta Burg* (*Planet of Storms*). Queen of Blood and *Voyage to the Prehistoric Planet* were both directed by Curtis Harrington, although he used the pseudonym John Sebastian for the latter. The third film was *Voyage to the Planet of Prehistoric Women*, directed by Peter Bogdanovich using the pseudonym Derek Thomas.**

March 4, 1966
*The Film Daily*
AIP STAGES RECEPTION FOR ANNETTE FUNICELLO
Annette Funicello, who is in New York to do a taping for this Sunday's Ed Sullivan TV Show, was given a reception at the Regency Hotel yesterday by American International Pictures, with which she has a non-exclusive contract.

With Miss Funicello to meet the press and fan magazine representatives was her husband-agent, Jack Gilardi.

Miss Funicello's next starring film under her AIP contract, *Fireball 500,* a musical about stock car racing in which Frankie Avalon, Fabian, and Aron Kincaid will be her co-stars, was the number on topic discussed at the reception. The film is slated to roll on the West Coast next week and to be released in June by AIP.

*Fireball 500* will mark Miss Funicello's seventh starring appearance in an AIP film. The Pathecolor-Panavision picture will be her first since she played in the company's *How to Stuff a Wild Bikini* about a year ago.. In the interim, she has been seen on the screen only in cameo flashes in AIP's *Ski Party* and *Dr. Goldfoot and the Bikini Machine*. Miss Funicello was forced into inactivity because of a date with the stork. The Gilardis' first child, Gina Luree, was born Oct. 17, 1965.

Miss Funicello also reported that after *Fireball 500*, she will star in AIP's *Robinhood Jones*.

After that, she will be starred by AIP in *The Jet Breed*. It was disclosed that other starring roles were being lined up by the company for her.

**Annette Funicello (1942-2013) appeared in ten AIP productions.**

March 28, 1966
*Boxoffice*
AIP'S NICHOLSON TO ROME FOR 'GOLDFOOT' FILMING
New York- James H. Nicholson, president of American International, and his actress-wife Susan Hart stopped off on their way from Hollywood to Rome, where he will be involved in pre-production work on *Dr. Goldfoot and the S-Bomb*, which will start filming there in April.

Susan Hart will play a machine-produced robot in the new *Goldfoot* picture; this following her role in *Ghost in the Invisible Bikini*, the company's April-Easter release. Vincent Price and Frankie Avalon, who will co-star in the new picture, which will be made in Panavision and Pathecolor, will leave for Rome late in March. *Dr. Goldfoot and the S-Bomb* is scheduled for release Thanksgiving 1966.


April 1966-

***The Ghost in the Invisible Bikini***
"There's something BLOOD CURDLING for everyone!"

Produced by James H. Nicholson and Samuel Z. Arkoff Directed by Don Weis
Starring Tommy Kirk, Deborah Walley, Susan Hart, Boris Karloff, Aron Kincaid

**Despite the announcement that she would star in the Dr. Goldfoot sequel, Susan Hart never made another movie for AIP following *The Ghost in the Invisible Bikini*. This was at the insistence of Sam Arkoff, who resented her marriage to Jim Nicholson. After appearing in episodes of the TV series *The Wild, Wild West* and *Death Valley Days*, her acting career was over.**

***The Dirty Game*** (formerly announced as *File 777*)
"THE REAL TRUE STORY... behind the girls... glamor and gimmicks of the world's most dangerous business... SPYING!"

Produced by Richard Hellman    Directed by Terence Young,
Christian Jaque, Carlo Lizzani
Starring Henry Fonda, Vittorio Gassman, Annie Girardot, Robert
Ryan

From the pressbook-
FAST, FURIOUS ACTION SPEEDS *DIRTY GAME*
Fast and furious action spanning two continents as Allied
counter-intelligence battles enemy agents is the basic ingredient
of American International's *The Dirty Game.*

The adventure thriller stars Henry Fonda, Robert Ryan,
Vittorio Gassman, Annie Girardot, and Bourvil.

*The Dirty Game* tells the exciting story of the tough and
dangerous daily work of professional spies- depicted with no holds
barred and stripped of the glamour of many other films on the
same subject.

May 1966-

### *The Great Spy Chase*
"RUN... love takes you where the spies are... PURSUE... women
who are curved like weapons... HIDE... with the one you seek...
and the sparks fly upward... *The Great Spy Chase*. Thru the back
alleys of Beirut... into the boudoirs of Rome!"

Produced and Directed by Georges Lautner
Starring Lino Ventura, Bernard Blair, Francis Blanche, Mireille
Darc, Charles Millot

May 2, 1966
*The Film Daily*
AIP STEPS UP WITH $3 MIL. BUDGET PIC
Hollywood- American International will co-produce a new $3
million motion picture, the first in company history at so large a
budget, it was announced Friday by AIP top executives James H
Nicholson and Samuel Z. Arkoff.

The film, to be made in association with Harry Alan Towers

on location in Ireland this summer, is Jules Verne's *Rocket to the Moon* with a cast that so far includes Terry-Thomas, Gert Frobe, and Lionel Jeffries.

May 9, 1966
*Boxoffice*
AMERICAN INT'L BUDGETS $16 MILLION ON NINE
PRODUCTIONS FOR 1967
Hollywood- American International Pictures, with a 1967 production schedule calling for a $16,000,000 outlay on nine productions- three of these each in the $3,000,000 class- is entering the "grand scale phase" of company development, it was announced here by James H. Nicholson, president, and Samuel Z. Arkoff, vice president.

The three productions in the $3,000,000 class will begin with the Jules Verne science fiction classic *Rocket to the Moon*, slated to start location filming in Ireland in August. The other multi-million dollar productions, now in final negotiations, include the screen adaptation of a major Broadway musical classic and an ultra-spectacular musical comedy. One will be made in Europe and the other in Hollywood.

Four Hollywood-based productions, each costing more than $1,000,000, will be led off in July with filming of the NASCAR auto racing thriller, *Malibu 500*. This will be followed by a $1,250,000 as-yet-untitled "high camp hillbilly comedy" to start in September and the $1,000,000 horror suspense mystery *IT*, based on the Richard Matheson original story, "Being," shooting simultaneously. The fourth Hollywood production will be *Girl in the Glass Castle*, scheduled to start in November. Two big overseas co-productions include the $1,350,000 H.G. Wells classic *2067 A.D.- When the Sleeper Wakes*, to be made in London utilizing a profusion of special effects, and the million-dollar remake of the horror classic *The Golem*, to be filmed in Europe in November.

The company has a record 11 features "in the can" for release during the remainder of 1966 and early 1967. These include *Fireball 500*, stock car racing film; the Roger Corman shocker,

*All the Wild Angels*, set for July release; the uncut English-language version of *La Dolce Vita; Bang You're Dead*, a chase yarn filmed in Marrekesh starring Tony Randall, Terry-Thomas, and Senta Berger; *Tokyo Olympiad; Tarzan and the Valley of Gold; War Italian Style; Trunk to Cairo*, filmed on location in Israel; *Violent Journey*, adapted from the bestseller "The Fool Killer"; *Frankenstein Conquers the World*, Tokyo-made production highlighting the Japanese use of miniatures; and *The Man from Cocody*, an action drama starring Jean Marais.

June 1966-

**Fireball 500**
"THEY LIVE FROM SPINOUT TO CRACK UP... and they love as fast as they can get it!"

Produced by James H. Nicholson and Samuel Z. Arkoff Directed by William Asher
Starring Frankie Avalon, Annette Funicello, Fabian, Chill Wills, Harvey Lembeck, Julie Parrish

Film Review- *Fireball 500*

*New York Times* (November 24, 1966) by Bosley Crowther
*Fireball 500*, a real turkey about stock racing, is one tough old bird that should have been cremated, not cooked. With those teenage singing idols Frankie Avalon and Annette Funicello at the helm, this asinine little package from American International thudded into the circuits yesterday.

It has one thing alone to recommend it- some fast-flying documentary footage in color of racing autos in whizzing tangles on various tracks and speedways.

For some odd reason, Mr. Avalon, as an ace driver, and the mewing Miss Funicello are officially pried apart, paring off with Julia [sic] Parrish and Fabian, if anybody cares an iota.

June 16, 1966
*The Film Daily*
AIP SETS $19-MILLION BUDGET- NICHOLSON &
ARKOFF IN EXPANSIVE MOOD; MAJOR STATUS
NEXT? by Edward Lipton
American International Pictures, with half a dozen top-budget
productions due next year, has upped its overall production budget
for the next twelve months to $19 million. This does not include
the costs of films it will distribute only. The increased AIP activity
was outlined at a trade press luncheon in New York yesterday by
President James H. Nicholson and executive vice president Samuel
Z. Arkoff.

Nicholson and Arkoff, in a private interview with *The Film
Daily*, noted the expectation that within four or five years, the
company will be making its pictures at the budget level of a top
major today. They also detailed company thinking with regard to
an upcoming changeover to an emphasis on "protest" pictures.

"The tastes of youth in motion pictures vary and change
quickly, just as they do in music," Nicholson stated. "Three or four
years ago, surfing songs were popular. Today, ballads and protest
songs are increasingly popular. It's as though the youthful audience
has swerved from its interest in jiggling on the sand."

Nicholson pointed out that future AIP productions would be
in three directions, "protest, soap opera, and action," in order to
attract today's young audience.

The AIP president cited *Fireball 500, Wild Angels,* and *Rebel
500* as pointing toward this type of film. In the planning stages,
according to Arkoff, is a picture on LSD. Still others may deal
with young marrieds.

Nicholson and Arkoff noted that as part of the company's
higher-budget co-productions program, AIP will put at least six
productions into the works for release next year. In the multi-
million dollar class will be *Rocket to the Moon* for release next
Easter, starring Bing Crosby, Terry-Thomas, Alfred [sic] Hyde-
White, and Gert Frobe. Other big pictures include *Guns of Anzio*
with Richard Widmark and *The 1,000,000 Eyes of Sumuru,* to
be made in Hong Kong with British, German, and Hong Kong
interests.

AIP, which is now deriving some 50% of its revenue from some 5,000 drive-ins, is planning to distribute 19 or 20 pictures a year in addition to such pix as *Macabro* and *Sex and the Teenager* via its Trans American subsidiary.

Yesterday's luncheon was attended by Peter Fonda, star of *Wild Angels*, which deals with motorcycling youth, and AIP contractees Mary Hughes and Sally [sic] Sachse.

June 20, 1966
*Boxoffice*
AIP ALLOTS $19,000,000 ON 20 FILMS FOR '66-67
New York- American International's production commitment for 1966-67 has been hiked to $19,000,000 from the previously announced $16,000,000, James H. Nicholson and Samuel Z. Arkoff told the tradepress at a luncheon at the Warwick Hotel Wednesday, June 15.

The new production schedule will comprise 20 features, including five top-budget pictures:

*Rocket to the Moon,* based on Jules Verne classic to be shot entirely in Ireland; *Guns of Anzio,* a war spectacle to be filmed in Italy; *2267 A.D.- When the Sleeper Wakes,* based on H.G. Wells classic to be filmed in Prague; and a fourth just set, *The 1,000,000 Eyes of Sumaru,* based on Sax Rohmer story, which will be an American-English-German co-production starring George Nader, Wilfred Hyde-White, and Shirley Eaton, to be filmed in Hong Kong starting in July. The fifth, Edgar Allan Poe's *The Gold Bug,* will be made in Toronto this fall with Vincent Price starred.

In addition to *Fireball 500* and *The Girl Getters* for June release, *The Wild Angels,* set for July, plus *Bang Bang You're Dead,* set for national release in August. The AIP releases for the rest of 1966 are *What's Up Tiger Lily?* in color with Woody Allen starred for September release; *Dr. Goldfoot and the Girl Bombs,* in color starring Vincent Price and Fabian, in November; and *Circus of Blood,* in color starring Christopher Lee and Leo Genn, and *Voyage to a Prehistoric Planet,* in color starring Basil Rathbone and Faith Domergue, a horror combination for December.

Already set for Hollywood filming are *Rebel 500*, a stock car racing picture in color and Panavision starring Fabian and set for January 1967 release, and *The Hatfields and the McCoys*, a musical in color and Panavision starring Frankie Avalon and Annette Funicello.

July 1966-

### The Wild Angels
"Their credo is violence...Their God is hate and they call themselves THE WILD ANGELS"

Produced and Directed by Roger Corman
Starring Peter Fonda, Nancy Sinatra, Bruce Dern, Diane Ladd

Samuel Z. Arkoff: "I think it was *Life Magazine* that had a cover on the Hell's Angels. I looked at the cover and said 'Jesus, this is a natural.' So we called up Roger Corman. I'm sure people from other companies saw that cover too and maybe they didn't think twice about it because it was a tough subject."

Charles Griffith (Writer): "I based the screenplay on stories that Roger and I heard hanging around the Angels at a little place in Venice called The Gunk Shop. Roger went down there once and he sat with a grin from ear to ear the whole evening. They were all so funky- putting us on. I recorded a lot of the speech. It was pretty obvious what sort of people they were, but it was what they believed they were that was interesting."

Film Reviews- *The Wild Angels*

*Time* (September 9, 1966)- VAROOM WITHOUT A VIEW
For the first time since *The Wild One* (1954), Hollywood has moved in for a closeup of the big, barbaric motorcycle gangs of Southern California. Directed by Roger Corman, a cut-rate

314

master of the macabre who seems to work better with spiders than he does with actors, *The Wild Angels* is a sleazy, synthetic retread that will probably take a long skid through U.S. grind houses. However, the film may well make a mark in Europe- the Italians have selected it to represent the U.S. at the Venice Film Festival- where a large audience likes to be shown how beastly Americans are.

*Newsweek* (August 15, 1966)- FALLEN ANGELS
"One of our saving graces," [Sam] Arkoff says, "is that we look upon this most ridiculous of businesses and our own role in it with humor." But the company has lost its sense of humor, and its innocence, in the process of growing up and undertaking supposedly adult themes. This ugly piece of trash, in which aspiring Fascists wear Iron Crosses and decorate their haunt with swastikas, revels in the shock value of murder, mob violence, gratuitous brutality, and a squalid rape in a chapel during a funeral. De Sade would have stayed for two shows.

*Independent Film Journal*- Some advance spectators were completely repelled by it, but let this reviewer go on record as saying that *The Wild Angels* is a masterpiece and the controversy surrounding it is all to the good. AIP heads Nicholson and Arkoff deserve credit for the tremendous courage involved in financing so strong and outspoken a motion picture.

*Los Angeles Times*- *The Wild Angels* is an exciting, original film that captures an authentic slice of contemporary American life that speaks volumes for the world we live in today.

**Frankenstein Conquers the World/Tarzan and the Valley of Gold**
"The Biggest BLOCK-BUSTER COMBO of the Year!... from American International"

*Frankenstein Conquers the World*
Produced by Tomoyuki Tanaka  Directed by Ishiro Honda

Starring Nick Adams, Tadao Takashima, Kumi Mizuno, Yoshio Tsuchiya

*Tarzan and the Valley of Gold*
Produced by Sy Weintraub  Directed by Robert Day
Starring Mike Henry, Nancy Kovack, David Opatashu, Manuel Padilla Jr, Don Megowan

Film review- *Tarzan and the Valley of Gold*

**Mike Henry in *Tarzan and the Valley of Gold*.**

*New York Times* (March 30, 1967)
*Tarzan and the Valley of Gold* does offer a few random amusements for the adult patron who, by some peculiar twist of fate, happens to see the picture unaccompanied by a small child. There is, for example, that memorable moment when this jet-age

Tarzan, who has been wearing a wash n'wear suite and carrying a briefcase, prepares to pursue the villain into the Mexican jungles.

"All I need," he says grimly to his friend, "is a knife, some rope, and a piece of soft leather."

In the next scene, he is wearing a loincloth, which just goes to illustrate the theme of this curiously witless updating of Edgar Rice Burroughs: You can take Tarzan out of Africa, but you can't take Africa out of Tarzan.

*Macabro* (a Trans American release)
"See the World in the Raw!"

Produced by Guido Giambartoleomei    Directed by Romolo Marcellini
Narrated by Marvin Miller

From the pressbook-
*MACABRO* CAMERAS PROBE MAN'S FESTIVALS AND FETISHES
A camera's-eye view of some of man's strangest festivals and fetishes rolls across the screen when the new Trans American shocker opens.

A follow-up of such pictures as *Mondo Cane* and *Taboos of the World*, this new offering is highlighted by such spectacles as a festival in which tiny children are hung as decorations on a parade float, much like baubles on a Christmas tree.

Educational as well as entertaining, *Macabro* was obviously filmed under secret circumstances. The film is one of the most comprehensive and shocking to ever probe into the weird ways of some of the world's people and far outdistances anything that has been done before.

*The Film Daily*
July 1, 1966
AMERICAN INTERNATIONAL ENDING DUBBING; ALL FILMING IN ENGLISH
by Louis Pelegrine
American International Pictures is "getting out of the dubbing

field" and henceforth, all its product "will be shot in English." AIP's decision to take this step was reported by Stanley E. Dudelson, vice president of American International Television, at a press luncheon at the Absinthe House that had been set up for the purpose of announcing AI-TV's achievement of a new peak in production and acquisition activities.

Dudelson explained that AIP is giving up "ordinary" dubbed films because it believes that "the market for such pictures is disappearing." According to him, the company feels there are so many badly dubbed films that the motion picture business is being harmed.

August 1966-

***Bang Bang You're Dead*** (aka ***Our Man in Marrakesh*** )
"STRANGE GIRLS IN HIS ROOM... LOADED GUNS IN HIS BACK... looks like it'll be a bang-up vacation!"

Produced by Harry Alan Towers  Directed by Don Sharp
Starring Tony Randall, Senta Berger, Herbert Lom, Wilfred Hyde White, Terry-Thomas

August 5, 1966
*The Film Daily*
WINTERS VICE CROSBY IN *ROCKET TO THE MOON*
Hollywood- Jonathan Winters, going into orbit recently in his movie career, is being wooed to replace Bing Crosby in the forthcoming Harry Towers multimillion dollar space feature *Rocket to the Moon*. Deal, which would have Winters playing P.T. Barnum, is contingent on switching the launch date of *Rocket to the Moon* to next spring.

September 1966-

September 12, 1966
*Boxoffice*

## AIP SELLS 'WILD BIKINI' TO CBS-TV FOR 1967
New York- American International Television has sold *How to Stuff a Wild Bikini*, color film released to theaters in 1965, to the CBS-TV network for telecasting "sometime in 1967," according to Stanley Dudelson, AI-TV vice president.

The sale of *Wild Bikini* follows that of *Beach Party*, which was released to theaters in 1963, also to CBS for telecasting in 1966. Other AIP films in the "Beach" series are currently being negotiated for, Dudelson said.

*Watu-Hatari*, an African jungle adventure series to be co-produced with Associated British Pathe, will start shooting on location in Kenya in October for a minimum of 26 half-hour color shows and in late October, AI-TV and ABC-TV of England will begin co-production of *The Solarnauts*, a science fiction half-hour series in color, in England.

September 16, 1966
*Boxoffice*
## NICHOLSON ANNOUNCES AIP'PROTEST' FILMS
Hollywood- American International will embark immediately on an expanded program of so-called "protest" motion pictures dealing dramatically with realistic commentary on our society and times, company president James H. Nicholson told a luncheon press conference at the Beverly Hills Hotel on Tuesday, September 11.

Outstanding in the "new protest" feature lineup for 1966-67 will be a new imaginative, but hard-hitting drama titled *The End*, which deals with a completely automated society existing 2,000 years hence, which is completely dependent on exotic and bizarre stimuli as a way of life. Roger Corman, producer-director of *The Wild Angels*, will produce and direct. Charles Griffith is currently writing the screenplay. The premise will bear a striking resemblance to the inner decay which marked the fall of the Roman Empire.

Included in the same category of upcoming films will be *The Trip*, another Roger Corman production which deals with the controversial hallucinatory drug LSD. Griffith is also writing this screenplay. The picture will be filmed on actual locations and technically accurate environment in January.

A third shocking commentary on our modern society will be *Sunset Strip*, a world of the long-haired, teenage kooks who apparently exist in another dimension. Robert Kaufman is currently writing the screenplay.

September 26, 1966
*Boxoffice*
AIP TO HAVE MINIMUM OF 21 FILMS FOR YEAR

**Although much of this lengthy article merely reiterates what was said in the June 20, 1966 *Boxoffice* article AIP ALLOTS $19,000,000 ON 20 FILMS FOR '66-67, there are still some new bits of information worth including.**

*Psycho Circus*, starring Christopher Lee, Leo Genn, and Margaret Lee, together with *Gill-Women*, starring Mamie Van Doren, will form the horror-science fiction combination for release in December.

An April special will be *The Glass Sphinx*, which begins filming in color and widescreen in Cairo, Egypt on October 12 with Dana Andrews, Anita Ekberg, and Luciana Paluzzi in the starring roles.

Three additional films are now in preparation, which will round out the company's heavy schedule of releases for the year. These include *2267 A.D.- When the Sleeper Wakes*, based on H.G. Wells classic to be filmed in color and starring Vincent Price; *The Puppet Masters*, an adventure horror feature which will be produced in color and Panavision; and *Sunset Strip*, a "protest" drama spotlighting the long-haired teenagers.

September 29, 1966
*The Film Daily*
AIP LAUNCHES FIRST GLOBAL SALES CONFAB
New York- AIP played host to the National Association of Theatre Owners convention delegates last night at a "champagne party" in the Imperial Ballroom of the American Hotel. The party brought to an end the opening day of NATO's first annual convention.

September 30, 1966
*The Film Daily*
AIP WANTS EVERY MONTH A MOVIE MONTH
New York- A suggestion that "the exhibitors and distributors sit down right now while NATO is convening and hatch out a workable plan for a Movie-of-the-Month program for every month of the year" was voiced yesterday by American International President James H. Nicholson.

October 1966-

*Nashville Rebel*
"The explosive story of a guy with a guitar... and GUTS!"

Produced by Freda Niles  Directed by Jay J. Sheridan
Starring Tex Ritter, Waylon Jennings, Sonny James, Loretta Lynn, Porter Wagoner

**This film introduced Country Western singing star Waylon Jennings as Arlin Grove, a wandering guitar player who eventually becomes a sensation at the Grand Ole Opry. Jennings liked the title of the film so much that he adopted it as his moniker. AIP often paired the film with *Door-To-Door Maniac*, which had been previously released by Sutton Pictures in 1961 as *Five Minutes to Live*. This movie introduces Johnny Cash playing a crazed killer.**

*Door to Door Maniac*
"It could be your street... your house... your life! When the bell rings... DON'T ANSWER!"

Produced by James Ellsworth  Directed by Bill Karn
Starring Johnny Cash, Donald Woods, Cay Forester, Pamela Mason, Ronnie Howard

*What's Up Tiger Lily?*
"WOODY ALLEN STRIKES BACK! Are you getting more

loving but enjoying it less? Try Woody Allen's sure-fire technique of how to make love without getting a headache"

Produced by Henry G. Saperstein and Woody Allen
Special Material by Woody Allen
Vocal Assists by Julie Bennet, Frank Buxton, Louise Lasser, Len Maxwell, Mickey Rose
Starring Tatsuya Mihashi, Akiko Wakabayashi, Mie Hama, Tadao Nakamura

Film Review- *What's Up Tiger Lily?*

*Time* (October 14, 1966)- JAP JAPE
Woody Allen, as televiewers know, is an anonymous little giggle merchant who looks like a slight defect in the wallpaper pattern and makes funnies that are so far out they sink before the slow boat gets there.

Woody has now discovered a gold mine: the movie business. And in *Tiger Lily*, this baby-faced bagman has pulled off the hat trick. He has made a movie without spending money- in fact, he has made a movie without even making a movie. For about $66,000, advanced by producer Henry Saperstein, Allen bought up a ludicrously lousy Japanese thriller. For a couple of thou on top of that, he eliminated some Japtrap, erased the Japanese talk, and dubbed in some English dialogue that transforms the story into Allengory and the characters into kooky-yacky.

The joke, of course, goes on too long (80 minutes) and when the spectator tires of it, he can't help noticing what Allen's annotations cannot entirely conceal: the original film. It's terrible.

*Boxoffice*
October 10, 1966
AIP EXECUTIVES SEEK MOVIE OF MONTH PLAN
New York- Samuel Z. Arkoff lauded exhibitors for their exceptionally progressive merchandising approach to the Movie Month drive, citing the impressive box office figures coming in on AIP's Movie Month release, *What's Up Tiger Lily?*, as a direct result of aggressive exhibitor campaign follow-through.

"All we did at American International," Arkoff said, "was to prepare and present to exhibitors a novel approach to a most unusual entertaining picture. They took the ball and ran for a touchdown."

November 1966-

*Dr. Goldfoot and the Girl Bombs*
"Meet the Girls with the Thermonuclear Navels!"

Produced by Fulvio Lucisano and Louis M. Heyward  Directed by Mario Bava
Starring Vincent Price, Fabian, Franco and Ciccio, Laura Antonelli

**Poor Fabian is waylaid by the dreadful comedy team of Franco and Ciccio in *Dr. Goldfoot and the Girl Bombs*.**

Film Review- *Dr. Goldfoot and the Girl Bombs*

*Los Angeles Times* (December 2, 1966) by Kevin Thomas
Each week brings a new James Bond takeoff that is even worse than the last. So it's meaningless to say that *Dr. Goldfoot and the Girl Bombs* hits rock bottom- though how a science fiction spoof could be lousier staggers the imagination.

December 1966-

***Trunk to Cairo***
"WHAT WAS IN IT? Big enough for a body... heavy enough for a bomb! Did it hold a nation's future or another's fate... where did it come from... and who knows its deadly secret?"

Produced and Directed by Menahem Golan
Starring Audie Murphy, George Sanders, Marianne Koch

December 12, 1966
*Boxoffice*
AIP PLANS 19 RELEASES JANUARY-OCTOBER
Los Angeles- American International will launch the new year with the heaviest production-distribution schedule in its history with a minimum of 19 features slated for release from January through October it was announced here Tuesday, December 6, by president James H. Nicholson. Of the 19 projects, 12 are scheduled to go before the cameras between now and September with seven of these productions between December and March. Four new feature films projects were also announced.

The four new features announced were *The Black Jacket Girls*, drama scheduled for September shooting; an untitled action drama to roll in March; *The Island of Amazons*, next August in Mexico; and *The End*, a drama of the future to go before the cameras next September. These will all be filmed in color and Panavision.

# CHAPTER FOURTEEN
# 1967

January 1967-

*Hallucination Generation* (a Trans American release)
"TONIGHT you are invited to a 'PILL PARTY.' You will experience every jolt... every jar of a Psychedelic Circus... The Beakniks... Sickniks... and Acid Heads... and you will witness their ecstasies, their agonies, and their bizarre sensualities... You will be hurled into their debauched dreams and their frenzied fantasies! For the adult minded... the revealing story of today's... *HALLUCINATION GENERATION!*"

Produced by Nigel Cox  Directed by Edward Mann
Starring George Montgomery, Danny Stone

*War Italian Style*
"BUSTER KEATON... fighting the funniest fracas in North Laffrica!"

Produced by Fulvio Lucisano  Directed by Luigi Scattini
Starring Buster Keaton, Franco and Ciccio, Martha Hyer, Fred Clark

January 9, 1967
*Boxoffice*
SKOURAS ON 61-DAY TRIP FOR AIP EXPORT
New York- Daniel P. Skouras, director of foreign sales and distribution for American International Export Corp, left on a 61-day around-the-world junket Sunday, January 8, during which he will visit 17 cities to herald the company's lineup of production for 1967.

Skouras will present AIP's new product brochure, which presents, among others, *War Italian Style*, Buster Keaton's last film; *Trunk to Cairo*, the new Audie Murphy film; *The 1,000,000 Eyes of Su-Muru*; *The Glass Sphinx*, starring Robert Taylor and Anita Ekberg; and *Ride the High Wind*, starring Darren McGavin, all of these filmed in Europe.

Other AIP pictures Skouras will discuss are Hollywood-made, including *The Hatfields and the McCoys*; *The Trip*, dealing with LSD, which was produced and directed by Roger Corman with Peter Fonda starred; *Thunder Alley*, starring Annette Funicello and Fabian; and *The Devil's Angels*, a drama in the vein of *The Wild Angels*. Two other AIP "protest" films are *Sunset Strip* and Sam Katzman's *Riot on Sunset Strip*.

MILTON MORITZ BECOMES AMERICAN INT'L V-P
Hollywood- Milton Moritz, national director of advertising and publicity for American International Pictures, has been appointed a vice president of the film company. The new vice president has occupied his present post as national director of advertising and publicity for the film company since 1958.

March 1967-

*Thunder Alley*
"Their God is speed... Their pleasure an 'Anytime' girl!"

Produced by Burt Topper  Directed by Richard Rush
Starring Annette Funicello, Fabian, Diane McBain, Warren Berlinger, Jan Murray

*Riot on Sunset Strip*
"The Most Shocking Film of Our Generation!"
Produced by Sam Katzman  Directed by Arthur Dreifuss
Starring Aldo Ray, Mimsy Farmer, Michael Evans, Laurie Mock, Tim Rooney

**Mimsy Farmer (born 1945) appeared in *Riot on Sunset Strip* and *The Devil's Angels*.**

*Riot on Sunset Strip* operates on a level of absurdity almost on a par with that classically bad movie *Valley of the Dolls*. Quite simply, it must be seen to be believed. Three bands are featured in the movie, The Standells, The Chocolate Watchband, and The Enemies. The singer in the latter band, Cory Wells, went on to become a member of Three Dog Night.


April 1967-

*It's a Bikini World* (a Trans American release)
"The BIKINI-BUNNIES are Bustin' Out All Over!"

Produced by Charles S. Swartz  Directed by Stephanie Rothman
Starring Deborah Walley, Tommy Kirk, Bob Pickett, Suzie Kaye

Although *It's a Bikini World* has many of the same elements as AIP's other "Beach" films, including stars Tommy Kirk and Deborah Walley, for some reason, they chose to distance it from the series by releasing it through their subsidiary company Trans American. The movie also features the singing groups The Animals, The Toys, The Gentrys, and The Castaways.

*Devil's Angels*
"GET OUT OF THEIR WAY... if you can!"

Produced by Burt Topper  Directed by Daniel Haller
Starring John Cassavetes, Beverly Adams, Mimsy Farmer

Film Review-*Devil's Angels*

*New York Times* (October 5, 1967)- A CYCLE GANG INVADES NEIGHBORHOODS AGAIN
Judging by what happened yesterday in *Devil's Angels*, even American International must be getting fed up with the current onslaught of movies about motorcycle hoodlum gangs, which started with two of the company's own products. The company has now piously shifted gears, at least temporarily.

Whereas those other exercises were plain sickening in their stress of violence and presented their protagonists in grudging, graphic admiration, this one tones them down, at least until the final eruption. The gang here, called the Skulls, are just exuberant, misunderstood boys at heart, it seems, under the leadership of John Cassavetes, a firm-spoken, clean-cut type.

May 1967-

*The Million Eyes of Su-Muru*
"She rules a Palace of Pleasure... for women!"

Produced by Harry Alan Towers  Directed by Lindsay Shonteff
Starring Frankie Avalon, George Nader, Shirley Eaton, Wilfred Hyde-White

*Psycho-Circus* (aka *Circus of Fear*)
"The most horrifying syndicate of evil in history!"

Produced by Harry Alan Towers  Directed by John Moxey
Starring Christopher Lee, Leo Genn, Anthony Newlands, Suzy Kendall, Klaus Kinski

From the pressbook-
CIRCUS WINTER QUARTERS FORM LURID BACKDROP FOR MURDER AND INTRIGUE IN AIP's PSYCHO-CIRCUS SHOCKER
Deep in the heart of London's Royal country, not far from Windsor Castle, the Queen's country residence, is a circus. Not the usual kind, with tinsel trimming for the kids at Christmas, but a circus stripped of all its glamour and glitter. Here at Winkfield is where one of the greatest shows in the world, Billy Smart's Circus, comes to hibernate and take stock of itself before the hectic Yuletide season.

This is the setting of American International's new thriller film *Psycho-Circus*, starring Christopher Lee, Leo Genn, with Anthony Newlands, Suzy Kendall, and Margaret Lee.

Real life circus king Billy Smart agreed to give the film's producer all of the technical assistance he required to heighten the dramatic realism of the circus background.

The film shows some of the acts in preparation and members of the talented Smart family and their personnel appearing as themselves alongside the principal actors.

*Teenage Rebellion* (aka *Mondo Teeno;* a Trans American release) "THE TRUTH... a factual report on the "NOW" generation... whose battle cry is 'MAKE LOVE- NOT WAR!"

Produced and Directed by Norman T. Herman
Narrated by Burt Topper

AIP News Clips.

AIP issued a monthly company newsletter, *American International Pictures News Clips,* to their employees and select theatre owners. The May 1967 issue (Volume 3, No. 3) featured the following:

On the Scene with News Clips (a monthly column with words of wisdom from Sam and Jim)
AIP Releases Parade of Select Specials for Greatest Season in Company History
Salli Sachse Upped to Star Billing in "Trip"
Madrid Filming Augments AIP's World-Wide Operations
Hollywood "Turned On" by Corman's Wild Psychedelic Nightclub in Center of Town
Eyes of Texas Focus on Fabian Tour, [Leon] Blender Round-Up
Cheesecake of the Month (featuring photos of bikinied babes from AIP films)
Promotion of the Month- First Psychedelic Paint-In

May 5, 1967
*Time* -Excerpts from the article "Z as in Zzzz, or Zowie"
The old team of Bunkum & Ballyhoo isn't dead. The fact is, they're working in Hollywood making what is known as Z pictures.

Bunkum is fast-talking James Nicholson, 50; Ballyhoo is fast-talking Samuel Arkoff, 48. They are the president and chairman of American International Pictures. Since 1954, they have reeled out 130 low budget, lowbrow features, grossed about $250 million, and built AIP into the nation's largest independent film company.

For adults, the Z picture stands for zzzz, but for teenagers, it's strictly zowie. It goes with such titles as *The Brain Eaters, Bucket of Blood,* and *Little Shop of Horrors* **(this was not an AIP movie)**. AIP's classic horror title was *I Was a Teenage Werewolf,* which caused traffic jams at drive-in theaters and earned $2,000,000. Similarly, AIP has made quick killings on bargain-basement Biblicals (*Goliath and the Barbarians, Goliath and the Sins of Babylon*), on way-outer spacers (*Angry Red Planet, Battle Beyond the Sun*), and teenage topicals (*Dragstrip Riot, Reform School Girl*).

AIP's cinemologists are sharply aware that kids are the big

movie market nowadays. "And, " explains Arkoff, "they don't want message pictures. They want pure escapism, a never-never land without parents, without adults, without authorities. Kids get lectures from their parents all the time. They don't want to hear them from us."

May 22, 1967
*Boxoffice*
'TV TAIL WAGGING THE THEATRICAL DOG' SAM ARKOFF OF AIP TELLS PRESS
New York- "The TV tail is wagging the theatrical dog," is how Samuel Z. Arkoff, chairman of the board of American International Pictures, summed up the present state of affairs to trade reporters on Thursday, May 11, following a national exhibitors and all-media press luncheon at the Plaza Hotel here and a screening of AIP's biggest production of all time, *Those Fantastic Flying Fools*.

AIP will be co-producing with a French company a version of Poe's *The Gold Bug*. AIP has made eight or nine other films, all hits with the general market, based on Poe tales.

On the home front, AIP box office veteran producer-writer-director Roger Corman will follow *The Trip* with another film in December. The company will concentrate on contemporary and timely themes with films like *The Mini-Skirt Mob*, shooting in August, and another tentatively titled film, *The Be-Ins*.

June 1967-

***Those Fantastic Flying Fools*** (aka ***Blast Off***)
"The most fabulous entertainment event of the year!"

Produced by Harry Alan Towers  Directed by Don Sharp
Starring Burl Ives, Troy Donahue, Gert Frobe, Daliah Lavi, Terry-Thomas, Lionel Jeffries

Film Reviews- *Those Fantastic Flying Fools*

*Time*(June 16, 1967)- LOONY & LUNAR
*Those Fantastic Flying Fools* is a spirited spoof in the Jules Verne
Vernacular. The background is Victorian, the project loony, the
destination lunar, and the fun is in the jocular vein of Mike Todd's
memorable *Around the World in 80 Days.*

By drawing a heavy-handed parallel with the contemporary
space race, the film's message- what mortals these fools be- nearly
scrubs the project. But the detailed sight gags and the cast's
irrepressible energy provide a variety of lunatic fringe benefits.
Like the rocket, they go a long way.

*New York Times* (October 19, 1967) by Bosley Crowther
The credits for *Those Fantastic Flying Fools,* the period comedy
which opened here yesterday, say that Peter Welbeck's original
story was "inspired by the writings of Jules Verne." That, however,
is only part of the truth. It seem to also have been inspired by *Those
Magnificent Men in Their Flying Machines,* which, in its turn, had
been more than a little inspired by Michael Todd's extravagant
version of Verne's *Around the World in 80 Days.* The inspiration is
now running somewhat thin.

The producers of this colorful rehash, however, have had the
intelligence- if not exactly the originality- to hire Terry-Thomas
and Gert Frobe to carry the comic burden in this turn-of-the-
century farce having to do with the launching of the world's first
moon rocket.

Burl Ives plays Phineas T. Barnum, who is somewhat less
famous as a Verne hero than Captain Nemo.

### Hells Angels on Wheels

Produced by Joe Solomon  Directed by Richard Rush
Starring  Adam Roarke, Jack Nicholson, Sabrina Scharf

**Although it had been announced as a forthcoming AIP
production in February 1966, *Hells Angels on Wheels* was
produced by Joe Solomon's company Fanfare Films and released
by U.S. Films in June 1967. In 1969, AIP acquired the rights**

to the movie and released it as part of their "Big 3 Cycle Rider Spectacular" along with *The Wild Angels* and *The Glory Stompers*.

July 1967-

July 10, 1967
*Boxoffice*
DELORES TAYLOR, PRODUCER FOR AIP, SAYS SOCIAL FILMS MUST ENTERTAIN
by Jim Watters
New York- Women producers are a rare breed. A fortnight ago, a petite blonde, born and reared in South Dakota, was in New York for the first press screenings of a film which officially marks her debut into the male-dominated ranks of motion picture producers.

Not only is Dolores Taylor the antithesis of what one would expect of the "executive producer" of *Born Losers*, she is also very attractive, quite young, probably 32 at the most, and very well informed about current affairs. She is, needless to say, also very interested in movie-making. Along with her husband, Tom Laughlin, the star of the picture, they have formed Otis Production with a number of film projects in the works.

According to Miss Taylor, young people in Hollywood as in New York and every other major city in the world are more and more interested in film as a means of expressing something of value without the limitations often placed on commercial moviemaking. *Born Losers*, while exploiting the nth degree all the sex and sadism of the subject matter, does so within the context of a very moral and affirmative concept.

The picture was actually begun in 1965 before the first motorcycle film was released. That was *The Wild Angels*, one of AIP's biggest commercial and critical successes. AIP took over the film after its completion.

AIP's advertising carries the line "Recommended for Mature Audiences" although Miss Taylor thinks that teenagers will be the backbone audience of her film. She believes that it is easier to make a point and even preach in a dark movie house via a fiction film than from a pulpit or social meeting and that is why *Born Losers* "hits hard," according to Miss Taylor.

July 17, 1967
*Boxoffice*
ROGER CORMAN EMPHASIZES REALISM IN MAKING HIS FILM *THE TRIP*
by Jim Watters
New York- Producer-writer-director Roger Corman always makes good copy for reporters when he comes to town. He was in rare form at the trade and foreign press luncheon hosted by AIP last week. Corman, controversial and articulate as ever, told the gathering that he himself had taken a "trip" before making *The Trip*, first film to dramatize the hot subject of LSD.

"Nothing like it in the world," Corman said, describing the experience as "a dream carried a hundred times further" and "beyond capturing on film," although he has tried to do just that in his newest film.

As for his film, the original story was thrown out and he started anew after his personal experience with the drug. When asked about the controversial nature of the film, he said he would never take a stand or preach in a picture; at best, "a slight subjective point of view" could be detected on his part in all his work.

Corman expects *The Trip* to be his most successful picture and AIP seconds that opinion. For ten years now, he has had no written contract with the company, but comes and goes and then returns, always able to make "with a free hand" his own films for AIP. He was responsible for many of the horror cycle and the Edgar Allan Poe pictures, which were very successful commercially and "helped put AIP on the road to the profitable and valuable company it is today."

August 1967-

*The Trip*
"A Lovely Sort of Death"

Produced and Directed by Roger Corman
Starring Peter Fonda, Susan Strasberg, Dennis Hopper, Bruce Dern, Salli Sachse

Charles Griffith: "Roger [Corman] thought that reading Timothy Leary's book was all the research he needed to do. I convinced him that he needed to drop acid. Roger took acid with some milk and we hung around in the woods. Nothing happened. 'I've been swindled,' he said, in a rage about how he'd bought this acid and nothing was happening. He finally calmed down and was sitting there sort of staring. 'Excuse me a moment,' he said. He lay down on his face on the ground and was gone. It was the best trip I ever saw anybody have."

Roger Corman (Producer-Director): "I was the most conservative of a very wild crowd. What started out as a couple of us going to Big Sur ended up as a caravan when they found out I was going to take LSD. There must have been twenty people or more. We had to draw up the equivalent of a production schedule- who was going to be taking acid at what time. When I was coming down from the acid, the thought occurred to me that there was no particular reason to go back to Hollywood. No particular reason to exist in the real world at all."

Film Reviews- *The Trip*

*New York Times* (August 4, 1967) by Bosley Crowther
In trying to visualize a notion of what Peter Fonda goes through when he embarks on an LSD trip, Roger Corman has simply resorted to a long succession of familiar cinematic images accompanied by weird music and sounds.

Is this a psychedelic experience? Is this what it's like to take a trip? If it is, then it is all a big put-on. Or is this simply making a show with adroitly staged fantasy episodes and good color photography effects?

In my estimation it is the latter. And I would warn you that all you are likely to take away from this picture is a painful case of eye-strain or perhaps a detached retina.

336

*Films and Filming* (June 1969) By Colin Heard

Roger Corman's film, refused a certificate by the British censor, reproduces the sensations of an LSD trip with remarkable accuracy. Technically, the film is a dazzling and brilliant work. Corman brings off the stunning effects with a skill that places him securely among the most interesting of all "visual" directors.

*Playboy-* The real impact and import is that, for the first time, Hollywood has tuned into the vibrations- good and bad- humming hallucinogenically through the nation.

**Peter Fonda in *The Trip*.**

**Forty years later, Roger Corman and Peter Fonda expressed their displeasure with AIP's tampering on *The Trip*.**

*Daily Variety* (November 8, 2007)
1967: *The Trip* falls flat.
FONDA, CORMAN FEEL FILM EDIT IS A 'COPOUT' by Army Archerd
*The Trip* is over, but the memory of the LSDeep-seated film lingers

on- not too pleasantly with both Peter Fonda and Roger Corman. Both feel- and independently- the finale was compromised by American International. Or, as Fonda says, "It was a 'copout.' The audience should have been permitted to make its own decision. It's very important for the moral commitment of the story." Producer-director Corman also objected to the alteration in the scene described to us by Fonda: "It changed the meaning of the picture."

September 1967-

*The Born Losers*
"Which One of You Cats IS FIRST?"

Produced by Don Henderson  Directed by T.C. Frank
Starring Tom Laughlin, Elizabeth James, Jeremy Slate, William Wellman, Jr., Jane Russell

Film Review- *The Born Losers*

*New York Times* (August 19, 1967) by Bosley Crowther
Yesterday's losers, as opposed to *The Born Losers*, were the hapless people who trooped into the theatre to see a sickening little motorcycle melodrama from American International Pictures that is also a trailing catchall of most motorcycle films clichés to date.

The whole business is laboriously detailed in E. James Lloyd's screenplay even as it piously pleads for personal change. But it is difficult to have empathy for the victimized youngsters after seeing them half-naked in beachwear, coyly edging up to the cyclists.

Tom Laughlin stoically plays a war veteran recluse who almost single-handedly squelches the gang. A battered-looking Jane Russell makes a brief, growly appearance as one of the parents.

October 1967-

*House of 1000 Dolls*

"MISSING! Have you seen this girl?... Just one of thousands of young girls who 'disappear' each year- victims of a tragic traffic in beauty and human flesh!... What happens to them? Where do they go?"

Produced by Harry Alan Towers  Directed by Jeremy Summers
Starring Vincent Price, Martha Hyer, George Nader

Film Reviews- *House of 1000 Dolls*

*Motion Picture Herald* (November 15, 1967)- That mischievous team of Vincent Price and AIP have this time around given us a contemporary drama about white slavery. For the most part, it is fun to watch the magnificently caped Price, cane in hand, carry on once more in his inimitable tongue-in-cheek style.

*New York Times* (March 14, 1968) by Howard Thompson
The dolls are a clutch of scantily-clad beauties- 20 or so, not 1,000- held captive in a Tangier mansion prior to a white slavery shipment by Vincent Price, heh-heh, and his partner, Martha Hyer.
A vacationing couple, George Nader and Anne Smyrner, trailed by the police, investigate a friend's murder. The search leads to the house. The rest is routine sleuthing, double-crossing, and chasing until Mr. Price does a swan dive four flights downward.

November 1967-

***The Glory Stompers***
"It's the 'Black Souls' vs. the 'Stompers'... in the deadliest cycle gang war ever waged!"

Produced by John Lawrence  Directed by Anthony Lanza
Starring Dennis Hopper, Jody McCrea, Chris Noel, Jock Mahoney

*Vincent Price* (1911-1993) was involved with twenty-six AIP productions, including voiceovers for *Taboos of the World* and *Spirits of the Dead.*

Film Review- *The Glory Stompers*

*New York Times* (March 28, 1968) by Howard Thompson
MOTORCYCLE GANGS
*The Glory Stompers* is the latest little motorcycle jamboree from American International Pictures. This one is just about rock bottom with two gang of filthy, lecherous young animals, the Glory Stompers and the Black Souls (all white), warring against each other with time out for orgies.

The grim irony of this trash is the contrast of the pretty pastoral backgrounds, in color, and the hog-wild behavior, led by

1967

such people as Dennis Hopper and Jody McCrea with Chris Noel and Sondra Gale as the main mixed-up girls.

December 1967-

*Sadismo* (aka *Mondo Sadismo;* a Trans American release)
"See: The Rack-Thumb Screw-Iron Maiden-Torture... Drugs That Make Men Slaves... Bizarre Human Sacrifices... Today! A frank, authentic catalog of cruelty! Actually filmed in the dark corners of our so-called 'civilized world'!"

Produced by Salvatore Billittieri
Narration by Burt Topper and Terry Telli

December 8, 1967
*Boxoffice*
'MONDODRAMA' PACKAGE ADDED TO AIP LIST
Los Angeles- American International Pictures, which has been packaging similarly themed films for exhibition for several years, has added its list a special grouping of three films described as shocking and bizarre and called "Mondodrama." The three features encompassed in the package all for the price of one are *Taboos of the World, Ecco,* and *Macabro,* filmed in quaint places throughout the world and showing certain pagan customs and rituals.

Other packages available from the company include the dusk-to-dawn horror combination of Edgar Allan Poe classics, *The Masque of the Red Death, The Comedy of Terrors, Tomb of Ligeia, Tales of Terror,* and *War Gods of the Deep.* Another package, a Rollorama Show, consists of *Rock All Night, Shake Rattle and Rock, Rock Around the World,* and *Dragstrip Riot.* A dusk-to-dawn bill advertising "beach-niks, surfers, ho-dads, and gremmies" consists of *Beach Party, Muscle Beach Party, Bikini Beach, Pajama Party,* and *How to Stuff a Wild Bikini.* A "mighty blook and guts show" comprises *Submarine Seahawk, Paratroop Command, Suicide Battalion,* and *Tank Battalion.* And a second horror and thrill show package includes *Blood of Dracula, It Conquered the World, Night of the Blood Beast,* and *The Headless Ghoul* [sic].

341

Additionally, year after year, AIP releases its top Edgar Allan Poe screamer package, labeled "5 Masters of Horror," comprising of *House of Usher, The Raven, Premature Burial, The Pit and the Pendulum,* and *The Haunted Palace.*

# CHAPTER FOURTEEN
# 1968

January 1968-

*The Cobra*
"Danger, Dames, and Sudden Death! These Are the Fangs of The Cobra!"

Produced by Fulvio Lucisano  Directed by Mario Sequi
Starring Dana Andrews, Peter Martell, Anita Ekberg

January 1, 1968
*Boxoffice*
AIP ACQUIRES RIGHT TO THREE CUE FILMS
New York- American International Pictures has acquired the rights to three productions from Commonwealth United

343

Entertainment, Inc. for U.S. theatrical distribution. The three-picture deal includes *Cervantes* and *The Desperate Ones*, both produced in Spain in color and widescreen, and *The Day the Hot Line Got Hot*, currently filming in Barcelona with Charles Boyer, Robert Taylor, and George Chakiris.

The AIP-CUE agreement marks the second distribution package to be effected between the two companies. AIP previously released ten films acquired from CUE, then the Landau-Unger Organization, all of which are currently in television release by AIP's television subsidiary.

AIP chairman of the board Samuel Z. Arkoff and president James H. Nicholson said that release plans for *Cervantes* call for the "largest advertising and promotion budget in the company's history." *Cervantes* stars Horst Buchholz, Louis Jordan, Jose Ferrer, and Gina Lollobrigida.

January 22, 1968
*Boxoffice*

AIP ALLOTS $22 MILLION FOR PRODUCTION IN 1968
Hollywood- American International Pictures has announced its releasing program for 1968, which represents an all-time record investment of $22,000,000. James H. Nicholson, president, and Samuel Z. Arkoff, chairman, said that this year's product expenditure represents a larger figure than product allocations for the first six years of operation combined.

The AIP heads, who left for European production centers, outlined the prominent releases as follows: A topical special, *Wild in the Streets*, produced personally by Nicholson and Arkoff with Barry Shear directing; *Cervantes*, a $5,000,000 production of large magnitude depicting the romantic adventures of famed Spanish soldier-poet Miguel Cervantes; and *The Desperate Ones*, action suspense drama filmed in color.

In preparation for summer release is an important comedy drama, *Three in the Attic*, which will be produced and directed by Richard Wilson in color. Also currently in production is *The Day the Hot Line Got Hot*.

Additional films on the program are *Maryjane*, shock drama in color starring Fabian and Diane McBain; *Psych-Out*, a modern anti-establishment drama produced by Dick Clark and starring Susan Strasberg, Dean Stockwell, Jack Nicholson, Bruce Dern, and Adam Roarke which Richard Rush directed; *Hell's Racers*, an action drama located around the famous auto racing circuit in Europe and starring Fabian and Mimsy Farmer; and *The Wild Eye*, filmed in color and scope and encompassing a shocking expose of the "Mondo" breed of spectacular filmmakers.

Completing the AIP releasing schedule as blueprinted through September are *The Conqueror Worm*, horror suspense drama patterned after the Edgar Allan Poe series of AIP films starring Vincent Price; *Hell's Belles*, a cycle feature which will be produced by Burt Topper and directed by Rod Amateau; and *Acapulco Gold*, a suspense drama dealing with the traffic of marijuana.

Release dates for the balance of the year were yet to be definitely set for such properties as *Blood Mama, The Day the Hot Line Got Hot, The Reincarnation, Hawaiian Beach Bum, Mondo Amour, The Gold Bug, The Marquis de Sade, The Day It All Happened Baby,* and *The Hatfields and the McCoys.*

February 1968-

## Maryjane

"It is illegal to possess MARYJANE, yet it is found in every high school corridor! The shocking facts behind the marijuana controversy!"

Produced and Directed by Maury Dexter
Starring Fabian, Diane McBain, Michael Margotta, Kevin Coughlin, Patty McCormack

Film Review- *Maryjane*

*New York Times* (March 14, 1968) by Howard Thompson
*Maryjane* is uneven on several counts as an indictment of "pot" usage by teenagers. With a theme right out of yesterday's newspaper, this little picture could have gone places. Considering how American International has previously gone hog-wild in

sadism and sex, notably in those motorcycle frolics, the tone here is surprisingly restrained. Unfortunately, the dialogue is generally wooden, the pace is static, the acting is generally second-level. Even so, the unmasking of the pusher is a devastating shocker that almost makes up for everything else.

**Diane McBain (born 1941) starred in *Thunder Alley, Maryjane,* and *The Mini-Skirt Mob* for AIP.**

February 5, 1968
*Boxoffice*
ERWIN A. LESSER HEADS TRANS AMERICAN SALES
New York- Erwin A. Lesser has been appointed sales manager of Trans American Films, American International subsidiary, now

set to go into full operation handling "specialized distribution" of top "specialized" product.

At a press conference for the tradepress January 30, Lesser announced the first three films of the company's projected five films scheduled for release in 1968. Alain Robbe-Grillet's *Trans Euro Express* will be the first release on the company's agenda in mid-April.

*Succubus*, which was produced by Atlas Films in Munich, is the second film which should be ready for mid-summer release. Starring French actress Janine Reynaud, *Succubus* was directed by Jess Franco and is the first co-production effort with Trans American Films.

*Dante's Inferno*, to be produced in Hamburg, Germany, in English language from an original screenplay by Gary Russoff, will be the third film. Shooting will begin in June.

Lesser emphasized that Trans American product differs from AIP product in that it requires special handling, which he considers the original meaning of "art house" films.

## NATO BOARD SALUTES AIP FOR AID TO INDUSTRY

New York- The National Ass'n of Theatre Owners board of directors meeting at Paradise Island, the Bahamas, paid special tribute to American International Pictures and that company's board chairman Samuel Z. Arkoff and president James H. Nicholson "for constructive an significant contributions to the prosperity and well being of the theatre industry."

March 1968-

### Wild Racers

"FROM STOCK CAR TO GRAND PRIX... show him a curve and he'll take it"

Produced by Joel Rapp  Directed by Daniel Haller
Starring Fabian, Mimsy Farmer

April 1968-

*Psych-Out*
"These are the PLEASURE LOVERS!"

Produced by Dick Clark   Directed by Richard Rush
Starring Susan Strasberg, Dean Stockwell, Jack Nicholson, Bruce Dern, Adam Roarke

*The Wild Eye*
"HE USED A CAMERA LIKE MOST MEN USE A WOMAN... You will see the strange secret world of the men who make 'that kind of film'... men who take pleasure from pain... and the women who love them for it!"

Produced by Georges Marci  Directed by Paolo Cavara
Starring Philippe Leroy, Delia Boccardo, Gabriele Tinti

April 1, 1968
*Boxoffice*
AIP BUDGETS $5,000,000 FOR TWO MAJOR FEATURES
Hollywood- American International Pictures executives James H. Nicholson and Samuel Z. Arkoff announced that back-to-back production on two major feature films will be launched by AIP in June. The two films, *The Marquis de Sade* and its sequel, *Justine*, will be made on an approximate budget of $5,000,000.
     Since announcement of the scheduled *Marquis de Sade* property, Richard Matheson has turned in his finished screen treatment. *Justine* is based on the novel of that title by the Marquis de Sade. Both films will be in color and scope.

May 1968-

*Wild in the Streets*
"The Old Tigers are scared baby!"

**Christopher Jones as Max Frost in *Wild in the Streets*.**

Produced by Samuel Z. Arkoff and James H. Nicholson  Directed by Barry Shear
Starring Shelley Winters, Christopher Jones, Diane Varsi, Hal Holbrook, Millie Perkins

Film Reviews- *Wild in the Streets*

*New York Times* (May 30, 1968) by Renata Adler
Events overtake fantasy so quickly now that any movie about the generation gap ought to be dated almost before the titles run out, but *Wild in the Streets* is a kind of instant classic. Blunt, a little

preachy, a product of American International Pictures (of beach party and teenage werewolf fame), the movie is philosophy with dual exhausts and a very clear logic about where things lead.

The writing (by Robert Thom, on the basis of his own short story) is often marvelous.

*The Hollywood Reporter- Wild in the Streets* is one of American International's most ambitious and expensive productions, but it assumed a look several times its budget through extensive and diverse set-ups, admirably researched and utilized newsreel footage, and the presence of a sizable recruitment of authenticating media personalities.

### The Savage Seven

"YOUR TOWN could be their killing ground... *The Savage Seven*... deadliest of all that violent breed!"

Produced by Dick Clark  Directed by Richard Rush
Starring Robert Walker, Larry Bishop, Joanna Frank, John Garwood, Adam Roarke

From the pressbook-
ADAM ROARKE'S EARLY LIFE SPRINGBOARD TO TOUGH GUY ROLE IN *THE SAVAGE SEVEN*
It wasn't planned that way, but Adam Roarke's early conditioning proved a first rate training ground for his chilling role of the outlaw motorcycle gang leader in *The Savage Seven*, dramatic thriller released by American International.

In *The Savage Seven*, filmed in color, Roarke appears in the most rugged role of his film career, sharing starring honors with Robert Walker, Joanna Frank, John Garwood, Larry Bishop, Max Julien, and Richard Anders, among others in the strong cast.

Roarke, who is a strapping six-footer, was born on Aug. 8th in the tough Bay Ridge section of Brooklyn. He was taught early to steal and fight and did both well.

*The Savage Seven* was produced by famed television personality Dick Clark and directed by Richard Rush from a screenplay by Michael Fisher and story by Rosalind Ross.

EXPLOITATION-
Secure the cooperation of local motorcycle club members to
appear on local radio shows for interviews. They would naturally
discuss the good side of motorcycling and also would bring in
mentions for *The Savage Seven.*

Film Review- *The Savage Seven* and *Wild in the Streets*

*Time* (May 24, 1968)
Some pictures are put-ons that seem to plead for a tacit
agreement with their audience: what is to be viewed is beneath
contempt, therefore it is beyond criticism. Two current examples
come from American International, the studio that perfected the
beach boy epic.
*The Savage Seven* begins with a bare-chested Indian looming
in the foreground, knife in hand. Another brave leaps forward
and they begin to grapple to the death. Then comes an offscreen
voice, "Will you guys quit screwing around?" The time is the
present and the Indians are a bunch of tribesmen trapped in a
California poverty pocket. From out of the hills comes the Enemy,
on wheels- and suddenly the ignoble savages find themselves in a
stereotypical motorcycle picture. It all ends as it began, in chaos,
proving itself ideal kapok to fill out the lower end of double bills
at drive-ins.
The top half of the bill might well be *Wild in the Streets*. The
thesis of the movie is that the U.S. is ripe for a teenage entertainer-
turned-politico. The central character is a delinquent (Christopher
Jones) who caterwauls his way into the hearts of young America.
An opportunistic Senator (Hal Holbrook) gets a law passed that
enfranchises 15-year-olds. They elect Jones President and suddenly
he-and-shedonism is for everyone under 35. Ultimately, Jones
finds himself surrounded by hostile children, who bring the joke
full circle by insisting: "Everybody over ten ought to be put out
of business." Everybody would include the operators of American
International. That could be the greatest put-on of them all.

351

### The Mini-Skirt Mob
"THEY PLAY AROUND WITH MURDER LIKE THEY PLAY AROUND WITH MEN! They're hog straddling female animals on the prowl!"

Produced and Directed by Maury Dexter
Starring Jeremy Slate, Diane McBain, Sherry Jackson, Patty McCormack, Ross Hagen

June 1968-
### Angels From Hell
"When he wanted a girl HE GRABBED ONE... When he wanted a cop HE BOUGHT ONE! He's a CYCLE PSYCHO!"

Produced by Kurt Neumann  Directed by Bruce Kessler
Starring Tom Stern, Arlene Martel, Ted Markland, Stephen Oliver, Paul Bertoya, Jimmy Murphy

Film Review- *Angels from Hell* and *The Mini-Skirt Mob*

*New York Times* (October 24, 1968) by Howard Thompson
CYCLIST DOUBLE BILL
Two reels of celluloid junk called *The Mini-Skirt Mob* and *Angels from Hell* unwound in succession yesterday on a circuit theatre double bill.

Both American International packages transparently pay awed tribute to a motorcycle gang, a repulsive roundup of young humanity. *Angels* simply gathers up some stale leftovers from the film company's other cycle sagas as the gorillas and their girls wallow around in a suburban shack and wage war on helpless civilians and the local police. As the gang leader, Tom Stern somehow manages to suggest that he might do very well in another picture.

*The Mini-Skirt Mob* is simply a monotonous exercise in sadism as a bunch of girl cyclists and their male partners torment a honeymooning couple. *Mini-Skirt* is sickening. *Angels* is merely dull.

352

August 1968-

*Conqueror Worm* (aka *Witchfinder General*)
"LEAVE THE CHILDREN HOME... and if YOU are SQUEAMISH... STAY HOME WITH THEM!"

Produced by Louis M. Heyward  Directed by Michael Reeves
Starring Vincent Price, Ian Ogilvy, Rupert Davies, Hilary Dwyer

From the pressbook-
SORCERY AND WITCHES FLOURISHING BUSINESS IN JOLLY OLD ENGLAND
In the sixteen forties, when Matthew Hopkins, Oliver Cromwell's self-appointed "Witchfinder General," stalked his evil and sinister way through the towns and villages of Eastern England, the practice of witchcraft was a crime punishable by death.

Hopkins, whose story has now been brought vividly to the screen in American International's horror thriller *The Conqueror Worm*, starring Vincent Price, used this fact to his own profit and aggrandizement by branding many innocent Roman Catholics as "witches" and putting them to agonizing torture and death by hanging and burning.

Since those days, witches, wizards, and sorcerers have flourished in England with impunity. Today, it is estimated, more witchcraft- and its more sinister corollary, Black Magic- is practiced in Great Britain than during the whole of the sixteenth and seventeenth centuries.

SEAT SELLING SLANTS
Contact local museums to arrange for a lobby display of torture equipment, such as Iron Maiden, witches dunking stool, etc.

Film Reviews- *The Conqueror Worm*

*New York Times* (August 15, 1968) by Renata Adler
*The Conqueror Worm* stars Vincent Price and features any

number of attractive young aspiring stars who seem to have been cast (by American International Pictures, which produced the film) mainly for their ability to scream. Vincent Price has a good time as a materialistic witch hunter and woman disfigurer and dismemberer and the audience seemed to have a good time as well.

*Hollywood Citizen News* (May 17, 1968)- A disgrace to the producers and scriptors and a sad commentary on the art of filmmaking. A film with such bestial brutality and orgiastic sadism, one wonders how it ever passed customs to be released in this country.

**The Young, the Evil and the Savage** (aka **Naked You Die**)
"SLAVES to their own STRANGE DESIRES! Prey to the nameless terror that stalks an 'exclusive' girl's school"

Produced by Lawrence Woolner and G. de Blasio
Directed by Anthony Dawson
Starring Michael Rennie, Mark Damon, Eleanor Brown

*Helga*
"This film shows scenes never before shown... from the conception to the birth of the baby. For the first time- the complete, intimate story of a young girl."

Produced by Karl-Ludwig Ruppel
Directed by Erich F. Bender
Starring Ruth Gassman, Eberhard Mondry, Asgarda Hummel

October 1968-

**Born Wild** (aka **The Young Animals**)
THE WILDEST of the YOUNG ONES!"

Produced and Directed by Maury Dexter

Starring Tom Nardini, Patty McCormack, David Macklin, Joanna Frank


November 1968-

*Killer's Three*
"One had the GUTS, One had the GUNS! The GAL they had between them!"

Produced by Dick Clark  Directed by Bruce Kessler
Starring Robert Walker, Diane Varsi, Dick Clark, Norman Alden, Maureen Arthur

Film Review- *Killer's Three*

*New York Times* (June 19, 1968) by A,H. Weiler
*Killer's Three*, which makes a vague pass at mountain folklore, has Robert Walker, son of the late actor and Jennifer Jones, Dick Clark, the platter spinner and darling of TV's teenage swingers, and Diane Varsi running afoul of the law just after World War II. Seems that Mr. Walker, who doesn't want to haul illicit corn likker no more, tries to steal $200,000 from his boss's safe with the aid of his wife, Miss Varsi, and his pal, Clark. They'll all go to California with the loot, where, it says here, the living is easier.
  Well, it doesn't work and while our harried trio, according to the background song, "never meant to kill anyone," they leave a pretty bloody trail for the posse to follow. Miss Varsi loves her little boy, but chooses to follow her man and gets shot for the devotion. Mr. Walker, strikingly reminiscent of his late father in appearance, is simply phlegmatic more often than not. And Mr. Clark, wearing glasses, a mustache, and a doleful expression that fits his laconic dialogue, is mowed down in the climactic battle, which, of course, has no connection with the fact that he's also the film's producer.

November 4, 1968
*Boxoffice*
AIP REPORTS MOST SUCCESSFUL YEAR; TO RELEASE
18 FEATURES IN 1969
Hollywood- The most successful year in the 15-year history of
American International Pictures was heralded by Samuel Z.
Arkoff and James H. Nicholson, chief executives, at a press
luncheon in the Lanai Terrace Room of the Beverly Hills Hotel
here Wednesday, October 30.

Profits thus far for the year, which ends in February, are double
that of any previous year in the company's history, the executives
said.

Through October 1969, AIP will release 18 features, nine of
them to be made in the U.S. and five in Europe. *De Sade* is a co-
production of AIP's wholly owned subsidiary, Transcontinental

Films, and a German company. Eleven of the features will
be before the cameras by February; four are in the planning and
writing stage.

November 25, 1968
*Boxoffice*
The London Report by Anthony Gruner
ON *DE SADE* SET- Samuel Z. Arkoff, American International
Pictures board chairman, and Louis M. "Deke" Heyward, AIP's
director of European production, took time out from shooting on
the set of *De Sade* to chat with two of the film's stars, Keir Dullea
and John Huston. The film is being personally produced by Arkoff
and James H. Nicholson, AIP heads, and is being directed by Cy
Endfield with Heyward as executive producer.

December 1968-

**Three in the Attic**
"Paxton Quigley's crime was passion... and his punishment fits
exactly!"

**Sam Arkoff with John Huston and Keir Dullea on the set of *De Sade*. Photo courtesy of Photofest.**

Starring Yvette Mimieux, Christopher Jones, Judy Pace, Maggie Thrett, Nan Martin

Film Review- *Three in the Attic*

*Chicago Sun Times* (December 20, 1968) by Roger Ebert
*Three in the Attic* is a frustrating movie because it could have been so good and occasionally is so good and yet it finally loses its nerve and collapses into a routine gutless exploitation picture.

Still, before the collapse sets in, there are a couple of fine comedy scenes and performances which are likely to surprise you. The premise is also promising: Paxton Quigley (Christopher Jones) is the archetypal fraternity stud, the guy who goes with three girls at once and is (as the ads say) a legend in his own time.

The seductions and the casual heartlessness that makes them possible are handled with an out-front sort of frankness that is both funny and true.

Now if *Three in the Attic* had simply stuck to this theme and played it straight, it could have been a great movie. Since moving out of its crab-monster and beach-party bag, American International Pictures has shown a certain daring in handling social themes (*Wild in the Streets, The Wild Angels, The Trip* ), but all three of these movies--and now this one too--chickened out of the implications of their subject matter and wound up with flabby, inconclusive second halves.

In *Three in the Attic,* it would have been good if Quigley had continued to juggle his three girls until some sort of inevitable, embarrassing, comic, tragic conclusion. But instead, the plot dives into fantasy and the three girls kidnap Quigley and keep him captive and try to love him to death and the movie falls to pieces.

Film Review- *Three in the Attic* and *Queen of Blood*

*New York Times* (February 27, 1969) by Renata Adler
*Three in the Attic* casts Christopher Jones (of *Wild in the Streets*) as a college boy who sleeps with three girls- one black, one Jewish, and one Yvette Mimieux, who finally abduct him to an attic and try to do him in from sexual hyperesthesia.

The movie, which was made by American International Pictures for the drive-in set, has a little touch of *The Touchables,* some *Joanne,* generation gap, hippiedom, college, McLuhan, and Kierkegaard, all wilted and stale.

*Queen of Blood* has a much more lively plot. A sickly greenish Martian woman (Florence Marley), who is rescued from a space crash by earth astronauts (John Saxon, Judi Meredith, Dennis Hopper), turns out to thrive on blood, lay eggs in aspic, and be a hemophiliac in chlorophyll.

They feed her with the spaceship's supply of plasma through a straw, but she drains another victim and nearly finishes a third.

The eggs in aspic, larvae by this time, are ultimately conserved by the late Basil Rathbone, an earth scientist, for study. "They're scientists, Allan. They know what they're doing," Miss Meredith says.

By this time, Jim Nicholson was playing an increasingly smaller role in the running of AIP.

Sam Arkoff was now Chairman of the Board with controlling interest in the company. With Nicholson taking a backseat, publicity articles which had previously charted the company's (and Nicholson's) movements in minute detail became less and less prevalent. In his autobiography, Sam Arkoff says, "In his middle fifties, Jim decided he wanted more out of his life than long workdays and the administrative responsibilities of running a film company."

# CHAPTER SIXTEEN
# 1969

Trade ad-
From the film company with the future look... American
International Pictures
   69/70
   *deSade*
   *Angel, Angel, Down We Go*
   H.P. Lovecraft's *Dunwich*
   *Blood Mama*
   Emily Bronte's immortal *Wuthering Heights*


January 1969-

***Cervantes*** (aka ***The Young Rebel*** )
"The Young Rebel from LaMancha"

Produced by Miguel Salkind  Directed by Vincent Sherman
Starring Horst Buchholz, Gina Lollobrigida, Jose Ferrer, Louis
Jourdan

*The Brute and the Beast* (aka *Massacre Time* )
"What kind of men LIVE ONLY TO KILL?"

Produced by Oreste Coltallacci  Directed by Lucio Fulci
Starring Franco Nero, George Hilton, Nino Castelnuovo

March 1969-

*The Devil's Eight*
"They're the EIGHT you'll love or hate!"

Produced and Directed by Burt Topper
Starring Christopher George, Fabian, Tom Nardini, Leslie Parrish,
Larry Bishop, Ralph Meeker

Film Review- *The Devil's Eight*

*New York Times* (June 19, 1969) by A.H. Weiler
*The Devil's Eight* are, for the record, a crew of road gang
convicts surreptitiously freed by Federal agent Christopher
George to get the goods on moonshiner Ralph Meeker and
governmental higher-ups on the take. Their training would be
worthy of commandos versed in brawling, breakneck car handling,
grenade throwing, machine gunning, and sundry diversions.
   The carnage among these unshaven hard guys is continuous, as
is the action, under rudimentary direction.

April 1969-

*Hell's Belles*
"MEET THE DEBUTANTE in a LEATHER SKIRT. Too

Young... Too Tough... Too Itching for Action to Look for it--
She'll make it Where she is!"

Produced and Directed by Maury Dexter
Starring Jeremy Slate, Adam Roarke, Jocelyn Lane

Film Review- *Hell's Belles*

*New York Times* (April 30, 1970) by Roger Greenspun
(reviewed with *Cycle Savages*)
*Hell's Belles,* operating in mountainous Arizona, involves
Jeremy Slate as an improbable cowboy cycle champ in a one-man
vendetta against an outlaw cycle pack who've stolen his prize bike.
There are fewer beating in this number and perhaps the
scenery is a mite prettier in color, but a fairly sane viewer gets the
feeling, even as our hero varooms into the sunset on his retrieved
bike, that only devout worshipers of violence and, say, Harley
Davidsons, would give a fouled spark plug for either *Hell's Belles*
or *Cycle Savages*.

*Succubus* (a Trans American release)
"This motion picture is the story of a kind of woman you may not
have known even existed."

Produced by Adrian Hoven  Directed by Jess Franco
Starring Janine Reynaud, Jack Taylor

From the pressbook-
CONTROVERSIAL FILM- EROTIC DREAMS, EROTIC
REALITY: WHERE DOES ONE BEGIN, THE OTHER
END?
Dreams are not merely shadows, but have their own important
reality and significance, a truism found not only in Freud, but in
untold works of art, including certain motion pictures.
This is brought out vividly in the new controversial drama
*Succubus,* starring Janine Reynaud.
"I hope to become the first lady of the horror sex film," said
Janine with a wink during an appearance at the Berlin Film

Festival, where the film was shown out of competition and where Janine was called the festival's "most exciting figure."

April 7, 1969
*Boxoffice*
*HELGA* SUCCESS PROMPTS AIP TO MAKE SERIES OF SEX-EDUCATION FEATURES
by Syd Cassyd
Hollywood- Continuing American International Pictures' successful format of series of films on the same theme, James H. Nicholson, AIP president, has announced that the company will follow the same type of pattern on the sex-education film *Helga*.

The success of the picture has induced Nicholson and Samuel Z. Arkoff, AIP executive vice president, to become co-producers of two additional "Helga" films. The second, which is currently being readied for release, is being titled *Michael and Helga* and the third will be *Helga and the Sex Revolution*.

Originally, the AIP toppers had heard of the success of *Helga* and flew to Germany and brought it back last year. Since then, the film has become one of the top ten grossers of all time in Europe and it is currently bringing in record grosses in many situations in the United States.

### Michael and Helga

"An ADVENTURE into the UNEXPLORED LANDS of LOVE! Parents: Only you can judge if your children are mature and intelligent enough to view this revealing film."

Produced by Rolan Cammerer  Directed by Erich F. Bender
Starrign Ruth Gassmann, Felix Franchy

Film Review- *Michael and Helga*

*New York Times* (September 4, 1969) by Howard Thompson
*Michael and Helga* is a sincere, methodical, and unsensational film lecture on sexuality. Made in German with a whole string of doctors listed in supervisonal credits, the color feature has been

rather awkwardly dubbed in English when called for and has English narrators chiming in.

The import is a dignified, old-fashioned lecture in nice color, using documentary footage, a few dramatic snippets of a self-conscious couple called Michael and Helga, obviously played by nonprofessionals, and a flow of statistics.


May 1969-

*Destroy All Monsters*
"The MONSTERS are in REVOLT... and The World is on the brink of DESTRUCTION!"

Produced by Tomoyuki Tanaka  Directed by Ishiro Honda
Starring Akira Kubo, Jan Tazaki, Yukiko Kobayashi, Kenji Sahara

**Destroy All Monsters is another entry in Toho's Godzilla series. In Japan, the film was known as *Charge of the Monsters* or *Monster Invasion*.**

*God Forgives... I Don't* (aka *Blood River*)
"They call him Pretty Face... and his credo is simple and short and sweet!"

Produced by Enzo D'Ambrosio  Directed by Giuseppe Colizzi
Starring Terence Hill, Frank Wolf, Bud Spencer


June 1969-

*The Oblong Box*
"Edgar Allan Poe's classic tale of THE LIVING DEAD!"

Produced and Directed by Gordon Hessler
Starring Vincent Price, Christopher Lee, Hilary Dwyer

Film Reviews- *The Oblong Box*

*New York Times* (July 24, 1969) by A.H. Weiler

The British and American producers, who have been mining Edgar Allan Poe's seemingly inexhaustible literary lode like mad, now have unearthed *The Oblong Box* to illustrate once again that horror can be made to be quaint, laughable, and unconvincing at modest prices. All things considered, however, *The Oblong Box* (the coffin in this cheerless charade) might have been better left interred.

*Monthly Film Bulletin* (July 1970)- *The Oblong Box* is firmly stamped with the vigor and assurance that one is coming to associate with the horror films of Gordon Hessler.

**Hilary Dwyer (born 1945) appeared in five AIP British productions.**

*Chastity*
"She's not just a girl... she's an experience! Pick her up if you dare!"

Produced by Sonny Bono  Directed by Alessio de Paola
Starring Cher, Barbara London, Stephen Whittaker

Film Review- *Chastity*

*New York Times* (August 9, 1969) by Vincent Canby
The film, which was written and produced by Sonny Bono, stars only Cher, a tall, graceful girl with long black hair and a lovely impassive, oval face. Chastity wears tight brown slacks, a tight mauve jersey top, and an air of arrogant indolence as she hitchhikes around the Southwest, searching for life's meaning and being generally disagreeable to the unfortunate people who pick her up. Mostly, however, *Chastity* is like a small child's frown-solemn and innocent.

June 9, 1969
*Boxoffice*
NICHOLSON AND ARKOFF FETED AT VCI CONVENTION
Hollywood- James H. Nicholson, president, and Samuel Z. Arkoff, chairman of the board of American International Pictures, were presented special awards by Variety Clubs International at the 42nd annual VCI convention here. Outgoing VCI president Ralph W. Pries presented engraved silver cigarette boxes to the AIP heads for contributing a 50-minute Variety Clubs documentary.

AMERICAN INT'L OFFERS FIRST PUBLIC STOCK SALE
Washington- A planned 300,000 share combination offering of American International Pictures, Inc. common stock, representing the initial public sale of the common, was registered with the Securities and Exchange Commission.

NEW *WUTHERING HEIGHTS* TO BE FILMED BY AIP
Hollywood- American International Pictures has completed

arrangements for filming and worldwide distribution of a multi-million dollar production from Emily Bronte's classic novel *Wuthering Heights* with distribution in the United Kingdom set with Anglo Amalgamated Film Distributors Ltd.

The AIP heads announced that the new *Wuthering Heights* will be an updated, contemporary version of the classic and has been treated accordingly in the screenplay by Meade Roberts.

A major all-star cast will be assembled for the new *Wuthering Heights*, which will begin filming in September on location in London and Ireland.


July 1969-

### Spirits of the Dead (aka *Histoires Extraordinaires* )
"Edgar Allan Poe's ultimate orgy dissects the anatomy of terror!"

Produced by Raymond Eger  Directed by Federico Fellini, Louis Malle, Roger Vadim
Starring Brigitte Bardot, Alain Delon, Jane Fonda, Terence Stamp, Peter Fonda

Film Reviews- *Spirits of the Dead*

*Motion Picture Herald* (July 23, 1969)- *Spirits of the Dead* is an ambitious attempt by three of Europe's most capable and respected directors to wed the approach and techniques of art film to the horror-fantasy material of Edgar Allan Poe. Their success in this enterprise is difficult to estimate since AIP, in picking up the American distribution rights, has apparently tried to tailor it to a less sophisticated shocker-exploitation audience.

*Time* (September 12, 1969)- The credentials are impressive. Federico Fellini, Louis Malle, and Roger Vadim, each directing a brace of international superstars in a loose adaptation of a Poe story, seem to promise one of the better anthology films. But the ads have something else in mind. "Edgar Allan Poe's ultimate orgy of evil and unbearable horror!" they shriek, conjuring up images of a dawn-to-dusk scare show at the local drive-in. Obviously, the distributors were afraid of something- probably the spooks the *Spirits of the Dead* promises, but never actually delivers.

*Los Angeles Herald Tribune*- The original idea was quite insane: Round up three famous European directors, surround them with beautiful people, mix Gothic horror, and then force-feed the whole conglomeration to a shell-shocked audience.

*Los Angeles Times*- The only real accomplishment of this shoddy trilogy is to make Roger Corman's Poe pictures look awfully good in comparison.

August 1969-

***Angel, Angel Down We Go*** (aka ***Cult of the Damned***)
"Can a sophisticated young man find happiness in the arms of an entire family?"

Produced by Jerome F. Katzman  Directed by Robert Thom
Starring Jennifer Jones, Jordan Christopher, Holly Near, Lou Rawls, Roddy McDowall

Film Reviews- *Angel, Angel Down We Go*

*Variety*- Miss [Jennifer] Jones, apparently uncertain as to what her role is supposed to be, wavers between sensuality and matronliness.

*The Hollywood Reporter*- Miss Jones' once mannered twitch has become an unpleasant snarl, in no way softened by the lines she is forced to mouth.

*New York Times* (February 4, 1971) by A.H. Weiler (reviewed as *Cult of the Damned*)
Holly Near, as the plump daughter of Jennifer Jones and millionaire Charles Aidman, has trouble respecting her parents.

Matters aren't helped when she becomes involved with Jordan Christopher and his group. And they're further confused when Christopher entices mama and, in the end, is eyeing papa. It's disjointed fare, despite a plethora of anti-establishment remarks, that leaves little impact even on a willing viewer.

### De Sade

"The Most Distinguished and Daring Film Entertainment of The Year!"

Produced by Samuel Z. Arkoff and James H. Nicholson  Directed by Cy Endfield
Starring Keir Dullea, Senta Berger, Lilli Palmer, Anna Massey, John Huston, Sonja Ziemann

From the pressbook-
*DE SADE* FIRST MOVIE TO SERIOUSLY PROBE LIFE OF FRENCH REVOLUTIONARY
American International's elaborate film production *De Sade* is the first film, surprisingly, to attempt a serious probe into the nature of a notorious Frenchman of grossly underrated historical importance, the Marquis de Sade, according to the extraordinary film's director Cy Endfield.

"In many ways, sadism is a perfectly just epitaph, but de Sade's life is more than a pre-Freudian textbook of passion and violence; it is also a highly contemporary story of protest," the director stated.

His only serious criminal excesses were distributing dangerous aphrodisiacs to Marseilles prostitutes and (reputedly) violently abusing one called Rose Keller.

One thing cannot be held against him, however. He could write sensitively when the mood took him. On a good day, de Sade was even known to write humorously, although his own story, now brought to the screen at long last, was very far from funny.

PROMOTION SUGGESTIONS
Dress six girls in the *De Sade* fashion, leather skirts, boots, and bolero jackets; they carry whips and hand out heralds. On their backs, each girl carries a letter of the title.

Film Reviews- *De Sade*

*New York Times* (September 26, 1969) by Vincent Canby
*De Sade*, which the producer's press agent once described as "A film biography of the great 18th century writer and sadist," is not quite as silly as it looks and sounds, but it comes very close. It successfully reduces one of the most fascinating figures of world

371

literature to the role of a not-so-straight man in a series of naughty tableaux vivants.

According to Cy Endfield, who directed the film, and Richard Matheson, who wrote it, the extent of Sade's inhuman, perverted, unnatural, lecherous, depraved behavior was a fondness for bare bosoms and round bottoms.

*Time* (October 24, 1969)- The new movie biography called *De Sade* is painful. Keir Dullea appears as the troubled marquis and his vulpine, immobile face helps him to range between anger and pitiful pleading with indifference. The orgies are only slightly more titillating than a *Playboy* centerfold and a good deal less polished. According to this film, the marquis' most notable contribution to esoteric eroticism was spreading jam on women's nipples.

**John Huston, in drag as a gypsy fortune teller, and Keir Dullea in *De Sade*.**

August 4, 1969
*Boxoffice*
AIP ANNOUNCES 21 FEATURE RELEASES JANUARY
'69 THROUGH APRIL '70
Hollywood- American International Pictures, with seven films released since January 1, has announced that it will have a total of 21 pictures in release for the year 1969 and extending through April 1970.

All but two of the 14 "quality" features slated between now and April 15 have been completed with work on the other two to begin within 60 days.

Important properties in the planning stage include seven best-selling novels, such as a contemporary film version of the Emily Bronte classic, *Wuthering Heights;* the Angus Hall novel, *The Late Boy Wonder;* William Maidment's *The Adultress; Public Parts and Private Places,* novel by Robin Cook; Robert Kyle's *Venus Examined;* the B.F. Jones novel *Implosion;* and Peter Saxon's suspense novel, *Scream and Scream Again,* which recently completed filming.

On the immediate AIP schedule yet to be filmed are *Lay Me Down to Sleep, Cry of the Banshee,* and *Sand Bum.*

Set for September release is *The Lonely Hearts Killers,* based on a Lonely Hearts Club murder case, produced by Warren Steibel and directed by Leonard Kastle. In October, AIP will distribute *Two Gentlemen Sharing* and in November, the company will release *Dunwich,* starring Sandra Dee and Dean Stockwell, directed by Daniel Haller.

The first release for the new year will be *Explosion* with Don Stroud and Gordon Thomson starred. Also set for January is *Savage Wild,* filmed in the Canadian wilderness. February releases include *Scream and Scream Again,* starring Vincent Price and Christopher Lee, and *Mafia,* starring Franco Nero and Lee J. Cobb.

Concluding the list are *Bloody Mama,* scheduled for March, and *Lola,* set for April.

**The Lonely Hearts Killers became The Honeymoon Killers and it was distributed by Cinerama Releasing Corp. in February 1970.**

September 1969-

*Hell's Angels '69*
"THIS WAS THE RUMBLE THAT ROCKED LAS VEGAS!
For a wild, wild weekend and the deadliest gamble ever dared!"

Produced by Tom Stern  Directed by Lee Madden
Starring Tom Stern, Jeremy Slate, Conny Van Dyke, Steve Sandor

Film Review- *Hell's Angels '69*

> *New York Times* (September 11, 1969) by Roger Greenspun
> *Hell's Angels '69* uses that noted law-and-order group, the Oakland, Calif., Hell's Angels, as heroes in a dismal story that wastes most of its attention on the villains. By now, their physical resemblance to lovable teddy bears may well have affected the Angels' self-image, but not, I hope, to the extent that they continue to submit to such degrading elevation in American folk-demonology.
> *Hell's Angels '69* more than lacks in character and conviction what it attempts to make up in a sucker's-eye view of Vegas casinos and timid glances at bike-groups' mores. Only Miss [Connie]
> Van Dyke emerges, her acting ability still in question, but her physical presence superb.

*Two Gentlemen Sharing*
"One was Black... one was White... but they had one thing in common!"

Produced by J. Barry Kulick  Directed by Ted Kotcheff
Starring Robin Phillips, Judy Geeson, Hal Frederick, Hilary Dwyer

Film Review- *Two Gentlemen Sharing*

> *New York Times* (September 18, 1969) by Vincent Canby
> *Two Gentlemen Sharing*, the British film which opened yesterday, is a movie about confused identities, a theme that may

have reached its most perfect cinematic expression in *The Prisoner of Zenda. Two Gentleman Sharing,* however, is not about look-alikes in Ruritania. Rather it takes place in London and concerns two men who share similar identity crises, if you believe that social and sexual identity crises are similar, which I don't. The movie itself is like a mixed metaphor. I mean it's unsatisfying because it's basically invalid.

September 29, 1969
*Boxoffice*
The London Report by Anthony Gruner
PRESS HONORS ARKOFF
Prior to the screening of *Angel, Angel Down We Go* at the Edinburgh Film Festival, Samuel Z. Arkoff, American International Pictures chairman of the board, was honored at a festival press reception.

October 1969-

October 20, 1969
*Boxoffice*
NEW AIP SUBSIDIARY
In Hollywood, American International's company heads Samuel Z. Arkoff and James H. Nicholson officially welcomed aboard George Sherlock, newly appointed general manager of American International Records, the film firm's new subsidiary.

November 1969-

November 3, 1969
*Boxoffice*
AIP EARNINGS FOR SIX MONTHS RISE, EXPECT 20 RELEASES IN CURRENT YEAR
New York- American International Pictures has reported revenues totaling $11,893,000 for the six months ended August 30, 1969. This compares with $9,897,000 for the same period in 1968.

AIP's releasing schedule for the current year will consist of approximately 20 feature motion pictures. Among these films in various stages of production and being readied for release in the next fiscal year are Roger Corman's *Bloody Mama*, starring Shelley Winters, and *Cry of the Banshee*, from an Edgar Allan Poe story "Valley of Unrest," starring Vincent Price.

Relative to future product, the company has accelerated plans for many important film projects. These include *Wuthering Heights*, the Emily Bronte classic, to be adapted to modern times and film techniques; an untitled sequel to AIP's successful *Wild in the Streets; When the Sleeper Wakes*, from H.G. Wells' classic; and *Christmas With Grandma*, an updated version of "Hansel and Gretel."

November 17, 1969
*Boxoffice*
ARKOFF, NICHOLSON PLAN STEP-UP OF AIP PRODUCT
Washington- American International Pictures hosted its 14th annual exhibitors' luncheon for the more than 1,500 attending the 1969 convention of the National Ass'n of Theatre Owners here on Tuesday, November 11. AIP heads Samuel Z. Arkoff and James H. Nicholson welcomed the throng and called themselves "the oldest incumbent management in Hollywood."

Nicholson said that now is the time for AIP to step up the quality and quantity of its product lineup rather than cutting back, as many of the majors are planning.

Shelley Winters, star of AIP's upcoming *Bloody Mama*, was then introduced. She spoke of AIP's admirable policy of giving young talent a chance and said she had learned the importance of the exhibitor through her 20 years in the industry.

December 1969-

December 22, 1969
*Boxoffice*
AMERICAN INT'L MOVES TO NEW HEADQUARTERS
Beverly Hills- American International Pictures has completed its

long-planned move of home office facilities and personnel and is now established for business at new headquarters located at 9033 Wilshire Blvd. in Beverly Hills. The new phone number is 278-8118.

The move to the new four-story American International building ended an eight-year tenure in former AIP headquarters at 7165 Sunset Blvd. in Hollywood.

AIP heads Samuel Z. Arkoff and James H. Nicholson said the move fulfills a progressively increasing need for expanded physical facilities to match the company's rapid growth in the entertainment industry and signified a new era in the firm's corporate development.

In addition to executive, sales, legal, accounting, production, music, and advertising, the new American International building encompasses quarters for the company's West Coast television division, cutting rooms, and art department.

The former AIP building in Hollywood has been purchased by Transcontinental Entertainment Corp.

**Another decade came to an end and, despite the box office failure of _De Sade_, AIP was still on an increasingly upward trajectory in the motion picture industry. But the next few years would bring about some devastating changes on both personal and professional levels for Sam and Jim.**

**Ingrid Pitt, Hammer and AIP's new Sex Symbol
for the Seventies.**

# PART THREE

**THE SEVENTIES- From Anti-Establishment to the Mainstream**

"Twice the TERROR... Ten Times the SHOCK!"

**Bigger budgets and Blaxploitation. Times change and AIP is there to exploit every new trend. The company moves into the big league, but a lengthy partnership dissolves.**

# CHAPTER SEVENTEEN
# 1970

AIP exhibitor's manual for 1970-
ANY WAY YOU LOOK AT IT... IT'S AMERICAN
INTERNATIONAL IN '70

During the Sixties, American International grew from the *Wunderkind* of the movie business into a viable, active, substantial film company with a reputation for profitable product and unexcelled exhibitor relations.

Our *new look* which we showed you last year hasn't worn off a bit. In fact, as you will see in the following pages, in this first year of the new decade, that *new look* shines brighter than ever.

Now in release:
H.P. Lovecraft's Classic Tale of Terror and the Supernatural!
THE DUNWICH HORROR

THE SAVAGE WILD... where the trails end and the adventure begins!

Here is the horror that nightmares are made of! SCREAM AND SCREAM AGAIN!

Twice Banned in Europe, now it can be seen here! BORA BORA.

March

To Mom with love from the boys... say it with bullets... Shelley Winters as BLOODY MAMA.

Up tight against a wall of defiance where a careless word or a casual kiss becomes a lighted fuse... Jules Bricken's EXPLOSION!

April

Twice the Terror in this Shock Combination! THE CRIMSON CULT and HORROR HOUSE!

The Wildest Bunch of the "70's! THE CYCLE SAVAGES!

WITCHCRAFT '70... a startling documentary film by Gigi Scattini

May

He just might break the world's record! 24-HOUR MAN.

Everyone knew <u>why</u> but the bridegroom! WEDDING NIGHT.

June

A funny, far out, flatulent look at the future. GAS!

Edgar Allan Poe's CRY OF THE BANSHEE. The scream that kills!

Trade up... before your present model needs a major overhaul! WIFE SWAPPERS.

July

ANGELS UNCHAINED... They ride again!

What they didn't dare in The Attic they're doing down in The Cellar! UP IN THE CELLAR.

August
THE VAMPIRE LOVERS... The most erotic chapter in the Book of the Undead.
CRUNCH! When an irresistible movement meets an immovable resistment.

Coming
MAFIA... Uncle Mario wants <u>you</u>!

More to come
A Bullet for Pretty Boy, Beach Bum, The Adultress, H.G. Wells' When the Sleeper Wakes, Wuthering Heights, Murders in the Rue Morgue, Dante's Inferno, Public Parts and Private Places.


January 1970-

Trade magazine announcement-
AIP AND HAMMER TO PRODUCE "VAMPIRE LOVER" IN ENGLAND
A co-production agreement has been reached between American International and Sir James Carreras of Hammer Films, London, for the filming of *The Vampire Lover* [sic] it was announced by AIP heads Samuel Z. Arkoff and James H. Nicholson. The film will be produced in London by Carreras and Roy Ward Baker directing. Set for a February start, the picture stars Peter Cushing, Dawn Addams, Kate O'Mara, Madeleine Smith, and continental sex image Ingrid Pitt.

*Fearless Frank/Madigan's Millions* (Trans American releases)
"The Most Incredible Comedies Ever Laughed At!"

*Fearless Frank*
Produced and Directed by Philip Kaufman
Starring Jon Voight, Monique Van Vooren

*Madigan's Millions*
Produced by Sidney Pink  Directed by Stanley Prager
Starring Dustin Hoffman, Elsa Martinelli, Cesar Romero

The new decade for AIP got off to an inauspicious start with a pair of lame comedies which had been purchased to capitalize on the success of *Midnight Cowboy*. Jon Voight made his motion picture debut in *Fearless Frank* in 1967. Dustin Hoffman had appeared in the Italian production *Madigan's Millions* in 1968. AIP press screened the double bill in Los Angeles on December 10, 1969, and it went into general release in January 1970.

*The Savage Wild*
"A Trackless Land of Violent Splendor! They Challenged the Last Wilderness!"

Produced and Directed by Gordon Eastman
Starring Gordon Eastman, Carl Spore, Maria Eastman

From the pressbook-
FAMED WORLD EXPLORER INVADES ANIMAL KINGDOM
Eminent photographer, writer, lecturer, and film producer Gordon Eastman brings another noteworthy film drama of unexplored wilderness and wildlife to the screen in American International's *The Savage Wild*.
The exciting film focuses on the adoption of a brood of wild wolf puppies by Eastman during his camera invasion of the wild animal kingdom in Canada's wilderness. The film took over two years of filming to complete.

SEAT SELLING SLANTS-
Contact local sportsman lodges in your area. Aside from catering to your regular audiences, don't forget that over 80 million Americans are avid followers of outdoor game.

*The Dunwich Horror*
"A few years ago in Dunwich, a half-witted girl bore illegitimate twins. One of them was almost human!"

Produced by James H. Nicholson and Samuel Z. Arkoff Directed by Daniel Haller
Starring Sandra Dee, Dean Stockwell, Ed Begley, Lloyd Bochner, Donna Baccala, Sam Jaffe

From the pressbook-
WERE DEMONS THE ORIGINAL HIPPIES?
In American International's supernatural thriller *The Dunwich Horror*, there are several scenes where frizzle-haired demons participate in ritualistic orgies.

The demons were hand-picked by Director Daniel Haller from among several communities of hippies who have flocked into the forest and coastal area of Mendocino county in northern California.

Those picked were not selected because of acting ability, but because their weird hairdos or scraggly beards made them look like demons with very little additional makeup.

Film Review- *The Dunwich Horror*

*New York Times* (July 9, 1970) by Howard Thompson
It is probably just as well that H.P. Lovecraft, the highly esteemed novelist of the supernatural, is no longer around to see the film version of his "Dunwich" exercise. Whatever the worth of his story, the picture is nothing more than standard, old-fashioned haunted house spookery tricked up with jumbled, garish color effects and clanging music intended to convey an army of demons on the loose.

February 1970-

*Scream and Scream Again*
"Shock After Shock To Leave You Numb With Terror!"

Produced by Max Rosenberg and Milton Subotsky  Directed by Gordon Hessler
Starring Vincent Price, Christopher Lee, Peter Cushing, Judy Huxtable, Michael Gothard

Gordon Hessler (Director): "[Max] Rosenberg and [Milton] Subotsky didn't understand the film at all and were continually trying to interfere. Deke [Louis Heyward] finally had them barred from the set. I am very pleased with this film."

From the pressboook-
A GRUESOME THREESOME
The world's three leading exponents of the gentle art of horror, Vincent Price, Christopher Lee and Peter Cushing, team together for the first time in American International's suspense drama *Scream and Scream Again.*

"But," says their director Gordon Hessler, "I don't really think I would describe it as a horror film."

Hessler (once associated with Alfred Hitchcock in Hollywood) says he would call the picture a modern detective thriller, but adds: "It does have some rather grisly scenes in it, which come under the horror heading."

Two examples from the "non-horror" drama include a killer committing suicide by jumping into an acid vat and a series of macabre transplants used to build a perfect human body organ by organ! "It has," says a slightly tongue-in-cheek Hessler, "all the undercurrents that horrify in the traditional horror story."

SEAT SELLING SLANTS-
Insert the word WARNING in all newspaper ads and on poster paper. Advertise a nurse in attendance. Caution those with weak hearts to BEWARE.

Film Reviews- *Scream and Scream Again*

*Hollywood Reporter* (February 10, 1970)- *Scream and Scream Again* has the successful touch of the vampire, the scientist perfecting the perfect race of beings, dismemberings, some lovely nude bodies, and a continuous guessing game as to what's going on throughout its 94 minutes.

*Los Angeles Times* (February 21, 1970)- *Scream and Scream Again* is a superb piece of contemporary horror, a science fiction tale possessed of a credibility infinitely more terrifying than any of the Gothic witchery of *Rosemary's Baby*.

*New York Times* (July 9, 1970) by Howard Thompson
*Scream and Scream Again* proceeds to unwind British-style, crisply, puzzlingly, and with some restraint. And the plot, which Christopher Wicking has adapted from a novel by Peter Saxon, begins to loop into a good, tight knot after the director, Gordon Hessler, bears down hard and graphically on a countryside pursuit by the police of a young mod-type killer.

February 16, 1970
*Boxoffice*
ARKOFF ADVISES EXHIBITORS TO APPEAL TO CURRENT TASTES TO BE SUCCESSFUL
Dallas- Decrying the signs of panic in Hollywood, the expenditure of vast sums on "blockbuster pictures," and the production of so-called "family pictures," Samuel Z. Arkoff, chairman of the board of American International Pictures, told the NATO of Texas convention here Wednesday (Feb. 4) that "today the audience is fragmented- and with the exception of the big and successful picture that may, by its special elements, appeal to many different groups, one must take aim at a special group in order to be successful."

The successful pictures, he continued, are those that appeal to not the entire family, but to a sizable but fragmented group and today's producers cannot make films to please everyone.

Of AIP and the future, Arkoff said, "We are doing business at the same old stand in the same way- growing naturally," adding, "We are continuing to put all our profits in the picture business. This is the only business we are in. We have the utmost confidence in the picture business- and so should you."

## AIP SALES CONFERENCE IN HOUSTON FEB. 23

Hollywood- American International Pictures sales executive and key personnel totaling approximately 75 representatives from all sections of the United States and portions of Canada will convene in Houston, Tex. Feb. 23 through March 5 for AIP's annual national sales conference at which sales policies and procedures for the company's elaborate 21-feature releasing program through September of 1970 will be outlined.

March 1970-

### Explosion

"KISSING OR KILLING... if it feels good... do it!"

Produced by Julian Roffman   Directed by Jules Bricken
Starring Don Stroud, Gordon Thomson, Richard Conte, Michelle Chicoine, Robin Ward

**Don Stroud (born 1943) appeared in seven films for AIP.**

From the pressbook-
*EXPLOSION* X-RAYS TODAY'S DRAFT-DODGING PROBLEM!
Jules Bricken's film *Explosion*, filmed in color, starring Don Stroud, Gordon Thomson, and Richard Conte, is a contemporary drama which probes the troubled center of today's restless youth movement and current explosive reactions to the draft problem.

*Explosion* unfolds the shocking story of an American draft dodger who bitterly resents the death of his older brother, who was killed in action in Vietnam. As a result, he rebels against his family and the Establishment and eventually comes to a tragic crisis.

Stroud's meteoric career has been recently highlighted by star appearances in... *tick... tick... tick* and an indelible role in AIP's *Bloody Mama.*

EXPLOITATION
*EXPLOSION* is current newspaper headline material- use this theme to sell the picture, headline special screenings for adult groups, and enlist the aid of your local radio station and newspapers to interview viewers to find out their feelings as they leave the theatre.

**Bloody Mama**
"When it comes to killing... Mama knows best!"

Produced and Directed by Roger Corman
Starring Shelley Winters, Pat Hingle, Don Stroud, Diane Varsi, Bruce Dern, Robert DeNiro

Film review- *Bloody Mama*

*Time* (May 11, 1970)- *Bloody Mama* is a lurid little number featuring Shelly Winters doing her smothering mother thing as the nefarious Ma Barker. You can tell she's mama because she is older than just about anyone else in the cast. Presumably, she should know better. A hapless and bloody rehash of *Bonnie and Clyde*, *Bloody Mama* features Shelley as the head of a small criminal band of psychopathic wastrels, four of whom are, incidentally, her sons. Producer-Director Roger Corman has made some tricky, sinister horror movies in his time (*The Tomb of Ligeia, The Masque of the Red Death*), but the hysterical vulgarity of *Bloody Mama* suggests he is more at home with crypts than crooks.

**Shelley Winters and Pat Hingle in *Bloody Mama*.**

March 6, 1970
*Boxoffice*
AIP TO TAKE OVER U.S. DISTRIBUTION OF COMMONWEALTH UNITED FILMS
Hollywood- American International will handle U.S. theatrical distribution of Commonwealth United Entertainment films under the terms of an agreement announced here Friday (March 3) by Samuel Z. Arkoff, AIP chairman; James H. Nicholson, AIP president; and Oliver Unger, CUE division chief executive officer.

The agreement involves 43 films, 27 of which are now in release. The 16 films not yet released are completed and ready for release.

Nicholson and Arkoff stated: "We are most proud to handle this lineup of product, which is one of the most important groups of films of any company in the industry. These new releases will in no way affect AIP's present production and release schedule, but will augment it at a time when Hollywood has been affected by a lull in production. This is extremely important, since a steady flow of top box office films to the nation's theaters is a vital stimulus to the industry."

The 16 films awaiting release include *Venus in Furs, Battle of Neretva, Julius Caesar, The Cannibals Among Us, Tam Lin, Dorian Gray, The Promise, Legion of the Damned, Strangers at Sunrise, Triangle, That Lady from Peking, The Savage Season, Freelance, Count Dracula, Tiki Tiki,* and *Anna Karenina.*

Trade ad-
American International is proud to be the exclusive U.S. Theatrical Distributor for Commonwealth United films, including:

*The Magic Christian, Viva Max, Venus in Furs, Battle of Neretva, Julius Caesar, The Cannibals, Tam Lin...* and many, many more!

It's AMERICAN INTERNATIONAL in '70.

April 1970-

*The Cycle Savages* (a Trans American release)
"HOT STEEL BETWEEN THEIR LEGS... THE WILDEST BUNCH OF THE 70's!
Roaring through the streets on chopped down hogs! SAVAGE!

Produced by Maurice Smith  Directed by Bill Brame
Starring Bruce Dern, Chris Robinson, Melody Patterson

Film Review- *The Cycle Savages*

*New York Times* (April 30, 1970) by Roger Greenspun
That minuscule subdivision of our youth, the mobile mobsters who reportedly dote as much on mayhem as they do on roaring motorcycles, get ample opportunity to display inane, destructive

madness in *Cycle Savages*. *Cycle Savages*, set in Los Angeles, has a gang led by an unshaven psychotic, played in unbelievably paranoiac style by Bruce Dern, dedicated to white slavery and to destroying a young artist who's done some incriminating sketches of them. There's a plethora of senseless beatings, torture, love making, and robbery to say nothing of a gang rape before these crackpot cyclists are unseated or killed.

May 1970-

*Horror House/The Crimson Cult*
"All new! NIGHTMARE combination of SHOCK and TERROR!"

**Both films in this double feature program were filmed in England as co-productions with Tigon British Films.** *Horror House* **was originally titled** *The Haunted House of Horror* **and** *The Crimson Cult* **was** *Curse of the Crimson Altar.*

*Horror House*
Produced by Tony Tenser  Directed by Michael Armstrong
Starring Frankie Avalon, Jill Haworth, Dennis Price, George Sewell, Mark Wynter

From the pressbook-
FAMED HAUNTED HOUSE USED IN AIP's *HORROR HOUSE*
The northwest English coastal resort of Southport, setting for American International's *Horror House*, is rich in eerie period manor houses which provide a spine-chilling background for 24-year-old British writer-director Michael Armstrong's psychological suspense drama of a séance and murder involving a mixed group of adolescents in a gaunt haunted house.

Chosen for the exteriors in *Horror House* was the Gothic-style manor house Band Hall at Bretherton, an imposing 17th Century estate owned by Lord Lilford, where the unit spent five nights of location shooting.

Michael Armstrong (Writer-Director): "Arkoff and Nicholson were not the kind of people you messed with."

*The Crimson Cult*
Produced by Louis M. Heyward and Tony Tenser  Directed by Vernon Sewell
Starring Boris Karloff, Christopher Lee, Mark Eden, Barbara Steele, Michael Gough

From the pressbook-
*CRIMSON CULT* STARS CINEMA MONSTERS BORIS KARLOFF AND CHRISTOPHER LEE
Boris Karloff was the first to portray Mary Shelley's monster on the screen in the original *Frankenstein* in the early 1930s. Some 20 years later, Christopher Lee's career was to be given the same kind of impetus by the same role when, after a series of telling but minor parts in films, Chris decided to enter the fantasy world of the macabre as Frankenstein's monstrous creation in *The Curse of Frankenstein*. This led to many more excursions into the sinister and brought Christopher to the title "The Crown Prince of Terror," second only in rank to Karloff. Both stars currently share starring honors in American International's horror-suspense drama *The Crimson Cult*.

Film review- *The Crimson Cult*

*New York Times* (November 12, 1970) by Roger Greenspun
I should be hard-pressed to defend *The Crimson Cult* on any grounds other than affection for the subject and for some of the cast. The special appeal of *The Crimson Cult* may be the last performance of the late Boris Karloff. He plays Professer Marshe, an ancient beneficent believer in the black arts, and his role holds no surprises. But Karloff himself, cadaverous and almost wholly crippled, acts with a quiet lucidity of such great beauty that it is a refreshment merely to hear him speak old claptrap. Nothing else in *The Crimson Cult* comes close to him- though there is Barbara Steele in greenface playing Lavinia, a glamorous 300-year-old.

*Wedding Night* (aka *I Can't... I Can't* )
"Her doctor knows! Her priest knows! Why can't she tell her husband? Every loving couple should see this film before it's too late."

Produced by Philip N. Krasne  Directed by Piers Haggard
Starring Dennis Waterman, Tessa Wyatt, Alexandra Bastedo

From the pressbook-
FILM SPARKS CONTROVERSY
The question which provided the crux of the controversy surrounding the popular *Forsyte Saga* series on TV is likely to be raised again by the showing of American International's *Wedding Night*.

The question posed by both productions is "can a husband be guilty of rape where his wife is concerned?" For JOE, played by Dennis Waterman of *Up the Junction* fame, and his bride MADY, played by Tessa Wyatt, the situation following Joe's attempt to take his rights by force looks equally black.

*Wedding Night* traces the consequences of a young and conventionally devout Irish girl being witness to her mother's fatal miscarriage, an event made the more traumatic because it occurs on Mady's own wedding day.

May 4, 1970
*Boxoffice*
AMERICAN INT'L CHARTS 32 RELEASES TO BE AVAILABLE NEXT 12 MONTHS
Hollywood- With a total of 32 pictures scheduled for release between April 1970 and April 1971, American International Pictures chairman of the board Samuel Z. Arkoff and president James H. Nicholson on April 29 announced the company's most ambitious release schedule at a press conference at the Beverly Hills Hotel. Twenty-seven of the films have been completed and five are currently shooting or are in pre-production stages.

Terming this "one of the most exciting periods in the industry's history," Arkoff and Nicholson continued: "Certainly, it is a period of change... and our company, along with most of the forward-looking creators of entertainment, welcomes the challenge."

May 10, 1970
*Boxoffice*
AIP OFFERS 'HEIGHTS' AS VCI FUND RAISER
San Juan, Puerto Rico- American International Pictures president James H. Nicholson and chairman of the board Samuel Z. Arkoff, hosting their company's luncheon before 500 Variety Club International members at the Americana Hotel here Monday (May 4), announced that AIP would make available its forthcoming films, *Wuthering Heights*, to be premiered worldwide under sponsorship of all local Variety tents. This unique action, the AIP executives said, was in consideration of VCI's philanthropic activities promoting the welfare of youth around the world.

Still in production on the Yorkshire moors of England, *Wuthering Heights*, which stars Anna Calder-Marshall and Timothy Dalton, is not slated for release until January 1971. Thus, said Nicholson and Arkoff, plenty of time is available for proper planning to insure the success of each benefit premier.

Delegates attending the AIP luncheon viewed a specially produced five-minute featurette containing scenes already shot for the picture, introducing characters and action and narrated by Art Gilmore.

June 1970-

*Count Yorga Vampire* (aka *The Loves of Count Iorga*)
"A TALE OF UNSPEAKABLE CRAVINGS... The Most Terrifying Experience of Your Life!"

Produced by Michael Macready  Directed by Bob Kelljan
Starring Robert Quarry, Roger Perry, Michael Muphy, Michael Macready, Donna Anders

Film review- *Count Yorga Vampire*

*New York Times* (November 12, 1970) by Roger Greenspun

Count Yorga's ambience is pure Hollywood and the seamy elegance of Robert Quarry's performance as a mysterious medium who has a handy supply of spirits of the dead lying around downstairs exactly compliments that ambience. Bob Kelljan's direction, often resourceful, does especially well by Quarry's disdainful civility- particularly toward Dr. Hayes (Roger Perry), his principal adversary- during their long, tense conversations that are the greatest pleasure in the movie.

June 15, 1970

*Boxoffice*

SONY'S VIDEOCASSETTES INTEREST AIP HEADS

Hollywood- The huge line at the Sony exhibit of its home tape cassette was swelled by the many exhibitors from the Variety Tent 25 luncheon on Wednesday (June 10). James H. Nicholson, president of American International Pictures, told *Boxoffice* that he and Samuel Z. Arkoff, AIP board chairman, are going to Japan at the invitation of Messrs. Ibuka, president of Sony, and Morita, executive vice president.

One of the developments in their video tape machine, which will come on the market in 1971, according to an informed source (Nicholson), is the capability of holding down the running of certain programs more than once.

June 23, 1970

*Boxoffice*

Beverly Hills- American International Pictures has stepped up its production pace to make the next six months the most active period in company history, it was announced by Samuel Z. Arkoff, chairman of the board, and James H. Nicholson, president, who outlined a concentration of projects which will find thirteen pictures completed or in post-production by the end of September.

Three films are already up before AIP cameras with *Up in the Cellar* in Las Cruces, N.M.; *Unchained,* on assorted desert locations in Arizona; and *Wuthering Heights,* on England's Yorkshire Moors.

Two films are slated for a June 15 start. *Murders in the Rue*

*Morgue,* based on the Edgar Allan Poe classic, and *Crunch,* a comedy to be directed by Jerome Kaufman.

Veteran director Gerd Oswald is currently scouting New Mexico locations for *Bunny and Claude,* crime satire starring Bette Davis in an offbeat role as a gun toting harridan. The film rolls in July.

In addition to *Bunny and Claude,* production will start in July on *Busy Bodies,* starring Diana Kjaer and Marie Liljedahl, and *I'll Marry You with Diamonds,* to be directed by Robert Fuest.

Vincent Price goes before the cameras in August for his starring role in *Devilday,* based on Angus Hall's novel; and George Pal will produce and direct *When the Sleeper Wakes,* based on H.G. Wells' classic. A third film, *Blood Sport,* is also scheduled for the month with Norman Herman producing.

Nicholson and Arkoff will put two films before the cameras in September, *Dante's Inferno* and *Beach Bum.*

Arkoff and Nicholson pointed to the lineup as an example of the company's emphasis on diversification.

July 1970-

### *A Bullet for Pretty Boy*
'THE SAGA OF PRETTY BOY FLOYD who stole more money... loved more girls... killed more men than most laws allow."

Produced and Directed by Larry Buchanan
Starring Fabian Forte, Jocelyn Lane, Astrid Warner, Adam Roarke

From the pressbook-
"PRETTY BOY FLOYD" AS REAL AS DEATH
Realism is the main ingredient of *A Bullet for Pretty Boy.* American International insisted that the biography of Charles "Pretty Boy" Floyd be authentic and producer-director Larry Buchanan went to Texas to capture the actual locales in the color drama of crime and death.

Fabian Forte, who depicts Floyd, is the former singer who turned to acting and has established a steady career in demanding roles. He was pleased that *A Bullet for Pretty Boy* had the physical feeling and appearance of 1934 and observed, "I have to keep reminding myself at the end of the day that this is 1970 and that I can shave with electricity and watch TV and drive a car with air conditioning."

### *24 Hour Lover* (aka *Crunch!*)
"HE JUST MIGHT BREAK THE WORLD'S RECORD!... if he could only remember to keep score."

Produced by Rob Houwer  Directed by Marran Gosov
Starring Harald Leipnitz, Sybille Marr, Brigitte Skay, Monida Lundi

### *Cry of the Banshee*
"Edgar Allan Poe probes new depths of TERROR!"

Produced and Directed by Gordon Hessler
Starring Vincent Price, Essy Persson, Hugh Griffith, Elisabeth Bergner, Hilary Dwyer

Film reviews- *Cry of the Banshee*

*Variety* (July 30, 1970)- Vincent Price is again the medieval evil. The production creates a very believable look of the Middle Ages with outdoor scenes particularly having the rich earthy red and brown hues of early Dutch paintings.

*New York Times* (December 17, 1970) by Vincent Canby
"You may have heard that they think of me as some kind of monster in the village," Vincent Price intones rhetorically in *Cry of the Banshee*, thereby unwittingly setting a comedy tone to this ersatz excursion into the dark past. It's hardly a revelation. The film is only mildly diverting and scarcely a tribute to that old-time religion or ritual murder. Mr. Price, a veteran of a score of these hapless horror items, plays it all with proper pseudo gusto.

July 3, 1970
*Boxoffice*
MORE PRODUCT, BIGGER PROFITS FOR AIP, ARKOFF,
NICHOLSON TELL STOCKHOLDERS
Hollywood- Stockholders of American International Pictures,
in their first annual meeting here on Monday (June 29), heard
forecasts of top profits and a product flow of 27 to 30 features for
the 1970-71 fiscal year in reports given by chairman of the board
Samuel Z. Arkoff and president James H. Nicholson. The session
was held at Pacific's Beverly Theatre.

Arkoff reported that AIP "is in good shape" with the largest
supply of completed pictures in its history, including many of the
16 pictures obtained from Commonwealth United.

Nicholson outlined AIP's aim to provide feature films on
subjects of appeal to modern patrons and told the shareholders,
"Our future production plans stress quality and diversity. A good
example of what we mean by quality and diversity is *Bunny*. This is
an action-comedy we are getting ready to film with Bette Davis."

Nicholson also cited *I Shot Down the Red Baron*, to be directed
by and star Academy Award winner Cliff Robertson; H.G. Wells'
*When the Sleeper Wakes;* Poe's *Murders in the Rue Morgue; The
Hatfields and the McCoys*, to be written and directed by Ted Flicker,
who has just completed *Up in the Cellar.*

Arkoff, Nicholson, senior vice president Leon P. Blender,
senior vice president and treasurer David J. Melamed, and vice
president Milton Moritz were reelected directors of the company.

A product reel showing scenes from *Wuthering Heights,
The Battle of Neretva, Julius Caesar,* and *Gas!* was viewed at the
conclusion of the meeting.

July 20, 1970
*Boxoffice*
These are excerpts from two articles by the AIP execs.

RELEASE OF NEW FILM EACH WEEK IS SET AS GOAL
FOR THE '70s
by Samuel Z. Arkoff, Chairman of the Board, American
International Pictures

Product shortage will be the big problem of the Seventies, American International Pictures believes. And as an exhibitor-oriented production company, we are as anxious to solve this as any theatre owner is.

We promise to try. To the extent that, if we succeed, all of us will enjoy greater success.

Right now American International has a bigger, deeper, and broader schedule of pictures we will make than ever before in our 16-year history. And we are considering "outside" and "independent" productions more seriously than ever before. And, with arrangements such as the one we have made with Commonwealth United, we are prepared to offer a selection of star names that compares favorably with that of any other organization in the business.

Cliff Robertson, Charlton Heston, Bette Davis, Jason Robards, and Shelley Winters are just a few of the stars who are being seen or will be seen in our films.

Every day, we read of product on cutback by some other studios, of postponed or cancelled films. We are in the business at American International of making sure that films are made. We don't have sound stages and we don't want them because, generally speaking, the best motion pictures are made where the action really is, where life really is. American International has a goal for the Seventies- to be able to release at least one good picture every week. Will you help us?

## DIVERSIFIED FARE FOR ALL PATRONS WILL INSURE BETTER BUSINESS

by James H. Nicholson, President, American International Pictures
Selectivity is the secret for the Seventies as far as American International Pictures is concerned. Business is good and will be better if we and other filmmakers are more careful in our selection of topics and in bringing them to the screen with quality.

American International is careful not to just make a slate of pictures. Instead, we try to have a diversity of entertainment ready to meet the needs of all exhibitors and all audiences. Everything from *Count Yorga Vampire* to *Wuthering Heights*, from *Angel*

*Unchained* to Bette Davis in *Betty* [sic] *and Claude,* from *Up in the Cellar* to Cliff Robertson in *I Shot Down the Red Baron- I Think.*

People throughout the world are becoming increasingly interested in a broader range of subjects. This is good for society, we believe, and good for the entertainment business.

Motion picture companies everywhere are striving as never before to create unusual entertainment that covers a broad spectrum of audience interests. At American International, we are trying to have exciting entertainment ready for those who prefer uninhibited versions of the classics, like *Wuthering Heights* and *Murders in the Rue Morgue,* or youth dramas, like *Angels Unchained* and *Beach Bum,* or sex comedies like *Up in the Cellar,* or bizarre subjects like *de Sade '71.*

Tomorrow looks good. Exhibitors and producer-distributors working enthusiastically and imaginatively together will continue to enjoy success and will provide more enjoyment than ever for a responsive public.


August 1970-


***Up in the Cellar*** (aka ***3 In the Cellar***)
"IT'S NICE REVENGE IF YOU CAN GET IT! Colin Slade is out to seduce the charming wife, beautiful daughter, ravishing mistress of his worst enemy. What a way to get even!"

Produced by Samuel Z. Arkoff and James H. Nicholson Directed by Theodore J. Flicker
Starring Wes Stern, Joan Collins, Larry Hagman, Judy Pace, David Arkin, Nira Barab

From the pressbook-
JOAN COLLINS SHAPES UP
Joan Collins, who will be seen co-starring with Wes Stern and Larry Hagman in American International's *Up in the Cellar,* has an aversion for biographies written by studio publicists.

Looking at one recently, which listed her measurements as 39-20-36, she said, "Obviously you exaggerated."

The publicist replied, "Obviously nature did the exaggerating." Miss Collins read further, "She is wealthy, successful, tempestuous, and rebellious." Brightening, she nodded her head. Apparently, she agreed with that description of herself.

*Up in the Cellar* was written for the screen and directed by Theodore J. Flicker, in color.

**Up in the Cellar is based on the novel *The Late Boy Wonder* by Angus Hall. AIP also bought the rights to his novel *Devilday*, which they filmed in 1974 as *Madhouse*, starring Vincent Price, Robert Quarry, and Peter Cushing.**

September 1970-

*Boxoffice*
September 7, 1970
AIP TO RELEASE 25 FILMS IN 1971; CURRENT YEAR IS BEST IN ITS HISTORY
By John Cocchi
New York- American International Pictures' cash position is the best ever and the company is enjoying the greatest year in its 17 years of existence. At a luncheon at New York's Regency Hotel, board chairman Samuel Z. Arkoff and president James H. Nicholson, who jointly founded AIP, made this statement, then gave a brief history of the company, referred to its present solid financial status, and outlined the future release schedule. Also present was Roger Corman, the producer-director-writer who has made some of the biggest hits AIP has had. The company plans to release 26 features in the 1971 calendar year.

Nicholson declared, "Our policy is to fill a void." When a particular type of film isn't being made available, then AIP supplies it, he explained. In the past, the company has had only one or two special productions a year, but by the end of 1971, there will be seven to nine important films in release.

The American International release schedule is broken down this way:

September: *GAS-S-S-S* and *Julius Caesar*
October: *The Vampire Lovers*
November: *Dorian Gray* and *I Am a Groupie*
January 1971: *Wuthering Heights, Wild Arctic*, and *Mafia*
February: *Dracula #1, The Battle of Neretva*
March: *Baby Bride* and *Bodies Busy*
April: *Incredible 2-Headed Transplant* and *Bloody Judge*
May: *Bunny O'Hare* and *The Switchers*
June: *Barracuda 2000* and *Murders in the Rue Morgue*
July: *Dr. Phibes* and *Beach Bum*
August: *Gingerbread House* and *Tam Lin*
September: *I Shot Down the Red Baron- I Think* and *G.O.O.*
(*Galactic Octopodular Ooze*)

### *Julius Caesar*

"Never before a Caesar so powerful! Never such a cast of international stars!"

Produced by Peter Snell  Directed by Stuart Burge
Starring Charlton Heston, Jason Robards, John Gielgud, Richard Johnson, Diana Rigg

From the pressbook-
THE WORLD OF ANCIENT ROME BROUGHT TO LIFE
IN *JULIUS CAESAR*
The assignment of bringing to life the world of ancient Rome went to Julia Trevelyan Oman and Maurice Pelling for the new American International screen version of the William Shakespeare classic *Julius Caesar*.

The problem for producer Peter Snell was to match the dignity and importance of the performances with equally impressive settings. The largest sound stages in London were to be
used and extensive battle sequences to be photographed on location near Madrid.

The solution was the cooperation of Miss Oman and Pelling. The production was something special and together they gave it that special touch.

EXPLOITATION
Prior to your engagement, in order to create excitement, have your ushers and usherettes dressed in toga costumes with armor.

Film review- *Julius Caesar*

*New York Times* (February 4, 1971) by Howard Thompson
"Ye gods! Must I endure all this?" understandably bellows Cassius (Richard Johnson) in the last lap of the third filming of William Shakespeare's *Julius Caesar.* The new movie moves sluggishly as directed by Stuart Burge. As the center of the whole thing, [Jason] Robards is incredibly dull and wooden as Brutus, the "noblest Roman of them all." [Charlton] Heston supplies laconic bite and delivers a good, ferocious funeral oration.

**The all-star cast for *Julius Caesar:* Richard Johnson, Robert Vaughn, John Gielgud, Diana Rigg, Jill Bennett, Richard Chamberlain, Charlton Heston, Jason Robards.**

## *GAS-S-S-S*
"This film contains: PHOTOGRAPHY, BIOGRAPHY, GEOGRAPHY, PORNOGRAPHY
(...but not necessarily in that order!)."

Produced and Directed by Roger Corman
Starring Robert Corff, Elaine Giftos, Bud Cort, Country Joe and the Fish

Film reviews- *GAS-S-S-S*

*Variety-* Obviously aimed at the youth market, it will take some very tolerant youngster to sit through this poorest of the [Roger] Corman films.

*New York Magazine-* There's a cool overlay and a serious undertone to the fun and games that give one an insight into the youth level that has long been Corman's forte. It's worth seeing for this alone.

*Films and Filming-* The film has a lightness of touch and controlled wit rarely encountered in U.S. parodies.

**GAS-S-S-S was the end of Roger Corman's directing career with AIP. In his autobiography, he says, "I turned in the final cut, left for Europe, and changes were made without my knowledge. When I saw what AIP did to my film, I realized we had come to the end of the line as a team."**

*The Swappers* (aka *Wife Swappers;* a Trans American release)
"Remember what all the guy next door wanted to borrow was your lawnmower?"

Produced by Stanley Long  Directed by Derek Ford
Starring James Donnelly, Larry Taylor, Valerie St. John, Dennis Hawthorne

From the pressbook-
FILM REVEALS SEX GAMES
The search for thrills by married couples out of boredom or rebellion against accepted standards is explored in Trans American Films newest release, *The Swappers*.

The result reveals a number of extra-marital sex games couples play which go beyond the practice of exchanging mates.

In addition to presenting two couples who swap partners occasionally, the film describes a routine in which a group of married couples meet and play a voyeuristic game in which a different wife is expected to perform for the group at each gathering.

SEAT SELLING SLANTS
For opening night, advertise in advance that two couples can gain admittance to the theatre for the cost of one couple. Thereafter, instead of having a single admittance price policy for this engagement of *The Swappers*, introduce a 'SPECIAL' TWO COUPLE price policy, also suggesting that the couples **swap** partners when they are seated!

*Venus in Furs*
"The coat that covered paradise, uncovered hell! A masterpiece of supernatural sex!"

Produced by Harry Allen Towers  Directed by Jess Franco
Starring James Darren, Barbara McNair, Maria Rohm, Klaus Kinski, Dennis Price

Film Review- *Venus in Furs* and *The Swappers*

*New York Times* (September 10, 1970) by Roger Greenspun
*The Swappers* and *Venus in Furs* are R-rated exploitation films in a double bill that opened yesterday at neighborhood theaters. Considering the bland nature of the sexual infusion in these movies, it seems to me that there is less harm in what sin may do to the suburbs than in what the suburbs are doing to sin. *Venus in Furs* features much inept fancy moviemaking, some semi-nudity, and virtually endless confusion. *The Swappers*, on the other hand,

features some semi-nudity, no fancy moviemaking, and much literalistic simplicity.

October 1970-

*The Vampire Lovers*
"EVEN THE DEAD CAN LOVE... and with lifeless lips drain the living of their passion and their blood."

Produced by Harry Fine and Michael Style  Directed by Roy Ward Baker
Starring Ingrid Pitt, George Cole, Kate O'Mara, Peter Cushing, Dawn Addams

*The Vampire Lovers* was the only co-production between AIP and the great British horror movie company Hammer, although AIP did pick up some of their other films for U.S. release. James Nicholson agreed for AIP to put $400,000 into the production. AIP's chief of production in Europe, Louis M. Heyward, was given script approval and general casting duties, but other than that, the filming was left to Hammer with little interference from AIP. Failing to foresee the big box office success of *The Vampire Lovers*, AIP decided to pass on financial involvement with the sequel *Lust for a Vampire*.

From the pressbook-
*THE VAMPIRE LOVERS* A FAMILY AFFAIR
Imagine a whole family of vampires terrorizing an entire district in middle-Europe in the eighteenth and early nineteenth centuries and there you have the bloodshot theme of *The Vampire Lovers*, American International's new shock piece.
Based on a story by Irish writer J. Sheridan Le Fanu, *The Vampire Lovers* sheds such new light on the vampire business that it makes the nefarious activities of Count Dracula look almost anemic.
The first part of the grisly narrative concerns the hunting down and destruction of the vampire family by a man whose sister has

been a victim. He seeks out their graves and rams stakes through their evil hearts.

But one grave escapes his frenzied work, that of a girl called Mircalla, who uses her compelling sensuous beauty to trap new victims.

The girl is played by Ingrid Pitt, electrifyingly beautiful new American International discovery, and the film focuses on her bloody vampiric activities and the trail of horror she spreads through the countryside.

**The glamorous cast of *The Vampire Lovers:* Ingrid Pitt, Madeline Smith, Kate O'Mara, Pippa Steele, and Kirsten Betts.**

EXPLOITATION-
When not at the theatre, your employees, dressed in vampire outfits, can parade through your town, passing out chocolate candy kisses. The person can be bannered with theatre and playdate information as well as come copy that might read as follows: "Not all kisses are as sweet. Come find out why."

Film Reviews- *The Vampire Lovers*

*Los Angeles Times* by Kevin Thomas
An excellent horror film- what makes for really good horror is not great quantities of blood and guts spilled across the screen, but the sense of pathos and loneliness surrounding the monster-heroes. A rare and pleasurable experience done with intelligence and taste.

*Films and Filming* by Richard Weaver
A package deal of thrills from the first co-production involving the two giants of horror film productions, AIP and Hammer, where sex is deeply implanted to the horror theme with the emphasis being on the former much to the neglect of the latter. Prior to the credit sequence, the film opens on an encouraging note, but it is a false indication because what follows turns out to be disappointing by comparison.

*New York Times* (February 4, 1971) by A.H. Weiler
Vampire Story With a New Angle
Roy Ward Baker, the director of the British-made *Vampire Lovers*, and his writers have had the diverting temerity to present their chief vampire as a photogenic temptress with distinct Lesbian drives. Ingrid Pitt is a vampire to delight any red-blooded Peeping Tom despite her German-accented English. Vampirism, which has become a silly business on screen, is, at least, easy on the eyes in this case.

*L'Incroyable Cinema* (Spring 1971) by Alan Dodd
It seems Inexplicable that it should be necessary for no fewer than three writers, of which Tudor Gates must take chief blame,

to compile this dreary-sounding script. Things are not helped any further by the uninspired photography of Moray Grant nor the irritating editing. Roy Ward Baker has directed it with such lack of luster effort that it shows in the dullness in so many scenes.

*Cue Magazine*
Vampirism is given a novel lesbian touch. Smoothly and stylishly directed by Roy Ward Baker, this Hammer film has the classic constituents of teeth, fog, caresses, stakes through the heart, and garlic flowers. It also has a bevy of beautiful women and some decent acting.

## *Mafia*
"MAFIA means MURDER... and EXTORTION... and TERROR... and VIOLENCE and other profitable enterprises!

Produced by Ermann Donati and Luigi Carpentieri  Directed by Damiano Damiani
Starring Lee J. Cobb, Claudia Cardinale, Franco Nero, Nehimiah Persoff

From the pressbook-
*MAFIA* BECOMES CHILLING CRIME SYNDICATE THRILLER
"Mafia," one of the most feared words in our modern lexicon, becomes the subject of a motion picture shock thriller entitled *Mafia*, with Claudia Cardinale, Franco Nero, Lee J. Cobb, and Nehemiah Persoff in the starring roles.

In American International's suspense drama, *Mafia*, a vividly chilling account is given of the Mafia's sinister operations in blocking investigations into a huge road construction racket and a murder. The exotic Italian star, Miss Cardinale, is innocently caught in a frightening trap between the syndicate and the police.

The exciting drama was filmed in color and directed by Damiano Damiani. It is based on the successful book *Day of the Owl* by Leonardo Sciascia.

SEAT SELLING SLANTS-
Arrange for a classified newspaper ad contest by inviting the readers to "expose the MAFIA."

Subject of the search would be to find the letters from the title which are printed in various ads throughout the classified section. Of course, the page headline should be "EXPOSE THE MAFIA." Promote prizes for the local winners.

October 5, 1970
*Boxoffice*
39-HOUR FILM PROGRAM IN SALUTE TO AIP
Albuquerque- "Film Revival of a Generation," a 39-hour marathon motion picture program offering continuous showings of 34 different American International features, was staged here by Commonwealth's State Theatre, beginning at 7:30 p.m. on Friday, October 2.

The films, covering the 17-year history of AIP, were divided into eight groups:

Group A. In the Beginning, the tough rock- *Fast and Furious, Rock All Night, I Was a Teenage Werewolf, Hot Rod Gang.*

Group B. Escape of the '50s, the horror cycle- *How to Make a Monster, Horrors of the Black Museum, Bucket of Blood, Circus of Horrors.*

Group C. Beasts and Muscles, the early '60s- *Goliath and the Barbarians, Konga, Marco Polo.*

Group D. A New Discovery of Evil, Edgar Allan Poe- *House of Usher, The Pit and the Pendulum, Premature Burial.*

Group E. Surf and Sand, California bubble gum- *Beach Party, Bikini Beach, How to Stuff a Wild Bikini.*

Group F. Cycles and Bad Guys, the beginning of violence- *The Wild Angels, Born Losers, Glory Stompers.*

Group G. A New Generation, the beautiful people- *Wild in the Streets, The Trip, Riot on Sunset Strip.*

Group H. American International Now, getting it together in the '70s- *Three in the Attic, de Sade, Bloody Mama, Up in the Cellar.*

The fact that AIP's *Bunny O'Hare* was shooting here, with Bette Davis, Ernest Borgnine, Jack Cassidy, Joan Delaney, and Jay

411

Robinson in town at the same time, brought the theatre salute to the proportions of a civic event.

*Boxoffice*
October 27, 1970
AIP SPECIAL PUBLICATION CALLED BOXOFFICE DIGEST
Hollywood- American International's graphics section, part of vice president Milton Moritz's advertising and publicity department, has prepared a special publication called Boxoffice Digest, which is being given to key press and exhibitors throughout the United States and Canada. The magazine is larger than *Life*, although slimmer, and has full-page layouts on several AIP releases.

Films proclaimed are *Wuthering Heights, Murders in the Rue Morgue, Dorian Gray, Bunny O'Hare*, Commonwealth United's *Julius Caesar, I Shot Down the Red Baron- I Think, Dr. Phibes, Beach Bum, Gingerbread House*, Commonwealth United's *Battle of Neretva*, and *G.O.O.- Genetic Octopodular Ooze*.

DAUGHTER OF AIP CHAIRMAN, DONNA ARKOFF, MARRIES
London- Donna Arkoff, daughter of the chairman of the board of American International Pictures, Samuel Z. Arkoff, was married here Friday, October 6 to entertainer Michael Pinder, member of the singing group the Moody Blues. Mr. and Mrs. Arkoff and their son Louis of Studio City, Calif., were in attendance. The Pinders will reside in London.


November 1970-

*Witchcraft '70* (a Trans American release)
"A wild, weird world of bizarre practices and savage pleasures actually filmed as they exist today in the cities and suburbs of our civilization!"

Produced by P.A.C.-Caravel  Directed by Luigi Scattini and R. L. Frost

Narrated by Edmund Purdom

From the pressbook-
*WITCHCRAFT '70* REVEALS PERILS OF THE OCCULT
The strange and weird world of the occult with its modern day witchcraft and hallucinatory phenomena presents a bewildering and hypnotic kaleidoscope in which today's youth can lose themselves and sometimes lose their lives, according to massive evidence recently uncovered by authorities and news media researchers.

Startling and garish aspects of this new cultism, which is sweeping the land and engulfing its young disciples in orgiastic sex ritual and sacrificial murder, are seen in Trans American Films' shocking film x-ray of today's greatest scourge, *Witchcraft '70.*

EXPLOITATION-
Dress young, attractive young ladies into professional-type uniforms pertaining to various types of positions, e.g. a white uniform to represent a nurse, etc. (other professions might be secretary's, teacher's), and have them parade all over your town passing out imprinted flyers or cards that read: "During the day I'm a (nurse), but come see what I do at night!"

*Bora Bora*
"Banned twice in Europe. First she tried all the islands, then all the islanders."

Produced by Alfredo Bini and Eliseo Boschi  Directed by Ugo Liberatore
Starring Haydee Politoff, Corrado Pani, Doris Kuntsmann

From the pressbook-
*BORA BORA* DARING SAGA OF LOVE IN POLYNESIA
*Bora Bora* is a romantic adventure filmed on location in Polynesia, in and among the coral reefs, jagged peaks, and azure blue waters that had so attracted Gauguin, Cook, and Stevenson.

The American International release stars Haydee Politoff, Corrando Pani, and Doris Kunstmann. *Bora Bora* is a name

413

evocative of the lure in the 19th century of the South Seas, a lure which extended not only to pirates and whalers, but to the artistic, literary, and scientific community as well.

*Bora Bora* is an exciting story of a marital breakup on the coral shoals of the Polynesian island and the exotic love complications which evolve among the natives as the couple become lost in a sea of sensuality.

EXPLOITATION-
Arrange a special screening for all the travel agents in your town. Present each female guest with a colorful "lei" to created atmosphere- and then follow up by having newspaper coverage as the guests are leaving the special screening.

December 1970-

*I Am a Groupie* (aka *Groupie Girl;* a Trans American release)
"There are all kinds of Groupies... from Plaster Casters to Freakers from Super-Mamas to Rock Geishas- but we all have one thing in common: What we collect ain't autographs!"

Produced by Stanley Long  Directed by Derek Ford
Starring Billy Boyle, Donald Dumpter, Richard Shaw, Esme Johns

From the pressbook-
GROUPIE DEFINED
What is a "groupie."
It is probably not in known dictionaries; however, the definition of a "groupie" is graphically presented in Trans American Films' new release called, aptly enough, *I Am a Groupie.* The film describes a "groupie" as one of the thousands of young girls who become fascinated with the itinerant rock music bands touring the country and join them in their travels as super-fans, ready to satisfy their every whim. They serve the musicians as maids, errand girls, and bed partners with eager fervor, but are often treated with cruel indifference and discarded when their presence becomes bothersome.

414

Starring Esme Johns, the film was directed by Derek Ford from a script by Ford and Suzanne Mercer.

### *Angel Unchained*
" This is the HELL RUN that you make alone!"

Produced and Directed by Lee Madden
Starring Don Stroud, Luke Askew, Larry Bishop, Tyne Daly, Aldo Ray

Film Review- *Angel Unchained*

*New York Times* (December 17, 1970) by Vincent Canby
There's little power in *Angel Unchained*, in which Don Stroud, the titular, disenchanted motorcyclist, latches on to a hippie commune and invites his erstwhile cycling pals to help the commune guys and dolls make it agriculturally. The new gimmick here is a decibel-filled, motorized joust between cowhands, who ride dune buggies, not pintos, and the cyclists, all of which ends

in inconclusive disaster. Mr. Stroud says wearily at one point, "I don't know, man, I'm all strung out." He's absolutely right. *Angel Unchained* just leaves you tired.

# CHAPTER SEVENTEEN
# 1971

January 1971-

*Boxoffice*
January 4, 1971
METHOD TO PREVENT FILM PRINT DAMAGE
IMPROVED BY J. H. NICHOLSON OF AIP by Syd Cassyd
Hollywood- Out of the wide experience and background of James
H. Nicholson, president of American International Pictures, comes
one of the profound contributions to the art of motion picture
projection, particularly relating to protection and preservation of
valuable prints and maximum enjoyment of the film by audiences.
The idea is simplicity itself, involving an additional 25 feet of leader
film added to the print to prevent scratching from cinch-winding.

In the firm's production projection room at its headquarters
on Wilshire Blvd., Beverly Hills, Nicholson, a one-time theatre
projectionist in his younger days, explained the system to

*Boxoffice* as he demonstrated how it had been added to all prints of *Wuthering Heights*. Testing two prints, one without this added leader, which is regular blank stock from the film laboratory, the research findings in practice turned up the following conclusions:

The print with the leader was run through the projector and rewound 30 times without a scratch. The other print, with normal length leader, was filled with scratches. Extending the findings, Nicholson predicted that there was a possible 25 percent increase in the life of the print.

## REMAKE OF POPULAR FILMS TO BE POLICY OF AIP

Hollywood- "Popular films should be remade periodically just like plays are presented time and again with new casts and new approaches to appeal to contemporary audiences- and American International is embarking upon a program to do precisely this."

Disclosure of this policy and other changes was made at an extemporaneous press meeting by James H. Nicholson, president, and Samuel Z. Arkoff, chairman of the board of AIP, at a Beverly Wilshire Hotel party in honor of Timothy Dalton, who depicts Heathcliff in the company's new film *Wuthering Heights*.

Dalton, who joined Arkoff and Nicholson in answering all questions posed by newsmen, revealed a unique arrangement between himself and AIP under which he stands ready to star in any of the company's films which both he and the studio consider suitable. "*A Tale of Two Cities* is likely to be next," Dalton said, "and we are talking about *Les Miserables*." Both are being adapted by Patrick Tilley, who wrote the *Wuthering Heights* script from Emily Bronte's novel.

Arkoff and Nicholson said that AIP "will continue to release the 'young-at-heart' type of films as it has in the past, often acquiring instead of producing them, but will concentrate production efforts on important properties which we hope will have strong general appeal worldwide. Among these will be *The House of the Seven Gables* and *The Scarlet Letter*."

February 1971-

*Wuthering Heights*
"Emily Bronte's defiant young lovers live again in a new and different look at an immortal classic."

Produced by Samuel Z. Arkoff and James H. Nicholson  Directed by Robert Fuest
Starring Anna Calder-Marshall, Timothy Dalton, Harry Andrews, Hugh Griffith, Ian Ogilvy

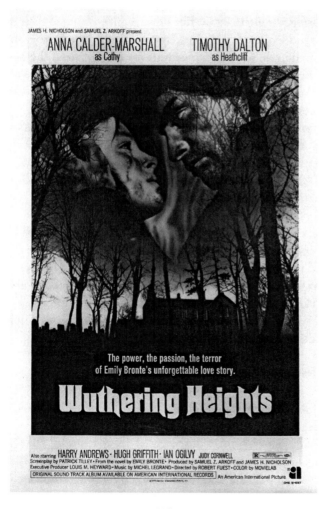

From the pressbook-
*WUTHERING HEIGHTS* REALIZATION OF
PRODUCER'S PET PROJECT
A new film of *Wuthering Heights*, one with which today's young
audiences could identify, has long been a pet ambition of producers
Samuel Z. Arkoff and James H. Nicholson.

They had in mind the kind of youthful approach and casting
which Zeffirelli gave his film of *Romeo and Juliet*.

They had planned, originally, to cast established major
star names in the roles of Heathcliff and Catherine, the young
lovers whose violent, extraordinary love-hate relationship is what
*Wuthering Heights* is about. But subsequently changed their minds.

"It suddenly dawned on us," they declared, "that a story so well-
known and one of such explosive force did not need the booster-
aid of big names. It already had this dynamic, built-in power of its
own. What it needed simply was a carefully handpicked cast of
first-rate and highly gifted performers."

Filmed in mid-winter on the rugged Yorkshire moors where
Emily Bronte set her story, *Wuthering Heights* was directed by
Robert Fuest from a screenplay by Patrick Tilley. Louis M.

"Deke" Heyward, American International's European
production chief, was executive producer.

**In a 1996 interview with "Deke" Heyward, he told me a
different story. "Sam Arkoff and Jim Nicholson told me that if I
moved to England, they would allow me to film a property that
was very important to me. It was my dream to remake *Wuthering
Heights*. As the years passed, they kept putting me off. Finally,
I had to sell the project to them as a horror film, which was
something they could understand."**

Film Review- *Wuthering Heights*

*Time* (March 1, 1971) by Stefan Kanfer- ROMANTIC
BACKLASH
*Wuthering Heights* is not without its redeeming factors. The
principal one is Anna Calder-Marshall. As Cathy, she lends her
role a cast of palpable tragedy and dignity. Though director

[Robert] Fuest seems to leave his players to their own devices, he has a fine camera eye.

Seldom does the film equal its pictorial quality. But perhaps *Wuthering Heights* was, like its principals, frustrated from the start. Its distributors, American International Pictures, saw it as "a youth oriented picture," suggesting groovy moors and Now people suffering Then hang-ups.

Its significance is, finally, not aesthetic, but historic. AIP, former king of motorcycle and beach blanket flicks, has become a leader of the romantic backlash. In one fell swipe, it has disavowed its sleazy origins, bypassed the grind houses, and landed the distributor's dream. *Wuthering Heights* will open at the ultimate Temple of Memory, Radio City Music Hall.

### *Dorian Gray* (aka *The Secret of Dorian Gray*)
"Eternal Youth is the Ultimate Perversion."

Produced by Harry Alan Towers  Directed by Massimo Dallamano
Starring Helmut Berger, Richard Todd, Herbert Lom, Maria Liljedahl, Margaret Lee

From the pressbook-
*DORIAN GRAY* DISPLAYS TODAY'S BEAUTIFUL PEOPLE
The new breed of hedonists who inhabit the pleasure spots of Europe are displayed in American International's feature, *Dorian Gray*.

Where in earlier years the world's royalty and heads of state once relaxed in verdant and sun-baked gardens and beaches, today's pampered pleasure seekers are shown as the over-rich in wealth or beauty who form a clique known as the "beautiful people."

Photographed in Otello Spila, breathtaking vistas of these famed spas are beautifully portrayed. It is in these plush backgrounds that a good deal of the story of *Dorian Gray* takes place. It describes the escapades of a man gifted with eternal youth, his age and the horrors of his depredations registered only on a portrait painted of him when he was still young and innocent.

Helmut Berger stars in the title role with Richard Todd and Herbert Lom sharing the leads.

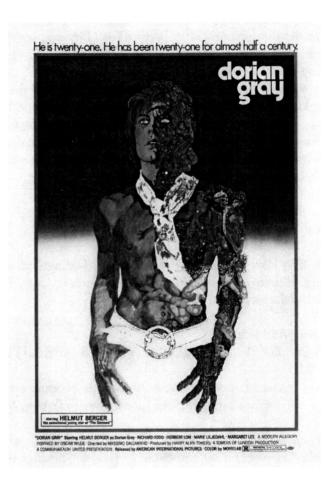

EXPLOITATION-
Your high schools and colleges, English, Literature, and Drama department chairmen should be contacted with the possibility of special screenings for students. In addition, contact should also be made to the instructors of these subjects, again with the possibility of a special screening for them alone.

It is highly unlikely that any responsible education department chairmen would have recommended that their students see this incredibly sleazy R-rated movie.

Film Review- *Dorian Gray*

*New York Times* (December 10, 1970) by Vincent Canby
Massimo Dellamano's semi-nude, semi-swish *Dorian Gray* is so dull as to defy description, though not contempt. Calling itself "A modern allegory based on the work of Oscar Wilde," the film is a little weak on allegory, but terrifically strong on modernity-moving in the more than twenty-year decline and fall of Dorian's portrait from the London of, say, 1969, to the London of, say 1970. The film itself, in the manner of much recently imported European pornography, is at once under-sexed and over-decorated- and unless flashing strobe lights are your idea of sin, you are unlikely to be titillated.

## *The Battle of Neretva*
"Among all the wars since time began, all the defeats and victories, there is no equal to this chronicle of raw courage and stubborn savagery!"

Produced by Steve Previn  Directed by Veljko Bulajic
Starring Yul Brynner, Sergei Bondarchuk, Curt Jurgens, Sylva Koscina, Franco Nero, Orson Welles

February 8, 1971
*Boxoffice*
IFIDA TO PAY TRIBUTE TO ARKOFF, NICHOLSON
New York- Samuel Z. Arkoff, chairman of the board, and James H. Nicholson, president of American International Pictures, will be specially honored by the International Film Importers and Distributors of America for "extraordinary global filmmaking" at the association's upcoming international film awards dinner, it is announced by Manny Reiner, dinner chairman.

The presentation of plaques to the two AIP principle executive officers will be made on Friday evening, February 26, in the

Imperial Ballroom of the Americana Hotel in New York during IFIDA's 11th annual dinner citing outstanding motion picture achievements for 1970.

February 15, 1971
*Boxoffice*
ARKOFF CHASTISES EXHIBITORS FOR GRIPES ON TRADE TERMS, PROMOTION NEGLECT
Dallas- Samuel Z. Arkoff, chairman of the board of American International Pictures, speaking before the 600 exhibitors attending NATO of Texas second annual convent here Wednesday, February 3, took exhibition to task for its failure to pay "distributors what they are honestly entitled to for their pictures" and stated that it is "shameful" that distribution must spend huge sums policing theaters to "get a fair count at the box office."

Arkoff concluded by telling the showmen, "You exhibitors have the responsibility of giving each picture what it deserves, meaning imaginative promotion, attractive presentation, and the film rental it individually deserves."

March 1971-

*Blood and Lace*
"Behind a veil of lace TERROR hides its face! And MURDER waits from behind a mask of unspeakable evil!"

Produced by Ed Carlin and Gil Laskey  Directed by Philip Gilbert
Starring Gloria Grahame, Milton Selzer, Len Lesser, Melody Patterson, Vic Tayback

*The House That Screamed*
"ONE BY ONE THEY WILL DIE! Only the killer knows WHY and HOW and WHO is next!"

Produced by Anabel Films  Directed by Narcisco Ibanez Serrador
Starring Lilli Palmer, John Moulder Brown, Cristina Galbo, Mary Maude

*The House That Screamed* is the 1969 Spanish horror film *La Residencia.*


April 1971-

*The Incredible 2-Headed Transplant*
"One brain wants to love... one brain wants to kill!"

Produced by John Lawrence  Directed by Anthony N. Lanza
Starring Bruce Dern, Pat Priest, Casey Kasem, Albert Cole, John Bloom

Film Review- *The Incredible 2- Headed Transplant* and *The House That Screamed*

*New York Times* (July 22, 1971) by A.H. Weiler
Incredible, even an indulgent viewer must conclude, is the precise word for *The Incredible 2-Headed Transplant* and *The House That Screamed,* the dual helping of jerry-built horrors that was dished up in pleasing colors at local houses yesterday. Unfortunately, this potentially mixed bag of abnormal surgery and abnormal education merely adds up to tepid, not divertingly chilling fare. Two flawed heads, like two flawed films, are not better than one.


May 1971-

*The Abominable Dr. Phibes*
"Dr. Phibes has great vibes."

Produced by Louis M. Heyward and Ronald S. Dunas  Directed by Robert Fuest
Starring Vincent Price, Joseph Cotten, Hugh Griffith, Terry-Thomas, Virginia North

Film Review- *The Abominable Dr. Phibes*

*New York Times* (August 5, 1971) by Roger Greenspun
Wait until you see the London digs of Vincent Price in *The Abominable Dr. Phibes*. Anyway, that house is a sight, got up like a gaudy discotheque suggesting the 1930s with a pink organ hooked up to the telephone. The plot, buried under all the iron tinsel, isn't bad. But the tone of steamroller camp flattens the fun. Price finally climbs into his own grave to the tune of "Over the Rainbow." Up the creek is more like it.

**Although Sam Arkoff was initially unimpressed with *The Abominable Dr. Phibes*, he quickly changed his opinion when it became one of AIP's biggest successes. "Deke" Heyward said, "At first Sam Arkoff hated the film and wanted his name taken off it, but when he realized what a potential success he had, Sam decided to put his name back on."**

**Joseph Cotten and Vincent Price in *The Abominable Dr. Phibes*.**

June 1971-

*The Hard Ride*
"TWO PRETTY CLASSY MACHINES. It will take <u>some kind</u> <u>of man</u> to handle both."

Produced by Charles Hanawalt  Directed by Burt Topper
Starring Robert Fuller, Sherry Bain, Tony Russel

*Pacific Vibrations*
"Like Woodstock on a Wave- Entertainment Weekly"

**Pacific Vibrations is a surfing documentary produced, directed, written, and photographed by John Severson. It was produced in conjunction with Surfer Magazine. The movie features music by Cream, The Steve Miller Band, Wolfgang, Ry Cooder, Crosby Stills & Nash, and Sky Oates.**

June 7, 1971
*Boxoffice*
VINCENT PRICE HONORED AT 'PHIBES' PREMIERE
Hollywood- Hollywood Boulevard lived again as it did for the big, colorful enthusiastic premieres of the 1930s at American International's charity world premiere of *Dr. Phibes* at Pacific's Pantages Theatre recently. One hundred and eight popular actors and actresses attended to honor Vincent Price on the occasion of his 100th motion picture. Army Archerd interviewed "names" from Allyson (June) to Worley (Joanne).
    Actress Virginia North, who stars in *Dr. Phibes*, flew in from London for this premiere, which benefitted Variety Clubs International's Boys Club in East Los Angeles.
    Price was honored with plaques presented by supervisor Ernest Debs for the Los Angeles County board of supervisors and Mayor Samuel Yorty, who declared the event "Hollywood Salutes Vincent Price Week."
    James H. Nicholson, president of American International Pictures, participated in the premiere. Samuel Z. Arkoff, chairman

427

of the board of AIP, was in London preparing for the production of *The Return of Dr. Phibes.*

July 1971-

July 5, 1971
*Boxoffice*
'HEIGHTS' AIDS VARIETY
The Royal Premiere at London's ABC 2 Theatre of *Wuthering Heights* was given as a benefit recently for the Variety Clubs of Great Britain through the auspices of American International Pictures.

## RECORD NUMBER OF RELEASES SCHEDULED BY AIP FOR SECOND HALF OF YEAR

Hollywood- American International Pictures is releasing a record number of features during the second half of 1971, it was revealed by AIP president James H. Nicholson and by chairman of the board Samuel Z. Arkoff at the annual shareholders meeting June 28 held at National General's Fine Arts Theatre in Beverly Hills. The total of 28 films being released in 1971 is the most ever in the company's 18-year history.

*Bunny O'Hare* and *Murders in the Rue Morgue* are for July release, *The Return of Count Yorga* and *Chrome and Hot Leather* in August, *The Year of the Cannibals* and *Some of My Best Friends Are...* in September, *Tam Lin* and *Dagmar and Co.* in October, *Lizard in a Woman's Skin, Carry On Camping,* and *Wild Arctic* in November, and three in December, *Gingerbread House* and the rerelease double feature of *Wild in the Streets* and *The Wild Angels,* plus (not counted among the 28 features) a four-unit festival of former AIP favorites starring Vincent Price, Christopher Lee, and Boris Karloff.

Arkoff and Nicholson stated that *"Wuthering Heights* is doing record business for us worldwide. It recently opened in England and Australia and is grossing more than any other American International attraction to date. This classic is proving very profitable as well as prestigious, and has encouraged us to go ahead with *The House of the Seven Gables, Camille,* and others in the classic vein."

*Dr. Phibes,* which also is proving to be a strong grosser, will have at least one sequel, *Dr. Phibes Rises Again,* now being written by James Whiton for October production.

*Carry Nation* and *Barracuda 2000 A.D.* also are expected to be in front of the cameras during the remaining months of 1971 and *Gingerbread House* is now being completed. Other films may be started by AIP during this time and many new releases will be added through co-productions and acquisitions.

July 12, 1971
*Boxoffice*

ARKOFF AND NICHOLSON ARE PIONEERS OF THE YEAR

New York- Charles A. Alicote, president of the Motion Picture Pioneers, Inc. has announced that Samuel Z. Arkoff, chairman of the board of American International Pictures, and James H. Nicholson, president of AIP, have been chosen Pioneers of the Year for 1971.

Arkoff and Nicholson were chosen unanimously by the directors of Motion Picture Pioneers because of their outstanding and continuous service not only to the film industry, but to charitable causes throughout the world. Through Variety Clubs International, for instance, the two men and American International have helped raise literally millions of dollars for needy children in America and other countries.

They will be presented their awards at the annual Pioneers dinner celebration November 22 at the Americana Hotel here.

"We honor Jim Nicholson and Sam Arkoff on behalf of the entire motion picture industry," Alicote said. "These two dynamic showmen started their company in 1954 when business was at its worst in our branch of entertainment. Their vision and statesmanship, plus good, sound dollars-and-sense moviemaking, have been an inspiration to us."

TITLE CHANGE
*Doomsday 2000 A.D.* is the new title of the next science fiction feature to be filmed by American International Pictures. Formerly entitled *Barracuda 2000 A.D.*, the James Whiton screenplay will be shot in the U.S. this autumn for release in 1972.


August 1971-

*The Return of Count Yorga*
"A terrifying tale of unearthly hungers!"

Produced by Michael Macready  Directed by Bob Kelljan
Starring Robert Quarry, Mariette Hartley, Roger Perry, Yvonne Wilder, Edward Walsh

Film Reviews- *The Return of Count Yorga*

*New York Times* (February 3, 1972) by Howard Thompson

430

Skip, if you can, *The Return of Count Yorga*, a dull, amateurish vampire brew.

*Cinefantastique* (Spring 1972) by Robert L. Jerome
As a follow-up film, it suffers a familiar stigma, too much money, but too little inspiration. The production dress is, visually, a distinct improvement over the initial feature and a couple of better-known supporting actors (Walter Brooke, George Macready) appear in the cast, yet the crude, poverty-row vitality which made the original something of a "sleeper" is absent.

*Yog- Monster from Space* (aka *Space Amoeba*)
"SPEWED FROM INTERGALACTIC SPACE to clutch the planet earth in its...TERROR TENTACLES! The most fantastic science adventure ever filmed!"

Produced by Tomoyuki Tanaka and Fumio Tanaka  Directed by Ishiro Honda
Starring Akira Kubo, Atsuko Takahaski, Kenji Sahara, Yoshio Tsuchiya

From the pressbook-
NEW MONSTERS FROM OLD FOR NEW MOVIE
A new assortment of monsters were created to raise havoc with the world's populace in American International's latest science fiction release, *Yog- Monster from Space*. However, they were created from "monsters" which have been a part of the earth's fauna for eons.

Thus the world's population becomes threatened by not-so-jolly green giant squids, crabs, and turtles.

Filmed in widescreen color, *Yog- Monster from Space* was produced by Toho International Company, a Japanese production and distribution organization which has created some of the most realistic and famous science fiction thrillers to hit the screens of the world. An earlier production, *Godzilla vs. The Thing*, was also released by American International.

EXPLOITATION-
Exterminator Tie-up- Have a local exterminator display signs on his truck panels stating: WATCH *YOG- MONSTER FROM SPACE* THREATEN OUR HOMES AT THE BIJOU THEATRE...
BUT LET US ATTACK THE   MONSTERS THAT THREATEN YOUR HOMES FROM WITHIN.

Film Review- *Yog- Monster from Space*

*New York Times* (August 5, 1971) by Roger Greenspun
Commandeering an unmanned Jupiter-bound rocket, a little cloud of shimmery blue spangles turns it around and rides it back to earth. The little blue cloud is in fact a militant astro-quasar bent on world domination. And though he is never introduced properly, I should guess that he is called *Yog- Monster from Space*, after the movie of the same name, which opened yesterday.

Yog lands near a Pacific island, a paradise but for its hyperactive volcano. He then occupies, in turn, the bodies of a huge, sub-zero, land-walking, man-eating octopus; an enormous hairy crab;
    a super-turtle; and a happy-go-lucky, but somewhat unscrupulous resort hotel promoter.

About the trouble he causes and the troubles he is caused, let there be silence. The crab, the turtle, and the hotel promoter are nothing much. But the octopus, sensuously swaying on its eight legs, its red-and-white eyes flashing over the treetops, a swarm of bats circling its head, though not exactly lovable, it is at least- well- a little sexy.

September 1971-

*Murders in the Rue Morgue*
"A sigh of PASSION! A scream of TERROR! and the scratch of claws on the cobblestones. These are the sounds of MURDER in the RUE MORGUE!"

Produced by Louis M. Heyward  Directed by Gordon Hessler

Starring Jason Robards, Christine Kaufmann, Herbert Lom, Michael Dunn, Lilli Palmer

From the pressbook-
EDGAR ALLAN POE SAGA *MURDERS IN THE RUE MORGUE* FILMED ANEW BY AMERICAN INT'L
One of the most frightening of Edgar Allan Poe's terror tales, *Murders in the Rue Morgue,* was recently filmed again by American International.

Shot in Spain with Jason Robards, Christine Kaufmann, Herbert Lom, Adolfo Celi, Michael Dunn, and Lilli Palmer sharing cast honors, the story describes a horrible fantasy which mingles with terrifying facts at a theatre of the macabre in Paris during the turn of the century.

Directed by Gordon Hessler, it was produced by Louis M. Heyward from a screenplay by Christopher Wicking and Henry Slesar.

EXPLOITATION-
Street Bally- Have a man draped in ape costume and carrying a mannequin dressed in a negligee stroll through busy section of town. Sign on his back states: FOLLOW US FOR MORE SHOCKING SIGHTS IN *MURDERS IN THE RUE MORGUE-* NOW PLAYING.

Film Review- *Murders in the Rue Morgue*

*New York Times* (February 3, 1972) by Howard Thompson
The entire film is a gorgeous eyeful in excellent color with lavish period decor and costumes and some perfectly beautiful dream montages. And under Gordon Hessler's intelligent direction, the suspense deepens, as do some enigmatic characters. Two in particular are well played by Herbert Lom and Michael Dunn. For that matter, [Jason] Robards looks considerably more alive than usual and Miss [Christine] Kaufmann is quite good.

*Chrome and Hot Leather*
"Don't Muck Around With a Green Beret's Mama!"

Produced by Wes Bishop  Directed by Lee Frost
Starring William Smith, Tony Young, Michael Haynes, Peter Brown, Marvin Gaye

Film Review- *Chrome and Hot Leather*

*New York Times* (March 16, 1972) by Roger Greenspun
*Chrome and Hot Leather* is a stupid motorcycle movie in which four clean-cut Green Beret sergeants hunt down and, so to speak, pacify a gang of riders partly responsible for the death of the fiancée of one of the sergeants. The film provides a certain amount of bare-armed machismo and, depending on your taste for male muscle (mine is pretty negligible), has almost nothing to recommend it.

*The Year of the Cannibals* (aka *I Cannibali* )
"When Sex and Violence are games of skill and Murder a delightful kind of recreation."

Produced by Bino Cicogna and Enzo Doria  Directed by Liliana Cavani
Starring Pierre Clementi, Britt Ekland, Tomas Milian

**The Year of the Cannibals is a 1970 Italian film which is an updated version of Sophocles' play *Antigone* set in 1991.**

September 6, 1971
*Boxoffice*
ARKOFF CRITICIZES NEW CODE HEAD FOR 'CHANGES IN RATING SYSTEM'
Hyannisport, Mass.- Samuel Z. Arkoff, chairman of the board of American International Pictures, speaking before the Theatre Owners of New England here Thursday, August 26, directed heavy criticism at Dr. Aaron Stern, new head of the Code & Rating Administration, for setting up what Arkoff termed the new Stern

System, effecting changes in the code and rating system "without the consent and approval of the rest of the industry."

Arkoff blasted at Stern's announced plans for film ratings, charging, "He is using the whole country as a guinea pig for his own psychiatric beliefs. He has even gone so far as to state that there is no precedent prior to July 1, 1971. This means that Dr. Stern, if his own pronouncement is to be believed, is now the dictator of what teenagers under 17 may see in motion picture theaters in this country."

Arkoff charged that Dr. Stern's "new emphasis seems to be in areas such as questionable psychiatric motivations which never have been of concern before" even in the days of the Will Hays code.

"To me," Arkoff said, "this is an absolutely terrifying concept, alien to America. Such prohibitions would probably include taboos on dramatizations of anti-war rebellion, abortions, new family relationships, minority rebellion, drugs, etc."

**Sam Arkoff had every reason to worry as the last paragraph just about sums up all of AIP's motion picture output at the time and the new ratings system would have restricted the attendance of their target teenage audience.**

September 13, 1971
*Boxoffice*
AIP'S GROWTH BRINGS NEW LONDON QUARTERS
London- James H. Nicholson, president of American International Pictures, here for a "housewarming" of the company's new European production headquarters in Berkeley Street, told newsmen and guests that the move from its previous offices had been necessitated by AIP's rapidly increased production activities over the last two years coupled with current new expansion and that planned for the future. Co-hosting the affair with Nicholson was Louis M. "Deke" Heyward, AIP head of European production, who is in charge of the new headquarters.

Nicholson also announced the production by AIP over the next five months of four important new films: Nathaniel Hawthorn's classic *The House of the Seven Gables*, starting this month; Duma's

*Camille,* starting in October, for which discussions were under way for Mia Farrow to play the role made famous by Greta Garbo; *Elmer,* science fiction subject starting in November; and *Dr. Phibes Rises Again,* starting in January, a sequel to the current *The Abominable Dr. Phibes.*

Guests at the "housewarming" included film stars Judy Cornwell, Hugh Griffith, and Virginia North, who appeared in such current AIP films as *Wuthering Heights, Whoever Slew Auntie Roo?,* and *The Abominable Dr. Phibes.*

October 1971-

**Bunny O'Hare**
"Enjoy those 'Golden Years' with the Bunny O'Hare old age pension plan!"

Produced and Directed by Gerald Oswald
Starring Bette Davis, Ernest Borgnine, Jack Cassidy, Joan Delaney, Jay Robinson

Film Review- *Bunny O'Hare*

*New York Times* (October 19, 1971) by Vincent Canby
INDOMITABLE BETTE DAVIS IN GIMMICK COMEDY
*Bunny O'Hare,* directed by Gerald Oswald, a man whose strengths have never been in comedy, is a gimmick comedy, unusual in the fact that to be told, its gimmick is to know the very worst there is about the film. Everything else is an improvement.

As Bunny O'Hare, Miss [Bette] Davis plays a member of the Silent Majority who takes to robbing banks, disguised as a hippie, with the collaboration of a real bank robber played by Ernest Borgnine. As I said, the gimmick is dreadful. Miss Davis, however, gives a performance that may be one of the funniest and most legitimate of her career.

*Bunny O'Hare* is nonsense of a quite acceptable order filled with absurd chases and stock characters who have been conceived and played with affection.

Sam Arkoff: "We found that big names often have big heads and when they create problems, they're usually big ones. That was the case with *Bunny O'Hare*. In retrospect, *Bunny O'Hare* was not only the wrong vehicle for AIP, but it was wrong for Bette Davis, too."

***Dagmar's Hot Pants Inc.*** (a Trans American release)
"A satisfied customer is our most important product!"

Produced and Directed by Vernon P. Becker
Starring Diana Kjaer, Robert Strauss, Anne Grete, Inger Sundh, Tommy Blom

From the pressbook-
WORLD'S OLDEST PROFESSION USES NEWEST METHODS
Love marches on!
A demonstration of how the world's oldest profession keeps pace with the latest practices in improving service to its customers is illustrated in a scene from *Dagmar's Hot Pants Inc.*, Trans American Films' new sex farce.

Localled in Demark, the spicy comedy describes the misadventures of a young call girl when she attempts to sell her list of clientele to a competitor. In one scene, she is hailed by a sister sinner who has mechanized her methods to the extent of using a motorcycle equipped with a commercial band radio on which she can receive orders for "service" in the field and satisfy customer needs with dispatch.

Diana Kjaer, the Swedish sexpot who sparked up the film *Fanny Hill*, portrays the young lady who is trying to unload her following.

EXPLOITATION-
Blushing Patron Gag- Have red light spots placed above exit door

to play on faces of customers leaving the theatre. Sign above exit facing street should announce: Through these portals pass the blushingest patrons in town... the ones who saw *Dagmar's Hot Pants Inc.*

*1,000 Convicts and a Woman*
"White Man... Black Man... ANY MAN! The story of a Nympho!"

Produced by Philip N. Krasne  Directed by Ray Austin
Starring Alexandra Hay, Sandor Eles, Harry Baird

Film Review- *1,000 Convicts and a Woman*

*New York Times* (August 18, 1972) by Howard Thompson
You'll be wasting your time and money on junk like *1,000 Convicts and a Woman*. Subtitled "The Story of a Nympho," it has a warden's poisonous teenage daughter wiggling around a kind of country club prison until the joint more or less caves in. About seven panting inmates are all we see, not 1,000. That's seven too many.

*Some of My Best Friends Are...*
"Love... It Takes Two People... Any Two."

Produced by Marty Richards and John Lauricella  Directed by Mervyn Nelson
Starring Fannie Flagg, Carleton Carpenter, Sylvia Syms, Candy Darling, Dick O'Neil

November 1971-
*Carry On Camping*
"FUN and GAMES in the GREAT OUTDOORS!"

Produced by Peter Rogers  Directed by Gerald Thomas
Starring Sid James, Charles Hawtrey, Joan Sims

**Although *Carry On Camping* had previously been released in the U.S. by the Rank Organization in 1969, AIP picked up**

This is the place that separates the men from the "boys".

## Some of my best friends are...

"SOME OF MY BEST FRIENDS ARE." Starring FANNIE FLAGG · CARLETON CARPENTER · SYLVIA SYMS · CANDY DARLING · DICK O'NEIL. Executive Producer JOSEPH RHODES · Produced by MARTY RICHARDS and JOHN LAURICELLA · Directed by MERVYN NELSON. Written by MERVYN NELSON · [R] · COLOR BY MOVIELAB · AN AMERICAN INTERNATIONAL RELEASE

this movie for re-release. At the same time, they also acquired the rights to *Carry on Doctor*, which had previously been shown in the U.S. in 1968, and the new film in the series, *Carry on Henry VIII.* AIP would release these two "Carry On" films the following year.

November 29, 1971
*Boxoffice*
AT THE PIONEERS ANNUAL DINNER- ARKOFF,

## NICHOLSON EXPRESS FAITH IN INDUSTRY FUTURE

New York- Samuel Z. Arkoff and James H. Nicholson, chairman of the board and president, respectively, of American International Pictures, were honored as motion picture "Pioneers of the Year" here Monday (November 12) at the 33rd anniversary dinner of the Foundation of Motion Pictures Pioneers, Inc. at the Americana Hotel.

Speaking to the 600 film industry leaders gathered to pay them tribute, Nicholson and Arkoff expressed their confidence in the future of theatre business, stating: "With luck, there is prosperity ahead. Our definition of luck is when preparation meets opportunity. When we started in 1954, the cries of depression and woe were as great as today. Actually, like now, it was the best of years and it was the worst of years.

"Now in late 1971, we repeat what we have said before. This industry is not dying. If we are truly Pioneers, then we must adapt and change- to be worthy of the name- for none of us were born to this. We pioneered."

Nicholson accounted for his successful relationship with Arkoff by stating that each had a "mutual respect for the other's talents and an understanding of our weaknesses."

It was a night for indulgent humor, mostly at AIP's expense. Master of ceremonies Monty Hall introduced Vincent Price, star of so many of AIP's successful horror films, who said, "I've been with them so long, I feel like I'm dug up every time they cast me."

A five-minute series of representative clips from AIP films, called "The Word," was also shown, consisting mostly of screaming ladies and screaming motorbikes.

December 1971-

### Kidnapped

"The Story of a Girl's Love, a Boy's Courage and a Rogue's Reckless Daring. A savage, passionate, thrilling story from the immortal pen of Robert Louis Stevenson."

Produced by Frederick Brogger  Directed by Delbert Mann

Starring Michael Caine, Trevor Howard, Jack Hawkins, Lawrence Douglas, Vivien Heilbron

From the pressbook-
*KIDNAPPED-* GRAND SCALE ALL-FAMILY ADVENTURE FILM
Penetrating the realm of grand scale adventure, a neglected source of screen entertainment in these days of "cinema verite," dramatic relevance, and message films, American International's *Kidnapped,* with a formidable cast headed by Michael Caine, Trevor Howard, Jack Hawkins, and Donald Pleasance, opens today.

Based on Robert Louis Stevenson's two novels, *Kidnapped* and *David Balfour,* its story of the guerilla warfare staged by rebellious Scottish highlanders against England's rule and the colorful adventures of David Balfour and Catriona Stewart at the side of the folk hero Alan Breck has captivated readers for generations. It is now splashed against the majestic mountains and sea coast of Scotland with all the eye-filling scope of Panavision's wide screen.

EXPLOITATION-
Bagpipe Music- Bands featuring Scottish pipers are prevalent and if your locality has one available, their music and costumes would provide a strong attraction to passersby.

Film review- *Kidnapped*

*New York Times* (December 24, 1971) by Roger Greenspun
Everything bespeaks low budget in the sense that many of the shots making up individual sequences don't fit together and that some of the costumes don't fit at all. Except for the locations, which are real, and the color, which is color, the whole thing suggests the dim listlessness of the late late show edging toward the catatonia of 3 A.M.

# CHAPTER NINETEEN
# 1972

1972 turned out to be a pivotal year in AIP's history because in January, Jim Nicholson told Sam Arkoff that he would be leaving AIP. According to Arkoff's autobiography, Jim told Sam that he was tired of the hectic pace and only wanted to produce a couple of pictures a year. Sam countered by saying, "Why don't you make the pictures you want to produce at AIP?" but Nicholson wanted out. Things had never been the same between Sam and Jim after Jim's divorce from Sylvia and marriage to Susan Hart. In his autobiography, Roger Corman also explained, "Jim Nicholson had become a true- and increasingly conservative- pillar of Hollywood's professional and civic community. Arkoff remained liberal."

January 1972-

January 24, 1972
*Boxoffice*
NICHOLSON TO ESTABLISH OWN PRODUCTION
FIRM
Hollywood- James H. Nicholson, president of American
International Pictures, plans to establish his personal production
company in the near future, it was jointly announced by Nicholson
and Samuel Z. Arkoff, chairman of the board of American
International Pictures.

His first production will be H.G. Wells' *When the Sleeper Wakes*
for AIP.

No date has been set for this move and will depend upon the
transfer of those duties with which Nicholson has been involved.
At that time, he will relinquish his post as president at AIP, but
will continue to remain a director and continue to promote the
welfare of the company he and Sam Arkoff founded in 1954.

"Because of our close personal relationship over the many
years," Arkoff stated, "I naturally regret Jim's decision. Jim will
still be with us in an advisory capacity, member of the board of
directors as well as a large stockholder."

**A number of items in the above article don't ring true given
what has since been said about Nicholson's split from AIP.
When Nicholson and his wife divorced, she got half of Jim's 345
shares of AIP stock in the settlement. Because of this, Jim no
longer felt he was an equal partner in AIP and Arkoff's position
in the company changed from vice president to chairman of the
board. Although Arkoff never spoke badly of Nicholson in later
years, there was obviously resentment in both parties at this
point in time.**

**In 1972, American International Television made a large
number of movie packages available to local TV stations as
well as syndication packages of previously shown TV series. As**

444

**listed in AIP's brochure "American International Television Presents," these were:**

*Films for the '70's-* Super-stars guaranteed to grab the largest share of primetime audiences

in 26 fast-moving, diversified, high-quality color features with top production values.

*Strongmen of the World-* 26 features in color depicting invincible feats of strength of the strongest and mightiest heroes of the past.

*New Color Adventure-* 33 color tales of adventure, spellbinding excitement, barbaric tortures, fights to the death.

*Amazing '65-* 19 features with all the exciting elements of the best in science fiction.

*Amazing '66-* 20 weird, way out science fiction at its explosive best.

*Amazing Adventures 1967-* From tales of suspense and science fiction to the rock n roll swingers; from secret agent adventures to the jungles of lost worlds; all this in 26 rip roaring action films in color.

*Amazing Adventures 1966-* 20 high adventure- roaming the exotic lands of the world... safaris after wild game... enticing temple dancers and Marco Polo, explorer extraordinaire... the fierce action of war in the jungle.

*Top Secret Adventures-* 20 of the lethal world of the secret agent- their fearless exploits- their torrid love affairs!

*Dominant 10-* 10 fast-paced, exciting stories, top drawing names.

*Young Adult Theatre-* 26 swinging, action-packed films in color.

*Holiday Storybook of Fables-* 13 where the screen awakens to a big, wide, wonderful world of enchantment.

*Real Life Adventures-* 6 high adventure, fierce action, all color documentaries.

*15 New Science Fiction-* 15 spine-tingling features.

*Sci-Fi '70-* Combining the most exciting elements of the scientific mysteries of the atomic age- the unknown unexplored galactic empires; their incredible technologically advanced civilizations; strange forms of life- in 14 features, all in color.

Special Feature- *Love, Hate & Dishonor*

445

One-Hour Program

*The Avengers* (83 Shows)- 26 B&W and 57 Color

Effervescent as champagne... sly as a furtive wink... hard as diamonds... and cool as a blue steel gun barrel.

Half-Hour Programs

*Prince Planet* (52 B&W Animated Shows)

A brand new thrill-packed adventure cartoon series.

*Johnny Sokko & His Flying Robot* (26 color live-action shows)

Here's the excitement-filled adventure series Johnny Sokko, about a real live boy, whom children will identify with, and the gigantic flying Robot, his computerized friend.

*Adventures of Ozzie & Harriet* (200 B&W Shows)

Four generations of Nelson's... in one of the longest running, highest rated, fully sponsored family entertainments ever!

5- Minute Cartoon

*Sinbad, Jr.* (130 Color Episodes)

130 brand new five-minute swashbuckling, action-packed, seafaring cartoons in glorious color with full animation.


February 1972


**Godzilla vs. the Smog Monster** (aka **Godzilla vs. Hedorah**)

"The GREATEST duels The DEADLIEST. Out of Pollution's depths it slithers! Breathing Poison... Leaving a wake of deadly slime... Destroying all in its path!"

Produced by Tomoyuki Tanaka  Directed by Yoshimitu Banno
Starring Akira Yamauchi, Hiroyuki Kawase, Toshie Kimura, Toshio Shibaki

From the pressbook-
ANTI-SMOG CAMPAIGN FEATURED IN LATEST GODZILLA ADVENTURE
Modern day problems of smog and pollution form the basis for the latest screen monster adventure featuring Godzilla, the towering

hero of American International's latest film, *Godzilla vs. the Smog Monster.*

In the spectacular thriller, the forbidding prehistoric beast takes up the cudgels for ecology when he pits his forces against the corrosive effects of pollution. The menace of pollution appears in the form of a massive hunk of animated sludge which flourishes on the wastes of a big city and revels in the contaminated smoke of its factories.

EXPLOITATION-
Godzilla Cocktail- Have a local bar owner create a new mixed drink labeled the "Godzilla Cocktail... it clears that five o'clock smog from your brain"... for use in promoting his cocktail hour offerings. Gag should be of interest as a humor item to local newspaper columnists and radio and television commentators.

Film review- *Godzilla vs. the Smog Monster*

*New York Times* (July 6, 1972) by Vincent Canby
*Godzilla vs. the Smog Monster* is an English-dubbed Japanese film about a creature that lives on sludge. Godzilla, a sort of Japanese Smokey the Bear, hates pollution and saves the day, clumping around the countryside on his hind legs, looking as embarrassed and pious as an elderly clergyman at a charity masquerade ball.

March 1972-

*Who Slew Auntie Roo?* (aka *Whoever Slew Auntie Roo?*)
"Say Goodnight to Auntie Roo, Kiddies... It's dead time!"

Produced by Samuel Z. Arkoff and James H. Nicholson  Directed by Curtis Harrington
Starring Shelley Winters, Mark Lester, Ralph Richardson, Judy Cornwell, Michael Gothard

**Jim Nicholson had been so impressed by Curtis Harrington's *What's the Matter with Helen?* that he hired the director and star**

447

Shelley Winters to make a film for AIP. The property that Jim had in mind was a story by David Osborn called *The Gingerbread House*, which was a horror variation on the fairy tale *Hansel and Gretel*. The filming was done by AIP's British production unit in conjunction with Hemdale Films.

The formidable Shelley Winters (1920-2006) appeared in four AIP productions.

Film Reviews- *Who Slew Auntie Roo?*

*Milwaukee Bugle American* (January 19, 1972) by Curtis L. Carter

*Who Slew Auntie Roo?* at the Capitol Court Theater is another of those films about which the only pertinent question is, WHY? There is no apparent reason why a responsible filmmaker would waste talent and resources on such a mediocre venture. Throughout, there are various shock techniques, designed to thrill persons who enjoy the macabre. However, the measures are only half-hearted. The film is unfortunately sufficiently restrained in horror to get by the GP censors, but quite capable of giving pointless nightmares to children who happen to attend.

*New York Times* (March 16, 1972) by Roger Greenspun

*Who Slew Auntie Roo?* opens up the full scope of Miss [Shelley] Winters' acting talent, which is insufficient reason for making a movie.

### Wild in the Sky

"Come along for the ride, Baby... You're gonna love it! Josh has the plane and the H-Bomb and he's gonna blow Ft. Knox higher than you've ever been."

Produced by William T. Naud and Dick Gautier  Directed by William T. Naud
Starring Brandon DeWilde, Keenan Wynn, Tom O'Connor, Dick Gautier, Robert Lansing

### Frogs

"Nature strikes back! And mankind faces the... FROGS!"

Produced by George Edwards and Peter Thomas  Directed by George McCowan
Starring Ray Milland, Sam Elliott, Joan Van Ark, Adam Roarke, Judy Pace

Film Review- *Frogs*

*New York Times* (July 6, 1972) by Vincent Canby
IN 'FROGS,' THE ANIMALS DO IN RAY MILLAND
*Frogs*, which is not to be confused with *The Birds* for an instant, is an end-of-the-world junk movie, photographed rather prettily in Florida and acted by [Ray] Milland as if he were sight reading random passages from the dictionary.

March 6, 1972
*Boxoffice*
NEW TAYLOR-LAUGHLIN FIRM IN TIEUP WITH AIP FOR PRODUCT RELEASE
Hollywood- Tom Laughlin, chairman of the board of Taylor-Laughlin Enterprises, announced February 29 the establishment of a new major distribution company, Taylor-Laughlin Distribution Co.

In a joint statement by Laughlin and Samuel Z. Arkoff, chairman of the board of American International Pictures, and Delores Taylor, president of Delores Taylor Productions, it was announced that American International will handle the sales and servicing of films being released through the Taylor-Laughlin Distribution Co. Distribution will be through AIP's 29 exchanges in the United States, the largest number of domestic exchanges in the motion picture business.

*The Trial of Billy Jack* will be the first Taylor-Laughlin feature to be distributed by American International under the new setup. AIP will handle up to eight films from Taylor-Laughlin annually in addition to its own growing number of releases.

Arkoff stated, "American International Pictures is delighted to be reunited with Delores Taylor and Tom Laughlin, as we were originally associated in the distribution of their picture *Born Losers.*"

**For some reason, AIP's deal with Taylor-Laughlin fell through and *The Trial of Billy Jack* was eventually released by Warner Bros. in 1974. That same year, AIP reissued *Born Losers* with a new ad campaign: "Back by popular demand... *Born***

*Losers...* the original screen appearance of Tom Laughlin as Billy Jack."

*Boxoffice*
MAJOR WINNERS OF IFIDA AWARDS
New York- One of the highlights of the annual dinner of the International Film Importers & Distributors of America, Inc. at the Hotel Americana on Friday, February 25, was the presentation to Nat Cohn and Bernard Delfont of Anglo-EMI with a special citation in recognition of their producing and distributing quality films in the world market. Samuel Z. Arkoff, AIP board chairman, presented the citation.

April 1972-

### Dr. Jekyll and Sister Hyde
"PARENTS: Be sure your children are sufficiently mature to witness the intimate details of this frank and revealing film."

Produced by Albert Fennell and Brian Clemens  Directed by Roy Ward Baker
Starring Ralph Bates, Martine Beswick, Gerald Sim, Lewis Fiander

From the pressbook-
FAMED HORROR SCENE IS SWITCHED IN *DR. JEKYLL AND SISTER HYDE*
A startling variation of Robert Louis Stevenson's famous scene depicting the noted Dr. Jekyll transformed into a monster is presented in *Dr. Jekyll and Sister Hyde,* American International's
thrilling new film shocker. Instead of turning into a hairy be-fanged beast, the misguided doctor's potion changes him into a gorgeous, sexy brunette with full blown feminine charms... but murderous ideas.
British star Ralph Bates portrays Dr. Jekyll in the film and raven-haired Martine Beswick plays his alter ego. It becomes a "double-threat" combination as young ladies in the neighborhood

become victims of his side of the bi-play and young men are lured to their doom by her villainous intents.

The American International release is a Hammer Film production produced by Albert Fennell and Brian Clemens.

**AIP's ultra-lurid advertising does an injustice to the excellent Hammer Film *Dr. Jekyll and Sister Hyde*.**

EXPLOITATION-
Brother and Sister Twins- Offer free passes to all brother and sister twins who appear at the box office with birth certificate proofs of their relationships. Stunt can be a source of newsworthy photos. Elaboration of the gag by having the twins dress up in costumes resembling those worn by the stars of the film would multiply the value of the idea and possibly attract coverage by local television stations.

Film reviews- *Dr. Jekyll and Sister Hyde*

*Variety-*
As with Hammer horror pix, production values and performances are of a high standard. Director Roy Ward Baker has set a good pace, built tension nicely, and played straight so that all seems credible. He tops chills and gruesome murders with quite a lot of subtle fun. Ralph Bates and Martine Beswick, strong, attractive personalities, bear a strange resemblance to each other, making the transformations entirely believable.

*Cue Magazine*
Under the direction of Roy Ward Baker and with a screenplay by Brian Clemens, Robert Louis Stevenson's oft-told tale is reduced to the utterly banal. Ralph Bates makes like a serious scientist as he spouts asinine dialogue. At least attractive Martine Beswick has been engaged to play Sis, so the film isn't a complete drag.

*Los Angeles Times* by Kevin Thomas
JEKYLL DOES HIS/HER THING
As the title *Dr. Jekyll and Sister Hyde* rather literally indicates, the latest variation on the Robert Louis Stevenson classic tale of split personality involves the transformation of a man into a woman. What the title doesn't suggest is that this elegant period picture is actually a satisfying horror entertainment, stylish rather than simply campy. Roy Ward Baker, a gifted horror specialist, directs Brian Clemens' clever script with such authority and imagination that he easily achieves a willing suspension of disbelief.

April 10, 1972
*Boxoffice*
TRADE LEADERS FETE JAMES NICHOLSON FOR AIDING VARIETY CLUB PROJECTS
Beverly Hills, Calif.- Some 800 persons from the show business world turned out on Wednesday (April 5) to honor film producer James H. Nicholson at a Variety

Club of Southern California Ten 25 luncheon in the Grand Ballroom of the Beverly Wilshire Hotel here.

Nicholson, presently an international vice president of Variety Clubs International and past chief barker of Tent 25, was lauded for his longtime support of Variety's charitable activities on behalf of children and for helping to organize the Variety Tent in Hawaii.

A plaque presented to Nicholson at the affair carried the inscription:

"To James H. Nicholson, whose inspirational leadership in showing the way to help those less fortunate has made all our lives fuller and meaningful and who is the living embodiment of the word 'humanitarian.'"

Among the dais guests were two fellow Variety Clubs International officers and Samuel Z. Arkoff, chairman of the board of American International Pictures and a longtime partner of Nicholson. Seated at the head table were Dorothy Lamour, Annette Funicello, Harvey Lembeck, Fabian Forte, Les Baxter, Roger Corman, and Morey Amsterdam, who served as master of ceremonies.

Nicholson, founder with Arkoff of American International Pictures, recently resigned as president of the firm to concentrate on independent production.


May 1972-


*Blood from the Mummy's Tomb/Night of the Blood Monster*
"TWO HIDEOUS TALES of TERROR! A severed hand beckons from an open grave as the Bloodiest Butchers in history turn the screen into a Slaughterhouse!"


From the pressbook-
HORROR FANS DELIGHT IN LOCAL SCREEN TWIN-BILL
A combination of thrillers to please the taste of screen horror fans opens when the American International double feature of *Blood from the Mummy's Tomb* and *Night of the Blood Monster* begins its local run.

Describing the reincarnation of an evil but beautiful queen of ancient Egypt, *Blood from the Mummy's Tomb* relates how her modern counterpart, portrayed by raven-haired British beauty Valerie Leon, carries out the deadly curse pronounced by the curvaceous cadaver before she was entombed.

The hectic with hunting days of 17th century England are recaptured in *Night of the Blood Monster,* which describes the burnings and tortures which took place under a sadistic magistrate of that period.

*Blood from the Mummy's Tomb*
Produced by Howard Brandy  Directed by Seth Holt
Starring Andrew Kier, Valerie Leon, James Villers, Hugh Burden, George Coulouris

Film reviews- *Blood from the Mummy's Tomb*

*Variety*
Polished and well-acted, but rather tame Hammer horror entry. The blood-spattered story is confusing with its involvement in Egyptology and the occult, but it provides a quota of chills and gory murders and as a programmer should fit in with the cult for such pix.

*Films and Filming*
Valerie Leon is stunningly deadpan come blood or tempest; she fills out her dual role as amply as could be wished.

*Night of the Blood Monster*
Produced by Harry Alan Towers  Directed by Jess Franco
Starring Christopher Lee, Maria Schell, Leo Genn, Maria Rohm, Margaret Lee, Hans Hass

**Night of the Blood Monster** is the Spanish horror movie *The Bloody Judge.*

*Pick Up on 101*
"Anybody's Back Seat will do... so long as he's going her way."

Produced by Christian Whittaker and Ed Garner   Directed by John Florea
Starring Jack Albertson, Lesley (Anne) Warren, Martin Sheen

May 1, 1972
*Boxoffice*
VARIETY INT'L HONORS NICHOLSON, ARKOFF
New York- Outgoing president James H. Nicholson and chairman of the board Samuel Z. Arkoff of American International Pictures paid tribute to each other and to their support of the Variety Clubs at the AIP luncheon held Tuesday, April 25, the second full day of activities at Variety Clubs International's 45th annual convention.

Nicholson, who is about to start production of his first independent film for release by AIP, said that he and Arkoff will always be friends and that he will always be a part of AIP. He pledged that the company will continue to support Variety Clubs, adding that AIP is "the company with a heart and  I'm sure it always will be."

May 29, 1972
*Boxoffice*
AIP NOW DISTRIBUTING OVER 35 FEATURES
Hollywood- Samuel Z. Arkoff, chairman of the board of American International Pictures, stressed that AIP is the only major film company which- through its 29 domestic film exchanges- is capable of distributing over 35 feature films a year.

"American International Pictures," said Arkoff, "plans to be at the center of this revitalization and resurgence in the motion picture industry." Arkoff announced an exciting array of forthcoming pictures, including *Boxcar Bertha, Blacula, The Sandpit Generals, Dr. Phibes Rises Again,* and *Dillinger.* He also stated that the '70s will go down in history as one of the film industry's most exciting and progressive decades.

*Camille* will begin shooting in Europe in October with "two very exciting international stars" in the lead roles, according to Arkoff.

June 1972-

*Lola*
"She's almost 16. He's almost 40. It may be love, but it's definitely exhausting!"

Produced by Clive Sharp  Directed by Richard Donner
Starring Charles Bronson, Susan George, Orson Bean, Honor Blackman, Michael Craig

**Lola is the 1970 British film *Twinky*.**

*Boxcar Bertha*
"KISSING and KILLING... One was her hobby, the other more like a business..."

Produced by Roger Corman  Directed by Martin Scorsese
Starring Barbara Hershey, David Carradine, Barry Primus, Bernie Casey, John Carradine

**Boxcar Bertha is Roger Corman's follow up to *Bloody Mama*, but in this case, he only produced the film, leaving the directing chores to Martin Scorsese.**

Roger Corman: "I had no intention of doing any more films with AIP. I did *Bertha* only because Sam had asked me."

Film reviews- *Boxcar Bertha*

*Chicago Sun Times* (July 19, 1972) by Roger Ebert
*Boxcar Bertha* is a weirdly interesting movie and not really the sleazy exploitation film the ads promise. I have a notion that Roger Corman, American International's most successful producer of

exploitation films, sent his actors and crew South with the hope of getting a nice, simple, sexy, violent movie for the summer trade. What he got is something else and something better. Director Martin Scorsese has gone for mood and atmosphere more than for action and his violence is always blunt and unpleasant, never liberating and exhilarating.

*New York Times* (August 18, 1972) by Howard Thompson
Set in the South and Southwest of the Depression years, this is the drama of two derelict criminals and sweethearts who finally meet a horrible doom. Does that sound familiar? Well, *Bonnie and Clyde* still leads the parade. However, while there is a striking similarity in general content, the new, more modest film stands curiously on its own.

June 12, 1972
*Boxoffice*
AIP SCHEDULES NINE IMPORTANT FILMS FOR RELEASE IN THE NEXT THREE MONTHS
Hollywood- Samuel Z. Arkoff, chairman of the board of American International Pictures, has announced an "impressive list" of pictures for release this summer with nine films slated to hit the nation's screens during the next three months.

*Boxcar Bertha*, produced by Roger Corman and directed by Martin Scorsese, goes into national release tomorrow (13).

*Dr. Phibes Rises Again*, sequel to last year's successful *Dr. Phibes*, will be available starting July 5 with Vincent Price repeating the title role.

*The Thing With Two Heads*, in which Ray Milland and Rosey Grier provide the two heads, will be released July 12.

The first black vampire film, *Blacula*, will be released July 26 with William Marshall in the title role.

Hall Bartlett's *The Sandpit Generals*, based on a novel by Jorge Amado, will be released August 2.

*The Deathmaster*, terror feature starring Robert Quarry, will be released August 9.

*F.T.A.*, which Arkoff termed "our most unusual film," will be available during the summer, recording the experiences of nine entertainers providing humor and music near military bases.

*Slaughter*, filmed in and around Mexico City in Todd-AO 35mm, will be released August 30 starring Jim Brown.

*The Devil's Widow*, starring Ava Gardner and Ian McShane, is set for release September 20.

AIP also is considering several independent productions for summer release and Arkoff said it is likely that two soon will be acquired. He added that the total summer schedule marks a concerted drive by AIP to win as much as possible of the coveted "kids-are-out-of-school" playing time, traditionally the company's most profitable season.

June 19, 1972
*Boxoffice*

## SALES, MARKETING TO SHARE ATTENTION ON NICHOLSON'S NEW APC FILMS

A press luncheon at the Beverly Hills Hotel here Thursday (June 8), hosted by James H. Nicholson, provided full details of the film executive's announcement of formation of his own production company, Academy Pictures Corp., which will release its product through 20th Century-Fox.

Nicholson said he would limit APC's output to three- possibly four- pictures per year, making only as many "as I can give my complete personal and undivided attention to."

The formation of APC represents Nicholson's first separation in 18 years from the partners and associates with whom he organized American Releasing Corp. and then American International Pictures. This was indicated when Nicholson, some months ago, made known his impending resignation from the AIP presidency.

## SAMUEL Z. ARKOFF NAMED PRESIDENT OF AIP

Hollywood- Samuel Z. Arkoff, co-founder of American International Pictures, has taken over the duties of president of the company in addition to continuing in his present position as chairman of the board.

Arkoff has been a producer or an executive producer on most of AIP's films since the company was formed in 1954.

He succeeds James H. Nicholson, who recently resigned as president of the company to enter independent production.

Arkoff will continue to headquarter in the AIP building in Beverly Hills.

July 1972-

*Dr. Phibes Rises Again*
"DEATH! TORTURE! MURDER MOST FOUL! Dr. Phibes is amusing himself again."

Produced by Louis M. Heyward  Directed by Robert Fuest
Starring Vincent Price, Robert Quarry, Peter Cushing, Beryl Reid, Terry-Thomas

From the pressbook-
*PHIBES* PHANS WIN NEW FILM LOOK AT HERO'S SKULLDUGGERY
Elated with the horrendous effect his skullduggery had on his audiences in *The Abominable Dr. Phibes*, the inventive doctor returns with a new batch of outlandish horrors in *Dr. Phibes Rises Again*. Each of his nasty tricks is a masterpiece of brilliant devilry and worth of standing alone as the piece de resistance of any horror flick. Combined as they are in this latest gory go-round, they make a veritable feast of cinema fascination.

Vincent Price again portrays the Machiavellian master, lending his inimitable savoir-faire to the proceedings. Produced by Albert Fennell [sic], the film is directed by Robert Fuest, who also directed the initial *Phibes* effort.

EXPLOITATION-
Women's Lib Controversy Stunt- The character of Vulnavia, played by Australian beauty Valli Kemp, is an ideal example of female servitude as she plays background music to Dr. Phibes' nasty machinations, pops grapes in his mouth, and provides gorgeous

feminine comfort in complete silence to the master criminal. Have pretty girls picket your theatre with signs stating
"Dr. Phibes is a chauvinist male monster... Free Vulnavia!"

**Vincent Price in *Dr. Phibes Rises Again.***

Film review- *Doctor Phibes Rises Again*

*New York Times* (January 11, 1973) by Vincent Canby
The movie, about a search for an ancient Egyptian Geritol formula, displays a good deal of wit in its amused affection for awful movie styles of the 1930s. *Dr. Phibes Rises Again* makes the usually dumb mistake of aspiring to be camp. Mysteriously, a lot of it works, probably because Robert Fuest, the director, knows just how long to hold an effect before it wilts.

*Dr. Phibes Rises Again* was the last AIP film to have the "James H. Nicholson and Samuel Z. Arkoff Present" credit. Henceforth, Arkoff's name would appear alone.

### The Thing With Two Heads

"The doctor blew it- He transplanted a WHITE BIGOT'S HEAD on a SOUL BROTHER'S BODY! Man, they're in deeeeep trouble!"

Produced by Wes Bishop  Directed by Lee Frost
Starring Ray Milland, Rosey Grier, Don Marshall, Robert Perry, Kathy Baumann, Chelsea Brown

Film review- *The Thing With Two Heads*

*Chicago Sun Times* (October 10, 1972) by Roger Ebert
The most incredible thing in *The Thing With Two Heads* is not the transplant, however, but what happens next. Within hours after [Ray] Milland's head has been screwed on, the two-headed escapee is on a motorcycle and being chased by no less than 14 police cars. Every one of them is destroyed during the chase, a process that takes so long that seven, or even five, squad cars might have been enough.

August 1972-

### Blacula

"BLOODSUCKER! Deadlier than Dracula! Warm young bodies will feed his hunger and hot, fresh blood his awful thirst!"

Produced by Joseph T. Narr  Directed by William Crane
Starring William Marshall, Denise Nicholas, Vionetta McGee, Thalmus Rasulala

*Blacula* was AIP's first major entry in the Blaxploitation market, although *The Thing With Two Heads* has definite Blaxploitation elements. AIP would become the leading producer of films in this genre. A sequel to *Blacula* called *Scream Blacula Scream* was released in 1973.

**William Marshall and Vonetta McGee in *Blacula*.**

Film review- *Blacula*

*New York Times* (August 26, 1972) by Roger Greenspun
YES, THE VAMPIRE IS BACK IN LOS ANGELES
Anybody who goes to a vampire movie expecting sense is in serious trouble and *Blacula* offers less sense than most. But it

does provide such bits of knowledge as the "well-known fact" (not well-known to me) "that vampires multiply geometrically..." or the useful information that a silver cross will also work against Third-world vampires from emergent African nations.

### The Deathmaster

"EYES LIKE HOT COALS! FANGS LIKE RAZORS! The Deathmaster has escaped from his grave!"

Produced by Fred Sadoff  Directed by Ray Danton
Starring Robert Quarry, John Fielder, Bob Pickett, William Jordan, Betty Anne Rees

From the pressbook-
STAR OF VAMPIRE FLICKS IN NEW SCREEN THRILLER
Robert Quarry, who has won screen renown for his convincing portrayals as a member of vampire nobility, stars again in a new, equally horrifying role in *The Deathmaster*, American International's new screen shocker.

It was his initial efforts as a merchant of menace in *Count Yorga, Vampire*, an earlier American International release, which launched the actor into the milieu of the horror film. He had established himself with film producers as a thoroughly trained and tested professional in film and stage performances, a record which strangely enough featured many roles in Shakespearean plays. But the success of his work at generating goose pimples in that first shocker sparked a second assignment in *The Return of Count Yorga* and this third project for the releasing company.

Film review- *The Deathmaster*

*Chicago Sun Times* (September 14, 1972) by Roger Ebert
*The Deathmaster* is a vampire movie that has moved into neighborhood theaters under cover of darkness (naturally). [Robert] Quarry is an old hand at the vampire game by now. The two superstars of the horror genre are Christopher Lee and Peter Cushing, but Quarry has been moving up fast in the last year or two. Anyway, in *The Deathmaster*, Quarry arrives at dawn in an old

coffin that floats up on the beach at Santa Monica. What follows is pretty routine. I counted seven chases down the same length of subterranean cavern. It is not a very long length, but what they do is photograph a guy running down it one way and then cut to the other end of the same passage and have him run back. That way, it looks twice as long as it is, which is how the movie feels.

*Slaughter*
"Jim Brown is SLAUGHTER... It's not only his name, it's his business and sometimes... his
PLEASURE!"

Produced by Monroe Morrison  Directed by Jack Starrett
Starring Jim Brown, Stella Stevens, Rip Torn, Don Gordon, Cameron Mitchell

AIP had another big Blaxploitation box office success with *Slaughter.* The following year, they released a sequel, *Slaughter's Big Rip-Off.*

Jim Brown as *Slaughter.*

465

Film review- *Slaughter*

*New York Times* (August 17, 1972) by Roger Greenspun
Except as another instance in the continued misuse of Stella Stevens, a talented and beautiful actress, there is almost nothing of interest in Jack Starrett's *Slaughter*. As the principal bad guy, Rip Torn plays as if evil were his only vocation. For the Creature from the Black Lagoon, this might be a good characterization. Jim Brown plays Slaughter as if he hated doing it, which is to his credit. Among other indignities, he is subject to racial insults on the order of "Just who do you think you are, boy?"- which put *Slaughter* perhaps five years behind current fashions in movie bigotry.

*The Wild Pack* (aka *Sandpit Generals*)
"Their Law is Lust! Their God is Violence! Their Prayer is a Four Letter Word!"

Produced and Directed by Hall Bartlett
Starring Kent Lane, Tisha Sterling, John Rubinstein, Butch Patrick, Alejandro Rey

September 1972-

*The Devil's Widow* (aka *Tam-Lin*)
"She drained them of their manhood... and then of their LIVES! The story of the kind of woman few people even know exists."

Produced by Alan Ladd Jr. and Stanley Mann  Directed by Roddy McDowall
Starring Ava Gardner, Ian McShane, Cyril Cusack, Richard Wattis, Stephanie Beacham

From the pressbook-
THE DEVIL'S WIDOW BASED ON ANCIENT SCOTTISH BALLAD
The screenplay for *The Devil's Widow*, American International's

exciting drama, is based on an ancient folk song called "The Ballad of Tam Lin." The lyrics for the ballad were created so long ago that the ballad's author is unknown; however, it is believed that Robert Burns first put the words to paper, thus recording the song for posterity.

Typical of so many of the ancient poems, the words describe a story of love and violence in relation to how a fierce fairy queen got a young lord in her power and refused to relinquish him until her evil was challenged by the knight's pretty sweetheart. The spelling of the name Tam Lin is a Gaelic version of Tom Lynn.

In the American International release, Ava Gardner portrays the evil queen, modernized in the character of a rich and attractive widow who holds power over the young Tom Lynn with her wealth until a lass arrives to complicate her plans. British male star Ian McShane portrays Tom Lynn and the role of the maiden is played by Stephanie Beacham.

Directed by Roddy McDowall, his first effort on a theatrical motion picture, it is a Jerry Gershwin- Elliott Kastner production.

EXPLOITATION-
"Widow" Bally- Have young women dressed in mourning clothing, including black dress and capes with dark veils, walk through the busy section of town. Lettering showing the title *The Devil's Widow* and playdate information should be applied across their chests and back to tie the clothing with the engagement.

October 1972-

***Baron Blood*** (aka *The Torture Chamber of Baron Blood*)
"THE ULTIMATE IN HUMAN AGONY! With Instruments of TORTURE ghastly beyond belief!"

Produced by Alfred Leone  Directed by Mario Bava
Starring Joseph Cotten, Elke Sommer, Massimo Girotti, Antonio Cantafora, Alan Collins

Film review- *Baron Blood*

*Chicago Sun Times* (October 10, 1972) by Roger Ebert
The publicity for the movie warns against the possibility of "apoplectic strokes, cerebral hemorrhages, cardiac seizures, or fainting spells" during the movie, but they're just trying to make themselves look good. The only first aid they really need is hot coffee for the patrons who doze off.

November 1972-

*Carry On Doctor/Carry On Henry VIII*

AIP paired the 1968 film *Carry On Doctor* with the latest entry in the long running series, *Carry On Henry VIII* (known simply as *Carry on Henry* in England). The new film was a spoof of the 1969 Richard Burton/Genevieve Bujold starrer *Anne of the Thousand Days*.

*Carry On Doctor*
Produced by Peter Rogers  Directed by Gerald Thomas
Starring Frankie Howerd, Sid James, Charles Hawtrey

*Carry on Henry VIII*
Produced by Peter Rogers  Directed by Gerald Thomas
Starring Kenneth Williams, Sid James, Charles Hawtrey

*Unholy Rollers*
"A Locker Room Look at the Toughest Broads in the World!"

Produced by Jack Bohrer and John Prizer  Directed by Vernon Zimmerman
Starring Claudia Jennings, Louis Quinn, Betty Anne Rees

Film review- *Unholy Rollers*

*Chicago Sun Times* (January 4, 1973) by Roger Ebert
I went to see *Unholy Rollers* partly because of my fond memories of Claudia Jennings as Playboy's Playmate of the Year. Miss Jennings was all golden and sleek in Playboy. You know, the kind of girl you'd never allow to open the door of her own Lamborghini. That makes her performance in *Unholy Rollers* all the more astonishing. How can I describe it? She plays a very tough broad and turns in the hardest, most vicious female performance in a long time. That's one of the most interesting things about *Unholy Rollers*- that it doesn't go all soft and sentimental around the edges.

### *The Dirt Gang*
"GOD HELP THE FUZZ that flashes a badge on the 'Dirt Gang'! He'll get a face full of bloody tread and marks of a 250 lb. dirt bike right where he doesn't need it."

Produced by Joseph E. Bishop and Art Jacobs  Directed by Jerry Jameson
Starring Paul Carr, Michael Forrest, Ben Archibek, Michael Pataki, Nancy Harris

From the pressbook-
OFF-ROAD CYCLES FEATURED IN NEW *DIRT GANG* FILM
A new breed of motorcycle which has achieved immense popularity among the nation's bikers is featured in *Dirt Gang*, American International's new action-adventure.

Called, appropriately enough, a dirt bike, it is intended for high-speed off-road travel along dirt trails and over open fields. As a result, it is a marked contrast to the high power, heavy "choppers" which are designed for speed on the smooth, straight lanes of a paved freeway.

**The Dirt Gang was the last in AIP's long running series of motorcycle gang pictures.**

December 1972-

*An Evening of Edgar Allan Poe*

**Vincent Price in *An Evening of Edgar Allan Poe*.**

Produced and Directed by Ken Johnson.
Starring Vincent Price

This 53-minute color film was produced for television by Ken Johnson and AIP. It is a one-man show with Vincent Price enacting four Poe stories: The Tell-Tale Heart, The Sphinx, The Cask of Amontillado, and The Pit and the Pendulum. The costumes were designed by Price's wife at the time, Mary Grant, and Les Baxter provided the original background score. The show was filmed in 1970, but not televised until December 1972. It continued to be shown in syndication from 1973 to 1976.

December 18, 1972
*Boxoffice*
JAMES NICHOLSON DIES; IN INDUSTRY 40 YEARS
Hollywood- James H. Nicholson, 56, president of Academy Pictures and former president of American International Pictures, died at UCLA Medical Center on Sunday (December 10) following surgery for a brain tumor. Funeral services were conducted on Wednesday (13) at Inglewood Park Cemetery. The eulogy was delivered by Samuel Z. Arkoff, his longtime associate.

In 1954, Nicholson and Arkoff founded American Releasing Corp., which soon became American International Pictures. With Arkoff as chairman of the board, Nicholson produced or co-produced over 150 films in his capacity as president. Starting with such fare as *Machine Gun Kelly, Five Guns West,* and *Dragstrip Riot,* AIP was built into its present position as a major independent producing company. In recent years, the company has turned out the popular "Beach Party" movies and such heavier fare as *Wuthering Heights, Wild in the Streets, De Sade,* and the *Dr. Phibes* films.

Nicholson resigned as president of AIP in June 1972 to organize Academy Pictures, releasing through 20th Century-Fox. The company's first film is the as yet unreleased *The Legend of Hell House.* The other Academy Pictures, which have not been put into production, have also been scheduled for release by 20th-Fox, but AIP could conceivably step in and distribute them.

Nicholson had his first contact with the film world when he ushered at San Francisco's El Rey Theatre in 1933. He was later a theatre circuit owner, film salesman, publicist, copywriter, and projectionist.

Nicholson was active in philanthropic work. For many years, he had been a leading figure with the affairs of Variety's international Heart Awards committee for charity achievements. He was a chief Barker of Variety Club of Southern California, Tent 25, and the personal donor of three Sunshine Coaches for handicapped children in the Los Angeles area. Last March, Tent 25 honored him with a luncheon.

Nicholson's showmanship and industry leadership had been honored frequently by exhibitor organizations. In November 1971, he and Arkoff were jointly honored in New York by the Motion Picture Pioneers as "Pioneers of the Year."

Nicholson leaves his wife, actress Susan Hart, their son James; three daughters by a previous marriage, Mrs. Luree Holms, Loretta Nicholson, and Mrs. Michael Sobel, all of Los Angeles; a sister, Elizabeth Nicholson; and ten grandchildren.

Honorary pallbearers at the funeral were David Melamed, Joseph and Milt Moritz, Leon Blender, Michael Zide, Norman Herman, Al Simms, and Salvatore Billitteri.

**And thus ended the Golden Years of American International Pictures....**

**James Harvey Nicholson (1916-1972)**

# PART FOUR

# CHAPTER TWENTY
# 1973

# JIM NICHOLSON
# AFTER AIP

WHEN JIM NICHOLSON LEFT AIP, HE TOOK WITH HIM TWO projects he was developing to be produced by his new company, Academy Productions, in conjunction with 20th Century-Fox. The first was *The Legend of Hell House,* a watered down version of Richard Matheson's 1971 horror novel, *Hell House.* It began filming in England in October 1972 under the direction of John Hough and starred Pamela Franklin, Clive Revill, and Roddy McDowall. Nicholson was the Executive Producer; however, he never lived to see the release of his first production independent of AIP. The picture came out in June 1973, six months after his death.

The second project was *Dirty Mary, Crazy Larry.* Based on a 1963 novel called *Pursuit* by Richard Unekis, the car chase story had been knocking around Hollywood for some time before

Nicholson optioned it. Nicholson hired John Hough to direct and cast AIP alums Peter Fonda and Adam Roarke to star. The movie went into production in the fall of 1973 and was released by Fox in May 1974.

Jim Nicholson's widow, the former Susan Hart, as an uncredited producer on these two films, diligently watched out for her husband's interests. She also continued his charitable work with Variety Club of Southern California, eventually raising enough money to create a pediatric heart wing at UCLA Medical Center in Los Angeles. She married Roy Hofheinz in 1981 and now owns the exclusive theatrical rights to several of AIP's most famous titles, including *I Was a Teenage Werewolf, I Was a Teenage Frankenstein, Invasion of the Saucer-Men, It Conquered the World,* and *The Amazing Colossal Man.*

# CHAPTER TWENTY-ONE
# 1973-1980

# AIP AFTER
# JIM NICHOLSON

AFTER JIM NICHOLSON DEPARTED FROM AIP THE COMPANY continued to prosper. Following the success of *Blacula*, AIP embarked on a series of Blaxploitation films thereby giving boosts to the careers of a number of black actors, chief among them Pam Grier and Fred Williamson. Between 1973 and 1978 AIP released no less than twenty Blaxploitation features.

AIP did not forget its horror/sci-fi roots and released such films as Brian DePalma's *Sisters* (1973), *Raw Meat* (aka *Deathline;*1973), *Squirm* (1976), *Tentacles* (1977) and a number of others. Bert I. Gordon returned to AIP for *The Food of the Gods* (1975) and *Empire of the Ants* (1977).

A partnership with the British company Amicus resulted in *Madhouse* (1974), which was Vincent Price's last film for AIP, as well as a trilogy of bigger budgeted fantasies based on the works of Edgar Rice Burroughs: *The Land That Time Forgot* (1975), *At the Earth's Core* (1976), and *The People That Time Forgot* (1977).

Attempts to get into higher budgeted film making such as *The Wild Party* (1975) and *Meteor* (1977) resulted in expensive flops. But *The Amityville Horror* (1979), which cost $4.7 million to produce, made $86.5 million in the U.S. alone.

February 3, 1975
*Boxoffice*
ARKOFF IS CHEERY ON BUSINESS OUTLOOK, FILMS NOW IN PRODUCTION AT AIP
Hollywood- Samuel Z. Arkoff, chairman and president of the board of American International Pictures, at a press conference luncheon at the Bistro in Beverly Hills January 23, reported that AIP recently completed the highest grossing nine months in its history.

The founder of 21-year-old AIP reminded, "We have come of age and we are in the position to take on all comers. We have the money, facilities, know-how, and organization to welcome any film project- regardless of cost- if we like the project and its potential."

**This last paragraph shows a trend which would occur again and again until Arkoff's death in 2001. Arkoff is listed as "the founder" of AIP rather than "the co-founder." As the years passed, Jim Nicholson's considerable and invaluable contribution to the company was pushed more and more to the background. In later years, Arkoff would often dismiss Jim as "a good man with titles" with Arkoff taking increasingly more credit for Jim's achievements. In his Foreword to the Museum of Modern Art's program for their 1979 AIP retrospective, Arkoff doesn't even mention Nicholson. The financial brain of the company had now become the creative force as well.**

March 26, 1979
*Boxoffice*
AIP, FILMWAYS AGREE TO MERGER
Los Angeles- Richard L. Bloch, chief executive officer of Filmways, Inc., and Samuel Z. Arkoff, chief executive of American

International Pictures, Inc., announced March 20 that the two companies have signed a merger agreement. Under the plan, AIP will become a subsidiary of Filmways.

June 4, 1979
*Boxoffice*
ARKOFF TO KEEP TITLE DESPITE AI's MERGER
New York- Samuel Z. Arkoff will retain his title of president and chief executive when the pending merger of American International into Filmways takes place. Arkoff currently serves as board chairman of AI in addition to his other duties. He will reportedly earn an annual salary of $225,000 with cost-of-living increases to be included.

Arkoff's five-year contract includes a clause that will allow him to terminate the contract after two years and become an independent producer for the feature film subsidiary of Filmways. In this case, Arkoff would receive profit participations on pictures produced by him in addition to his annual salary.

**In 1992, Sam Arkoff published his autobiography, "Flying Through Hollywood by the Seat of My Pants." In it, he had this to say about the merger with Filmways:**

"The merger was the biggest mistake of my life- but I figure everyone is entitled to one major mistake and this was definitely mine. [Richard] Bloch and Filmways had bought AIP because of what we had accomplished over the last quarter century; then they promptly tried to change us."

**Sam Arkoff sold his stock in Filmways in December 1980 and resigned from the company.**
**The final movie to have Arkoff's name on it before his departure from Filmways was Brian DePalma's *Dressed to Kill*. In his autobiography, he said of the film:**

"*Dressed to Kill* was a picture I was proud of, a truly brilliant film, full of unexpected plot twists and more thrills and heart-stopping moments than the roller coaster at Coney Island."

**Angie Dickinson is about to be murdered by a gloved killer in Brian De Palma's *Dressed to Kill*.**

On December 18, 2000, *Daily Variety* published the first in a series of "Legends and Groundbreakers" profiles. It was about the "Original Indie pioneer" Sam Arkoff. In the article, in reference to Jim Nicholson, Sam is quoted as saying: "I had the experience of making cheap pictures and Jim had the knowledge of distribution. That made a very good combination." What "cheap pictures" Sam had made prior to their involvement is open to question.

September 17, 2001
Excerpts from Sam Arkoff's *Daily Variety* obituary
ARKOFF MADE ART OF B-MOVIES by Richard Natale
Sam Arkoff, the gruff, outspoken producer and co-founder of American Intl. Pictures and the creator of hundreds of actions exploitation films in the 1950s and 1960s, has died. He was 83.

Arkoff claimed there wasn't enough sex and violence in movies, raising eyebrows. The word "art" never crossed his lips;

the stout producer, ever-present cigar in hand, was first and foremost a businessman. And as his low-budget, high return films demonstrate- *The Amityville Horror, I Was a Teenage Werewolf,* and *Muscle Beach Party,* as well as much of the early Roger Corman oeuvre- cost efficiency and exploitable elements were his hallmarks.

At the company's height, AIP's B-grade movies filled a niche between television and major studio product, becoming double-bill fodder for the nation's drive-ins and sub-run theaters. Arkoff was prescient in tapping the post-war youth market, attracting them with horror, action, and sexual innuendo- which would later filter up to the major studios.

Arkoff was always an opponent of what he called "runaway waste"- the skyrocketing budgets and marketing costs of movies. Unsuccessfully, he called for the enforcement of cost controls on movies. With them, he argued, films would wind up costing $25 million on the average by 1985.

His words were not heeded and Hollywood more than lived up to his predictions.

**One final note. The CD for the soundtrack of Les Baxter's score for *Bora Bora* was released in July 2012. In the liner notes, it says that the AIP films followed the "Arkoff Formula," which states that each movie should "contain the following elements: Action, Revolution, Killing, Oratory, Fantasy, and Fornication." It's almost as if Jim Nicholson never existed at all.**

# APPENDIX
# M.O.M.A

AMERICAN INTERNATIONAL PICTURES:
TWENTY-FIVE YEARS
A Retrospective at The Museum of Modern Art, New York
July 26- August 28, 1979

Excerpt from the program Preface:

Probably more has been written on the relationship between American movies and the American public than on any other subject in film. The topic is almost as old (or young) as is American cinema. At no point does this discussion become so lively and vigorous as when it pertains to American International Pictures, which in the past quarter-century has produced films that are as energetic and feisty as is the debate that attaches to them. Not only are these films rich in their depiction of our culture, but indeed they have played a not insignificant part in it. If *Beach Party*, *The Trip*, and *The Wild Angels*, among others, helped establish filmmaking trends by anticipating public interest, they also addressed something familiar in their audiences. Looking back, we are not surprised. The young filmmakers attracted to AIP were already moving to the beat of a changing America. The company itself was moving to the new tempo with its first release in 1954- *The Fast and the Furious*- a title that aptly describes the green years of the studio.

The films shown in the retrospective were:

*The Abominable Dr. Phibes, The Amazing Colossal Man, The Amityville Horror, Beach Party,*
    *Black Caesar, Bloody Mama, The Bonnie Parker Story, Born Losers, Boxcar Bertha,*
    *A Bucket of Blood, Chastity, The Comedy of Terrors, Cooley High, Dementia 13, Dillinger,*
    *The Fast and the Furious, Girls in Prison, Heavy Traffic, House of Usher,*
    *Invasion of the Saucer-Men, The Island of Dr. Moreau, I Was a Teenage Werewolf,*
    *Machine Gun Kelly, Master of the World, A Matter of Time, Night Tide, Panic in Year Zero,*
    *Psych-Out, Rolling Thunder, Sisters, Submarine Seahawk, Tales of Terror, Three in the Attic,*
    *The Trip, The Unholy Rollers, What's Up Tiger Lily?, The Wild Angels, Wild in the Streets,*
    *X The Man with the X-Ray Eyes*

# BIBLIOGRAPHY

Aaronson, Charles S., ed. 1970 *International Motion Picture Almanac*, New York: Quigley, 1969.

Arkoff, Samuel Z., with Richard Trubo. *Flying Through Hollywood by the Seat of My Pants*. New York: Birch lane, 1992.

Corman, Roger, with Jim Jerome. *How I Made a Hundred Movies in Hollywood and Never Lost a Dime*. New York: Random House, 1990.

Hunter, Tab, with Eddie Muller. *Tab Hunter Confidential*. Chapel Hill, N.C.: Algonquin Books, 2005.

McGee, Mark Thomas. *Fast and Furious: The Story of American International Pictures*. Jefferson N.C.: McFarland, 1984.

Williams, Lucy Chase. *The Complete Films of Vincent Price.* New York: Citadel, 1995.

# INDEX

*Guns of the Black Witch* 172
*Gunslinger* 31-32
Gurney, Robert J. 56,58,95
Guthrie, Lester D. 140

Hagen, Jean 183
Hagen, Ross 352
Haggard, Piers 394
Hagman, Larry 401
Hagopian, Berj 184,185
Hale, William 111,176
Haller, Daniel 212,274,284,293,328,347,385
*Hallucination Generation* 325
Halsey, Brett 81,103,301
Hama, Mie 281,322
Hammer Films 155,164,383,407,451
Hampshire, Susan 286
Hanawalt, Charles 426
Hancock, Hunter 59
*Hand, The* 153
*Hard Ride* 426
Harper, Kenneth 224,286
Harrington, Curtis 204,205,306,447,448
Harris, Nancy 469
Harris, Robert H. 88
Harrison, Richard 158,301
Harrison, Sandra 65,67
Hart, Susan 261,263,275,284,285,289,293,295,296,297,302,
303, 308,443,476
Hartley, Mariette 430
Harvey, Marilyn 73
Hass, Hans 455
Hattie, Hilo 75
*Haunted Palace* 212-215
Hawkins, Jack 441
Haworth, Jill 392
Hawthorne, Dennis 405
Hawtrey, Charles 438,468

Holm, Claus 142
Honda, Ishiro 265,280,315,365,431
Hopper, Dennis 205,306,336,339,341
*Horror House* 392-393
*Horrors of the Black Museum* 101,105-108,110
Hoshi, Yuriko 265
*Hot Rod Girl* 81-82
Houghland, Arthur 183
*House of Fright* 155-156
*House of 1,000 Dolls* 338-339
*House of Usher* 137-141,164
*House That Screamed* 424-425
Houwer, Rob 398
Hoven, Adrian 363
*How to Make a Monster* 88-90
Howard, Ron 321
Howard, Sandy 267
Howard, Trevor 441
Howerd, Frankie 468
Hoyt, John 85,217,267
Hudson, John 94,95
Hudson, William 60
Hughes, Mary 239,289,293,313
Hull, Henry 156
Hummel, Asgarda 354
Hunt, Ronald Leigh 153
Hunter, Bruce 205
Hunter, Tab 195,202,284,285
Huston, John 357,371,372
Hutton, Robert 136
Huxtable, Judy 386
Hyde-White, Wilfred 279,318,328
Hyer, Martha 243,244,260,326,339

*I Am a Groupie* 414-415
*I Was a Teenage Frankenstein* 64-66, 76,79
*I Was a Teenage Werewolf* 44,45,55-57,66
*Incredible 2-Headed Transplant* 425

Misano, Fortunato 182,236,272,273
Mitchell, Cameron 206,465
Mitchell, Mary 219
Mizuno, Kumi 316
Mock, Laurie 327
Moffa, Paolo 250
Mohr, Gerald 130,131
Mondry, Eberhard 354
Monlaur, Yvonne 134
Monteiro, Johnny 166
Montel, Lisa 46,91,93
Montgomery, George 325
Moody, Ron 225
Moore, Kenneth 258
Moore, Terry 136
Moorehead, Jane 62
Moreland, Sherry 243
Moritz, Joseph 5,9
Moritz, Milton 138,145,153,167,168,287,290,326
Morris, Barboura (aka Barboura O'Neill) 64,119
Morris, Chester 35
Morrison, Monroe 465
*Motorcycle Gang* 62-63
Moxey, John 329
Mullaney, Jack 295
Muir, Gavin 205
*Murders in the Rue Morgue* 432-433
Murphy, Audie 324
Murphy, Jimmy 103,352
Murphy, Michael 395
Murray, Jan 327
*Muscle Beach Party* 220,222,238-239,242-246
Musy-Glory, Vittoria 115

Nader, George 329,339
Nakamura, Tadao 281,322
*Naked Africa* 59-60
*Naked Paradise* 46-48,93

—

CPSIA information can be obtained at www.ICGtesting.com
Printed in the USA
BVOW03s0928091213

338256BV00008B/24/P